READ
WRITE
LEAD

///////////

REGIE ROUTMAN

READ, WRITE, LEAD

Breakthrough Strategies for Schoolwide Literacy Success

 Alexandria, Virginia USA

1703 N. Beauregard St. • Alexandria, VA 22311-1714 USA
Phone: 800-933-2723 or 703-578-9600 • Fax: 703-575-5400
Website: www.ascd.org • E-mail: member@ascd.org
Author guidelines: www.ascd.org/write

Gene R. Carter, *Executive Director;* Richard Papale, *Acting Chief Program Development Officer;* Stefanie Roth, *Interim Publisher;* Genny Ostertag, *Acquisitions Editor;* Julie Houtz, *Director, Book Editing & Production;* Darcie Russell, *Senior Associate Editor;* Georgia Park, *Senior Graphic Designer;* Mike Kalyan, *Manager, Production Services;* Valerie Younkin, *Production Designer;* Kyle Steichen, *Production Specialist*

PAPERBACK ISBN: 978-1-4166-1873-7   ASCD product # 113016   n6/14

Also available as an e-book (see Books in Print for the ISBNs).

Quantity discounts: 10–49 copies, 10%; 50+ copies, 15%; for 1,000 or more copies, call 800-933-2723, ext. 5634, or 703-575-5634. For desk copies: www.ascd.org/deskcopy

Library of Congress Cataloging-in-Publication Data
Routman, Regie.
Read, write, lead : breakthrough strategies for schoolwide literacy success / Regie Routman.
    pages cm
Includes bibliographical references and index.
ISBN 978-1-4166-1873-7 (pbk. : alk. paper)   1. Language arts (Elementary).   2. Language arts (Secondary).   3. Educational leadership.   I. Title.
LB1576.R7583 2014
372.6—dc23
                                                                                                      2014003413

23 22 21 20 19 18 17 16 15 14   1 2 3 4 5 6 7 8 9 10 11 12

For Frank

READ, WRITE, LEAD

Note

All references to research, quotations, and additional information related to the text may be found in the Endnotes.

Acknowledgments

Most of all, I owe a debt of gratitude to the extraordinary community of educators with whom I have had the good fortune to collaborate over many years. Generous and kind teachers, principals, administrators, coaches, and students continue to inform my work, cause me to think deeper, and ensure we jointly create hope and joy right along with effective literacy teaching, leading, and learning. Many of the voices of those educators are embedded in this book in their own words. I am grateful for their honesty, knowledge, and insights, all of which make the text richer and clearer. To most fairly recognize each one's talents, they are listed alphabetically.

Heartfelt thanks to contributors Shana Bowens, Lois Bridges, Debbie Fowler, Betty Hannaford, Charity Haviland, Gloria Heflin, Mike Henderson, Joyce Hyland, Lindsay Jacksha, Lori Johnson, Tracey Johnson, Melissa Kirkland, Danica Lewis, Andrea Lockhart, Machel Lucas, Sue Marlatt, Jamie Newman, Abigail Pinard, Marilyn Robbins, Susan Rodriguez, Greta Salmi, Kay Sprader, Sherri Steuart, Ann Thomson, April Waters, Heather Woodroof, and Robin Woods.

Many other contributors whose voices are integral to the text also served as reader-responders for a chapter or more or the entire book; where reader-response was the larger role, those acknowledgments follow. Thanks to principal Kim Ball for her kindness, insights, and amazing leadership; assistant superintendent Jason Drysdale for his broad vision and unfailing support; teacher-leader and grade 5 teacher Laurie Espenel for sharing her students, her enthusiasm, and her prodigious talents; principal Margaret Fair for her steadfast leadership; high school literacy coach and former principal Sandra Figueroa for her precious gift of daily friendship and ongoing collaboration in our joint work; literacy coach and teacher- leader Kate Gordon for her thoughtful comments in responding to the entire text and for her extraordinary leadership and generosity; scholar and researcher Elfrieda Hiebert for her outstanding work on the role of texts in successful reading; school improvement coach and former principal Barb Ide who read the entire manuscript and offered apt suggestions, always with wise perspectives and humor; adjunct university instructor and former principal Marilyn Jerde, cherished friend and colleague who provided invaluable feedback; director of teaching and learning Debbie Johnson, for her unwavering leadership, support, and good humor; English language development teacher Sharlline Markwardt, for her courage, commitment to students, and for willingly serving as my unofficial photographer; professional development coordinator and Reading Recovery leader Allyson Matczuk for her outstanding leadership and vision that made the work we did together in Winnipeg, Canada, possible and joyful; literacy coach Nancy McLean for her expert coaching with kindness and our special friendship; principal Matt Renwick for generously sharing his technology expertise; literacy coach and colleague Kathy Schmitt for wisely insisting I include a chapter on reducing the need for intervention and then carefully reviewing it; principal Trena Speirs for graciously sharing her experiences with leadership teams and PLCs; scholar, researcher, and dear friend Sheila Valencia for generously sharing her literacy and assessment expertise; teacher-leader and grade 1 teacher Lesley Vermaas for her graciousness, "can do" manner, and great instructional skill; national teacher and treasured friend and colleague Judy Wallis for her smart advice, attention to all important details, and her uncanny ability to always find within minutes any article or reference I have been unable to locate.

Heartfelt thanks also go to those educators, mentioned or not, who have helped shape my thinking and ideas over the last several decades. In particular, I am grateful to the staffs and students in all the diverse schools in the United States and Canada where I have conducted demonstration teaching and coaching residencies with the goal of increasing schoolwide literacy engagement, enjoyment, and achievement. Those residencies continue to be my most gratifying work, especially realizing what is possible for all learners, including our most vulnerable ones.

I am deeply appreciative of the entire ASCD team. From start to finish, the entire process has been immensely supportive. Acquisitions editor Genny Ostertag gently but firmly guided me in responding to the manuscript with great sensitivity and intelligence. Magnificent copyediting was done by Kathleen Florio and superb project management was carried out by Darcie Russell, who worked tirelessly to ensure every aspect of the book was as excellent and accurate as possible. An early conversation with Richard Papale, former publisher and now acting chief program development officer, continued to inspire me throughout the writing. Georgia Park, senior graphic designer, did a terrific job with the cover and interior design. As well, the talented design and typesetting team, production department, and all those at ASCD who worked to make the book as complete, organized, and attractive as possible deserve a big round of applause.

The process of writing requires determination and hard work, and—to keep going full speed ahead—breaks, good food, and good fun are also necessities. For that I am most thankful to my dear family and friends. Especially, spending time with Peter, Claudine, Katie, and Brooke always brings me joy. So does time with treasured friends in Seattle and across the country. Special mention goes to Harriet Cooper for her beautiful gift of our lifetime friendship. Finally, this book is dedicated to my husband Frank for his unwavering love, support, and generosity, which have made it possible for me to continue to teach and write and to live an interesting life.

Introduction:
Why This Book,
and Who Is It For?

This is a book about literacy and leadership. Through a lifetime of working in schools, one of my most powerful insights and core beliefs is that *teachers must be leaders, and principals must know literacy.* Without a synergy between literacy and leadership and a committed, joint effort by teachers and principals, fragile achievement gains do not hold. Although much has been written about leadership and learning as well as literacy and learning, little has been written about the crucial interconnection between literacy and leadership for ensuring that all students become effective readers and writers. That partnership is at the heart of successful schoolwide literacy and at the heart of this book.

This is a book about sustainable school change through professional learning. It is not professional development, per se, that leads to increased achievement but rather shared learning in a high-trust, schoolwide environment where everyone is committed to learning more and doing better for all students and teachers in the school. It is an embedded schoolwide culture of thoughtful professional learning, gained through informed debate, dialogue, and reflection, that leads to classroom application of more effective literacy instruction and assessment and, ultimately, higher student achievement, engagement, and enjoyment. In particular, it is the creation and sustained activity of Professional *Literacy* Communities, permeating all aspects of school life, that lead to improved student achievement across the curriculum. Although such cultures and communities of deep and ongoing learning are uncommon, they are essential for enduring and meaningful change. Any lasting improvement in literacy through implementation of the Common Core State Standards in the United States, the provincial curricula in Canada, or international benchmarks will depend on such collaborative communities.

This is a book about hope, learning energy, and possibilities. Key to its premise is the belief that each of us has the potential, if we become highly knowledgeable and committed to high levels of success for every student, to make change through our individual and collective actions, and that ultimately we can change the outcome for students, even in our most challenging schools. What has often been missing from our collective work is the unrelenting commitment to the belief that through our own agency and efficacy we can change preconceived expectations and results for students. Sometimes this means stepping out of our comfort zones to advocate for saner practices.

Ultimately we want students and teachers alike to become self-determining learners who set and then carry through on their own worthwhile goals and objectives, some of which extend beyond themselves. It's slow, plodding, messy work that is often discouraging, but it's essential for improving the lives of our students, many of whom deserve more than what they are getting in our still segregated schools of the 21st century.

This is a book about effective literacy practices and becoming literate. Although the latest standards raise the bar for student achievement and give us a clear blueprint for what we need to be teaching, the "how" of that teaching is not defined, which puts a huge responsibility—ready or not—on schools and districts. Furthermore, most often there has been no consistent or coherent professional development plan provided for changing local, national, and global education. Implementing standards in a manner that will actually improve education for all our students is up to us, so it's critical that we have the knowledge to do so.

My aim is to demonstrate what actions, habits, processes, and reading and writing practices are most crucial to teach and assess, and how to apply those literacy practices in a manner that engages all students and is respectful of their needs, interests, and cultures. It is not literacy practices, per se, that matter but practices that lead to developing literate and thoughtful individuals. These individuals are students and teachers who don't just know how to read and write but who are well read and knowledgeable; able to think, analyze, and support opinions and arguments through facts, experiences, and reasoning; and able to clearly articulate their thinking through writing and speaking. What matters is becoming literate to lead a full and meaningful life.

This is a book about how good teachers can become remarkable teachers. Through stories of teachers in diverse schools and examples of collaborative reading and writing work with students and teachers, this book demonstrates how literacy change happens. It specifies what it takes for us educators to move out of our comfort zones and shift our existing beliefs and practices to become more effective, efficient, and joyful teachers—all with the end goal of increased student learning across a whole school. It also highlights teachers who have become increasingly adept at combining advocacy and leadership in their instructional roles, and it presents their voices.

This is a book about effective leadership practices. A unique aspect of this book is that the focus on leadership includes teacher leadership, along with principal leadership, as essential to whole-school achievement. How teacher-leaders develop and their influence on a staff's cohesiveness and collaboration—and, ultimately, student and teacher achievement—are delineated. The necessity of a strong and active school leadership team and how that works are also fully discussed.

This is a book about how dedicated principals can become outstanding instructional leaders. Evolving stories of principals in diverse schools provide insights into the knowledge and practices that make it possible for a principal to begin to create a whole school of highly effective literacy teachers and teacher-leaders. Included are suggestions for how to coach a principal on what to look for in a classroom and how to give effective feedback that moves teachers and learners forward, so that the process of observing teachers, working with them, and coaching them in their own classrooms becomes a positive and respectful one for principals and teachers alike. And, most important, numerous examples show what it looks like and sounds like to create a highly effective, ongoing professional collaboration among the principal, teachers, and students that raises achievement and possibilities for all.

This is not a book about school reform. That is, this book is not about changing a whole system of schools through policies, politics, prescriptions, and new assessments proposed by states or the federal government. Historically, such efforts have cost billions of dollars and have had, at best, mixed results. Rather, this book is about school change and how thoughtful, committed educators can make a lasting impact through teaching and leading well—one school, one principal, one teacher, and one student at a time. This is a story about how worthwhile change can be sustained and how changes in one school can jumpstart change in other schools. This is a book for those of us who have an unwavering commitment to do the necessary and hard work of getting better at what we do and who have learned that a "quick fix" eventually just brings us back to the starting line. This is a book for those of us who believe that one person can make a difference that matters, and that it's essential that we at least try—and try and try again.

This is a book of stories, struggles, solutions, and strategies. Both practical and personal, my hope is that the classroom and school accounts of practicing teachers and leaders will inspire and inform you. Furthermore, my hope is that you will learn specifics for applying effective reading, writing, and thinking practices across the curriculum and come to understand the critical, intersecting role that smart and sensitive professional leadership plays. Conversations with many educators are honestly recounted in their own voices; in a few cases I have used pseudonyms. This is not an all-encompassing book. I have chosen to highlight the stories, factors, data, strategies, struggles, and successes that seem most critical for improving and sustaining schoolwide literacy achievement.

This is a book about joy in teaching and learning. Although we educators will continue to be bombarded by new initiatives and constraints—pressures such as unwieldy standards, complex performance evaluations, value-added data analysis, high-stakes testing, and more—it *is* still possible and necessary to find joy in what we do and to pass on that joy to our students. We must! As I was completing this book, an impassioned parent whom I encountered at an airport told me this:

> My daughter is about to go to college. She has a high grade point average and has taken many advanced placement classes, but she finds no joy in learning in most of her classes. She demonstrates little curiosity or the desire to discover information on her own. All the test prep and focus on standards and testing have leached the fun out of learning. Is she prepared for college? She's passed the courses, but, sadly, she no longer loves to learn.[1]

Her comments reminded me that if we just graduate students who have fulfilled requirements but lack curiosity and a desire and ability to be self-sustaining learners, we have failed. Many of the accounts in this book show how we can rediscover joy in our work for our students and ourselves.

This is a book for all educators—teachers, teacher-leaders, principals, coaches, literacy specialists, interventionists, administrators, curriculum directors—for all of us who want to do a better job in the schools where we work. It is for those of us who believe we have a shared responsibility to educate all children. Ultimately, of course, this is a book for our students and about how we can serve them better and ensure they learn more, no matter where they happen to live or go to school. Change is difficult and challenging, but with a dedicated and highly informed staff, great things can and do happen for students, teachers, and principals. I invite you, my esteemed reader, on the learning journey.

Quick Wins

Seeing ourselves as teacher-leaders and leader-teachers is a new role for most of us and a challenging one. Throughout the text, in addition to stories, strategies, data, and change processes related to literacy and leadership, many "Quick Wins" are provided in the margins of every chapter. These are practical, everyday ideas that are easy to implement, yield quick and reliable results, and help us educators to deal more effectively and efficiently with the nuts and bolts and nuances of effective teaching and leading.

Change is slow, and we need to be able to see some sign of progress and results for our efforts as soon as possible. A quick win promotes confidence that incremental progress is important and that long-term change is possible. As one principal noted, "Recognizing quick wins buys you a lot of money in the bank. The staff knows you're on their side. As a principal, quick wins are really important for moving the school forward."[2]

1

Literacy and Leadership: Change That Matters

Every one of us who deeply cares about equal educational opportunities for all students tries to solve the problem that won't go away: *How do we create schools and classrooms where all students thrive and become highly literate?* Despite reams of research, billions of dollars for new programs, a renewed focus on testing and evaluation, and massive professional development efforts, not much of substance has changed for a large proportion of our students, especially students of poverty and our Latino and black students.

Many of our schools remain segregated, with accompanying inequality of funding, while other schools are resegregating by race and class.[1] Income disparity has become a greater factor than race or color in the achievement gap.[2] In addition, the high school dropout rate in our cities is as high as ever, with students who are poor and minority much more likely than their affluent peers to drop out; the number of students of color who get to two- or four-year colleges, let alone earn a degree, is still dismally low; and teachers and principals are caught in the crossfire of who's to blame.[3]

For most of us who are conscientiously doing our jobs as best we can in a demanding culture of cumbersome rules and regulations, exacting standards and evaluations, growing diversity in students' language and culture, increasing class sizes—and working with the often devastating consequences of poverty on students' learning—it's important to stay focused on what we can do. This is no easy matter. It's easy to get discouraged and to blame factors outside our control for our students' low achievement. Despite pockets of success where students in some high-challenge schools beat the odds and become high achievers, placing the blame for low achievement on factors that we cannot control is still quite common.

What keeps me going and encouraged in the complex world of teaching and leading is the core belief that what we do greatly matters, not just to the future of our students, but to our nation and the world. John Dewey wisely stated more than a century ago, "What the best and wisest parent wants for his own child, that must the community want for all of its children. Any other ideal for our schools is narrow and unlovely; acted upon, it destroys our democracy."[4] What keeps me teaching and leading is the belief that one persistent, knowledgeable, caring person can and must make a difference. A statement by playwright Arthur Miller resonates: "The longer I worked the more certain I felt that as improbable as it might seem, there were moments when an individual conscience was all that could keep a world from falling."[5] At the very least, one person's commitment can change the projected results for one learner; and for that learner, whether it be a child or a teacher, the experience can be life changing. Such stories are woven through this book.

My goal in writing this book is to demystify the process of "getting better," to show through individual and collective stories, actions, practices, demonstrations, and shared experiences in diverse classrooms and schools how worthwhile literacy and leadership change can happen, one person and one school at a time. Highly knowledgeable teachers and leaders can and do create a culture of collaboration, professional learning, and trust that becomes the oxygen that breathes life and hope into learning. We can become energized and excited by the work itself and the results we get. We can replace fear with joy. We can create a whole school and community working together for a greater good. So how does that happen? A bit of background first.

Learning from Teaching and Leading

I am a teacher-learner with 45 years of experience in instructing, assessing, coteaching, coaching, leading, and learning in diverse schools and classrooms. I have been a classroom teacher of most of the elementary grades, a reading specialist, a Reading Recovery teacher, a teacher of children with learning disabilities, a mentor teacher and leader, a literacy coach, a staff developer, a literacy change agent, and an author of many books and resources for educators.

Since 1997 I have been conducting residencies in schools across the United States and in Canada. Most of these schools are diverse; that is, they serve large populations of students of color, second language learners, and highly transient students. Often these are also schools with large numbers of students from low-income households. I created this residency model when I realized no one was demonstrating for educators—showing them the what, why, and how of effective teaching and assessing practices— beyond the one-day or one-week inservice training sessions on how to use the newest adopted program or implement the latest standards.

In the teaching residencies, most of which occur over the course of a week, I assume responsibility for the classroom; that is, I do the teaching while the classroom teacher and other teachers are released to observe. Using what I call an Optimal Learning Model (described in detail in Chapter 2), I begin with demonstrations and shared experiences before gradually handing over responsibility to the teacher to "try and apply" with my coaching support. Fundamental to the residencies are the daily ongoing professional conversations in which we debrief, question, and discuss our work.

Over many years my perspective has expanded from the classroom to the school and, sometimes, the district, and from a focus on literacy to a focus on *literacy and leadership*. I have learned much about what works, why it works, and what needs to be done to raise and sustain whole-school achievement. Like you, I am still learning. I am passionate about improving the literacy and learning lives of students, as well as for us educators. I continue to rely on tried-and-true practices and to seek and try out new ideas based on my experiences, knowledge about literacy and leadership, collaboration with colleagues, professional reading, reflection, and current and relevant research.

Literacy Insights

My experience working in schools and collaborating and presenting at educational workshops and institutes has taught me that what works best for sustainable, long-term gains are interactive opportunities with school teams. Those teams include teachers and their principal, and, perhaps, coaches and curriculum specialists. Although literacy is the focus, the emphasis is on literacy in the context of whole-school achievement, as well as literacy that is supported by beliefs that align with robust practices and strong leadership. Likewise, I have learned that workshops dedicated solely to literacy—without consideration for whole-school learning—often leave individual teachers and principals satisfied with implementation of specific reading and writing strategies. However, even when such implementation is successful, the change that occurs is often superficial and limited; a new activity or strategy has been added to the teaching repertoire, but nothing more.

Lasting change depends on an entire staff working together to develop shared beliefs and to align them with research-based practices that move a whole school of learners forward, grade to grade, teacher by teacher. For example, I have observed that most teachers and principals hold and act upon a part-to-whole learning model and a belief system that supports teaching skills and strategies mostly in isolation. Yet teaching isolated skills actually slows down and diminishes the impact of the learning experience. To maximize full learning potential, our most vulnerable students in particular must experience how the skills are relevant and fit into a meaningful and authentic whole. Until a staff develops a belief system that contextualizes and integrates the teaching of skills and strategies into meaningful and whole texts, achievement continues to lag. Moreover, without well-developed and articulated shared beliefs, schools continue to rely too much on programs and resources to determine what to teach rather than seeking out resources that support their well-founded beliefs.

Meeting as a Professional Literacy *Community*

I have also learned that not only must the professional learning be ongoing (scheduled weekly and monthly), but professional conversations have to become infused into the daily life and culture of the school. That is, in addition to Professional *Literacy* Communities (which are discussed in detail in Chapter 6) in both horizontal and vertical teams at and across grade levels, the day-to-day work of the school must include supportive visits and conversations between and among the principal and teachers, observations and coaching by and with teachers and the principal, time for team planning, older students tutoring or coaching younger ones, and an ongoing, free flow of conversation about reading, writing, teaching, leading, assessing, and learning.

From researchers Kathy Au and Taffy Raphael, I have learned the need for building a staircase curriculum with clearly defined and high enough literacy benchmarks at every grade level.[6] Until teachers and principals see what excellence looks like and sounds like at every grade level and can articulate with deep understanding what they are seeing, expectations and progress for students will fall short. Developing benchmarks is a messy, complex task that requires knowledgeable teams to be able to look at student work, determine significant strengths and weaknesses, and set worthwhile goals. Once established, those reading and writing benchmarks need to align and increase in depth from grade to grade. Also, as teachers and leaders we need to ably demonstrate effective literacy practices through thinking aloud as we show how we read, write, speak, listen, analyze, and solve problems across the curriculum. At the same time, we need to establish clear objectives in a manner that is meaningful and relevant and likely to lead to increased student understanding and application.

Perhaps most important to the school change process, I have learned that literacy is not a strong suit for many principals even when they have solid leadership and organizational abilities. For example, I have worked with elementary school principals who were former music teachers, physical education teachers, and high school principals. They did not recognize the key literacy specifics to look for when they went into K–8 classrooms, and many could not effectively assess if the work was at a high enough level. Offering useful feedback and appropriate support to teachers was, consequently, limited. As a result, I created virtual literacy residencies, in the form of a video-based, embedded professional development series, as a companion for principals—as well as coaches and teachers—so that, as a staff, educators could view, discuss, analyze, plan, and apply effective literacy practices to the classroom.[7] Without deep knowledge about literacy, principals remain restricted in their quest to raise reading and writing achievement across a whole school.

Leadership Insights

I didn't know much about leadership when I began demonstration teaching in weeklong residencies. My first residencies involved a multiyear contract with one typical school in a high-needs district. I conducted two weeklong writing residencies each year at the school, one in the fall and one in the spring. The results were humbling. After four years there were some outstanding teachers of writing, as documented by high achievement scores on state and district tests, along with excellent daily writing. There were some teachers who hadn't moved much, and we still had a couple of resisters who hadn't budged. The principal was a strong leader in the sense that she knew a lot about literacy, entrusted many professional development decisions to a teacher-led team, and held regular professional development meetings. But—and this is a big *but*—she rarely got out of her office to go into classrooms. When I would return each spring, I learned that she didn't know that several teachers weren't teaching writing every day—an agreed-upon school belief—or that teachers hungered for affirmation for taking risks as writing teachers, or that one teacher was actively working against change of any kind. Also critical, because of the principal's absence from classrooms, she was unable to provide the feedback and coaching that are necessary for supporting teachers and staff in their efforts to continually improve.

In truth, not much writing progress was sustained, and looking back, I realize we didn't accomplish much for the amount of time, resources, and energy invested. My background was as a teacher, and instruction is what I knew. In those early residencies, I spent the entire morning instructing and coaching in a primary classroom and the entire afternoon instructing and coaching in an intermediate classroom. Although the principal was required to be part of the residencies, observing and participating with the teachers, I hadn't yet seen the principal as the linchpin in school literacy achievement.

The hardwiring of my thinking changed after I acknowledged and took responsibility for our failure to attain and sustain schoolwide achievement in those first residencies. I came to realize the crucial role of principal-as-literacy-leader in improving school achievement. In all residencies since then, I devote the entire afternoon to mentoring the principal, and that has made a big difference in our short- and long-term outcomes. (See www. regieroutman.org for more information about the residency model.)

I also learned that teachers need encouragement, demonstrations, and responsive coaching to step up to the plate as leaders. Once we teachers learn how to take on a leadership role and embrace it, the culture, collaboration, and achievement in a school change in many positive ways. Professional conversations go on all day long, between and among grade levels; the principal is seen as a supportive partner and not just an evaluator; teachers are eager to be coached and to share their ideas and questions; trust and respect increase throughout the building, and all students begin to thrive.

On a personal level, I learned that we educators need courage, stamina, and unrelenting determination to lead. A few years ago, in cooperation with Seattle University, I conceived and organized with five esteemed colleagues the first Urgency and School Change Conference. It was a huge challenge and undertaking, which included inviting notable national and international keynote speakers. Never having put on a national conference before, my colleagues and I were learning along the way. Early on in the process, when my husband and I were on vacation and unavailable, one of our most dedicated group members panicked that we would not be able get the number of attendees we needed to cover our considerable expenses. Meaning well, she communicated her fears to other members of our group, and the group concluded we should cancel the conference. Returning from vacation, I learned I had a benevolent but serious mutiny on my hands. I called each group member and spoke at length with each one.

Through persuasion, optimism, and sheer grit, I convinced them all that we would have a highly successful conference—and we did! It didn't matter that I didn't know with certainty if we could pull it off. What mattered was that without collective support and all of us confidently working toward the same worthy goal, we had no chance for success. I learned that people want to be convinced that the work they're doing is important, that their role is crucial, and that they can depend on the designated leader to help them reach the goal line. I also learned that as a leader I had to be willing to live with tension and uncertainty while doing everything possible to see a commitment through and ensure a successful outcome.

I further learned that being a decisive teacher-leader is very different from being a teacher-collaborator. At first I would allow our weekly planning calls to go on too long, listening hard and with an open mind to all viewpoints and trying to get our group to consensus. But often we had no consensus, and although it was difficult at first, I learned to say something like this: "Based on all the viewpoints that have been presented and discussed, it seems like such-and-such makes the most sense, so we're going to do thus-and-so." As a teacher, I was not used to making the final, important decision for a group of peers; my work in schools has always been based on a collaborative mindset and plan. That is, after presenting and discussing possibilities and options and reviewing data, the teachers and the principal decide the course of action that they believe is best.

So I understand firsthand how risky and hard it is for teachers to move into the unconventional role of teacher-leader—for example, to be willing to stand up and say, "This is what I'm seeing at our school. This is an important issue we all need to talk about, and here's what I'm thinking may be a possible solution." And I know from working with principals how difficult it can be to move into the role of respected instructional teacher and coach when their own literacy knowledge may be limited and their time in classrooms has been mostly dedicated to evaluating teachers. My hope is that this book will be a catalyst for moving the literacy and leadership connection to center stage, jump-starting significant professional conversations, increasing expectations for what's possible for all learners, and accelerating literacy and leadership for whole-school achievement and lasting change.

Prepare People for Worthwhile Change

Change is difficult for most of us, especially when the change is unexpected and pushes the boundaries of our comfort zones. Successful and lasting change depends on solid trust, high expertise by the change agents, excellent resources, sufficient time and practice for adjusting and learning, and a whole host of complex factors. It also depends on taking the time to reflect on where we are and where we want to be. A personal story gives some perspective on the process.

Recently my reliable MacBook Pro, my writing partner and preferred tool for all my composing, stopped functioning well. That is, programs were taking a long time to upload, I had to do more and more "force quits" because of constant freezes, and the constant starts and stops were interfering with my being able to work efficiently. Full disclosure: technology is not my strong suit, although I am constantly improving, thanks to occasional and ongoing help from a specialist, known in Mac lingo as an "Apple genius." Rhett Johnson has been the "genius" who patiently showed me what to do to move forward and who was my personal IT guy for almost a decade. He taught me what I needed to know that I couldn't figure out on my own and boosted my information technology confidence so that I could begin to troubleshoot some issues myself. Over many years, he earned my trust; that is, I came to depend on his ready support when I was confused and scared and knew that he would guide me through the rough patches with kindness and specific hands-on help, and without passing judgment on my "slow" learning.

However, I was unprepared for what happened when Rhett told me he'd need to "clean up" my desktop and reinstall the operating system and all my programs to get everything working efficiently again. What he didn't tell me was that some programs would look and operate somewhat differently because he was installing the latest versions. When I went back to use my rebuilt computer, I panicked. The familiar was now unfamiliar; the habitual actions and routines I depended on had shifted. I became physically uncomfortable and mentally exhausted trying to adapt to my new computer landscape. Truth be told, I wanted things exactly as they had been before the upgrade. I didn't see the new change as an advantage, and I was peeved at Rhett for making changes without my permission—all of which I told him.

> *Rhett*: "If I'd told you that some of your programs would be different and require some new learning, what would you have said?"

> *Regie*: "Keep everything exactly as it is."

> *Rhett*: "I want you to try out what you now have. I think you'll find that most of the changes are for the better, and with practice you'll actually see that. However, if you find you're not happy, I'll put everything back the way you had it."

All of us require an IT person—an intelligent, instructive, intentional, and inspiring teacher and leader, a guide-on-the-side to expertly shepherd us through a worthy change process. Because I trusted Rhett, in spite of my discomfort I believed him. In fact, I did come to appreciate and prefer the upgrades. Change and the unknown can be threatening to us, especially if those changes occur in an area where we do not have high confidence. Without colleagues we trust for support, we are unlikely to fully participate in a manner that benefits our students or us.

My recent computer experience caused me to deeply reflect on the school change process. I have organized those thoughts into a reflection sheet for thinking about leading a successful change effort. See "Prepare for Change" as a catalyst and self-reflection tool for sparking conversations and actions in your school and district. (See Appendix A for a related reflection sheet to use for an assessment and planning activity.)

Quick Win

Focus first on those teachers who are ready for needed change and willing to accept and work through the accompanying challenges. Give them full support and resources to be successful. They will positively affect a large percentage of the "wait and see" teachers, which also helps minimize distractions from naysayers.

Prepare for Change

- **Prepare people for the change process.**
  - Be explicit and transparent: here's what we're doing and why.
  - Communicate high and realistic expectations.
  - Allow sufficient time.
  - Maintain continual focus on the K–5, 6–8, 9–12 continuum.

- **Infuse optimism.**
  - Promote a "We can do it" spirit.
  - Be honest about tension in the change process—both the hard parts and the benefits. Infuse creative tension: paint a clear picture of where we are and where we want to be. People need to see the goal.

- **Build in ongoing support and collaboration.**
  - Provide PLCs and ongoing PD focused on literacy and shared learning.
  - Encourage coaching opportunities—release time to observe others and to coteach, attend grade-level meetings, and facilitate common planning times.
  - Make space for failure and problem solving.
  - Allow for sufficient pacing of the learning, including adequate practice time.

- **Establish a schoolwide culture that promotes trust and risk taking.**
  - Recognize people's strengths, interests, and needs.
  - Include personal and professional celebration.

- **Lead the change effort.**
  - Model your own thinking, questioning, and wonderings publicly.
  - Respect and listen to all viewpoints.
  - Recognize that, at some point, the leader has to decide.
  - Allow sufficient time and emphasis for the change effort.
  - Help people adapt and move forward.
  - Stay focused on the main goals.

- **How do we know we're learning more and getting better?**
  - Assess the depth and frequency of professional conversations.
  - Note the increase in knowledge and effectiveness of reading and writing practices.
  - Count the number of people on board with the change effort.

- **How do we know students are learning more?**
  - Collect evidence of everyday literacy work and communications, across the curriculum.
  - Gather evidence of students as self-determining learners.
  - Conduct assessments—formative, interim, summative.
  - Regularly review student work and data together.

In particular, my computer experience and many years of being an educator have convinced me that *without teachers and other stakeholders seeing and understanding the need for change, it is not likely to happen.* One teacher noted that the only reason her school agreed to examine how they were teaching writing in their failing school was fear of an instructional mandate from the district. Initially they did not believe that a whole-school professional development model based on authentic writing for audience and purpose would change anything.

For staff buy-in to occur, establishing the need for change must be agreed upon collaboratively. What is most compelling is to identify the need through data that teachers can see, interpret, understand, and talk about as a whole school. We have to "own" the data so the reason for change becomes transparent and even urgent. In addition, the professional development plan must be clear, reasonable, and well thought out, and it must include sustained time for shared learning and application of learning.

Put in Place a Solid Infrastructure

A school's infrastructure is the operating system that provides the expectations and tools for procedures, actions, collaboration, and language that all educators agree to abide by as members of the school community. Worthwhile change is unlikely to take hold without these foundational procedures and structures in place to ensure the effective and efficient functioning of the school. For example, without operating structures, many teachers wind up focusing on nuts and bolts of daily operating procedures, such as the master schedule and lunch.

When we educators are not apprehensive of the uncertainty that ensues from a disorganized or inadequate infrastructure, we can invest our full energies toward improving instruction and learning, and we are more flexible and willing to make worthwhile changes on behalf of our students. An underperforming or dysfunctional school must be made whole before serious learning can take place, and that wholeness starts with getting predictable structures in place.

Chief among these organizational and interactional elements of infrastructure are the following:

- Delineation of roles and responsibilities for teachers and leaders
- Common language and understandings about key literacy concepts and literacy beliefs and practices

Quick Win

Address the most pressing needs of the staff first—before addressing curriculum expectations. Those needs might include issues related to recess, buses, lunch, or common planning times. Knowing that as leaders we will immediately work toward resolution of pressing issues builds trust and energy for teaching and learning.

- Data review and response with examination and disaggregation of the data as a foundational step in beginning the school change process
- Schedules and room layouts that promote collaboration, coaching, and interaction between and among teachers and students
- Leadership and literacy groups such as a schoolwide leadership team, grade-level teams, and subject matter teams
- Resources (e.g., curriculum, texts, technology, educational specialists, classroom libraries, tutors) that give instructional support to all students to meet the school's and community's literacy aims
- Norms for optimal functioning and expectations for how we act with each other—organized groups and professional development (especially PLCs—Professional *Literacy* Communities)

Ideally, infrastructure would also include social services and community partnerships.

A strong infrastructure includes not just the tangible structures in the list, but also the intangible, psychological ones, such as these:

- A safe and orderly school culture of high trust and respect for all
- Equal opportunity for all students to learn
- A collective responsibility for the school's students

Quick Win

Look at the building layout as a way for improving trust. Do all you can to shape it so people can readily interact and easily run into each other, which encourages spontaneous discussions "on the fly" and builds collaboration and trust.

Because the ultimate purpose of a sound infrastructure is increased student learning, an expansive definition of infrastructure must include learning conditions that make student success more likely, such as fairness, some choice, meaningful dialogue, small-group work, daily routines, and well-managed classrooms. High-quality standards and curriculum are necessary, of course, but successful implementation is contingent on infrastructure, which is essential for accelerating and sustaining achievement.

Focus on Worthwhile Instruction and Learning

Without collective knowledge of how, what, and why to teach and lead, our work to improve our schools will not result in improvement, despite the presence of optimal organizational structures and processes. My teacher research and experience strongly suggest that without adequate literacy and instructional knowledge, change is superficial, at best. Our finest intentions can still keep us marching in place.

For example, for a teacher of writing who has a low level of knowledge, looking at student writing samples and analyzing them can be mostly a waste of valuable time; what the teacher can identify as strengths and needs is severely limited. That is, the focus is primarily on improving the mechanics of writing, such as spelling, punctuation, and grammar, without attention to craft, organization, and style, with the end result that student writing doesn't improve much overall. In addition, limited knowledge of teaching reading leads to an overreliance on core programs and teaching skills in isolation. Superficial teaching of reading comprehension and an undervaluing of the role of access to books students can and want to read also result. Scant time is provided for actual reading practice and enjoyment of reading texts, and students remain dependent on teachers, so they often do not become confident, self-directed readers.

Another common, time-consuming practice that may or may not have significance is crafting an inspirational vision, mission, or goals statement. Without a realistic plan of execution K–12, that important vision statement doesn't affect literacy achievement very much. Execution of the vision depends on clear understanding of the vision's goals, highly effective teaching and leading, and ongoing assessment—ideally across the entire district.

Making a worthy vision a reality includes but is not limited to a mindset and actions that value and focus on things such as these:

• Students before standards
• Students viewed as capable of high achievement
• Relevant, engaging, and challenging curriculum
• Common language and curricular understandings
• Celebrations before evaluations
• Formative assessments
• Coherence, consistency, and thoroughness at and across grade levels

One of the helpful things about the Common Core State Standards (CCSS) is that we get the full literacy picture K–12 in terms of expectations for students, learning outcomes, and samples of student work. This is a huge plus. So is the focus on bigger ideas underpinned by concepts that gradually become more complex but are meant to continually build on each other. Members of a self-sustaining school are keenly aware of the full picture of literacy, what comes before and after their grade level. But this is atypical for schools. A former middle school principal speaks to the narrow focus that is common in many schools:

> The two years I facilitated a K–12 curriculum committee for our cluster, the high school English department chair headed up the committee and had never seen 1st grade writing. The fluency of those young writers made her head spin! YES! All grade-level teachers should observe what great teachers can do with our youngest students.[8]

The caution is not to rely too much on any set of standards, resources, or research. The only way to achieve a healthy working balance is to become highly knowledgeable. That is, regardless of the curriculum or standards in place, we must know how and why to expertly instruct, assess, and adjust for optimal student learning and engagement. For many of us, our teacher and leadership education and ongoing professional learning have not adequately prepared us to be excellent at our craft.[9] One of the major goals of this book is to increase educators' effectiveness for the purpose of accelerating and enriching student learning.

Establish a Culture of Professional Trust

The importance of trusting relationships in creating a healthy school culture of high achievement cannot be overstated. Without trust, we cannot become a whole school of successful literacy learners, teachers, and leaders. Trust is the glue that makes all things possible. Without it, even worthwhile changes will not stick. Where trust is missing, fear is often present, and fear is a guaranteed antidote to learning. An absence of fear on the part of teachers and students is a prerequisite to raising expectations; feeling safe; having open and honest, healthy debate; and finding joy in learning. It is well-founded trust that allows us to be vulnerable and to take risks even when it may seem scary to do so.

I will never forget when a teacher spoke up for the first time in our after-school Professional *Literacy* Community. Victor was a teacher who struggled mightily with our change process in teaching writing and with moving his students forward. Although he attended every PLC meeting, took notes, cooperated with peers, and seemed attentive, it was impossible to know what he was thinking. That particular day, after he volunteered his thoughts aloud to the whole group, I said, "Victor, it's wonderful to hear your voice. What took you so long?" I have never forgotten his response.

He said, "I've been watching you. I had to be sure I could trust you." It was our third year working together at the school. He was now finally willing to fully participate in our whole-school change process, and his students finally began to make modest gains. The lesson here is that we cannot learn from people we do not trust. It's one of the reasons that it's so important to spend time getting to know people on a personal level before beginning to work with them in earnest.

Although having high knowledge of content and pedagogy is necessary for others to trust us, "We cannot trust even well-intentioned people if they are not good at what they are doing."[10] Being good at what we're doing includes being able to work effectively with *adult* learners. Two other stories come to mind.

A first-time principal replaced a successful and well-liked one in a high-achieving school, and I was surprised by the ongoing difficulties the new principal encountered. She was highly knowledgeable in literacy and educational issues and had published several articles about literacy in respected journals. I found her easy to talk to and assumed she would do well. Yet her first year was fraught with painful issues as several skilled teachers reacted badly to her critical stance when she was observing in classrooms and communicating with the staff. Rather than beginning by noticing what these teachers were doing well, the principal chose to focus on what needed improvement. In so doing, she alienated many teachers and had to work long and hard to regain trust.

Another example is when a highly knowledgeable classroom teacher became her school's literacy coach. Everyone expected that she would excel in her new role, but her critical though well-intentioned stance toward her peers led teachers to stop requesting her coaching support. Eventually, with feedback from others and more experience, she learned how to interact with adults in a highly positive and constructive manner. Although she ultimately became successful and highly regarded as a coach, that initial loss of trust took several years to rebuild.

Professional Trust: What It Is and Why It Matters

I first heard the term *professional trust* described by an excellent principal who stated, "Professional trust means that everyone on staff is committed to all students and trusts that all teachers will do an effective job."[11] That definition infers a trust between and among teachers at all grade levels and content areas and encompasses the belief that next year's teacher will continue to move students forward in a timely and expert manner. In other words, we all commit to being accountable for making sure our expectations and results for students are high enough, and we continue to build upon students' learning from previous grades and schools within our district. Without professional trust, schoolwide achievement is not possible or sustainable. And it is important to remember that *personal trust precedes professional trust and is its foundation.* Victor, in the aforementioned story, eventually came to believe (though he didn't say it in these exact words): "I can depend on you not to harm me or be dishonest. I can depend on you to accept me. I can trust the words you speak." Once we had that personal trust, professional trust began to develop. Without schoolwide trust, we educators are not likely to say what we don't know, to express our fears, or to speak up even when it's risky but important to do so.

Take Action to Promote Professional Trust

In a professional development meeting at a recent residency, it became apparent that a couple of teachers—one, in particular—were holding the school back. As a whole school, we were examining typical grade-level writing samples from our end-of-the-year writing assessments from the previous school year. The purpose was to note strengths and needs as a school and to see where we were doing well and where we needed to step up the writing instruction. After two years of an intense focus on writing, the school as a whole was making excellent strides as documented by evolving beliefs aligning with more effective practices, everyday writing, interim assessments, district assessments, and application of school-established benchmarks and the Common Core State Standards. In that professional development meeting, we celebrated the specifics of what was going well and then moved to where we could do better. Although it was difficult to do so, in the midst of our guided process of reviewing typical writing samples by grade level, I said something like the following to the staff:

> There's no blame game here, but the writing at one grade level looks very similar to the writing at the adjacent grade level. Unless we have steep enough steps between grade levels, we will not get the high schoolwide achievement we are seeking. So each of us needs to do whatever is necessary to ensure we are doing right by our students at our grade level.

In actuality, a couple of weak teachers were causing some teachers at other grade levels to carry more than their fair share of responsibility for moving students forward as writers. Although the staff was evolving to a high level of personal trust, the lack of movement in one particular grade level was eroding full professional trust. Overall, these were kind and caring teachers, and they were generous in sharing ideas with others and welcoming colleagues into their classrooms, but those carrying the heavier load were also feeling frustrated that not all their peers were moving forward in a timely manner.

After that PD meeting, one teacher in question approached the principal and requested a meeting with me. The teacher stated she knew she needed to do a much better job and wanted help on how to improve. With the principal present and with her prior approval, I said to the teacher:

> You've had enormous support now for more than two years. Your principal, the literacy coach, and staff have bent over backwards to give you materials, demonstration-teach in your classroom, coteach with you, give you constructive feedback orally and in writing, and help you move forward in countless ways. Now it's your turn to do the hard work required to become an excellent writing teacher. Put together a plan for what you're saying you're going to do next, and show it to your principal. Review the videos we've been watching, do the professional reading, go over your notes from past residencies, observe other teachers. It's up to you now.

I believe there comes a time when we must take a tough but fair approach to teachers who don't measure up after they have had excellent mentoring and lots of ongoing opportunities and support over time. Ultimately, it's about all of us truly assuming the responsibility to do our academic and personal best for our students through our deliberate and skillful actions.

In 40-plus years of working in schools, I have found there are few teachers—less than 5 percent—who do not improve. In my experience, it is almost always a rigid personality type that cannot change or does not want to change, but again these are rare instances. Sometimes these are teachers who are just waiting it out, believing and hoping that the present initiative or fad will eventually go away, as previous ones have. I have come to believe that after giving these teachers plentiful support, either they step up to the plate or we kindly find a way to minimize the damage. As leaders we have a professional responsibility to have hard, honest conversations when necessary. We cannot afford to have any "urgency killers" in our schools—those who fail to be personally accountable for their actions and students' low achievement and who take on the role of resisters, naysayers, or gossipmongers.[12]

A culture of trust provides the emotional infrastructure that makes risk taking and openness to change possible. As I've stated before, nothing sustainable is possible for whole-school literacy achievement without that personal and professional trust. As well, when we try to change too many things at once, we can become overwhelmed and may even wind up taking a step or two backward. When our anxiety goes up, we are reluctant to consider doing things differently. We often see this when a new and ambitious leader steps into an organization. Even if almost everyone acknowledges the need for change, if the leader moves too fast and before trust is established, the best of intentions can backfire. And once trust is broken, it's extremely difficult to reestablish. Here, the adage "slow down to hurry up" is apt; within a trusting and respectful culture, all things are possible and possibilities are limitless.

Patience is a necessity. Sometimes it may feel to us like a teacher is barely moving along; but for someone who has been teaching the same way with limited results for her whole career, even a small change, such as trying to give directions to students more succinctly, feels huge. It can also take time for teachers—even veterans who are unaware of what they don't know—to realize that change is needed and to act upon that knowledge. Noticing and recognizing teachers' efforts so they will be willing to risk making even the smallest change can spur them on. Acknowledging a teacher's comment of "I didn't know that" with a response such as "It takes courage to say that. Thanks for speaking up" encourages the teacher to take a risk. Of course, eventually we need to push for faster change and progress, but in the beginning, celebrating even the smallest victories can pay big dividends.

It is also true that we cannot always wait for our colleagues to be ready. To make needed changes that have a positive effect on student learning, we have to rely on those who are ready for change and continue to model and expect the same for those who are reluctant or fearful. For a few colleagues, unfortunately, that readiness never comes. Once we've examined the data and are clear on what's needed to move forward, we have an obligation to move ahead in a thoughtful manner while providing the needed support

Quick Win

Find ways to acknowl-edge all that is good and kind in students, families, colleagues, staff members, and community.

that successful and worthy change requires. However, we will not have even an opportunity for successful change if we fail to acknowledge the need for change, establish a solid infrastructure supported by a foundation of trust, and fully commit to the change process.

Become a "Positive Deviant"— A Force for Helpful Change

Over many years, I've observed and concluded that one of the most crucial factors—if not the most decisive one—that influences how well students achieve is the *expectations mindset* that we educators hold. I have never been in a school where expectations by the adults are too high. A school culture of low expectations is so pervasive that often we don't even notice it. Too often we have convinced ourselves that outside factors—not we educators—are responsible for low achievement. Although poverty, crime, inadequate parenting, and a host of society's ills prevent us from reaching and teaching every student every day, we must try—and continue to try and try again—to do right by and for all our students.

In addition to an excuses-and-deficit mentality that reinforces low expectations, a collective lack of a sense of agency often hampers our efforts; that is, many of us don't really believe we have the wherewithal to significantly influence student learning and achievement.[13] In his leading-edge book *Better: A Surgeon's Notes on Performance*, prominent physician Atul Gawande describes how the outcomes for some intractable diseases have drastically improved through hard-working, informed individuals who possess a mindset that does not accept failure and who work relentlessly to ensure things get better. Gawande uses the phrase "positive deviants" to refer to those who do whatever it takes to "make a worthy difference" and positively change the status quo. I adopt that term for us as committed educators. In schools where all students are viewed as having high learning potential, there is no blame/complain game. Instead, there is a collective, unwavering will and a collaborative effort to do whatever it takes to guarantee that all our students engage in meaningful learning. That collective will includes becoming as knowledgeable as possible about all aspects of literacy, leadership, and learning. Furthermore, worthwhile and sustainable change requires that we educators hold the belief that we have it within our power to positively influence our students' learning and life destinies. Our first step as educators is to acknowledge that we can do better for those we

Quick Win

Hire teachers who are curious, and assess their willingness to learn more and be part of a continuously learning culture of high expectations and ongoing collaboration. That positive mindset will make it easy for them to quickly adjust.

serve, even when we are teaching under challenging conditions. Despite the presence of real constraints that remain outside our control and that influence our students' ability to engage and achieve, there are actions we can take—individually and collectively—that can positively influence our students' abilities so they enjoy increasing success. First among these is altering our mindset as to what's possible.

Develop a Mindset for High Achievement

Our ability and willingness to see possibilities where adversity and diversity coexist determine how successful we will be as educators. We may care about our students, work hard, and be knowledgeable about literacy, but kindness, hard work, and knowledge do not suffice for raising achievement.

Recently I was at a high-needs school where two 1st grade teachers held very different expectation mindsets about the capability of their students. It was the second month of school, and both teachers had received all their students (with the exception of those new to the school) from the school's only kindergarten teacher, who taught two half-day classes. Although almost all the exiting kindergartners at the school were readers and writers, as confirmed by teacher observation and detailed data, the two 1st grade teachers viewed and perceived this group of students very differently.

One praised the kindergarten teacher and told her how thrilled she was that her job as a 1st grade teacher was much easier because the incoming 1st graders knew all their sounds and letters, formed letters correctly, and could fluently write a page or more of meaningful text. She was excited about how far she would be able to take her students and that she could focus on meaningful content from the start.

The other 1st grade teacher saw her students differently and described their performance as "very low" and as "sweet children with behavior problems." She noted that they could not write well, requiring her to take dictation for some. She was discouraged by how hard she perceived it would be to move her students forward. Although she expressed hope that her students would become better writers and readers, unless she could alter her mindset to a more positive one, her students' literacy progress would be constrained by her low expectations.

The first teacher in this story lived her school life as a positive deviant. She did whatever it took to move her students forward, including advocating for them, partnering her 1st graders with students in an intermediate-grades class who acted as peer tutors, assessing them day by day to be sure they were moving forward, and refusing to let any political and school issues distract her from a laserlike focus on high literacy achievement for every student. At the end of the school year, most of her 34 students were joyfully reading and writing texts well beyond grade level, as judged by various assessments, including school and district benchmarks and exemplars from the Common Core State Standards, standardized interim writing assessments, everyday reading and writing samples, and student self-assessments. Her high expectations for all children, her sense of agency that she could propel all students forward, and her whole-part-whole, meaningful instruction made excellent results likely, and she got them.

The second teacher worked diligently and had good intentions, but at the end of the school year her students' reading and writing competencies, as a whole, lagged far behind the first teacher's. In spite of her participation in embedded, high-level professional development dedicated to improving student learning, collaborative work across grade levels to develop shared literacy knowledge, a strong and supportive principal and literacy coach, and a school culture of increasing trust, the second teacher was unable to sufficiently modify her expectations mindset in a manner that would help most of her students soar. Her beliefs and low expectations about what her students could and could not accomplish remained static.

So, how do we get all staff members to alter their views for what's possible for students? It's no easy matter, and it starts with changing the culture of the school. By *culture* I mean the trust levels, collaboration, sense of agency and urgency, shared beliefs, knowledge level, feedback, and infrastructure that support high-level, embedded professional development aimed at improving reading and writing achievement across the curriculum, each and every day. By *culture* I also mean determining what kind of change is worthwhile and what mindsets, structures, systems, resources, and practices we need to keep in place, what we need to modify, and what we need to replace. By *culture* I further mean creating a whole-school community that works together to increase effectiveness, efficiency, and enjoyment for teachers, leaders, students, and their families. Much of this book centers on achieving a culture that supports optimal learning.

I have thought a lot about why the second teacher never became part of the school culture of high expectations and why she seemed to lack any sense of urgency. I believe, above all, she lacked the determination, commitment, and curiosity to learn more, which require welcoming divergent conversations and thought as well as openness to doing things differently. Lacking those characteristics herself, she was unable to instill them in her students and thus thwarted their optimal progress.

At a minimum, the interview and hiring process for new teachers and leaders must include, as a crucial component, finding out what the applicant is curious about, is studying, is thinking about, and is hoping to learn. Responses to the questions "What are you reading professionally?" "Who are some of your favorite authors?" "What are you wondering about?" and "What are you passionate about?" can tell us volumes.

Teach with a Sense of Agency and Urgency

A sense of complacency is the air we breathe in too many schools—our low- and high-achieving schools alike. In low-performing schools, we too often accept the fact that students are routinely two and three years below grade level. In high-performing schools where many students may come from affluent backgrounds, teachers often take credit for students' high test scores that may more realistically be the result of the wide literacy and learning opportunities families have provided to their children.

A story comes to mind. When teaching in a residency focused on reading, I was struck by the engagement and curiosity of a 1st grade student who enthusiastically responded to a nonfiction story about dogs of war that I had just read aloud to the class. (The book is *Nubs: The True Story of a Mutt, a Marine and a Miracle*.[14]) His participation at all levels—answering thoughtful questions, understanding vocabulary, and contributing to our shared writing summary—stood out among his peers. So I was surprised and disheartened to learn and to observe that this boy was the oldest and most struggling reader in the classroom. Because he did not yet know his letters and sounds, he was pulled out to work with an interventionist 30 minutes a day, during which he was drilled with flash cards and unavailable to benefit from high-quality classroom instruction in language arts.

As an alternative I suggested using vocabulary and pictures from the nonfiction book he appeared to relish—words and phrases such as *Humvee*, *war zone*, and *stray dog*—to teach him his letters and sounds, which I believed he would learn rapidly if meaning were attached to them. I remember feeling outrage that this intelligent boy was not receiving the support

Quick Win

Give a potential hire a professional article to read; then base part of the interview on discussing that noteworthy article, which will give some insight into whether the person is a good fit for the school's learning culture.

that would propel him forward. His teachers were kind and caring, but they did not yet see this student as highly capable. Moreover, their actions did not indicate an urgent need to hold themselves accountable for his lack of progress or to do whatever it took to ensure his immediate and fast progress as a reader.

Believing we have the wherewithal to increase achievement for all students is a big shift for many of us. As already stated but important enough to be restated, a lack of agency on the part of adults—that is, the belief that we cannot influence the learning and achievement of some of our students—is one of the major factors holding these students back.[15] Additionally, teaching with a sense of urgency is required.

Teaching with a sense of urgency means making every minute count. When teaching with urgency, we teach with a sense of relevancy and purpose, keep most demonstration lessons to 10 to 15 minutes, adjust our pacing, assess as we teach, and constantly rethink and revise as we go along. Teaching with urgency does not mean rushing through lessons; it does mean being mindful that how and what we are teaching in every instructional moment is worthwhile for our students. *We're not in a race to the top; we're on a journey to excellence.*

Ask Uncommon Questions

The questions we ask ourselves while planning, teaching, assessing, and reflecting show what we value, and ultimately those questions play a large part in determining our effectiveness as educators and "positive deviants." By effectiveness, I mean the beneficial and lasting influence and effect we are able to have on student engagement, learning, and achievement. That effectiveness does not come about through strict adherence to a particular learning target, standard, program, or set of criteria. The latter are important, of course, and can help us become more intentional and specific in our teaching and leading. However, the learning targets and objectives must not supersede our primary emphasis: the mental and emotional well-being and growth of our students. I believe that highly effective teachers ask different questions than typical teachers do—before, during, and after instruction. In fact, we are constantly questioning everything we do: *Why does this matter? Could it be otherwise? What other considerations are necessary? Is there a better way? How could we do this differently and more effectively?*

Before I teach literacy in any school residency, I spend many hours thinking and planning, on my own and with the teacher in whose classroom I will be demonstrating and coaching. Although I always have the curriculum, standards, and specific learning goals in mind, the students take precedence over those, and my primary planning questions to myself run along these lines:

- What topic, actions, and activities will fully engage the hearts and minds of the students so they will invest their full energies?
- What outstanding and relevant literature and resources will inspire and inform the students through rich language and ideas from various authors, genres, and formats?
- How can we best support all students to move their learning forward and encourage their success and independence?
- How will we know students are understanding and learning what we are teaching?

Some administrators and teachers complain they get "push back" if they try to deviate in any way from standard protocols and required resources. However, focusing on particular standards, learning targets, and outcomes does not guarantee a positive effect on student learning. As one principal from Wisconsin wrote to me:

Requiring teachers to rigidly adhere to a prescribed protocol for instruction can leach the life out of what makes learning so enjoyable: the interactions between teacher-student, student-student, and classroom-global community.[16]

Here's an example of what I'm talking about, taken from my work with the members of a K–12 school team who were committed to doing better for their mostly underachieving students in a large urban district. The leaders and teachers proudly described how anyone could walk into any classroom and know immediately by what's posted on the walls exactly what standard and learning outcome every teacher was focused on for that day. In particular, they took great pride in the standardization they had achieved; that is, all teachers at a grade level were working on the same goal. However, when I asked, "How is that working for you? Is student achievement going up?" they responded that a large proportion of students were still one to three years below grade level.

And here's another example. Recently an elementary coordinator wrote me of her concern that the district leadership expects teachers to know exactly what the learning target is for every learning task and to have those posted. Yet the same teachers do not know what knowledge their students possess or lack, and the teachers are not highly skilled in assessing their students or in knowing how to give effective feedback. This all too common practice of following procedures, standards, and resources without question, which can sound good and look impressive on the surface, may do considerable harm to students by taking the focus away from their most pressing learning needs and interests. We have only so much time, and we must apportion it wisely.

There is a big difference between posting clear learning goals (perhaps as "I Can" statements) and simply copying something from the district pacing guide. Learning goals can be linked to district and state standards, as well as student needs, but we educators have to be both knowledgeable and articulate to use learning goals so they actually help students learn more.

Keep in mind that in our role as positive deviants—that is, as productive teachers and leaders who put students at the forefront of all we do—we must advocate for and behave with a mindset that puts students first. That means asking questions that are uncommon for some of us as educators.

Uncommon Questions

- What do we really need to be doing, saying, and providing to ensure students understand, value, and can apply the academic expectations we set for and with them?
- What are we doing, saying, and providing that may work against optimal student learning?
- Are we emphasizing the wrong end goal(s)?
- Are we overly focused or overly invested in a structure, a process, standards, or a program?
- What might we do differently?
- What else do we need to consider?
- Are we succumbing to "group think" and failing to consider important alternatives?
- Does our instructional emphasis build on the student's self-esteem, transferable knowledge, and self-monitoring abilities?

Instead of thinking first about naming and posting learning targets, think first about making worthwhile learning visible, explicit, and comprehensible for students. We can, in fact, teach our colleagues and ourselves how to think, question, and teach more responsively. We must ensure that we are doing enough excellent demonstrating for learners—for example, through our explanations and thinking aloud, which show exactly what we expect students to be trying and applying in their own work. In addition, we must provide sufficient shared experiences and guided practice if we expect learners to be successful. Once we as educators are highly knowledgeable and are clear and articulate in our instructional intentions, posted learning targets can become somewhat redundant. At this point, we can find out what students are learning and why they are learning it by asking them.

Become a Teacher Who Also Leads

At schools where teachers are expert at their craft and students are high achieving, those teachers are also, almost always, teacher-leaders. To be clear, we are not talking about those teachers whose goal is to move into administration. A teacher-leader's primary job is still as a teacher of a group of students, but the job goes far beyond the classroom walls. It means seeing ourselves as concerned for all the school's students and being willing to share what we know, coach and coteach, help implement new initiatives, partner with teachers who may be at a different grade level, set up unconventional learning situations, speak up honestly in meetings when it's important to do so, and keep the good of the whole school uppermost in all our actions. Much of this book is about becoming a highly effective teacher who also leads, which is a necessity for raising and sustaining achievement schoolwide.

Becoming a teacher-leader requires extensive knowledge of relevant research and best practices and how to apply that knowledge in the classroom, superb skills in communicating and working with others, a mindset that puts students before standards, plus courage and stamina. That is, these are teachers who are willing to share what they know, collaborate with others, stretch their thinking, stand by their principles, advocate for their students, and see themselves and their work as part of a larger school purpose. Becoming a teacher-leader also means being willing to step outside our comfort zones and outside our classrooms. It means questioning the status quo when necessary, checking the research to ensure it applies to

Quick Win

Dress for success. The way we present ourselves sends a message to students and the public about our pride in our profession.

our specific population and context, looking carefully at the data and using them to improve learning, and suggesting and advocating for alternative approaches when necessary.

It can be difficult to take a stand on established policies that are harmful to the teaching profession and ultimately to our students' achievement and well-being, but sometimes there's no one else to do it, and we have to at least try. Jonathan Kozol wisely states, "Look for battles big enough to matter but, at the same time, small enough to win some realistic victories."[17] We'll never know if we can win an important battle or a small victory unless we confront the issues in a constructive manner and offer alternative actions.

An example of a courageous teacher-leader is Lori Johnson. When her district became overinvested in an evaluation program that was yielding numerical data that were not useful for improving reading instruction, she lobbied her superintendent, led the formation of a district advisory group, and caused the district to take another look at the program that was taking too much time away from instruction and that did not support what Lori knew and practiced regarding excellent reading instruction. She did all this in a highly professional and positive manner while recognizing and affirming district leaders and their intentions. The result of her unrelenting efforts—which was possible in no small measure because of the ongoing moral support of her principal, DeAnna Finger—was that her school was granted flexibility with how to use the required assessment. Like many teacher-leaders, Lori was a reluctant one. She did not start out seeking to be a leader. She felt compelled to speak out and take action because of what she believed—from years of professional study and teaching experience—her students most needed to develop as readers.

Here's another example. Sharlline Markwardt is an English language development (ELD) teacher who took a stand and lobbied her district for a "push-in" model rather than the traditional "pull-out" model for second-language learners. She invited her principal and the district's director of curriculum and instruction to observe firsthand the results she was getting when she supported her English language learners (ELLs) in the regular classroom, and those results included impressive data.

Working closely with the classroom teacher, Sharlline differentiated the curriculum all students were receiving to scaffold the learning for her English language learners. Not only was she then able to change the model at her own school, but she also convinced the district to change the model in every school. She offered and followed through on mentoring ELD teachers in other buildings by inviting them to observe her teach, debrief through professional conversations, and follow up with districtwide professional development. Sharlline notes:

> I knew something had to change, that what we were doing wasn't working. In looking at the whole-part-whole model, I realized that teaching ELD in a pull-out was about teaching just parts and not wholes. A classroom teacher took a chance on me and my idea of doing a language assessment on her whole class. What we found was that all of the non-ELD students scored somewhere on the language acquisition range, so we took the plunge, with administration support, and implemented ELD within content area teaching. The results have proven to be not just positive for ELD students, but the non-ELD students' writing improved as well.[18]

Becoming a teacher-leader also means speaking with clarity and knowledge, and communicating and collaborating in a respectful and effective manner. The teacher-leader who is able to be a force for positive change strives for a mindset of "we-we," not "we-they," and recognizes that all of us want students to succeed even if our means to that success differ. It is our close relationships with other teachers and administrators that give us our political power to make change. I have never seen a teacher who maintains low expectations for students or poor relationships with peers and administrators rise to become a leader who makes a positive and lasting impact in a school or district.

Perhaps most of all, we need to stay focused on solutions, stay upbeat (become a positive deviant), see our colleagues positively and as having good intentions, continue to generously share ideas, and listen to others with an open mind. Laurie Espenel is a teacher-leader who possesses all of these characteristics, along with being an excellent communicator. Having a strong relationship with her principal enabled Laurie to serve as a positive buffer and an advocate for both the principal and the teachers. In speaking of her role as teacher-leader, Laurie says:

> It's a role I come by naturally. I've never been afraid to bring up an issue that needed resolution. Also, the staff trusted me. I knew the feelings of much of the staff. Taking on the role of teacher-leader opened the

principal's door wider so there's better communication. The principal was more accessible because teachers' concerns were addressed in a way that made them feel they were being heard.[19]

Become a Leader Who Also Knows Literacy

My biggest learning lesson in working in diverse schools for the last two decades is this: *Teachers have to be leaders, and leaders have to know literacy.* I learned this lesson the hard way when, after focusing all my residency efforts on working with teachers, I realized the principal often did not know how to fully support teachers—what to look for in the reading-writing classroom, what to say to teachers to help them move forward, and most of all, what highly effective literacy instruction, learning, and assessment entailed. Although I had been demonstrating effective reading and writing practices with students in classrooms and then coaching teachers to take on that responsibility, I realized that nothing of significance would be sustained schoolwide until the principal could assume the role of effective literacy coach as part of being a strong leader.

A principal cannot bring a whole school of teachers from good to great without becoming a highly knowledgeable literacy expert, as well as a trusted leader and colleague. Without the principal knowing what's most important to look for and listen for in the literacy classroom and how to give honest and useful feedback and support to teachers, teachers and students won't improve much in ways that matter.

Barb Ide, a former elementary and middle school principal who works as a school improvement coach in a high-poverty urban school, is an excellent example of a principal who greatly increased her effectiveness when she expanded her leadership role to include literacy. She talks about how that increased knowledge—along with learning how to better support, trust, and communicate with her staff—changed things for teachers, students, the school, and herself as a leader:

> A new leader going into a successful school needs to observe and pay attention to the established culture. I followed this protocol in my first two schools, and it was a good decision! At my next school, I was sent in as a change agent and made a mess of things because I was accustomed to collaboration and trust. When some of the faculty met me with suspicion and resistance, I reacted with a heavy hand. I made a

rookie mistake by hearing only the contrary minority rather than seeking out the innovators and prospective leaders. After a couple of difficult years I shifted to a focus on literacy and delighted in our staff as we combined effort for positive change. An indicator of progress over the seven years at that school was the number of teacher-leaders who emerged, due in part to the literacy experience anchored in a culture of trust. Nearly a dozen future principals, assistant principals, and literacy coaches spread their wings with first-hand knowledge of the power of curriculum teams (PLCs) guided by a schoolwide focus.[20]

Sustainable, worthwhile change in our schools is not easy, but it is possible and necessary if we are to serve our students well and fairly. A premise of this book is that it is all of us working together as smart, inquiring, trusting educators with our primary focus on deep knowledge of literacy, instruction, assessment, and learning—not the latest standards, curriculum, evaluations, or tests—that matters most. For the high achievement, engagement, and joy in learning we all seek, not just for our students but for ourselves as well, it *is* within our power to make a worthy and lasting difference.

2

Responsive Instruction, Feedback, and Assessment

Before we can discuss what's most important to teach in reading and writing, we need to be sure our instructional focus is grounded in responsive and responsible instruction and assessment through application of a research-based learning model. Understanding and applying that model makes it possible for all learners—students, teachers, and leaders—to succeed. Therefore, this chapter begins by discussing some crucial teaching and learning principles as well as mindsets, actions, and core beliefs that underpin all responsible literacy teaching and leading across the curriculum. We then move to an emphasis on what I call the Optimal Learning Model, a foundation for all effective instruction and learning and for learners assuming increasing responsibility for becoming independent.[1] Finally, we turn to an in-depth focus on feedback, a recurring theme in this book. How, when, and where to give effective feedback is a complex undertaking but vital for accelerating learning and giving learners the tools and confidence to move forward.

Teach and Assess Responsively

Responsive teaching and assessing means we are always teaching for understanding, continuously checking for understanding, and adjusting instruction as needed. It's not enough to know how to do something; we have to know what we are doing and why we are doing it if we are to apply any "how to" in a worthwhile and sustainable way. Otherwise we remain stuck at a limited level of functional expertise and never reach the level of a knowledgeable expert, one who is able to adjust and innovate as the situation requires. This is as true for us teachers and leaders as it is for our students.

Underlying the highly effective teaching of reading and writing—along with listening, speaking, and thinking—are responsive and responsible practices, actions, and mindsets that we educators integrate into our daily instruction, assessment, and leadership. Chief among these are to

- Ask the essential questions first.
- Teach with authenticity.
- Plan with the end in mind.
- Provide more choice within structure.
- Hear all the voices.
- Embed formative assessment.

All the aforementioned actions and goals are connected to our beliefs and current knowledge and are the fabric of our daily teaching, leading, and successful interactions with students and colleagues. Although standards and curriculum guide our instruction, what and how we teach must be interconnected to the responsive practices that lead to high student engagement, achievement, and independence as learners. Again, the practices listed are those I keep in mind as a leader working with teachers as well as a teacher working with students.

Deeply connected to responsive teaching and assessing are holding high expectations that translate into relevant and appropriately challenging work. As noted in Chapter 1, after more than four decades of teaching, I have not yet been in a school where expectations are too high—and that includes affluent schools. Always, it's amazing what students and teachers can do when we empower them with the knowledge and tools to learn more easily and with greater engagement and enjoyment. As students demonstrate that they can do better, many teachers do raise expectations. However, learners shouldn't have to prove their worth before we give them the relevant and challenging work they deserve. Much of this book shows what is possible when we educators become highly knowledgeable.

Ask the Most Essential Questions First

Our inner conversations and the questions we ask ourselves before, during, and after instruction determine not only where we put our instructional emphasis but also how successful our students will be as learners. As effective and thoughtful teachers and leaders who apply the evidence we have related to student learning, we constantly think and rethink where to put our energies and efforts. I continually ask myself two big questions.

Two Big Questions

- What is the most important thing I need to do, right now, for this learner or group of learners to keep them engaged, to move learning forward, and to encourage independence?
- How much support—and what kind of support—does this learner or this particular group of learners need at this point in time to be successful?

I have similar inner conversations when I am coaching teachers and principals; that is, my focus is on the bigger picture and the end goal of their becoming confident, effective, and independent instructional learners, teachers, coaches, and leaders.

If we ask ourselves questions focused first on the learner and second on the content (see bulleted examples that follow), we are more likely to reach our objectives and learning targets, engage and motivate students, and zero in on students' needs and interests—all of which will enable us to accelerate learning and teach with urgency, enthusiasm, and authentic purpose. The secondary questions listed (in parentheses on p. 40) are necessary, but they are dependent on the first questions, which set the tone and create the conditions for successful learning. Some essential questions I continually ask myself follow on the next page.

Because standards are an important issue in today's schools, we need to think about how they relate to the questions we ask ourselves before, during, and after instruction. Although I teach with the big picture of the Common Core State Standards in mind and have a copy of the Anchor Standards for Reading and Writing (http://www.corestandards.org/) available on one double-sided sheet, those standards are mostly a check on my instruction. If we start out asking ourselves questions such as "How can I ensure my students have mastered a specific standard?"—for example, "citing textual evidence to support an argument" or "text structure"—we can wind up with a rigid approach that emphasizes teaching a set of subskills. Without deep, sustained reading and rich conversations on worthwhile

texts—accompanied by teacher demonstrations and guided practice—
students are not likely to progress very well as literacy learners.

Essential Questions

- "How do I engage students' hearts and minds so they want to read and
  write?" (Rather than "How do I raise achievement in reading and writing?")
- "How can I ensure that students will want to go on writing and have the
  energy to write?" (Rather than "How can I get this student, or this group of
  students, to improve his, or their, writing?")
- "What do I need to do to ensure that students are becoming increasingly proficient, independent, self-determining readers?" (Rather than "How can I fit in
  all my guided reading groups today?")
- "How can I easily assess what students are learning when they are working
  independently?" (Rather than "What management activities do I need to have
  in place to keep students busy while I meet with a group?")
- "How can I ensure that almost all students are ready to be released to write
  (or read) on their own, even if it takes more time today?" (Rather than "I've
  planned for the students to write today, and we have only 20 minutes left, so
  we need to get started.")
- "How can I have in-depth, public conferences with a few students in a way
  that all students benefit?" (Rather than "How can I fit in 25 conferences?")
- "What didn't I do (when a lesson goes badly) when students didn't 'get it,'
  and what do I need to do now to help students understand?" (Rather than
  "I taught it. What's wrong with the students that they didn't learn it?") Most
  often, I go back to the Optimal Learning Model (see p. 58) when teaching
  breaks down and learning doesn't occur.

As a staff, think about starting with the big question "What do we want
our students to know and be able to do as readers, writers, and thinkers?"
instead of "What standards do I need to teach?" Then, use the standards as
a framework and guide but not as a dictate of instruction or curriculum. Of
course, the more knowledgeable the staff becomes, the greater the chance
there is that the standards, or any framework, will be used in a manner that
increases student learning.

A significant consideration is that the essence of what we teach from
grade to grade remains constant. That is, we want all learners to read for

understanding and to write for authentic audiences and purposes. What changes are the complexity, sophistication, variety, and length of the texts; the amount of demonstrations, guided support, and practice students require to be successful; and our expectations and purposes for the learners' actions regarding use and application of genres, texts, resources, strategies, and self-monitoring.

Teach with Authenticity

Authenticity is key to everything we do and say each day when we seek to engage students, teach reading and writing, give feedback, and assess. No matter their age, students learn and retain more when they can apply engaging classroom instruction to real-world issues, they can collaborate with peers, they can participate in active learning, and they are taught how to learn, not just what to learn.[2] "Reading comprehension growth seems to be especially strong in classrooms employing more authentic literacy events," according to literacy researcher Nell Duke.[3] In fact, "providing students with real-world reasons for engaging with informational texts was the most significant factor in improving their reading and writing of these texts."[4] Teaching with authenticity also leads to greater inquiry by students.

We need to constantly ask, "How can we make what we are about to do as authentic and meaningful as possible?" That is, if we successfully address the larger questions, the details will be included. This kind of questioning is also connected to whole-part-whole teaching. That is, the most efficient way to teach all the necessary skills and strategies students need is to embed that intentional teaching into the daily reading and writing of whole, meaningful texts. In fact, at the end of a residency, when we assess and list all the skills and strategies we have "covered" and taught, teachers who were used to teaching skills in isolation are amazed and relieved (see chart on p. 42).

In authentic assessment the activity looks much like the instruction; that is, "the difference between instruction and the assessment of instruction vanishes."[5] This seamlessness is exactly what we see when we teach responsively. The instruction and assessment are interwoven, working together side by side and continuously informing us of where we need to go next to increase understanding and learning.

Even when it seems difficult to take required content and make it meaningful for students, we can create an authentic audience. For example, in teaching summary writing, 5th graders learning about the body systems such as the heart, lungs, and digestive system can create picture books for younger readers or "What I've Learned" letters to their parents. Such authentic writing can also serve as an evaluation for what students have learned. Along the same lines, book reviews by students (not book *reports*, which are found only in schools) can become part of a school's website of book recommendations across the grades or be featured in the school's library to entice readers, just as my local independent bookstore uses the reviews.

**Partial List of Skills and Strategies Taught
in a Two-Day Reading Residency (Nonfiction Focus)**

- Rereading to clarify meaning
- Slowing down to cement meaning
- Reading on to understand a concept
- Using surrounding context to figure out word meaning
- Using photos, captions, headings, and labels to enhance meaning
- Gaining background information on a website before reading
- Substituting a word that makes sense for an unknown word
- Self-checking and self-monitoring
- Noting author's purpose and point of view
- Noticing author's craft and applying to own writing
- Figuring out most important facts and restating in own words

---

Similarly, teachers of language arts, science, and social studies in middle and high school can also incorporate authentic literacy instruction into their required content. For example, social studies teachers teach students how to access, read, summarize, and discuss current events, and then connect the significance of those events to their history lessons and the world students live in. Authenticity is key for inspiring middle and high school students to do "the work" and to see how what they are learning in school is relevant to their futures.

Nell Duke and her coauthors have shown that when work is more authentic—that is, it resembles a real-world enterprise—students are likely to be more engaged and to achieve more.[6] After a while, teachers become skillful in finding ways to make curriculum more relevant to students. For example, in planning for an upcoming residency in a combined 4th and 5th grade classroom, we focused our reading and writing on "What does it mean to be a good citizen in our community?" The frontloading, which included immersion in relevant texts and noticing what authors do (and students might try), resulted in excellent student writing and a shift in the teacher's thinking. The teacher, Sherri Steuart, commented:

> When planning for the residency, I started to think even more deeply and critically about my practice. Rather than gathering books for a unit study, I centered my thinking around a question—"What does it mean to be a good citizen?" It wasn't simply a "unit"; it became an inquiry. Writing is more than studying a particular genre and having students create their own piece. This is where I think we teachers can get stuck. The residency experience reminded me to move beyond the bulletin board and view student writing as having a specific, authentic purpose for the real world.
>
> This residency also validated my strong belief that reading and writing go hand in hand. They are harmoniously intertwined and are taught in a dynamic fashion, rather than a linear set of activities. During this inquiry, we read several texts as "readers." Students interviewed their parents asking who they admired and why. We listed our connections, shared our thoughts, asked questions and made note of parts that tugged at our hearts. We also read these books as "writers." We charted the different techniques authors used. Students started to experiment with these techniques in their own writing. More importantly, students started to view each other as writing resources by using techniques created by their peers.[7]

How can we ensure that our teaching has the authenticity we strive for? Questions such as those in the section called "Self-Assessment for Authenticity in Teaching" (p. 44) can help keep things on track.

Plan with the End in Mind

In my current residency work in schools, most often I spend three days at a school in the fall, demonstrating and doing most of the teaching in the host classrooms. Then, when I follow up with a two-day residency in the spring, I begin the handover and gradual release of responsibility to teachers, and my role becomes more one of shared teaching and coaching.

(During the months between the first and second residencies, the teachers—with the support of the weekly PLCs—have been trying out and practicing what was demonstrated.) By far the most challenging part of the residency work is getting the overall planning right. The planning takes many hours and weeks and requires constant thinking. My biggest question is "What do we want the students to be able to do at the end?" (in this case, at the end of three days). Of course, the question takes into consideration the required curriculum and standards, but we don't begin there.

Self-Assessment for Authenticity in Teaching

- Does the goal, lesson, or activity reflect a real-world expectation and context?
- Is the work relevant to students' needs and interests?
- Are the resources of excellent quality?
- Are the audience and purpose meaningful?
- Is a whole-part-whole teaching philosophy embraced?
- Are we continuously checking for understanding?
- Is there time built in for sustained practice?
- Are there choices within structure?

In beginning our planning together for a recent residency in a 5th grade classroom, the teacher related how she and the students had been learning about body systems and were using that study to learn how to summarize. The teacher expressed frustration that the students were not that engaged in writing summaries about how the heart or lungs work, despite excellent instruction. While they dutifully did the work, they didn't see a real purpose for it. Both the teacher and students were frustrated by how long the work was taking. The main questions we asked when planning were these:

- How can we engage students' hearts and minds in a way that will make it easy to teach them everything they need to know as readers and writers, including summarizing?
- How can we connect reading with writing so students use more nonfiction in their writing (a CCSS goal that we were keeping in mind)?
- What supports do we need to provide so every student is successful?
- How will we check for understanding as we go along?

Coming up with a topic that could successfully answer those most important questions was initially one of the most challenging parts of the planning. Once the host classroom teacher and I were in agreement on bullying as a topic, everything fell into place. We chose bullying because it is a real-life concern that affects most students; it seemed a good topic for the beginning of the school year; it might prove to build a culture of kindness in the classroom and throughout the high-needs school; it could give students agency in their own lives. And, yes, we could also teach summarizing in a way that would be highly engaging and purposeful and also fulfill curriculum requirements.

Our highest priority was finding excellent literature that would provide the facts, perspectives, and information we needed. Without excellent, accurate, engaging texts and sources, we could not have followed through with our plan in a deep and meaningful manner. Here I want to underscore how crucial it is to have first-rate texts and resources to support teaching, leading, and student learning.

Our second priority was to leave enough time for frontloading—that is, assessing what students knew; immersing them in the topic; gathering information through reading and note taking; compiling important information and facts; and determining possible solutions. We allowed two full weeks before the residency for this necessary preparation work.

Looking back on this lesson study many months later, we realized that teaching with the CCSS in mind rather than using them (or any standards) as a starting point, we taught—and students practiced, with expert guidance from their classroom teacher, Laurie Espenel—several important skills. The students were reading a wide range of informational texts, including online resources; researching and taking notes; citing specific evidence from a text; performing a close reading of text; learning and applying new vocabulary; and building on prior knowledge. Not least of what students learned was how to collaborate, effectively communicate orally and in writing, listen to others' ideas and understand varying viewpoints, and present ideas clearly. All these essential skills are an integral part of the CCSS. However, if we had set out to teach each of these elements as a separate piece, we would have taken the joy, eagerness, and depth out of teaching and learning and squandered precious learning time.

Because summarizing, especially in writing, is hard to do well and would require much practice, it would not have been realistic to expect all

32 students to write summaries, on their own, in three days. The question we asked ourselves was "How can we best teach summarizing so all students experience success?" That led to putting the students in eight heterogeneous groups of four, which the classroom teacher balanced by gender, ability, and personalities.[8] Our goal and expectation was for each group to do a shared writing; that is, to collaborate to create one written summary.

The question we then asked was "What demonstrations and supports do we need to provide to ensure each group of four is successful?" That led to a fishbowl demonstration, in which the teacher chose four high-achieving students from different groups to model with me the procedures and actions we would expect from each working group. It's important to note here that we were not showcasing "fishbowl" as a teaching technique that is useful to have in our toolbox; we chose fishbowl because it seemed the best means to reach our end goal of having students successfully and confidently write short summaries.

The fishbowl demonstration included defining the roles of facilitator, scribe, and group members, and it took place in front of the whole class, with the rest of the students looking on and taking notes on the positive actions and behaviors they observed. (Their notes were our assessment for what the observing students noticed and learned.) An excerpt from one student's observation notes are presented on p. 47. What is striking is that this particular student is the one who had most bullied others. Yet the student saw the value of what we were doing, took it seriously, and eventually went on to become an excellent group facilitator and a more productive and kind class member.

When the work is authentic, the processes used can apply across a broad spectrum of curriculum and instruction. Note that the fishbowl and the following guidelines for conversations in small groups (p. 47) apply for literature, math, science, social studies, and other content areas. In fact, teachers report that teaching students to work in self-directed, heterogeneous groups pays big dividends. Not only are all students actively involved; teachers are free to walk around, monitor, and guide groups as needed.

A fishbowl demonstration before self-directed small groups begin their work.

A student's observation notes from a fishbowl observation.

General Guidelines for Small-Group Conversations

- Speak as if you are having a conversation with a friend or family member. No need to raise your hand.
- Make eye contact—with group members and with the speaker.
- Build on statements others have made; "I'd like to add on to…." "I disagree because…." "I'm not sure I understand what you're saying. Can you explain that?"
- Support statements with evidence.
- Assume a posture that shows engagement: sit up tall, lean into the conversation, listen attentively.
- Invite everyone into the conversation. "We haven't heard from…. Tell us what you think, or you can restate what someone else has said."[9]

Quick Win

Have multiple small groups operating at the same time once you have demonstrated and practiced how small groups are to collaborate. In 15–45 minutes, you can observe and guide each group, and every student gets to fully participate, whether it's in reading, math, social studies, or science.

Evaluation of Learning
October 1–3, 2012
Sandy Grade School, Sandy, OR

Name MADISON RIOS Grade 5th

Write down your thoughts on what you learned this week about writing, revising, editing, reading, thinking, conferring, working in a group, or anything that seems important to you.

I learned that I was a better writer than I thout. I fell like in the future I will have a book of my own in stores. My group of four made me fed great, included and a good writer. I liked having the group of four better than the table groops. I learnd about what

hapens in a fish boul. I felt excited fore all the ideas I came up with. and I felt good about it. It made me a evan beter writer then I use to be. I want to make more books now because I fell confident.

A student reflects on her learning at the end of a residency.

In the self-evaluations students wrote at the end of the residency, most of them indicated that participating in self-directed small groups was the highlight of the residency. They felt empowered. One student's reflection was typical for growth and confidence and is shown above.

Provide More Choice Within Structure

Teachers and administrators worry that if we give learners more options, we will lose control. Just the opposite is true. Allowing and encouraging some choice within a carefully defined structure promotes higher-level decision making and thinking and greater engagement for our students. When we teach explicitly, make the criteria for success visible, and give learners the necessary demonstrations, supports, and time and space to practice, giving some choice in the required activity yields better results. Notice that the use of the word *learners* in this discussion of providing more choice is deliberate; providing options is as critical for us educators as it is for our students.

Some choice makes it possible for all students to engage—that is, to willingly and enthusiastically do the work of applying their best efforts and abilities, and the same is true for adults. When we have to rigidly follow a protocol with no room for our professional judgment, many of us disengage or simply go through the motions to get the job done. An extreme and unsettling example is the way some current teacher evaluations rate teachers in unbending ways, forcing some to put on a "dog and pony show" in order to get a good evaluation. Another disturbing side effect of implementing uncompromising structures is that some teachers act robotically and have difficulty thinking for themselves.

Choice is often the game-changer for elementary, middle school, and high school students who are not thriving as readers and writers. Research from Peter Johnston and Gay Ivey, along with work from practitioners and teacher-researchers including Nancy Atwell, Donalyn Miller, Kelly Gallagher, Nancy Allison, and Penny Kittle, conclusively shows that when students are given interesting, personally relevant, and, often, "edgy" books—along with time and choice to read and discuss them with peers—they become engaged, proficient readers.[10] Research by Don Graves, Don Murray, Lucy Calkins, and others clearly indicates that choice in writing topics is essential and may be the single most important factor for engaging writers,[11] which then leads to their willingness to do the hard work of revision and editing.

Note that we would first demonstrate and explain our expectations, give students time to try out and practice the activity or assignment with our guidance, and then, with the students, establish basic criteria to be included in the work. But for many of our students, providing some choice makes the difference in whether they will succeed.

Here are some ways we can provide choice within structure in reading and writing:

Ways to Provide Choice Within Structure

- Write a book review on a recently completed favorite book.
- Self-select and read a nonfiction book, from a choice of several to many titles, to supplement and expand a required curriculum study.

Ways to Provide Choice Within Structure—(*continued*)

- Allow students more choice in daily writing, about 80 percent free choice (with less prompt-writing and no story-starters). That choice may include genres, forms, and presentation formats, such as charts, brochures, and e-presentations.
- Write with a partner or independently in a genre or form that has already been taught and practiced (to ensure quality and accuracy).
- Give more time for self-selected reading by having a rich selection of interesting texts for students to choose from (after first teaching and assessing that students know how to choose "just-right" books).
- Set up a reading log or reading record together; that is, negotiate with students what is to be included.
- Allow choice in a required research topic; that is, while everyone may be required to write about a person who influenced history, students get to choose from a wide range.
- Encourage publication in various formats, such as blogs, videos, social media, and graphics.

See Routman, 2005, *Writing Essentials*, pp. 177–178, for many more ideas.

In the bullying lesson described in the previous section, all the students working in heterogeneous groups of four were expected to cowrite one business letter to a self-selected audience summarizing a local bullying issue and proposing some solutions. (See the photo of the class-written chart of possible audiences for these letters on p. 51.) Each group chose the audience that mattered most to them and wrote a business letter describing the particular bullying situation. One of those letters appears on p. 52.

Each letter began with a required introductory paragraph, which was based on a rubric we jointly created:

Rubric for Introductory Paragraph on Bullying

- Grab the reader's attention in first sentence (for example, with a question or most interesting fact).
- Restate facts in another way to make them stand out.
- Combine important facts into one sentence.

We created the rubric after first doing a whole-class shared writing. A photo below shows the actual paragraph we wrote together in the shared writing session.

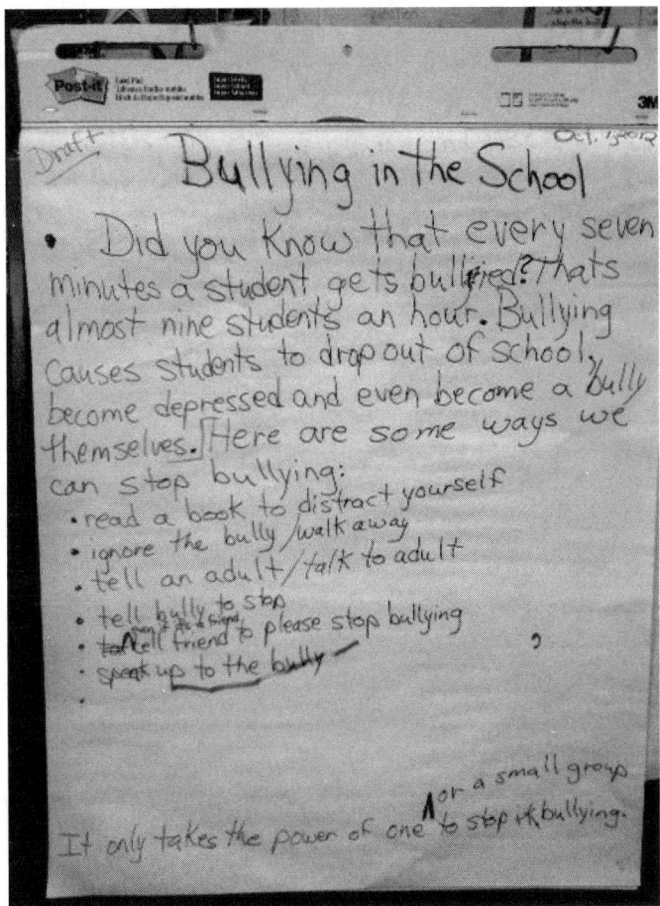

Example of whole-class shared writing.

Our shared writing led directly to the fishbowl demonstration of writing described previously. The eight self-directed, heterogeneous groups then met simultaneously to write their introductory paragraph and letter as the classroom teacher and I walked around, conferred, and offered guidance.

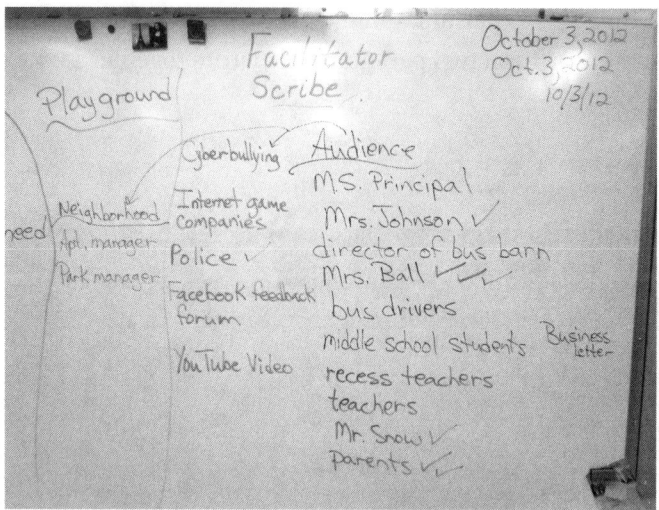

Students identify audiences for a letter related to school bullying.

Dear Student Council,

A bus full of action! Kids screaming, kids arguing, bus driver yelling at kids, and kids crying. That's why it's a bus full of action.

Now that we're 5th graders we think that we're the big cheese of the school but don't get carried away because right after that year we become the youngest again. We thought that the middle school kids were supposed to be the role models for the elementary students. Instead some middle schoolers are bullying, and the bystanders won't do anything about it because they're afraid.

We want to request a meeting with the student council and principals of both schools to talk about bullying on the bus and how it hurts everyone and how we can prevent it. We think that with communication we can figure out how to stop the bullies from bullying. Children shouldn't be afraid of riding the bus. We should all have a happy ride home.

Sincerely,

Sera, Braeja, Parker, and Riley

One group's letter to the middle school's student council.

Students were thrilled to receive written responses to their letters and to have their letters taken so seriously:

We wrote to the bus barn, the middle school, our principal, and many others. Surprisingly, we got a lot of responses. We got letters back, set up meetings, and the middle school even developed a lesson plan about bullying to help make it stop. We were shocked, surprised, and excited when we realized we had so much power! We also felt relieved that someone was willing to listen to us and help us with this problem.[12]

The director of buses came into their classroom to speak with the students about possible solutions, as did representatives from the middle school's student council and the teachers in charge of recess. Because students' concerns were heard, they believed their actions would cause positive changes—and they did. As one example, the principal of their elementary school told them she was receiving fewer referrals related to bus behavior, as well as fewer students being sent to her office for behavior issues. She credited the 5th graders' efforts for the reduction in bullying.

These students experienced an uncommon sense of agency in their young lives; that is, through their own efforts as readers, writers, and thinkers, they learned it was possible to initiate some positive changes to improve a dysfunctional system. Perhaps best of all, everyone at the school benefited from the work of these 5th graders. These students took their learning and advocacy across the school, starting with their interactive bulletin board "What do you stand for?" (see photo below). All students and visitors who entered the school would encounter this visual and written message emphasizing friendship, generosity, responsibility, and kindness, and viewers/readers were invited to add their own written thoughts. Teachers at every grade level extended the message of making friends, resolving conflicts constructively, and performing acts of kindness daily—all of which improved the school's culture. Because "the culture of a school plays an important role in the social choices students make,"[13] this last outcome is significant.

5th graders advocate for a school culture of kindness.

Quick Win

Say something personal and positive to every student every day, such as "I see you are interested in _____. Would you like to explore that further?" or "I noticed how you stayed with that problem and kept working on it even though it was hard for you. That kind of perseverance is what smart people and scholars do."

Quick Win

Have students evaluate their school experience. Whether from elementary, middle, or high school, interview students who are graduating or have them work in small groups of 3–4 to write an evaluation of their school experience:

• What worked really well for you at this school?

• What are your best memories?

• What specific suggestions do you have for what would make this school a better place for learning and getting along with others?

The audience for this evaluation is teachers and principals, and students will know that the school and future students will benefit from their experiences and that their ideas will be taken seriously.

Bullying, the topic that was the focus of our literacy work—in the residency and throughout the school year—is a crucial, real-world issue that causes lasting psychological harm. Research indicates that bullying profoundly affects a person's long-term functioning for both the bully and the victim.[14] I believe immersing Laurie Espenel's students in an authentic, worthwhile study where they had choice and understood the importance of their efforts will have a positive effect on them now and as adults—and the experience may help them be more caring individuals.

Hear All the Voices

Hearing all the voices, that is, ensuring that all learners feel safe and valued enough to share their thinking, needs to be one of our main goals for all learners—educators and students alike. When encouraged to speak their minds, some students' voices are initially barely above a whisper. Hearing all the voices means literally hearing learners speak in a voice loud enough for everyone to hear. It means being able to speak our beliefs, back up facts with evidence from texts and experience, and offer thoughtful opinions and arguments. We need to encourage and promote the inclusion of everyone's voice in discussion (whole class, small group, partner—both teacher- and student-led groupings), through literature conversations, curricular content discussions, and meaningful writing, to name a few examples. By promoting and modeling camaraderie and a high level of discourse, by teaching students to coherently explain the how, what, and why of the learning activity they are engaged in, and by supporting them as they attempt to participate, we validate and promote their thinking and foster problem solving. Moreover, we are creating a culture of respect where "teaching as conversation," not interrogation, is the norm.

One of our goals as educators must be to create learning environments that encourage student talk and honor students' thinking. It is true that the person who does most of the talking is the one doing most of the learning. That's because in the act of figuring out what to say, we are thinking, not just passively listening. One way to show respect for a student's thinking is not repeating what the student has just said. If the class knows we will restate a student's words, there's no reason for them to listen in the first place. Another way to hear all the voices is to accept students' thinking without judgment. We may help shape their thoughts, as in shared writing, but we make it known that students can risk sharing their thoughts without

Some Reasons We Don't Typically Hear All the Voices

- Teachers do most of the talking.
- Students are not in the habit of speaking up.
- Students don't believe they have anything important to say.
- Students are unsure of how to support their opinions.
- Students fear they may not have the response the teacher is seeking.
- Students lack the confidence to speak their thoughts.
- Students are in an environment that does not reward risk taking.

fear. As one student said in a small-group self-evaluation related to our work on bullying, "I learned not to worry about having the right answer."

It's not just students' voices that need to be raised. Teachers' voices need to be heard, too. Often it is fear of reprisals or lack of self-confidence that keeps us from speaking up. We all need to aspire to create school cultures where teachers and principals who have viable suggestions and solutions to problems, not just complaints, can honestly and respectfully speak up without fear of retribution.

Embed Formative Assessment

In teaching and assessing responsively, formative assessment is paramount. Formative assessment is the frequent classroom assessment that checks how our instruction is working based on what students are learning. That is, on a daily basis, we evaluate strengths and needs and continually modify our instruction and the type and amount of support we provide in order to increase learning and learner independence. The best formative assessment is learner driven, not just data driven, and includes self-assessment. We deliberately use the term *learner* and not *student* because formative assessment is not just for teachers working with students; it's also for leaders and coaches working with teachers and for students at the level of self-teaching. It's for all of us who seek to do better.

Formative assessment *is* what responsive teaching is all about; that is, our teaching is "contingent on, or responsive to, a student's responses during instruction." To be formative, an assessment "must actually be used to modify teaching to meet students' needs." Very significant, the effective use of formative assessment can close the achievement gap for students

Quick Win

Hold all students accountable for listening, which makes them more likely to listen and make appropriate remarks about what they have heard, for example, through "turn and talk." If one partner can't give a response, have the speaker or partner repeat the original statement. Then, expect the listening partner to repeat or put into his own words a meaningful response. Repeat as needed.

Quick Win

Do not repeat what a student says. Have the student say it again, louder. Once we repeat what the learner has said, listeners have no incentive to listen to anyone but us. Honoring the student as the primary speaker shifts the power from teacher to student.

who are low-performing.[15] I believe these statements are also true for principals and leaders working with teachers.

Ideally, as effective instructors and leaders, we are constantly and relentlessly assessing during our moment-by-moment teaching and leading, analyzing what our students are learning, and using that information to ask ourselves, "Are they understanding?" "How can we find out?" "What is the next step?" "What specific skill or strategy or action do we need to teach, reteach, or pursue?" That in-the-moment assessing means being able to do many things at once and recognizing the ongoing cycle of learning. It is not just establishing objectives and learning targets and checking for those. Simply saying we are doing formative assessment doesn't make it so.

One formative assessment I never leave out is to ask students at the start of every activity, "Why are we [am I] doing this… public conference, chart, study, lesson, demonstration?" If students are unable to state the purpose of the activity, it's unlikely they will apply what we are attempting to teach. For example, when I do a demonstration writing and think aloud as I write and revise, I say something like the following to students:

> The reason I'm thinking aloud as I write is because I want you to hear and learn how I work as a writer, so when you go to write your own piece you will know how writers think and work and can apply that to your writing.

Without that specificity, a student may think, "My teacher's up there talking to herself. I wonder why she's doing that" and, in turn, take little away from the demonstration. In addition, I ensure teachers also understand the purpose of an activity such as establishing shared beliefs as a staff, holding public writing conferences, and creating rubrics. Without that prior understanding and buy-in, investment and positive results are much less likely.

Formative assessment can include various contexts. Notice in the list "Some Possible Contexts for Formative Assessment" that the first six examples are actions the teacher leads, and the last three are actions students lead. Even when the student is in charge, the teacher would first demonstrate and have students practice with guidance what they are expected to know and do. Ultimately, we want students—and teachers, too—doing their own ongoing assessment and self-questioning to learn more, to seek and locate resources, and to be able to ask for the modeling, guidance, and specific support they need.

Some Possible Contexts for Formative Assessment

- Asking questions as we teach for the purpose of refining and redirecting our instruction based on what we learn while working with learners.
- Charting through shared writing what students know and notice before, during, and after a study; adding on to the chart as knowledge increases: "What do we know now?" "What else have we learned or figured out?" "What questions do we still have?"
- Modeling shared writing—for example, to parents or community members to use as an evaluation of what's been learned (this is also one way to create an authentic audience for required curriculum study).
- Conferring with students in public and in one-on-one conferences.
- Having students turn-and-talk before, during, and after a lesson, and then checking for understanding.
- Using students' oral and written responses to analyze strengths and needs and to adjust instruction to improve learning.
- Having students record observations from a fishbowl (e.g., as in the bullying example or from a demonstration, video, or oral presentation).
- Self-evaluating small-group work—oral or written by group or individuals.
- Self-checking by students—via room resources, word wall, using whiteboards for high-frequency words, rubrics, rereading—and adjusting, self-correcting as needed.

Quick Win

Use whiteboards for quick self-checking of spelling, word work, and math. Make statements such as "Check yourself." "Is it right?" "How do you know?" "Where can you find it?" "Fix it up."

Apply an Optimal Learning Model

An instructional, cyclical framework that I call the Optimal Learning Model (OLM) forms the foundation for all my teaching, coaching, and leading.[16] The OLM structure is grounded in a research-based, "gradual release of responsibility" instructional model,[17] and the focus is on the *learning*. Gradual release occurs as a result of the learning students do, which then makes it possible for them to work with more confidence and competence, increasing independence, fewer instructional scaffolds, and solid problem-solving abilities.

When we focus on the learning and the learner, we are appropriately responding to the student's needs and interests. We continually assess what the learner needs at this particular time in order to progress on the path from apprentice to expert. As instructors and mentors, we provide the demonstrations, support, scaffolds, resources, guidance, practice,

Quick Win

Apply the OLM in administrative meetings with the superintendent and other administrators and principals as a way to model excellent professional development and shared learning. When administrators experience the OLM firsthand, they work more effectively with principals and teachers.

reteaching, and so on that make it possible for the learner to attempt the task and follow through with reasonable success. *The OLM is responsive teaching in action.*

Optimal Learning Model (OLM)				
TO LEARNERS	**WITH LEARNERS**			**BY LEARNERS**
I DO IT	**WE DO IT**	→	**WE DO IT**	**YOU DO IT**
Demonstration	Shared Demonstration		Guided Practice	Independent Practice
TEACHER shows how to do it	**TEACHER** leads, negotiates, suggests		**STUDENT** takes charge, approximates, practices	**STUDENT** initiates, self-directs, self-evaluates
STUDENT listens, observes, minimally participates	**STUDENT** questions, collaborates, responds reading/writing	← HANDOVER OF RESPONSIBILITY	**TEACHER** encourages, clarifies, confirms	**TEACHER** affirms, coaches
INSTRUCTIONAL CONTEXT explanation, reading/writing aloud	**INSTRUCTIONAL CONTEXT** shared reading/writing		**INSTRUCTIONAL CONTEXT** guided reading/writing	**INSTRUCTIONAL CONTEXT** independent reading/writing

DEPENDENCE   INDEPENDENCE →

One of the key aspects of the OLM is the concept of refinement and adjustment. That is, when the learner's performance or understanding breaks down, we assess, analyze, and reteach. Traditional reteaching starts the lesson all over again. With the OLM, we refine and support in various ways in response to specific students' needs and interests *while* the student is engaged in the learning. Too often in teaching we isolate rather than incorporate the needed refinement into ongoing, meaningful instruction and learning.[18]

My favorite part of the OLM is celebration. It's where we start and where we end, and it's exemplified by these questions:

• What do we know?
• What have we accomplished?
• What has this learner done well or attempted to do?
• What can we learn and apply from what [learner's name] has done so well?

Celebrating and building on the learner's strengths as opposed to first highlighting deficits is a big shift for many teachers and leaders. Once educators integrate the OLM into all instruction across the curriculum, they find that teaching, leading, coaching, and learning become much more engaging, efficient, enjoyable, and successful for all. Let the celebrations begin![19]

Embrace Seamless Teaching

Understanding and applying the Optimal Learning Model can be the most significant shift teachers and leaders make in improving instruction and in refining their beliefs about teaching and learning. At first, many teachers see the model as a sequence of steps when, in actuality, application is a seamless, cyclical process based on learners' needs. Being able to effortlessly apply the model comes from professional study, teaching, reflection, collaboration with peers, and ongoing high-quality professional development—all of which make it possible for us as knowledgeable educators to think on our feet, solve problems in the moment, and quickly determine next steps, adjustments, and needs. The inner conversations we have may include questions such as these:

- What does the learner know and understand?
- How can we build on the learner's strengths? (For some, who already "know it," how do we offer enrichment?)
- Why and where is the learner having some difficulty?
- What supports are necessary? (For example, do we need more teaching, more guided practice, tutorials?)
- What's most important to do, provide, or say at this time?
- How will we know more learning is occurring?

These are the same kinds of questions we want learners to eventually ask of themselves as they become increasingly independent and self-sufficient. (See Appendix B for a chart to help plan instruction using the Optimal Learning Model.)

Ensure sufficient frontloading

An essential tenet of the OLM is ensuring that learners have sufficient frontloading *before* we expect them to try out an activity, assignment, action, or literacy task. This statement is as true for us as educators as it

Quick Win

Encourage teachers to self-evaluate their lessons for adequacy of demonstrations, shared experiences, and guided practice. If a lesson breaks down, have teachers reflect: "Where did the lesson falter?" "What did I leave out?" "What do I need to do differently?" "What supports do I need to put in place?"

is for our students. The better job we do at frontloading—providing the necessary groundwork that includes sufficient and effective demonstrations and instructional supports for a task, whether it be teaching how to problem-solve while reading a complex text or how to write an engaging lead—the more prepared and successful the learner will be. When a lesson falls short, I go back to the OLM and ask questions: "Where do I need to provide more support?" "What didn't I do to enable learners to meet success?" "What's the most important next step I need to provide?" I know the students are capable and will learn what I have set out to teach them if I consistently apply the OLM.

The OLM in action

At an Urgency and School Change Conference in Seattle, Washington, in March 2013, exit cards on the first day indicated that participants were confused about the OLM. On day 2, I revised my original plan and began the day by explicitly showing how I use the learning model for seamless, joyful teaching (I used poetry writing as my example):

OLM Actions

- Assess what students know.
- Immerse students in reading free-verse poems.
- Notice and name what poets do (including student poets).
- Demonstrate poetry writing.
- Share the writing and thinking to compose a class or group poem.
- Scaffold a few public conversations before expecting students to write independently.
- Write independently with sustained time provided.
- Confer with students.
- Celebrate writers' efforts.
- Teach and reteach skills and strategies, as needed.
- Assess what students now know.

Notice the verbs: *assess, immerse, notice and name, demonstrate, share the writing, scaffold, write, confer, celebrate, teach.* These action words and processes can be applied to all teaching and learning, and there is no correct sequence. For reading, the process is similar; we would substitute the words *reading* and *read* for *writing* and *write.* All the bulleted actions are repeated as necessary but not in any predetermined order. For example, continually assessing—and adding to a class chart, "What do we know about poetry?"—lets us know how much more immersion, demonstration, and scaffolding are necessary before expecting students to write successfully on their own. The OLM is cyclical, and continuous assessment and ongoing celebration of strengths are interwoven into the model.

Shift to Whole-Part-Whole Teaching

We often think that if we give our most struggling students isolated parts of whatever we are trying to teach them, that somehow all these parts will eventually come together as a whole. It rarely happens that way. We only confuse and frustrate learners and make it harder for them to progress. In fact, a part-to-whole approach with its emphasis on isolated pieces is one of the three most significant, research-based factors that hold students back and keep schools low-performing.[20] Richard Elmore uses the word "atomization" to denote teaching parts in isolation. (The other two most significant school-based factors cited are the adults' low expectations and low sense of efficacy.) Moving to whole-part-whole teaching and away from a skills-in-isolation approach goes hand in hand with the Optimal Learning Model. That is, we learn more—and more easily—when we start with a whole, meaningful text, process, or activity and embed within it the necessary skills and strategies the learner will need to achieve success. Many examples of whole-part-whole teaching are woven throughout this book.

Teaching content, genres, and processes as a whole entity instead of in pieces and parts leads to greater effectiveness, efficiency, and enjoyment. Even kindergartners—who embrace writing free-verse poems—quickly grasp the idea of playing with line breaks, white space, rhythm, word choice, punctuation, capitalization, titles, and endings all at the same time. If one of these areas needs special attention, we take it out of context and explicitly demonstrate and practice what students need to know. But that "isolated" teaching fits within the context of a meaningful whole, and so it makes sense to the learner. Conversely, when we teach each of these factors separately with the intention of linking them all together at the end, we slow down the instructional process and the learning and engagement. The most worrisome aspect of the piecemeal approach is that, for most of us, the parts only make complete sense when we can first grasp the whole.

Based on years of our own schooling and long-held beliefs, moving toward whole-part-whole teaching can be a challenging transition for many

Quick Win

List all the skills taught at the end of a lesson or unit of study when you have started with a big literacy question and whole text. Teachers are amazed at how much of substance has been taught, and it's always much more than what is covered through a subskills approach.

of us. However, the change can be felt almost immediately once we make the shift. That shift occurs when teachers internalize how much more—and more effectively—they can teach and that all the skills are being "covered."

Ongoing Cycle of Responsive Teaching: OLM

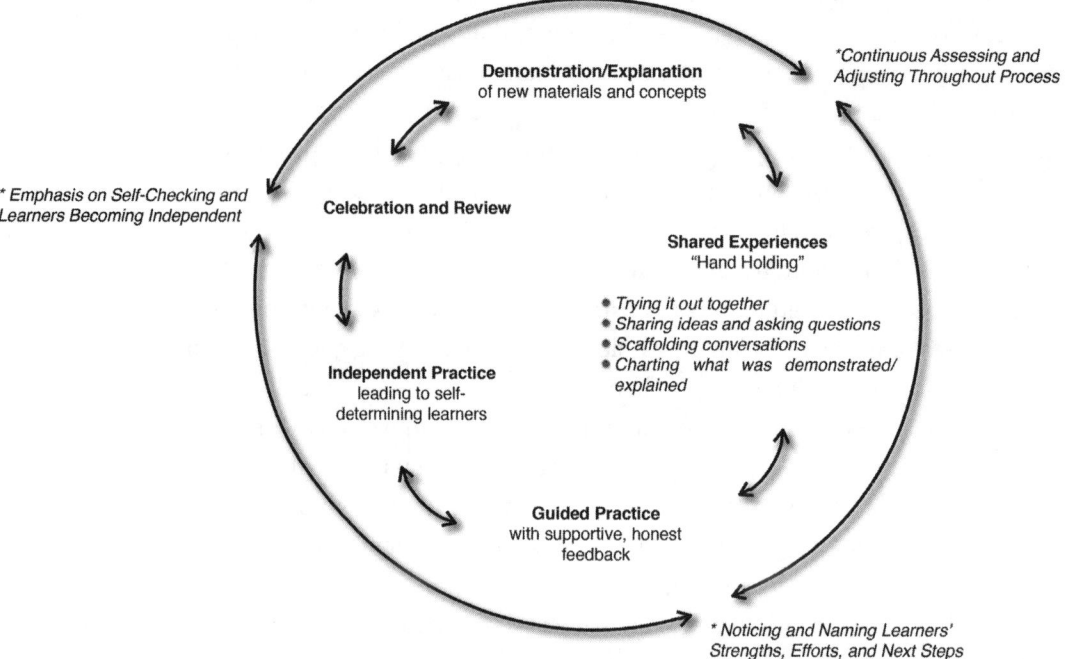

Kay Sprader is an instructional coach in an elementary school in the Fond du Lac School District in Wisconsin. Over 70 percent of the students in the school qualify for free and reduced lunch and are low-performing. She and her principal, Tim Schipper, concluded that only deep professional learning would make the impact needed to improve student learning. With their strong leadership and the support of district literacy specialist Kathy Schmitt, they instituted ongoing, school-based Professional *Literacy* Communities using the *Reading/Writing Connections* project as their foundation for professional development.[21] It took only two months for a change that Kay calls "transforming to all our teaching."

Kay comments on how the change has affected not just teaching but the culture of the school:

> *The Reading/Writing Connection*, more specifically the Optimal Learning Model, guided our thinking and instructional decision-making in ALL content areas—it became "how we did business"! During all-staff collaboration meetings our teachers learned about the inseparable relationship between formative assessment and instruction. Teachers brought assessment data (notes written during reading/writing conferences and observations made watching students learn) to grade-level team meetings to determine "next steps" along the I DO, WE DO, YOU DO framework. OLM transitioned from something we read about during professional development to a way of thinking; a habit of mind. It grew from an instructional model that "sounded good on paper" to the delicate balance of providing just enough, but not too much support as we guided each student toward independence.[22]

District leader Danica Lewis speaks to how the OLM focus has transformed the entire district's approach to student learning and leadership:

> New to the role of Director of Curriculum and Instruction, I examined our student learning results from several years' worth of data and was concerned about the lack of growth our students were demonstrating in the areas of reading and writing. Most of our nine elementary schools then spent the entire year exploring and practicing with the Optimal Learning Model. As principals became more adept at identifying teacher behaviors related to the OLM, their feedback to teachers became more specific, teachers were able to adjust their instructional techniques, and students' learning grew![23]

Rely on Excellent Demonstrations

A crucial missing piece for improving literacy instruction and learning is a visual and auditory one: the books and research on literacy make sense and can be applied to the full instructional context once we educators "see" the moves of effective teaching, "hear" the language of responsive and respectful teaching, and analyze what we have seen and heard. It was that realization that led me to create virtual residences—that is, ongoing video-based professional development for schools and districts so educators could see, hear, observe, reflect, analyze, plan, and—most important—apply the effective teaching and assessing practices that take place in diverse schools where students and teachers accelerate their learning.

Defining demonstrations

Demonstrations make visible and public for learners the effective actions and language of proficient literacy users. Explicit demonstrations by experts are the "show and tell" necessary for having learners successfully "try and apply" the behaviors we expect from them as thoughtful readers, writers, and thinkers. Here is where we make the learning intentions and what constitutes success clear, explicit, and transparent. Demonstrations are equally important for us as teachers, coaches, and leaders, along with sustained time to try out and practice with support.[24]

Talking and thinking aloud are crucial parts of demonstrations because they enable students—and the teachers we are coaching and mentoring—to know what we're thinking, how we're processing what's going on, what we're noticing, and how we are making our decisions. Our best demonstrations include making our reasoning visible, a necessity for helping poor readers become strategic. "Mental modeling makes visible invisible mental processes. This is in sharp contrast to modeling of procedures, which consists of telling students directions or steps to follow in completing a specific task."[25]

Demonstrations can be presented by teachers, leaders, experts, videos, texts, or audio modes, and they include but are not limited to the following:

- In-the-head thinking before, during, and after teaching
- Explaining ideas and processes
- Examining a passage, text, or process for a specific purpose
- Noticing what an author is trying to say and do
- Offering commentary on how, when, and why a text or process works well
- Providing necessary background information and essential vocabulary
- Showing exactly how to do something, for example, summarizing
- Modeling the strategic moves involved in problem solving
- Revising thinking for a more thoughtful, complete result
- Rereading and rewriting for clarity, accuracy, and meaning
- Seeking and using resources

Part of any successful demonstration lesson includes ensuring students understand and value the purpose of the demonstration. Otherwise you cannot assume application will follow. Begin with language that lets students know what you're about to undertake and why it's important. ("Here's what we're doing and why we're doing this.") After the demonstration, check to be sure students "got" the demonstration—even in kindergarten. ("What did you see me do?" "What did you notice?" "What will you try?" "What do you need to do first?") It may be useful to chart responses. Those responses serve as an assessment and as a possible rubric of criteria for what students are expected to do. Some examples of oral responses you might expect could relate to why all eyes need to be on the shared writing (to improve reading skills), where students can find words they need (to ensure independent use of room resources), why rereading is important (to figure out unknown words and clarify ideas), and so on.

Some tips to ensure demonstrations go well

Although one demonstration is rarely enough for our students or for us as educators, keep in mind that the demonstration is a means to an end—students becoming self-monitoring, self-directed learners. The demonstration is not the main event; the main event is having students able and willing "to try and apply" what we are teaching and to have sustained time to do it. Here are some useful tips:

- Time yourself, and don't go on too long—10–20 minutes is usually sufficient.
- Stop while energy is still high. You can return to the demonstration later or the next day.
- Leave the bulk of the literacy block for deliberate practice so students have sustained time to "try and apply," work through challenges, and self-teach.
- Stay in charge, and do not get distracted by taking responses and suggestions from students. (In this stage of the OLM, the teacher or expert does the thinking, reading, writing—showing how.)
- Do not assume learners benefited from the demonstration. Assess.
- Refine and reteach as necessary.

Provide More Shared Experiences

In a shared learning experience, an expert—usually the teacher—is in charge and does the actual reading and writing while encouraging and accepting responses from students. That is, the teacher or expert holds the pen or book and does the reading and writing while students are invited

Quick Win

Invite a student to lead a shared reading after teacher-led shared reading of a class-authored shared writing. Then, observe and ensure that all eyes are on the print and notice which students need guidance.

Quick Win

Accept all responses in a shared writing. It's a draft that can be fixed later. Acknowledging all students and encouraging everyone's voice is easy to do and pays big dividends in the long run.

to read along and offer ideas for writing. Successful shared learning experiences require a trusting, nonjudgmental classroom and school culture where risk taking is rewarded in a positive manner and the focus is on the thinking and not the "right answer." What's so powerful about shared experiences is that all students are encouraged to contribute, and we accept anything that makes sense as we help shape learners' thoughts. Students learn that their ideas and their voices are valued. Applying the Optimal Learning Model at the shared-experiences level increases enjoyment, confidence, and success for all students and teachers.

Doing more shared experiences has the potential to change the classroom culture—whether it be elementary, middle, or high school—to a more inclusive, risk-taking, and collaborative one. As students go through the grades, it's been my experience that doing activities with students—before we expect them to take on the task themselves—becomes rarer. That is, even when the teacher shows students how to do something or clearly explains a task, too often students are expected to get right to work on their own without sufficient scaffolding, "hand holding," and guided practice. What many students often need is much more time "doing it together" before working independently.

A terrific use of shared experiences is to do more guided small-group work with students. Especially for lessons that require close reading, note taking, analyzing, summarizing, report writing, or other multifaceted actions, moving too quickly from demonstration to small-group or individual guided practice can lead to disappointing results.

Examples of Shared and Guided Experiences

- Constructing a chart together of what was observed (to be applied and used by students as a reference)
- The teacher and one student demonstrating together for the whole class, following a teacher demonstration
- Conducting scaffolded conversations with students before they write (especially critical for second language learners who need to speak the language before they write it)
- Two students practicing an expected task (perhaps in view of the whole class with teacher guidance)
- The teacher doing a task with a small group
- A small group working on a task together, such as writing a report[26]

As one powerful example, the observation and use of fishbowl groups in the previously described bullying lesson set up a group structure that teachers continued to employ across the curriculum at all grade levels. Working with simultaneous, heterogeneous groups of three to four students can yield huge benefits:

• The responsibility is on the students to do the work.
• We have a record of the group thinking and process (our own anecdotal notes, a scribe's recording of group thinking, or other documentation).
• We are free to join one group and confer with other groups.
• Students employ reading, writing, speaking, and listening.
• Peer learning is strengthened.
• We can easily assess strengths, needs, and next steps.
• A limited time frame yields maximum participation by all students.

Some tips to ensure shared experiences go well

I sometimes describe the OLM model as "I do it. We do it. We do it. We do it. You do it." It is through shared experiences—the "we do it/you do it"—that the learner gets to try out new ideas, actions, and thinking without fear of failure or ridicule, so this stage is critical for learners' growing confidence and independence. All of the following tips apply to us educators as learners too:

• *Honor every learner's thinking.* For an off-the-wall response, say something like "Say more about that." "What makes you think that?" Accept any part of the response that you can; content can be revised later.
• *Put the language in their ears.* These scaffolded conversations are especially crucial for our second language learners and students who struggle. Help shape their thinking by saying something like "How about if we say it like this _____" or "What did _____ say next?" or "You can repeat what Carlos said or put it your own words. Carlos, could you say that again for Maria?"
• *Celebrate everything you can.* "I like the way you tried _____." "That can work." "That statement shows how carefully you've been listening."
• *Read and write about high-interest topics.* The more students—and we—value the task, the more likely we are to engage and put forth our best efforts.

> **Quick Win**
>
> *Send home class-authored, shared writing pieces* on a regular basis; doing so ensures that parents know what students are doing and learning in reading, writing, and the content areas.

- *Consider small-group work as an additional shared experience.* As noted, especially when the work is complex, it's productive to have students complete the task, or a part of it, as a group before expecting them to "try and apply" on their own.

Release students to practice in situations where they are in charge

Although shared experiences are a necessity for optimal learning, it is also the case that as well-intentioned teachers we sometimes keep students at the shared level too long. Often a teacher will say something like the following: "The results of the interim writing assessments are not indicative of the results I get in my classroom." Upon questioning and reflection, we determine that in the classroom, teachers are still doing much of the work by supplying resources, correcting errors, and giving the message that they are always available to help. Then, when students take a test and are expected to work independently, they have not internalized the expectations and habits for taking full responsibility through the rereading, problem solving, self-monitoring, and self-correcting that make it more likely we will get their best efforts.

Kindergarten teacher Melissa Kirkland put it this way after she saw in our writing residency what her students were capable of doing on their own:

> What stood out for me most during the residency was that students' confidence comes before their independence. I am amazed at the improved quality of their writing in just a few days. From holding them responsible for self-checking words during word work to having them understand "why" we listen during a public conference, it ups the expectations and puts the ownership of the learning back on the students…. I am now stopping and looking at the content of the writing, the language and vocabulary, and asking students relevant questions rather than putting a sentence in their heads. What really resonated with me is that if it's not their own language, they will not be able to read back their writing.[27]

By the end of the school year, Melissa noted how profound the results were in terms of what her students were now able to accomplish independently:

> We have just finished with our end of year writing sample, and I am absolutely amazed with what they are able to do on their own—it will

be exciting to see, with such increased expectations, what next year's writing samples will look like. They absolutely love reading and writing and are so confident in what they can do.[28]

Build in Sustained and Guided Practice

Without sustained practice, it's hard to become excellent at any craft. Any lesson, whether it is in music, sports, reading, or writing, will not lead to long-term improvement without substantial practice by the learner regardless of the excellence of the lesson. Yet, in school, extended practice time is often relinquished to fit in more guided reading groups, longer demonstrations, and more teaching of skills in isolation. It is, however, in the practice stage that our approximations grow closer to achieving the actual goal or task and learning target over time.

That practice needs to be deliberate and have the goal of improving performance. "It needs to be at an appropriate, challenging level of difficulty, and enable successive refinement by allowing for repetition, giving room to make and correct errors, and providing informative feedback to the learner."[29] Take a look at the OLM visual (see p. 58) and notice that in the guided practice phase the student is now in charge of holding the book and the pen and is doing the bulk of the thinking, reading, and writing work. Although we are technically still in a "we do it," shared learning stage, it's the "you do it/we do it" phase. Most of the responsibility for the learning and doing is now on the student, not the teacher. The teacher is the guide-on-the-side, monitoring to ensure that the student can do the work while giving the learner *occasional* support through explicit teaching, targeted guidance, and encouragement, only as needed.

If we've done our prior work well, with sufficient and effective demonstrations and shared experiences, learners are ready for this handover of responsibility. A previously cited example that brings guided practice to life is the self-directed small-group task that all eight groups of 5th graders successfully achieved in their work on bullying. They did the work!

A caution here is that guided practice often goes awry—that is, the teacher remains in charge. Guided reading is one common example in which far too often the teacher continues to do most of the work, for example, by supplying words and answers to questions, ultimately holding the learner back from becoming self-regulating. Also important to note here,

> ### *Quick Win*
>
> *Use classroom charts to record student responses* to validate and assess student learning and to document expectations. Charts, displayed on a stand or posted on the wall, are an easy reference and support for encouraging students to take more responsibility. Old-fashioned pen-and-paper charts work well because the learning record is visible and easy to refer back to.

the guided practice work has to be as authentic as possible and worth learners' time. For instance, spending most guided practice time on round-robin oral reading has not been proven to be useful.

Work Toward Independence in Learning

In order for learners—whether they be students or teachers—to work in the independent practice phase, they need to have acquired the problem-solving, self-monitoring, self-correcting behaviors necessary to do "the work" on their own. (By *work*, I mean meaningful work, not completing worksheets or other time-wasting activities.) That is, in doing the work, learners have the stamina, will, and expertise to find and use resources; self-evaluate; recognize their strengths and needs; set their own worthwhile learning goals; and work without expecting constant feedback and affirmation. To be independent learners, they also need to have the uninterrupted, peaceful time that can lead to sustained engagement and flow. The teacher or expert is still available to the learner; but unlike guided practice, where the expert is usually "right there," either side by side or roving the classroom, in the independent practice phase the expert is only infrequently available, often at designated times. In fact, the expert does not always need to be physically present. For example, the learner might access a video, turn to a guidebook, or query Google or another search engine and be able to understand, analyze, and apply information to continue learning.

Make independent practice meaningful

A school example of worthwhile independent practice is voluntary, independent reading, the mainstay of any well-developed reading program at all grade levels. If students are to gain in fluency, understanding, stamina, vocabulary, and knowledge, they must have acquired the engagement, habits, and skills of self-directed readers so they are able to read a massive amount of meaningful text on their own. The teacher, in this instance and for other subject matter, is available for assistance at limited times in the classroom and might be willing to be reachable by phone, e-mail, or social media on a controlled basis. It is important to note that homework also fits within the independent practice category. Homework is only beneficial if students have acquired the problem-solving skills to be able to do almost all the work on their own.

A real-world example of working independently, or at the independent practice phase, is the way I worked with my trusted editor and several colleagues in the process of writing this book. We were in contact only occasionally at prearranged times when my editor or colleagues offered specific guidance and clarity and responded to lingering questions. Before any contact, I sent them my carefully considered drafts with requests for specific feedback on content, organization, tone, and much more. I knew the responsibility for doing the work was totally mine. I had sufficient knowledge, experience, and resolve to "do it," but I still required intermittent advice, guidance, and support for the most optimal outcome.

Ultimately, we want all learners to move beyond being independent to becoming self-determining learners; that is, they have acquired the competence and confidence to be totally in charge of their own learning. They do not require a teacher or mentor to set their own worthwhile goals, to solve problems to achieve their ends, or to evaluate their achievements.

Reap the Benefits of the OLM

The goal of the OLM is more effective, efficient, and joyful learning—for students, teachers, and leaders. My esteemed colleague Kathy Schmitt calls the OLM "the heartbeat of the classroom." It makes all things in literacy and learning possible, across the curriculum. The OLM is consistent with research on excellent instruction and makes successful implementation of standards, resources, or any activity more likely. What follows are two stories that show some of those possibilities.

Debbie Fowler is an outstanding 5th grade teacher in Colorado with more than 20 years of teaching experience. She is greatly admired by colleagues throughout her district. In 2005 when we began our work together in her classroom as part of our whole-school writing residency, she did not yet see herself as a highly competent writing teacher. At her request, we focused on editing because her students—as well as most students schoolwide—exhibited poor spelling, conventions, grammar, and handwriting. Today it's a very different story. Year after year, almost all of Debbie's students score exceptionally high in editing and conventions on the state's high-stakes writing test, which has not been typical for comparable students in the district. Debbie comments:

> It's not just that my expectations are now very high and that I refuse to
> do for my students what they can do for themselves. I have also shown

them, over and over again, through demonstrating on my own writing, but especially through shared experiences, what I expect from them as editors. We discuss, come to agreement, and chart what they can and will do as editors; we edit together several students' papers before they work on their own; they see several public conferences before they have one so they know I expect them to come fully prepared. I have greatly slowed down releasing them to edit on their own by ensuring they have sufficient support and practice first. Then I have even been able to "hire" qualified students as peer editors. That's been a huge change. Also, the students take editing seriously because the writing we do is almost always for authentic purposes and audiences they care about or that they choose to write for. In the end, not only is improved writing and editing the payoff, it's also the boost in self-esteem that is evident when they come beaming with pride over the hard work they did.[30]

Perhaps equally as important as accelerating learning, applying the Optimal Learning Model increases enjoyment and success for both students and teachers. Marilyn Robbins has been teaching for over 30 years, with the last 20 in kindergarten. When I met her a decade ago, she did not see herself as a confident or happy teacher. At that time, she did not believe kindergarten students could write whole, meaningful texts or that they could do so independently. Today she is an exceptional and joyful teacher, her kindergartners are enthusiastic writers and readers, and she is completing a book on teaching writing in kindergarten!

Marilyn's big leap came in the spring of 2010 when she followed the OLM and what she had learned about writing for audience and purpose and had her students write reviews of favorite local restaurants. Each review was carefully written and then sent to the specific restaurant. Several of the restaurants prominently posted the child-authored review, to the absolute delight of the students and their teacher. The story even made the local newspaper. Marilyn noted at the end of that school year, "This year was the highlight of my career. I was able to move beyond the mastery level of teaching to truly making a significant impact on every student."[31]

Provide Effective Feedback

Intimately connected to applying the Optimal Learning Model is knowing how to give effective feedback. "Feedback is information provided by an agent (e.g., teacher, peer, book, parent, or one's own experience) about aspects of one's performance."[32] Essentially, good feedback is about having productive conversations. That is, from our feedback, the learner—whether the learner is the student, the teacher, or the principal—is encouraged, willing, and able to take specific actions to improve on the task or learning situation. Talking through and applying suggested actions may require support through demonstrations, shared experiences, lots of guided practice, or all three. But all of it is a two-way endeavor.

Quality teaching, coaching, and leading are dependent on our feedback abilities. In fact, learning how to give effective feedback is as important as any subject matter we teach. Yet giving useful feedback is one of the most elusive elements in teaching and learning. Because effective feedback is so critical to learning achievement, throughout the rest of this book, I demonstrate and discuss what effective feedback to both adults and students looks like and sounds like, and I also share current research and practices related to productive feedback. Some rich opportunities for providing feedback that propel learning and self-monitoring are further illustrated in such contexts as instructional walks, Professional *Literacy* Communities, and celebrations and suggestions in reading and writing conferences. Giving effective feedback is a sophisticated, learned skill that requires much modeling and practice—and that also includes feedback to the one learning to give it.

Apply Feedback Essentials

Most of all, for feedback to be effective, it must move learning forward in a positive way, be ongoing, and happen in a timely manner close to the actual teaching/learning experience. Knowing what to say and do—and how and when to say and do it—is an art and a craft that takes most of us years of experience to successfully develop. The content of our feedback and the manner of delivery are crucial for effectiveness, and they depend on pivotal elements that include the quality of the instruction, what the learner is doing well, and the learner's demeanor and self-esteem.

"*Less* teaching plus *more* feedback is the key to achieving greater learning."[33] Useful feedback is an absolute necessity for developing trust, enhancing learning, increasing risk taking, and raising achievement. Such feedback is crucial for learners' progress and social and emotional well-being. Learners do not become self-checking, self-regulating, and self-sustaining without effective feedback—whether given by others or themselves. These statements are as true for us educators as for our students.

Ensure feedback is helpful

Feedback can be helpful, unhelpful, or damaging. Helpful feedback is specific and actionable. Here's an example in response to a piece of writing:

In your opening paragraph, when you said _____ [restating actual language], I knew as a reader exactly what this piece was going to be about. I wonder if you might take another look at the title, which confused me because it suggests a totally different topic.

In contrast, unhelpful feedback is general and unspecific, with comments such as "I like your ending" or "You used good details." Looking at these comments, it's unclear how the learner can move the writing forward or even what the feedback means.

When we give feedback, it's not enough to say what needs improvement. We who give the feedback must be willing and able to suggest next steps and provide the needed support. We also need to check that the learner "received" our feedback, understands it, and has the tools to take action. Ask such questions as these:

- What did you hear me say?
- What are you thinking?
- What are the strengths we talked about?
- What kind of help do you need next?
- What will you do next?

Depending on the learner's response, we may need to repeat the feedback and assessment, often informally through questioning.

Ineffective feedback can harm the learner's progress if it is overly prescriptive, focuses on nonessential details, or winds up draining the learner's enthusiasm and energy to successfully tackle the task. Here's a sobering thought: 80 percent of the feedback elementary school students receive about their work comes from their peers, and most of that feedback is either incorrect or unhelpful.[34] So it is crucial that we demonstrate what useful feedback is—what it looks like and sounds like—and that we apply the OLM in teaching students how to give effective feedback before we encourage them to provide it to others.

Feedback essentials

Productive feedback is all about language and tone, what we say to the learner, how we say it, and how the learner receives it.

Quick Win

Teach even your youngest students the specific language of feedback for noticing and commenting on something positive. For example, "When you said _____ in your writing, those words let the reader know _____." Apply the OLM to teach students how to give effective feedback.

- The learning goal must be clearly understood and valued by the teacher and the learner.
- The feedback is specific to the task and lets the learner know how he or she is doing, beginning with recognizing and naming strengths.
- The language of the feedback is specific, relevant, and respectful.
- The learner understands the feedback and can apply it to reaching the agreed-upon goal(s).
- The feedback increases the learner's understanding of the task.
- The feedback enhances the trust between the giver and the receiver.
- The feedback is appropriate to the task and for the learner.
- The feedback causes the learner to respond positively.
- The feedback provides a clear roadmap for the most important next step(s).

Perhaps most important of all, the feedback must leave the learner with an "I can do it!" mindset and a disposition of sufficient energy and will to do the work. Without that positive spirit on the part of the learner as a result of the feedback, our comments will not help much and may, in fact, set things back by overwhelming or discouraging the learner. When we give effective feedback, we use language that is honest, supportive, and responsive, and most of this language is oral, clear, and straightforward.

Questions to keep in mind

It may be helpful to also keep the following essential questions in mind when giving feedback:

- What am I noticing about what the learner has done well or is attempting to do?
- What am I noticing about where the learner may be confused?
- What are the most important things I can do and say at this time to move the learner forward?
- How will the feedback help the learner progress toward the learning goal(s)?
- How will the feedback help the learner to become more confident, competent, and self-directed as a learner?

These questions are the ones I ask myself every time I confer with a student, a teacher, or a principal. Beginning with noticing what the learner is doing well requires the person giving the feedback to have a positive mindset—that is, to be able to first notice and emphasize strengths, not deficits.

Check that learners can apply the feedback

Eventually we want learners to be able to give their peers and themselves useful feedback. For that to happen, teachers and students first need to value and understand the feedback process. Students need to see us model it and make our thinking visible, and we need to assess what they've noticed us do, reteach as necessary, and provide lots of guided practice before we gradually hand over responsibility.

Here are some questions to have learners keep in mind when conferring with peers (or themselves, as ultimately we want students and all learners to self-direct their own learning):

• What do you notice that you've done well?
 (*What do I notice that I've done well?*)
• How are you moving closer to the learning goal?
 (*How am I moving closer to the learning goal?*)
• What's the most important thing you need to do next?
 (*What's the most important thing I need to do next?*)
• What questions do you have? What help might you need to move forward? Where and how can you find that help?
 (*What questions do I have? What help do I need to move forward? Where and how can I find that help?*)

These same self-reflection questions apply when we are coaching adult learners.

Use Effective Feedback to Build Professional Trust

Human beings are complex. To give effective feedback we must observe more than what the learner is doing or attempting to do academically. We must also pay close attention to the learner's nuances, posture, facial expressions, gestures, and other behaviors. We need to intuit what the learner is trying to tell us about the feedback he or she may be ready and willing to receive. Above all, we need to show respect.

A story of feedback to a teacher sheds light on this sensitive issue. It was my first year in a residency in a high-needs school. As part of the residency, the principal and I were spending the afternoons doing "instructional walks" (see Glossary and pp. 197–216). The purpose was twofold: to build trust with staff members whom I did not know and to model the language of effective feedback for the principal. When I walked into one classroom,

Quick Win

Make a "crib sheet" for students with questions to ask and to think about in giving feedback to peers or self while students are learning the process.

I could tell almost immediately by the teacher's nervousness—apparent by her fidgeting and comments centered on how her room looked—that she did not want feedback on her teaching. Taking my lead from her, I commented on what a beautiful space she had created in her teacher desk area. She beamed.

My comments to the teacher were truthful, but they did nothing to move teaching and student learning forward. What they did do was help the teacher relax a bit so the next time I entered her room she was not so nervous. Until I could begin to build a rapport with her and to earn her trust over time, she would be reluctant to talk about student learning and where she might need and want to improve her instruction.

Use effective feedback to build trust between principals and teachers

In a recent residency at a low-performing school, it took only a couple of days to see how splintered the staff was and how low the trust levels were. I observed that there were some physical areas in the school where some teachers did not feel welcome; the number of grievances to the union were disproportionately high compared to other schools in the district; certain teachers avoided some of their peers; and the principal was both loved and despised, depending on whom you talked to. Not surprisingly, there was little schoolwide personal or professional trust. And here's the sobering part. Once the trust between and among staff members and the principal is broken, it's extremely difficult to repair and rebuild it.

In this particular school, I was mentoring the principal through our daily instructional walks on what to look for in the literacy classroom and what to say to teachers and students. We were in a primary-grades classroom, and the teacher wanted to celebrate the writing her students were doing. She called on one of her students to read his piece aloud. As soon as the student completed reading the piece and before I could model what I might say to this student, the principal took over. All her comments, said aloud to the student in front of the whole class, related to what the student didn't do and needed to fix—raising his voice, holding his paper so we could see him, including more details in the writing. I watched the student's reaction to those comments and saw the student's demeanor, including his posture and facial expression, disintegrate from proud to troubled. The principal and I had the following conversation after we left the classroom.

Regie: So how do you think that went?

Principal: I think it went well.

Regie: Did you notice anything about the student's demeanor when you made your comments to him?

Principal: (Pause) Well, I guess he looked a little disappointed.

Regie: Why do you think that might be?

Principal: I'm not sure; maybe because he needed to correct a lot of things.

Regie: Do you think you could have done or said anything differently?

Principal: (Long pause) Maybe I could have said something about the writing that I liked.

Later that day, the principal pulled me into her office and with a pained expression said, "What I did to that student today, that's what I've been doing to many of my teachers." It was no accident that achievement was low, the school had cliques, many teachers did not trust the principal, collaboration was minimal, and teachers felt enormous pressure to raise test scores. The main message and feedback the principal had been giving to staff was: "You're not doing a good-enough job." And while we all need to improve and get better at our craft, if we want people to do better we have to first begin by recognizing and celebrating their strengths and their efforts. We cannot develop a culture of trust without it, and, as was emphasized in Chapter 1, without a culture of trust, schoolwide achievement is not possible.

Use effective feedback to support the principal

Being a principal or a leader of any kind can be a lonely job. The principals I have come to know well work long days, are dedicated to improving teaching and learning, and try to protect their staffs from all the crises and minutiae that are part of every leader's job. Often they receive little support or recognition for the hard tasks they tackle. Just as we want our principals and administrators to first notice our strengths, we need to show them the same respect and positive stance. The feedback and language we use with our leaders often determine how willing they will be to work with and for us as well as how flexible and open to change they may be. Kind words and gestures can work wonders.

Delores was an intermediate-grades teacher who approached me early during our first residency to request more observation time; that is, she and her middle-grade colleagues wanted to observe not only the scheduled intermediate-grades lesson but the primary-grades lesson as well. I suggested she talk with her principal, whom I had just met. She immediately replied that her principal would refuse to make any adjustment. At the time, I didn't know that Delores was a teacher who was in constant conflict with her principal; neither one spoke positively about the other. Here's what I said to Delores:

> I know your principal has tried very hard to work out a schedule that is fair and that works for everyone. Given all the demands of her job, I also know she doesn't have time or funds to hire additional substitutes. If you can figure out a way to make your request workable, without your principal's involvement of time and effort, I know she would be open to your suggestion.

Delores's immediate response was that her principal would never listen to anything Delores suggested. I insisted that if she presented a fair and easily workable solution that did not require any extra effort or funds on the part of her principal and spoke in a positive and supportive manner, her principal would most likely agree to the request. Sure enough, to Delores's surprise, the principal granted her request and thanked her for working out the details. As teacher-leaders, we sometimes need to provide a possible resolution to the problem we have presented to our principal and to be willing to work through the details to get the response we are seeking.

We also need to be willing to support our principals even when their actions may disappoint us. Anna was an experienced teacher who was new to a school that also had a first-year principal. Devastated by her first evaluation, in which it seemed to Anna that the principal only noticed and commented on small things that needed improvement, Anna began to take a negative stance toward the principal. When Anna approached me about her situation, I suggested she give her principal the benefit of the doubt and let the principal know how that same feedback could have been presented in a way that would have been beneficial. We practiced what she might say to the principal, which went something like this:

> I'm used to having my principal come into my classroom, and I welcome the opportunity to grow as a teacher. I hope you and I will develop a close working relationship. Last week when you gave me feedback on your observation, I would have appreciated hearing first

what you noticed that was going well. Then, it would have been easier for me to also hear where I needed to improve.

In both cases, relationships with the respective principals began to improve once feedback to and from the principal was stated in a positive manner. It is not only we teachers who need to learn how to give effective feedback to students. Through our mentoring and modeling and the language that we use, we can also support principals and leaders in their efforts to give and receive the kind of feedback and results we would want to receive ourselves.

3

Reading and Writing Priorities

When do they read? When do they write? These are the key questions we must continually ask ourselves to ensure that our students spend most of their time engaged in reading and writing meaningful texts and have some choice in the matter. As responsible educators, we must ensure that we become expert at instruction, useful feedback, and ongoing assessment so students can work productively and independently. In addition, we need to link speaking and listening skills to all literacy and communication.

It is a civic, moral, and national obligation that all of our students become fully literate so that they may seek, find, and enjoy the opportunities for rich and expanded lives that literacy makes possible. Learning to successfully read and write is just the beginning. A recent report, *The Heart of the Matter*, puts literacy and the Common Core State Standards in perspective:

> Although it is too soon to predict all the outcomes that will result from nationwide implementation, the proposed Core makes communication—reading, writing, and speaking—a fundamental element of education, opening doors for more advanced learning. It emphasizes literacy as a way of learning about the world; in other words, literacy is not the "end" but the beginning to a voyage of understanding.[1]

So although this chapter deals with effectively and joyfully teaching reading and writing, the long-range goal is that we and our students use literacy as a means to lead satisfying and meaningful lives. That is, through reading, writing, speaking, listening, and inquiry, we acquire knowledge, an appreciation for the written and spoken word, a love of literature, creative thinking, personal integrity, and a spirit of humanity that connects us to a world beyond ourselves, where we fully participate.

Quick Win

Keep demonstrations and minilessons to no more than 10–20 minutes. Stop while engagement is still high so students have sustained time and energy to write, read, and solve problems.

Sustained time for reading and writing continuous, meaningful texts every day—and time to talk about those texts—must be our first priority for turning students into readers, writers, and thinkers. It's all well and good to have effective guided reading lessons, demonstrations on effective writing, and conferences in reading and writing with students, but if students do not spend most of their time practicing and behaving as readers and writers— that is, reading and writing authentically throughout the day—they will never become proficient and joyful literacy users. In fact, students who are unexpectedly high achieving as readers and writers read and write text after text throughout the day; typical students spend more time on activities and "stuff" about reading and writing.[2]

Knowing how and what to teach does not depend on the latest standards and programs, or the newest resources. Those can be helpful for providing important frameworks and instructional guidelines, but they must not become the driving force. In a recent conversation with a new principal, when I asked him what his priorities were for the school year, he replied, "We're focusing on implementing each of the Common Core State Standards along with our new core reading program." Although he was kind and well intentioned, his priorities would put him on a path to exhausting his teachers and making little progress in literacy achievement.

By contrast, a well-informed and knowledgeable principal who had a thriving PLC culture in her school said this:

> We have to be really careful that when we ask teachers to spend time on things, it's got to be worth their effort and the students'. I'm convinced that strong test scores are a byproduct of excellent teaching. The key is our standards are higher than the CCSS. We check the CCSS to be sure we're not missing anything, but the CCSS do not drive our teaching.[3]

One of the most difficult things to do as a teacher and a leader is to prioritize what's most significant to say and do now and later, and what to leave out. The politics of literacy inside and outside our districts can make it extremely difficult to sift through all the demands and to focus on what's most essential. Deciding what and who needs our attention, in what manner and for how long, is no easy task. Yet to become highly effective, efficient, and skillful at whatever we do, we have to prioritize. It's a lot like being able to summarize—figuring out what's most important and what we can omit or ignore. We can't do it all. We only have so much time to make a worthy difference for our students.

In my previous books and resources (including those listed in References and Resources), I have written about and shown in great detail the research, instructional moves, skills and strategies, and day-to-day reflections and assessments that contribute to highly effective teaching of reading and writing. Here I want to discuss and explain the most crucial elements—those fundamentals that must have our closest attention in order to increase and sustain literacy achievement and enjoyment across the curriculum.

Even when required curriculum, standards, procedures, and learning targets constrict us, our absolute first priority must be students' optimal learning, well-being, success, and promising futures. How we prioritize depends largely on our beliefs and what we value. Therefore, this chapter begins with developing shared beliefs as a necessity for moving forward. We then move to a discussion of access to appropriate texts, because the texts we read and write determine our engagement, motivation, satisfaction, and achievement as readers and writers. Finally, we come to the topic of key priorities for writing for audience and purpose and reading to understand.

Develop Shared Beliefs

Coming together as a whole school around shared literacy beliefs and learning is a highly overlooked and undervalued endeavor. Yet it is an indispensable process. What teachers and leaders believe about a concept, an instructional approach, or a learning process greatly influences their degree of openness to new concepts, their flexibility, and their willingness to commit to new ideas. How beliefs evolve and change is a powerful indicator of how a school is growing.

Without agreement and cohesion across grade levels and across a district on what we believe about learning and teaching, we educators will continue to thrash around seeking the "perfect" solution, program, or resource to show us the way to raising achievement. Lacking strong inner convictions and deep knowledge, we rely on quick solutions, smartly packaged programs, and easy-to-get data to determine our beliefs and practices. Out of desperation, we purchase "stuff" without even knowing what we're buying. As well, we are more likely to be lured by quick and slick tech-based resources that yield ready numbers that may or may not be useful, solidly research based, or worth our time and the students: Several years down the road, we are often still marching in place. Programs have come and gone, we have given them a good effort, achievement has remained flat, and the whole time-consuming but ineffective process begins again.

To avoid the scenario just described, it's critical that we *make shared beliefs a first priority.* Establishing shared beliefs as a staff and putting them in writing guides us to make wise decisions and to question and not just blindly follow the program-of-the-moment. For example, No Child Left Behind put a huge emphasis on phonics, phonemic awareness, and fluency *before* focusing on meaning. Five years and billions of dollars later, we saw no increase in reading comprehension, which is to say we squandered a huge opportunity to do a whole lot better teaching reading to millions of students.

In a current example in the United States, the admirable intentions and promise of the Common Core State Standards are being co-opted by demanding accountability measures, which are leading to incessant test prep and testing in K–12 classrooms—which in turn are driving how the standards are being implemented in many cases. The only way for sanity to prevail is for us as knowledgeable educators to know and value what we believe and for those beliefs to align with effective, research-based, and experience-based practices.

Often we teachers and leaders have had so much fragmented professional development that we don't know what we believe. It is not unusual for a school to have multiple and conflicting programs operating at the same time. See the graphic on page 85 by esteemed educator and colleague Judy Wallis for "What Often Happens" in schools. Programs and resources take priority and set the course for instruction and assessment in most schools, when in fact "What Needs to Happen" requires just the reverse. That is, we need to shift our thinking and start with our informed beliefs, align those with best practices, and then carefully select resources that support our firm beliefs and aligned practices.

Without that mind-action shift, we will continue to identify and refer too many students as requiring intervention and special education labels and services, and we will continue thrashing about for solutions. Without a staff coming together around shared beliefs, the best we can hope for, as a school, are incremental shifts in practices rather than the fundamental changes that may be needed. Yet once we are clear on our beliefs and have had schoolwide discussions to establish them, we can properly put

Quick Win

Figure out your own top three beliefs in reading and in writing. Make sure they align with research and best practices.

standards, curriculum, programs, and resources in perspective; align our beliefs with best practices; and begin to move forward with sustainable, worthwhile change.

What Often Happens

What Needs to Happen

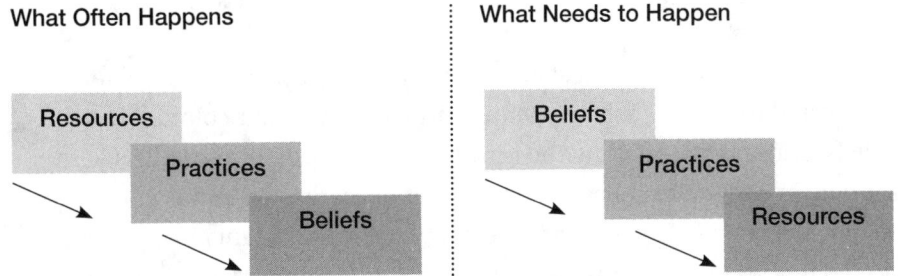

Start with Schoolwide Discussion of Literacy Beliefs

Begin any literacy change process with a whole-staff discussion of beliefs. Our beliefs reflect our convictions and what we value, and they guide our instruction. "Practices are our beliefs in action."[4] And we and our students are best served by not assuming that we know our colleagues' beliefs. As one literacy coach noted after leading her staff through discussion of their literacy beliefs, "I was surprised and humbled by how far we have to go. Our staff is more divided in their thinking than I realized." (See Appendix C for a suggested procedure for discussing and developing shared beliefs in reading.)

A common occurrence, early in a first literacy residency, is for teachers at the school to request "a list of skills to teach at each grade level, preferably in a predetermined order" and "strategies to put into practice right away." A discussion of beliefs is not yet considered a cornerstone of a successful school's operating system. But without shared beliefs that are articulated and applied schoolwide through practices that support those beliefs, we are likely to end up frustrated and treading water. New skills and strategies may be added to the teaching repertoire and we are staying afloat, but nothing of substance changes. As one teacher put it, "We've had no schoolwide conversation about beliefs for several years, and teachers are all over the place. Mostly, they are drilling kids to death."[5] Judy Wallis comments on what often occurs in schools that have not examined common beliefs.

Often what has happened is overdependence on an adopted resource and its associated practices. When a new resource is added, new practices accompany it, and teachers often wind up continuously implementing something new and replacing previous practices rather than refining. This frequently leads to teachers' disempowerment.[6]

Professional trust and instructional cohesion, which are crucial for raising and sustaining achievement, cannot exist without commonly held beliefs among a staff. Taking the time to deeply discuss those beliefs with the goal of coming to consensus is an essential early step in the whole-school literacy change process. One of the most significant changes that occurs in a school in flux is a gradual shift away from part-to-whole teaching and teaching skills or concepts in isolation, toward whole-part-whole teaching and teaching skills and concepts as part of a meaningful whole text or activity. In general, this schoolwide shift takes about one-and-a-half to two years to take hold. Literacy coach Kate Gordon describes what happened when staff at her school began to discuss their beliefs:

> We moved from "I have to prove that I know everything" to "We're a group of learners who want to do better." We realized we were all over the board with our beliefs and instruction. Once we took collective responsibility and embedded meaningful PD into our school, we began taking some ownership for needed change. That came through our conversations and wanting to be the best we could be as professionals. That all started when we began examining our beliefs.[7]

Agree to refocus instructional priorities

Instructional priorities begin to shift as staff members gradually come together around shared beliefs. For example, here's how 4th grade teacher Ann Thomson describes how a yearlong emphasis on teaching to the test and focusing on isolated parts of writing gradually shifted to teaching for authenticity and beginning with a whole, meaningful text:

> I was scared by the test and felt uncomfortable preparing kids for it. My colleagues and I did intense writing to a prompt. The kids hated it, and so did I. Writing and scoring all those papers wore them out, and then the kids didn't do well on the tests anyway. My biggest change came when I started applying the OLM and modeling for kids, writing in front of them. My beliefs began to shift along with my practices.

It's been wonderful to meet every week as a staff in our PLC and talk and work together with common goals, common language, and shared beliefs. I'm enjoying teaching a lot more now. I have more understanding of the big picture of everything. I do a lot of public conferring instead of "take home and correct." Regarding my lesson planning, I respond more to the kids now, what their needs and interests are.[8]

For principal Mike Henderson and his teachers, prioritizing instructional practices that most benefited student learning did not happen until the staff coalesced around shared beliefs. Until then, teaching test-taking strategies took center stage. However, once the staff shifted their priorities and developed a PLC culture, student growth soared. The staff moved from a rating of "underperforming" from the state department of education to a "B" rating for two years running. Here's how Mike describes the transformation:

Due to our focus on prioritized practices, teaching test-taking strategies has become obsolete. This used to be a practice fulfilled out of desperation and concern that our students wouldn't perform well on standardized tests. Desperation and concern have been replaced with confidence and trust that our teaching practices have such an impact on student thinking that they will naturally perform well during the state testing each year.[9]

Moving to the collective belief that the more effectively we teach students to write, the higher their test scores will be is not easy, even when mindless test prep has not yielded the results we seek. Results from the National Assessment of Educational Progress (NAEP, often called "the nation's report card") indicate that most students at grades 8 and 12 have the writing basics, but only about one-quarter are proficient in communicating to others—coherently, effectively, and accurately—when they write to persuade, explain, or convey experiences.[10] As renowned educator Grant Wiggins notes, what we are actually saying when we rely on writing formulas, prompts, and other counterproductive measures is "I have to teach *worse* to raise test scores; I have to teach poor writing to improve their writing performance. This is an error—and a grave one."[11]

It is no easy matter for a staff to coalesce around shared beliefs. We all hold strong beliefs based on a lifetime of experiences and deeply rooted ideas, many of which may reside beneath the surface. However, we each act upon our beliefs whether we can articulate them or not; they are part of our operating system. Professional development at many schools has concentrated on the procedural aspects of yet another new resource, so many of us are not used to thinking about our own beliefs and exemplary practices, or questioning adopted practices.

At first, it is not unusual for a staff to come to agreement on only one or two beliefs about reading or writing. Typically, the staff sees this low level of agreement as a discouraging negative, but it is a positive beginning and needs to be viewed as such and celebrated. In fact, for schools that have had lots of different and often superficial professional development offerings over the years as well as scant collaboration with colleagues, coming to agreement on only one or two beliefs is quite typical. A literacy coach from one such school said she and her colleagues began by identifying their common ground. "Even when our staff could find little in common with our beliefs, we could agree on the fact that we all want what is best for our kids."[12] Typically, revisited and revised lists of a school's beliefs evolve over time to include roughly 6 to 10 core beliefs that align with sound practices. (See the photo on this page for an example of one school's first efforts to establish beliefs about writing, prominently displayed in a school hallway.)

A school proudly posts results from its first shared beliefs discussion about writing.

Conduct an environmental writing walk

One reliable way to assess a school's beliefs is to do an environmental writing walk. On the elementary school level, my colleagues and I have found this activity to be a relatively accurate way to infer and discern the writing beliefs of a whole school. As we walk around the school, we notice the hallways and bulletin boards and assess the following:

- First impressions when entering the building
- Messages we are sending about writing
- Audience and purpose for posted work
- Access to readers—eye level, explanation of the work, legibility
- Quality of the work—content and craft, spelling and conventions, presentation
- Instructional practices and beliefs
- Expectations for students as writers

When the John de Graff School in Winnipeg, Manitoba, conducted such a writing walk, the result was a meaningful evaluation that included strengths, needs, and goal setting. See a sample evaluation at www.ascd .org/ASCD/pdf/books/Routman2014figures.pdf. Use password Routman 2014113016 to unlock the files.

Think about implementing a similar walk as a literacy assessment. How the walls change over the years is one quick and easy measure of a school's growing literacy knowledge and beliefs that reflect "best practices."

John de Graff's principal, Margaret Fair, comments on how the walks have influenced and represented her K–6 school's literacy journey:

> The environmental writing walks are one of the most helpful and motivating parts of our work on writing. We use them as a celebration of the wonderful writing that the students are doing. We also use them as a way to look for trends and consistency so that we can set goals for our teaching. Our focus on environmental writing walks that we do several times per year has really enhanced our writing project. It has given a real purpose and audience for students' writing and has transformed the culture of our school into being a place for communicating our ideas with writing."[13]

Quick Win

Highlight the positive when conducting an environmental walk in writing or reading and go with a small, knowledgeable team. When sharing results with staff, begin with celebration. Staff members will then be more willing to discuss school needs.

Conduct an environmental reading walk

Either separately or in concert with the writing walk, we notice school practices around reading that reflect beliefs, school strengths, and needs, and we prioritize what we need to focus on as a school. Here are some indicators to take into account:

- First impressions when entering building
- Messages we are sending about reading
- Instructional practices and beliefs (such as the alignment and grouping of practices and beliefs, including expectations for reading conferences, independent work, and free-choice reading)
- Expectations for students as readers
- Purpose and engagement (not just on-task behavior)
- Response to reading (thoughtful discussion, further reading, writing, literature conversations)
- Evidence of self-determining readers (assessment, self-monitoring, joy, flow)
- Access to attractive, organized, high-quality library that acts as a focal point of the school, offering students choice, selection, and an appropriate balance of fiction and nonfiction

In particular, notice the classroom library and whether or not it is visible, attractive, easily accessible to all, put together with student input, based on students' interests, balanced with high-quality and diverse nonfiction and fiction texts, leveled (an attribute that is *not* recommended), and part of a classroom reading area.[14]

See Appendix D for specifics on key actions and practices to look for in the reading and writing classroom.

Connect Beliefs with Excellent Instructional Practices

The transition to more meaningful beliefs and aligned practices goes hand in hand with a willingness to try out new practices. As noted earlier, modifying beliefs is a slow process that requires patience, professional conversations, an open mind, and deep reflection and questioning, along with being willing to try out "new" practices and to refine "tried and true" ones. "Research on attitudinal changes has long found that most of us change our behaviors somewhat before we get insights into new beliefs."[15] Although attitudes and beliefs change slowly, a culture of support and trust speeds up the process.

Machel Lucas was a grade 8 teacher when her beliefs began to shift through weekly, whole-school professional development that included support for application of new learning. Because of the ongoing professional development, discussion of schoolwide beliefs, and dissatisfaction with her system of conferring one-on-one with students at their point of need, she took a leap of faith and tried out public conferences after viewing a video that showed an example. To her surprise, "the results were ASTOUNDING!! I had not one behavior issue. Every student was engaged in a meaningful way."[16] Machel says it was her "dedication to growing as an educator" and her trust in the PD process that led her to take the risks involved in trying out an unfamiliar practice, which then led to rethinking long-held beliefs.

Because beliefs are reflected in practices, a teacher's beliefs are often transparent. For example, a teacher may say, "I believe students should write for an audience and purpose." Yet the bulletin boards in her room and in the hallway may display writing that has misspellings, is placed too high for potential readers to see, and mostly emphasizes isolated parts such as "vivid verbs." This teacher's beliefs are in transition, which is a normal part of the change process. Or, in another example, a teacher goes through the motions of making a shift from part-to-whole teaching without firmly believing in it, perhaps because the teacher is waiting for the "latest fad" to pass.

Holding beliefs that derive from valid and reliable research, growing knowledge, and experiences can give us the courage to successfully advocate for better practices. For example, teachers and administrators do begin to question the use of some widely used reading assessments, such as DIBELS and mCLASS, once they realize that the data they are receiving are not helping improve reading instruction and the research behind some assessments is not valid and reliable.[17]

Also, it is through wrestling with our beliefs and working to become more knowledgeable that we begin to become more effective as a staff and are able to talk about instruction and student work in a clear, consistent, and comprehensive manner. Important enough to be restated, once our beliefs are solid in a school and a district, we can effectively determine what practices support those beliefs and develop a curriculum that is in alignment. Then, even the best program becomes a resource or framework—but not the curriculum—for supporting our viable beliefs and vision.

Quick Win

Make your mental processes visible by explaining aloud reasons for what you're doing. Learners (students and teachers) are more engaged in learning and more motivated to do the work when they understand and value the purpose.

Articulate your beliefs

What follows are my most essential core beliefs about writing and reading and my instructional practices that support those beliefs. Throughout this chapter and book, I note how those beliefs are consistently translated into practice. Check as a school that your established beliefs and practices are being discussed and reviewed, are based on research and experience, and are in alignment across the grades. Until changing beliefs become visible in daily practices, those stated beliefs are just wishes.

My beliefs related to reading and writing are supported by research and more than four decades of experience, both of which drive my daily practices in planning, instruction, and assessment. Although I continue to refine these core beliefs, I make no abrupt swings based on politics, outside pressures, or new programs. My beliefs have remained solid for quite some time, based on a lifetime of teaching, learning, collaborating, and reflecting, and my practices align with those beliefs. Authenticity in teaching, learning, and assessing are intrinsically connected to my beliefs. When we apply real-world contexts, purposes, texts, practices, and resources, we get better results and higher student engagement. Also, deeply connected to my core beliefs is the conviction that we are all teachers of reading and writing, regardless of our grade level, content-area focus, or position we hold.

Connect beliefs with assessment that moves learning forward

An important learning for me has been that if teachers are not well grounded and knowledgeable about literacy, we can waste a lot of valuable time looking at student work. When I first began residency work and we looked at student work, teachers lacked the knowledge to notice and state learners' important strengths and needs. Schooled in a part-to-whole approach to teaching, which was reflected in their beliefs, they always focused initially on isolated parts that were easy to name and measure.

For example, the focus in writing would typically emphasize mechanics (capital letters, punctuation, complete sentences, grammar, and so on), with little mention of the craft of writing (leads, organizational structure, precise word choice, sense of audience, and so on). It typically took at least two years of ongoing, high-quality, embedded professional development for teachers to be able to look at student work through a different lens—one that noticed the whole of the work, the person behind the work, and the language that made the work unique. Being able to fully notice and name

> **Quick Win**
>
> *Use the language and contexts of the real world*—"book reviews" (instead of "book reports"), "great books" or "inspiring literature" (instead of "mentor texts"), "writing" (instead of "writing workshop"), "non-negotiables" (instead of "must-do's").

what the writer or reader is doing is highly sophisticated work that takes much modeling, practice, and feedback.

My Top Three Beliefs About Writing

- Students need to have sustained time to write every day for authentic and valued audiences and purposes.
- Focus on the writer first, the writing second.
- Connect reading with writing; notice what authors do.

Top Five Things I Do to Ensure Students Become Excellent Writers

1. Demonstrate that I am a writer and make visible the processes of writing; that is, the thinking, planning, revising, and editing.
2. Use excellent texts, including those by student authors, to showcase the craft as well as the nuts and bolts of writing with the goal of having students try out in their own writing what real authors do.
3. Guide students to choose topics for writing (choice within structure) and give students the time, space, resources, and tools to write in a variety of genres for real-world audiences and purposes.
4. Teach students the strategies and habits they need to communicate clearly, purposefully, fluently, confidently, and joyfully.
5. Assess and evaluate students regularly; note and celebrate strengths, give useful feedback, teach, set goals together.

Source: From *Writing Essentials* (2005, p. 8) and *Regie Routman in Residence* (2008) by Regie Routman; Portsmouth, NH: Heinemann. Copyright by Regie Routman. Adapted by permission.

Quick Win

Celebrate a student's writing by projecting it (with permission) via a document camera or other means so everyone can see the actual writing and key in on celebration points. Other students will be motivated to try some of the same techniques.

Quick Win

Teach students how to keyboard. Expect one page in one sitting by 3rd grade, three pages by 7th grade.

Limited literacy knowledge leads to constraint in how much we can do to help students improve and increases the likelihood of inflexible instructional practices. When what we see and believe about writing and reading is at the isolated-skills level and that's all we know how to do, then that's how and what we teach. It does not matter that we set new goals for students if those goals do not increase students' competency in meaningful ways.

We can assess our growing knowledge and sophistication about literacy teaching by the language we use in our classrooms and schools to describe what we see when examining and assessing students' writing and reading.

Quick Win

Chart strengths and needs in writing when looking at student work at and across grade levels. Notice the language used to describe students' strengths and needs, and use those findings to jumpstart discussion of schoolwide beliefs and accompanying practices and where change and professional development are most needed.

At first, many teachers focus on surface, easy-to-assess features such as mechanics, grammar, and spelling in writing; in reading that focus is often on correct reading of words, skills in isolation, and literal comprehension. As we become more knowledgeable about what's most important to celebrate and teach, the literacy elements we notice, name, and value become more high-level. For example, in writing, focus increasingly moves to writing craft, awareness of a reader, elaboration, and organization techniques. In reading, focus increasingly shifts to deep understanding of a text, finding evidence from the text to support thinking, and comprehension of a wide variety of fiction and nonfiction genres.

My Top Three Beliefs About Reading

- Establish an excellent classroom library of interesting and varied nonfiction and fiction texts and provide access and choice to all students.
- Provide sustained time for independent reading every day and monitor understanding through reading conferences and small-group work.
- Demonstrate strategies, processes, and habits of effective and joyful readers and guide students toward independent application.

Top Five Things I Do to Ensure Students Become Excellent Readers

1. Demonstrate that I am a reader and make visible my processes of reading, including the thinking, text selection, problem solving, and self-monitoring for understanding.
2. Work with students to provide an excellent classroom library.
3. Guide students to choose books they can and want to read and give students sustained, daily time to read them.
4. Teach students the processes, strategies, and habits they need to understand and enjoy texts.
5. Assess and evaluate students regularly; note and celebrate strengths; identify where students need support: give useful feedback, teach, and set goals together.

Source: From *Reading Essentials*: *The Specifics You Need to Teach Reading Well* (p. 43), by Regie Routman, 2003, Portsmouth, NH: Heinemann, and *Regie Routman in Residence: Transforming Our Teaching Through Reading to Understand*, by Regie Routman, 2009, Portsmouth, NH: Heinemann. Adapted by permission.

With increased knowledge and understanding—including focusing on a whole and meaningful text first—teachers are able to take their new insights and apply them to writing and reading conferences in an effective and efficient manner that increases student learning. Also vital, until we are skilled in knowing how to use and apply formative and summative assessments and to then instruct in a manner that improves learning, students' progress will remain limited.

Provide Access to Appropriate Texts

When the goal is to develop proficient, confident, joyful readers and writers, it's all about texts—the quality and quantity of meaningful, interesting texts that students can access. Underpinning everything we do as literacy teachers and leaders is our role in ensuring wide availability of appropriate texts and sustained time to write them and to read them. Here we must consider many vital text factors, including the following:

- Quality
- Language
- Meaningfulness
- Readability
- Difficulty
- Complexity
- Length
- Genre
- Format
- Text supports (e.g., visuals, organization)

In addition to curriculum requirements, we must also take into account readers' and writers' interests, needs, background, and culture. Providing students with texts they can read on their own with fluency and understanding is crucial for their development as readers.

It doesn't matter much what students read as long as they read. Researchers have found that middle schoolers who read comic books did more reading for pleasure and tended to do more book reading.[18] This was certainly true for me. I was an avid reader of Archie and Veronica and other romance comics as a young teenager and gradually made my way into higher-level fare. Today I am picky about what I read, and I credit years of light reading—comic books and series such as *The Box Car Children* and *Nancy Drew*—for turning me into a discerning reader. I also credit my grandmother, who continued to read aloud to me, all the way through my teens, the classics that I would never have picked up on my own.

Quick Win

Encourage parents and other family members to continue to read aloud to their children all the way through high school. Make the benefits of reading aloud known to families and caregivers; provide support and encouragement to families where reading aloud is not a familiar practice or habit.

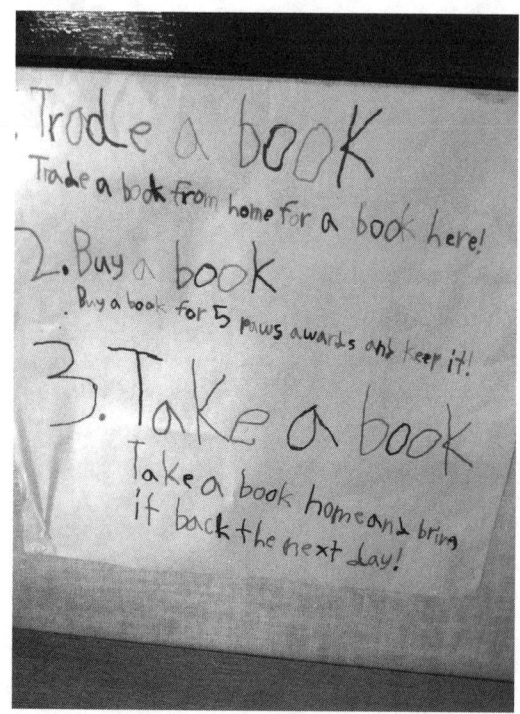

Two students, with the support of the school's literacy coach, initiate a book exchange to help equalize student access to books.

Ensure Access to Books for All Students

As access to books that students can and want to read is such an important issue for turning kids into readers, seek out as many ways as possible to make that happen, including publishing "second editions" of high-quality books students write. Keep in mind that a recent study by the Cooperative Children's Book Center at the University of Wisconsin found that less than 5 percent of children's books published in 2013 were about black or Latino kids. Therefore, it's up to us educators to do whatever we can to also ensure culturally relevant books are obtainable for our students—even if we have to write them ourselves.

As educators, we are also responsible for ensuring that books are readily and equitably available to all students in our schools. Access to reading materials is a continuing problem that limits progress in developing literacy. Especially in low-income areas, many students have few books in their homes, and books are much harder to find and purchase than in middle-class communities.[19] Sandy Grade School in Oregon addressed this challenge directly by setting up a book exchange in the hallway (see photos on p. 96). Significant as well, even though close to 25 percent of all public school children in the United States today are Latino, only 3 percent of children's books are by or about Latinos.[20]

Excellent classroom libraries with diverse and balanced collections are essential for promoting the massive amount of independent reading students need to do to improve and maintain comprehension, fluency, and vocabulary.[21] Electronic books are one way to increase access and interest, but most students still prefer holding and reading an actual book when they "read for fun."[22] Finally, it's up to us to ensure that our students read texts in which they see themselves and the diversity of the world, which encourages them to want to read and to become curious about other lives and new possibilities.

Use Riveting Literature

We can't teach a first-rate lesson with second-rate texts. Without fail, I seek outstanding literature for all the reading and writing I bring into classrooms. For that I rely on librarians, bookstores, book reviews, and recommendations from colleagues. As an example, in the bullying lesson described in Chapter 2, our teaching would have been very limited without access to outstanding literature. We needed both nonfiction and fiction literature for writing models, for examining decisions and choices authors make, for providing extensive information and research including reliable websites and videos, and for engaging students in up-to-date subject matter. The literature is not just the way we launch the work; it's what we use to sustain interest and build necessary background information, as well as help with motivation, engagement, and joy in doing the work.[23]

We must not underestimate the powerful potential of engaging books. Riveting literature and texts turn students into readers. By riveting literature, I mean any text—fiction, nonfiction, poetry, biography, history, science, and so on—that captures the heart and mind of the learner and serves as a springboard to developing the stamina, interest, and knowledge that can transfer to other kinds of reading. Our job is to continually guide each student to find that riveting literature and also to expand his or her choices to include a variety of texts and genres.

It is never too late to become a reader! As already noted, older struggling readers who have extensive opportunities for voluntary reading and access to interesting books of their choice do more reading and read better.[24] More than that: Research shows that when high school students read and discuss "intense," "compelling," and "edgy" books of their own choosing, they change in significant ways. Not only do they become engaged readers, they interact socially around the books. For example, they initiate talk and communicate openly about the books they are reading in and out of school with peers and family and may even take on the role of the characters. They also gain greater perspective on their own lives, become more attuned to the world, and see possibilities for shaping and transforming their social environment.[25] Not to be minimized, riveting literature influences the quality of writing that students of all ages do, especially when we teach them to notice and apply what effective authors do, including what student authors do.

A word about informational texts. There is no research that supports the notion that substituting informational texts for literature will improve students' college readiness. In fact, in school districts with "literature-rich" standards, students consistently score high on national reading tests.[26] While the latest standards in the United States do not specifically recommend that we reduce the amount of literature we teach, some have interpreted the increased emphasis on nonfiction to mean just that. In fact, it is close reading of much literature, such as riveting fiction, that helps prepare students to tackle more complex texts and issues, including informational ones.[27]

It is up to us as informed educators to ensure that we maintain a healthy instructional balance that includes fiction and informational texts as well as poetry and a wide variety of genres and formats. I also suggest we be less rigid in what we call literature. My preferred informational books are those that are literature, that is, narrative nonfiction that is beautifully crafted, has a vivid setting, a unique story to tell—a true history (his story or her story)—which is brought to life through well-developed characters that the reader gets to know as flesh-and-blood human beings. As an example, a recent favorite is the award-winning book *Behind the Beautiful Forevers: Life, Death, and Hope in a Mumbai Undercity* by Katherine Boo. More than

Quick Win

Become a reader. If you have not yet experienced the joy of being a reader, think about starting with children's literature. Ask a librarian, a colleague, or your students to recommend favorite short titles, including picture books, and start reading!

anything I've ever read, Boo's unflinching look at the devastating impact of extreme poverty on ordinary people informed me—in a way I will never forget—about the cruel and lasting consequences of severe economic inequality.

Establish Excellent Classroom Libraries with Students

Excellent classroom libraries, school libraries, and public libraries are the cornerstone of a successful school reading program. Until viable libraries are in place in the classroom, students are often relegated to lots of independent work *about reading*—filling in worksheets, doing skills work, responding to questions—with no substantial time devoted *to reading* sustained, interesting, self-selected texts that they can read with fluency and understanding. Once excellent classroom libraries are in place and we explicitly teach and assess students on how to select "just right" books, we can move to a focus on guided reading—but not guided reading as an end in itself; rather, guided reading as a means to helping students become more independent. That is, once we have checked how students are reading and comprehending during guided reading and we have supplied any needed support, we assign further reading—reading on, rereading, responding to reading—of continuous, meaningful texts.

Make excellent classroom libraries one of your highest priorities— ahead of the latest technology, resources, programs, and standards. It is only through wide, self-selected reading that we will produce proficient and joyful readers as well as writers. To obtain books for a classroom library, check school bookrooms and see which of the books you find there might be better used in classroom libraries. Borrow books from local public libraries, known for their generosity in loaning large numbers of books. Solicit donations from the community. Ask students to lend books from home. Use book fairs to buy engaging books at low prices. Share with administrators the extensive research on how wide reading can increase reading achievement[28] and strongly advocate for funds for rich and diverse classroom libraries. Be sure to include sufficient numbers of nonfiction texts to support students' interests in science and social studies topics. Finally, because "nearly half of today's [U.S.] children under 5 years old are nonwhite" and the publishing industry has not yet caught up to this changing demographic,[29] reserve a section of classroom libraries for class-authored and student-authored texts that fill that void.

Quick Win

Seek free and inexpensive ways to build classroom libraries, especially if you are a teacher new to a school and facing a stripped-down classroom. Some schools have worked with their local public and county libraries (or bookmobiles) to create "unlimited libraries" where teachers can request 30 or more titles on loan for their classroom. (Some book fairs, such as those sponsored by Scholastic, give away remaining titles at the end of the school year or offer deep discounts.)

Although it's time-consuming work that can feel chaotic at first, letting go of organizing the library and inviting students to participate in the process pays huge dividends. When students feel ownership of the classroom library, they are more likely to read more and to enjoy reading, and to have a sense of easy and equitable access to books. As a 2nd grade teacher noted, "Oh man, was it hard to let them make a mess! But they are so into it! They ask to go back and work on it every spare minute."[30]

Honor your students' preferences for topics, authors, series books, picture books, magazines, graphic novels, unique literary writing styles and forms, poetry, inquiry content, and more. Include a wide range of non-fiction and fiction texts, and don't hesitate to include sports magazines, comic books, manuals, audio books, and e-book readers. For example, it's well known that boys tend to prefer comic books, humorous novels, and sports magazines above other genres. "Boys like to read texts that will have an immediate payoff in conversations with friends."[31] For turning kids on to reading, it doesn't matter much what they read—or what device they read it on—as long as they interact meaningfully with texts that engage them. For older students and some younger ones, desire to read a book trumps all else.[32]

A strong recommendation is to organize your collection by students' interests and not by levels. Leveling all books in the classroom and classroom library is undemocratic and restrictive. Imagine being told upon entering a public library that we could only check out books at our predetermined reading level. We would be outraged! Although it makes some sense to rely on levels for guided reading instruction and assigned textbook reading, once students are readers—usually by the end of grade 1 or early grade 2—they can be taught to effectively choose books they can read and understand.

Guide Students to Choose Books They Can Read

Almost all the reading we do is voluntary, silent reading, and we get to choose what we want to read. Even when we may have job-related reading, we get to decide what we want to read for our own pleasure, information, and curiosity. It should not be much different for our students, but first we need to explicitly show them how to choose "just right" books and to follow up with guided practice.

Teaching students how to choose books they can actually read and understand is not as easy as it sometimes appears. Teachers can be lulled into a false sense of security when students can orally say how they choose books but can't actually do so on their own. In particular, in my experience, students seldom mention or apply actions related to understanding, so it is crucial we teach that most essential reading quality. Too many older students are fake readers who sit quietly and turn pages that they cannot read or understand. Taking students to the classroom library, school library, or book collection and explicitly showing them how to choose a book—with all students observing—and then following up with lots of shared and guided practice is a necessity for helping students understand that they must be able to the following:

- Choose a text that interests them.
- Read the title.
- Have enough background and experience to comprehend the particular text.
- Be able to decode almost all the words—at least 95 percent of them.
- Look through the text and read a few pages to "test" for "just rightness."
- Figure out most unknown vocabulary.
- Be comfortable with the format and amount and size of text on each page.
- Use the book's table of contents, layout, and organization to enhance meaning.
- Access the format for information, including the table of contents, graphs, charts, captions, and index.
- Understand the big and small ideas in the text.
- Self-monitor and self-correct while reading.
- Tell someone who has not read the text what it is about.
- Abandon a book that is too hard or is uninteresting.[33]

Once students have the "right" book, they need uninterrupted time to read it in a comfortable and peaceful setting. Sustained time to read continuous, meaningful texts, most of which are self-selected, must be the mainstay of any reading program, and this daily time should be substantial enough so students have time for deep engagement. Although shared reading and guided reading are important teaching scaffolds to support students' move to independence, without daily time for independent practice that is carefully monitored—mostly through one-on-one conferences—students are not likely to become fluent, comprehending readers.[34]

Quick Win

Teach this reading timesaver. Avid readers pile up books they want to read on their bedside tables. Instead, ask students to make a list of books they want to read, as a way to save time and help them anticipate their next read.

The volume of reading is also crucial for raising and sustaining reading achievement, but that volume must consist of books that students can read and comprehend. Students can only become self-teaching and self-regulating—learning new vocabulary and concepts, knowing when it's necessary to reread, adjusting rate to fit the purpose, and so on—when they can actually read and understand the texts. Too often students spend most of their time with books that are too hard for them, which can cause them to stall and regress as readers.

Understand Text Complexity

Text complexity and text difficulty are not the same, and knowing the difference matters. The complexity of a text is determined by the elements that reside within the text—sentence structure, organization, vocabulary, concepts, and so on—and that complexity remains the same regardless of the reader. A reader may find a complex text difficult, manageable, or easy to understand. By contrast, the difficulty of a particular text is determined by the reader; that is, it depends on factors such as the reader's prior knowledge, background, reading ability, engagement, and motivation.[35]

Although the Common Core State Standards place a huge focus on students reading complex texts, a caution is in order. We still have far too many readers who are receiving instruction using books that are too hard for them and who are choosing or being assigned books to read that are too complex and difficult. Too much emphasis on text complexity in the primary grades may actually hinder beginning reading proficiency. In addition, research does not support the claim that the CCSS-recommended increase in complexity of 3rd grade texts will lead to improved proficiency in higher grades.[36] Although the Common Core State Standards, curriculum, and other resources can provide a useful guide to the kinds of texts that are appropriate, we must not neglect valid and reliable research and our own informed professional judgment in making text decisions.

Rushing students into complex texts before they are ready will lead to more, not fewer, reading problems. For students from low-income families, emphasizing complex texts will only exacerbate the reading achievement gap between rich and poor.[37] Also, the more complex something is, the harder it is to reach the level of confidence and power that comes from knowing how to do something well.

Whether or not a text is suitable for a student depends on consideration of multiple variables, including—but not limited to—these:

- Interest in the topic, engagement
- Sentence structure and length
- Background knowledge of the learner
- Complexity and clarity of ideas and vocabulary
- Knowledge demands of the text, including language and literacy features
- Text support for figuring out unknown vocabulary and concepts, for example, supportive illustrations or in-text explanations
- Text genre, format, and structure
- Amount of scaffolding the learner will receive

Ultimately, well-informed teachers—often with the support of colleagues—must determine appropriate readability of texts for their particular students.[38]

Apply Reading Levels Judiciously

More than 30 years ago, in a high-poverty school where 50 percent of 1st graders were failing to learn to read, I led an effort away from core reading texts (what were then called basal texts) toward teaching reading with outstanding children's literature as the mainstay of the reading program. We teachers set up a school bookroom with a focus on natural language texts, predictable texts, and riveting children's literature. We ordered five copies of every book and leveled those books on our own, primarily for use in guided reading groups in the early grades. Because our main goal was to engage students in reading texts they could read fluently with enjoyment and understanding, our book collection centered on books that promoted those goals. The end result was dramatic; almost all the children became successful readers and writers.[39]

As part of our process, we established benchmark books for the end of each grade level by asking, "What book(s) would we expect a typical student to be able to read and understand by the end of grade 1, grade 2 and so on?" The exiting benchmark book for a grade level would also be the entering benchmark book for the next grade level. For example, the exiting benchmark book for grade 3 would also be the entering benchmark book for grade 4. In leveling and adding books to the school bookroom collection, we asked questions such as these: "Is this book as hard as _____?"

"Is this book as easy as _____?" "What are the particular supports and challenges the text provides for the reader?" In the mid-1980s, there were no commercially available leveled collections, so we used trial and error with students, our own knowledge as reading teachers, and common sense as we leveled many hundreds of books.

Because there is no proven scientific process for definitively leveling texts,[40] our subjective process worked well. We relied on high-interest topics and well-written, natural-language texts, and we paid close attention to print features, predictable structure and layout, content and ideas, large numbers of phonetically regular words, vocabulary and repetition of high-frequency words, length of text, and visual text supports such as pictures and photos. Most of our criteria turned out to be aligned with later research on excellent texts for beginning readers.[41]

Despite their usefulness, it is important to not rely too much on levels. Although a designated level can offer some helpful guidance, especially for instructional use for us teachers and for some struggling readers, a level by itself is often insufficient for matching readers with books they want to read. Regardless of the level provided by an outside source, we and our students need to look at the actual text and apply our own judgment. As students gain more experience with texts and improve as readers, they can do a better job choosing books for themselves than any formula can.[42]

Use caution with Lexile levels (which do not take into account text content, interest of the reader, or book design), computerized reading program levels, and leveled text in general, all of which may be useful for complexity of words and sentence structure but have not proven reliable for complexity of concept, which is far more important to a reader's understanding.[43] As an example, the parents of a middle school student were concerned that their daughter was not challenging herself as a reader. It seemed to them the books their daughter was choosing were "too easy." The teacher gave the parents a list of books at the student's Lexile level. Seeking my advice, the parents shared the list with me. Reading down the list, books about topics that were beyond the student's maturity level took me aback. Although the student would certainly be able to read all the words, the sophistication of topics beyond her emotional level made some of the books inappropriate.

Once students are readers, factors such as choice, interest, and background are far more important than a precise reading level. As already stated—but important enough to restate—it is advisable to organize classroom libraries according to students' favorite authors, series, interests, genres, and so on. If we've done our job as educators, students will be able to make appropriate text choices.

Expand Background Knowledge

Prior knowledge and experiences, familiarity with the particular genre, and general and academic language remain requirements for understanding fiction and nonfiction text, especially for the nuances, inferences, and analysis required by the latest standards and all good instruction. This is common sense; it's difficult to comprehend a problem or a text without sufficient background information. The answers do not lie in the text alone. Overemphasis on text-dependent questions and relying almost exclusively on the text itself for total understanding are not how competent readers and thinkers work. In fact, noted educator and scholar Jeffrey Wilhelm emphatically states, "The central lesson of my career is that the most important time to teach is *before* students undertake a new challenge. We must prepare students for success; we must be *proactive* vs. reactive in responding to students' needs."[44]

Teaching before students undertake a new challenge is exactly what we did in the bullying lesson described in Chapter 2 in order to ensure that students had the vocabulary, concepts, and background information they would need to tackle a tough issue.

> When students do not have the knowledge necessary to comprehend a particular text, such knowledge needs to be built; one cannot activate what is not there, and one cannot strategize about things one does not know.[45]

We began by assessing and valuing students' background knowledge and experiences. Then, as knowledgeable educators, we provided students the demonstrations, resources and information, shared experiences, strategic actions, and guidance that would allow them to work successfully at the information gathering we asked them to do. One result of building sufficient background knowledge was that students were able to ask more relevant and challenging questions—a hallmark of inquiring learners.

Integrate Social Media and Technology into Literacy

Social media provide the wide, authentic audiences and purposes that readily engage students in reading, writing, speaking, listening, thinking, and creating in ways that schools often do not. For example, students can post a blog or a classroom project on a safe interactive site for classrooms and students.[46] (One such site is Edmodo.) Some worry that allowing students to do the shortcut writing that social media encourage will derail their more formal writing required in high school and college. However, research shows just the opposite; more authentic writing through social media actually leads to better and more extensive writing in all genres, largely because students are so aware of their audience and purpose and also because they understand that different forms and purposes require different ways of writing. "Technology isn't killing our ability to write. It's reviving it and pushing our literacy in bold new directions."[47]

A survey of advanced placement (AP) and National Writing Project teachers led to the conclusion that the effective use of digital tools can be especially motivating to middle and high school students, encouraging them to express themselves creatively, collaborate more, and share their work with wider and more varied audiences.[48] The same statement holds true for elementary students, many of whom have grown up blogging, making videos, and connecting online as a part of their literacy lives. (See Appendix E for recommended technology tools and how best to use them.)

The caution is that simply promoting the use of social media and the latest technology tools does not guarantee increased engagement and literacy gains even though students hold positive views about such literacy applications. Too many of us educators apply new literacy tools in old ways, which then constrains the possibilities for our students.[49] We need to be up to speed in our own use of social media and technology, demonstrate to our students how to use social media and technology such as YouTube videos and blogs effectively and appropriately, and be continually open to seeing new possibilities. We need to take a lesson from our students who routinely write and communicate to persuade, debate, and inform using social media and to bring that enthusiasm for writing for real audiences and purposes into our classrooms and schools.

A sobering fact: Internationally, the highest-performing schools are not heavy into technology use. Spending on teacher pay and resources for neediest students comes first.[50]

Quick Win

Incorporate technology wisely. Use iPads or other technology to integrate photos, videos, and audio in your classroom and other presentations. Be sure technology use leads to interactive curriculum and increased learning.

Write for Audience and Purpose

I have deliberately placed the discussion of writing before the discussion of reading because writing has the power to quickly change a child's life in a way I have rarely seen happen with reading. In reading, the child has the text as an intermediary support. Writing has no such support, and that blank page or screen can be more daunting. Writing requires thinking, taking an idea and communicating it effectively. It is through writing that we figure out what we want to say. A student's ability to think rationally, argue with credible evidence, and speak eloquently to defend a position—all CCSS goals—are enhanced through thoughtful writing.

My recommendation is to make sustained time for daily writing a high priority and to consider writing in math, science, and social studies *writing*, and to not separate writing into journal writing, creative writing, and writing across the curriculum. Although "writing workshop" is a popular term, I call all writing work "writing" because that's what I call it as a writer.

Also, because writing takes so much mental and physical energy, consider scheduling it early in the day, especially for our youngest learners. Sadly, writing has often been given short shrift because of the link between what is tested and what is taught or valued; that is, where writing has *not* been tested, it has often not been taught or highly valued. The Common Core State Standards rectify this oversight and recognize that the act of writing promotes exploration and thinking, which are crucial for effective communication. However, it is up to us educators to ensure that writing is purposeful and relevant for students. In that regard, writing for audience and purpose is the umbrella for all writing and includes providing sustained writing time each day.

The continuing caution with writing is that we need to align sound writing beliefs with sensible, research-based practices K–12, but this discussion and alignment across elementary, middle, and high school rarely occurs. Without such alignment across all grades and disciplines, students become disheartened writers. As one middle school student wrote to me: "When we worked together in writing in grade 5, I loved writing. But in middle school, we were asked to write in a formula way, and I got very confused."[51]

Quick Win

Have elementary students keep all writing together—reading response, literature, science, social studies in one notebook—with dividers for sections for drafts, minilessons, and special formats (e.g., business letters). Writing is writing. Don't make "writing workshop" a separate activity.

Quick Win

Devote large amounts of daily time to actual reading and writing of continuous texts. Sustained, deliberate practice is a necessity for becoming expert.

Make Writing Authentic

All the writing we do in the world outside school is for an authentic audience and purpose. Even when we write notes or reflections, or keep a journal, we are writing for a real audience—ourselves. It is only in school that writing is often just for the teacher, to practice for a high-stakes test, or to fill up an empty space on a bulletin board or in a hallway. No wonder so much student writing never gets better; students are practicing what they don't know and what they don't care much about.

Successful teachers of writing strive for authenticity, engaging students in meaningful activity and teaching writing the way real writers work. Students will invest their full efforts in composing, revising, and editing when they value and understand the purpose and the audience for the writing. They will take responsibility for creating lively writing that engages readers through ideas clearly presented, well-crafted language, a well-organized flow of ideas, correct conventions and form, and so much more. This last statement also holds true for those who don't experience the "power of the pen" until later in life. Alfred Tatum has eloquently documented how African American male adolescents can be taught to write "to define themselves, to nurture their resilience, to engage with others past and present, and to build capacity for future generations of African American male writers."[52]

If students understand and value the purpose of the writing, they will put forth their best efforts, even on a writing assessment where they may not see their results. Appendix F is a standardized interim writing assessment that can be used to determine how well students are progressing schoolwide. Note how the specific purpose of the writing is read aloud to students to make it more likely they will invest their best efforts.

Some teachers find it difficult at first to take required curriculum and connect it with writing for an authentic audience and purpose. Some easy ways to start include shared writing on such topics as establishing classroom routines and procedures and how to solve problems related to classroom issues (audience: students); summaries and recommendations from content-area study around such issues as immigration, citizenship, and discrimination (audience: school community, news media, families, other students); and a "Welcome to Our School" book (audience: new families, real estate agents).[53]

Quick Win

Assign writing that gives kids agency in their lives (e.g., essays on bullying, resolution of classroom issues, authentic persuasive pieces).

Simplify the Teaching of Writing

We make writing harder than it needs to be when we focus too much on the parts, when we emphasize mechanics (spelling, capitalization) over content and form at the start, and when we lack sufficient knowledge for effectively teaching and assessing writing well. We also complicate writing for our students and ourselves when we lack cohesiveness of beliefs and practices from classroom to classroom and grade to grade in a school or district. In Chapter 6, I discuss how a Professional *Literacy* Community can serve as the school's foundation for improving teacher knowledge and student writing.

One proven way to simplify writing and increase results K–12 is to see all effective writing—and the teaching of writing—as interconnected, across the curriculum. That is, we accept responsibility for the fact that regardless of our content area, we must all be teachers of writing and that it's not necessary to create separate writing lessons and units every time we change genres or subjects. If we and our students internalize the strategic actions, intentional decisions, and habits of effective writers, we can easily transfer what we know to all writing. We do, of course, need to know and teach the specifics of each genre,[54] but what students learn about craft, leads, revision, and so on applies to all writing. The Summary of a Framework for Teaching Writing Genres (p. 110) shows common actions that make that transfer possible.

We also make writing more complicated than it needs to be by having students write so many long pieces. So much of what is important to teach about writing can be done by simplifying our work through having students write memorable short pieces.

Teachers and students alike find a powerful way to connect with peers through "snapshot writing," in which, for example, we create a mental picture about something revealing about ourselves—such as sharing an important memory, a hobby, a humorous situation, or a life-changing moment. A middle school teacher and literacy coach comments on the impact of this kind of writing:

> I can't quite capture the emotion I felt as I heard middle school math, science, social studies, art, and physical education teachers sharing their writing with other teachers, but it hovers around thrill and awe. I am still amazed how an act as simple as sharing written thoughts, ideas, and stories can create and strengthen bonds.[55]

Quick Win

Teach it first; label it later. Immerse students in a concept and process before naming the individual parts. This approach increases and speeds up understanding. For example, once students have seen, discussed, and understood the need for transitions as they occur in meaningful reading and writing, say something like, "Remember how the author used such-and-such words to let the reader know she was moving to a new idea or topic? That's called a 'transition.' Now you know what that's called and how and why to use transitions in your own writing."

Quick Win

Have students write mostly short pieces, which allows them to frequently practice and apply the entire authentic-writing process from planning to publication, instead of the more typical marathon report writing or extended unit study that limits how often students engage in the entire process.

Summary of a Framework for Teaching Writing Genres

- Find out what students know about the genre and chart their responses. (*assessment before teaching*)
- Gather many high-interest, well-crafted, and grade-appropriate examples of the genre and have students examine these materials with guidance. (*immersion, demonstration*)
- Discuss and chart "What makes a good _____? (*shared demonstration, ongoing assessment*)
- Think aloud and write in the genre (*demonstration*) and together as a class. (*shared demonstration*)
- Identify additional criteria for what to include when writing in the genre. (*shared demonstration, ongoing assessment*)
- Prepare to write. (*shared demonstration and guided practice*)
- Write for a sustained period in the form of the genre for an authentic audience and purpose. (*guided and independent practice*)
- Confer with students; teach what's needed; set goals together. (*shared demonstration, guided and independent practice, ongoing assessment*)
- Publish, present, and share with the intended audience. (*celebration and independent practice*)
- Encourage students to do more writing in the genre. (*independent practice*)

Source: From *Writing Essentials* (pp. 196-197), by Regie Routman, 2005, Portsmouth, NH: Heinemann. Copyright 2005 by Regie Routman. Adapted by permission.

Finally, if we consult anchor standards for writing as a guide (see http://www.corestandards.org/ELA-Literacy/CCRA/W), it's feasible to stay focused on the big picture and key writing areas and not get bogged down by minutiae (and the same is true for reading).

Become a Writing Role Model

Writing in front of our students, even if we do not see ourselves as "writers," is essential so they can see that the process is recursive and messy, a back-and-forth working through of thoughts and ideas to form an organized and engaging text for a reader. It is rare for writers to have everything worked out in their heads and then to seamlessly transfer their thoughts to the page. For most of us, even if we are seasoned writers, writing is often slow, plodding work. Our students need to see us tackle that process in all its complexity.

Quick Win

Teach students to skip lines when writing by hand and tell them why that matters. Acquiring this habit early on helps students understand and value that writers write for readers, and revision—which requires more space—may be needed for clarity, interest, and content accuracy.

Many years ago, renowned educator Frank Smith wisely said, "It's not that I like writing; I like having written." Surely that is true for many of us. The greatest satisfaction comes from knowing that our sustained, thoughtful efforts may yield a meaningful text that is purposeful and useful to our intended audience. Our students will follow us into the tough terrain called writing if they value and understand the purpose and audience for the work, the work is meaningful and doable, they have some choice in the topic, and we set them up for success with sufficient frontloading.

In the process of writing, we figure out what we want to say through an ongoing, nonlinear process of drafting our first thinking; rereading for clarity and for ideas on what to say next; rethinking our writing-in-process; revising by adding on, deleting, and changing words and ideas; reorganizing text so it's coherent and flows well; rereading for meaning and flow of ideas and language; and editing, both informally as we go along and "catch" errors and, formally, later on, as an intentional, final check for accuracy and precise word choice. None of this is easy, but the rewards are worth the effort. It's important for us to demonstrate for our students the work, process, and thinking writers do so they, too, can begin to see themselves as writers.

Keep the whole in mind

Remember to keep the focus on meaning and whole texts in such demonstrations. In teaching and assessing, emphasizing a whole-part-whole teaching approach is not only more effective and authentic; it's also more efficient and enjoyable for the long run. For example, teaching and analyzing writing by breaking it down to six commonly agreed-upon traits actually slows down the writing process and artificially limits what writers actually do, which is particularly egregious for writers who struggle.

Here's an illustrative story. In an intermediate-grades classroom where we were focusing on memoir, I spread out my demonstration writing over two days. Then, to show observing teachers and administrators how much teaching had taken place, I analyzed and assessed my writing according to the "six traits." Notice, I did not begin my teaching with six traits, teaching them in isolation as learning targets, or using them as curriculum, all of which fragments the writing and limits and slows the writer's progress. Appendix G shows a chart for the traits and the teaching points from my actual writing. Notice too that in the course of authentic writing, all the traits were "covered" but in an authentic manner.[56] (The same principles

---

Quick Win

Expect a core of high-frequency words to be spelled correctly—starting in grade 1—and hold students accountable, which saves time in the long run. For older students, employ a word wall dedicated to the current content study and expect those core words to be correctly spelled. Take words off the word wall once students have mastered them.

Quick Win

Have a student first read her paper aloud in a writing conference, and listen for the whole of the piece and what the student is attempting to say before offering comments. Focus on what the writing *does* (its impact on the reader) before focusing on what the writing *has* (organization, leads, punctuation).

hold true for reading. As proficient readers we don't read by only making connections, inferences, or predictions. Comprehending readers strategically and interactively apply all their knowledge and strategies in order to make sense of text.)

Tips on becoming a writing role model

Even if you are reluctant and fearful to publicly write, give it a sincere attempt. Students appreciate honest efforts. Not only that, but thinking out loud and writing in front of our students is the number one strategy for improving students' writing.[57]

- *Show students your writing process.* Do plan the piece in advance, for example, by jotting down some notes (I often use a Post-it or two for a short piece, though I may show an outline for a longer piece); but do the actual composing, thinking aloud, and revising-as-you-go on the spot. Students need to see our struggles. Don't worry about getting it "right."
- *Tell the whole story or topic first.* Not only does this help students "see" and understand the complete topic, describing the story or content aloud before you write helps you clarify your thinking and decide what to write. Often information and details emerge in an oral telling that you didn't expect. Also, you may write only a part of the whole oral text—a snippet, moment, paragraph, or chapter—but it will make sense because the students will know where that piece fits into the whole.
- *Time yourself.* Complete the writing in 10 to 20 minutes, on average. You want students to have the time, will, and energy for uninterrupted writing. Going on too long depletes energy for students' own writing. You can always revisit or continue the demonstration writing on subsequent days.
- *Focus on the content first.* Devote total attention to thinking about, drafting, rereading, and revising a coherent text. Doing that well requires full concentration and helps ensure students are initially focused primarily on ideas. (The exception would be kindergarten through early grade 1, where children also require a strong focus on letters, sounds, and basic words.)
- *Just write! Don't teach.* Keep thinking aloud and demonstrating with the goal of writing the best piece possible within the time frame; avoid trying to do too much, which confuses students and slows down the writing.
  - *Do say something like*: "I'm feeling stuck. I'm going to reread this to see what I want to say next" or "I'm not sure about my title. I'm not going to

worry about that right now" or "I want to let the reader know why this really matters to me."

   ○ *Don't say something like*: "I want you to notice that I started a new paragraph here" or "Why do you think I moved these words around?" or "Notice that I'm putting a capital letter here and I'm using commas in a series." Just do it without commenting on it!

- *Avoid distractions and stay in charge.* Remember that in the demonstration phase of the OLM, teachers are in charge of doing the thinking and the writing. Let students know their turn to write will come soon. If students raise their hands or call out a suggestion, say something like "It's my turn to do the writing now. Your turn will come later."

- *Assess what students took away from the demonstration.* Ask students, "What did you see me do?" "What did you notice?" Chart responses and assess if students are ready to write on their own.

- *Save final editing for later.* It doesn't really matter if the editing is excellent if the piece isn't worth reading. Students come to learn that editing really is the easy part once they have meaningful content. Also, writers tend do a better job on editing once the content is set if there's first an interval of even just a couple of hours.

- *Apply the OLM to editing.* With the student's permission, project his writing and show how to go line by line and reread at least several times to carefully check and fix spelling, punctuation, grammar, final word choice, and so on. Then, before having students work exclusively on editing on their own or with a partner, have one or more public, shared editing experiences with students. Once you have established reasonable but high editing expectations through the construction of an editing expectations chart, put the responsibility on students to do almost all the editing work, beginning in grade 2. Editing is about showing respect for the reader, and it's important to model for students how to take that responsibility seriously.[58]

- *Publish regularly.* Publishing writing at least once a month provides the necessary practice students need in revising and editing. Not only that, publishing texts for real readers motivates students to invest their full efforts. In general, go with short pieces, such as book reviews, editorials, poetry, letters, news stories, summaries, or group-written reports in which each group does one portion. Almost everything writers need to do can be taught in short pieces, which do not exhaust either students or teachers. Also, expand communication and publication to a variety of

> ### Quick Win
>
> *Don't allow students to waste time copying a paper* just to make it neater, which indicates that they equate revision with neatness. Revision is for content.

formats that appeal to students' oral and written online reading and writing activities: blogs, photo journals, interactive texts, videos, social media, podcasts, and so on.

• *Let students know you are a reader.* It is true that you can't be a strong writer without being a strong reader. Although we often artificially separate reading from writing, research supports the positive effects of interconnection on students' reading, writing, and comprehension skills.[59] In *On Writing: A Memoir of the Craft,* prolific author Stephen King talks about how being an avid reader all his life has greatly influenced his writing.[60] Walter Dean Myers in *Just Write: Here's How!,* an excellent book to share with middle school and high school students, discusses how the family stories he heard growing up and, especially, his time spent at the public library reading book after book allowed him to leave his limited world of poverty.[61] It was reading books that enabled him to see a way into a promising future as a writer. If you are not a reader, become one! Ask students for recommendations; also, see my reading blog on my website (www.regieroutman.org) for titles and reading habits.

Notice What Authors Do

Noticing and naming what authors do is vital for helping students become highly skillful writers. It's important to read aloud well-crafted fiction and nonfiction texts in multiple genres, and to point out how authors organize their text, engage their readers, choose their language carefully, and use elaboration and detail to expand on a topic. In doing so we let our students know that in the act of reading we not only follow the story and information in the text, we also pay careful attention to the intentional decisions authors make, and we consider trying out some of those same techniques (or words, format, visuals). Imitation is not only a high form of flattery; trying on the style of a writer helps us develop our own voice and style.

Use daily read-alouds, guided reading, shared writing, and other contexts to create continuous opportunities to be explicit about what authors do. Guide students to pay close attention in their own reading to the essential qualities of effective writing that authors apply—accuracy (facts, grammar, mechanics), clarity, relevancy, reasoning, meaningfulness, useful organization, convincing argument supported by evidence and presentation style—and to notice their technique. Point out and teach these qualities so students can understand, practice, and apply them in an integrated manner

Quick Win

Show excellent exemplars of student writing; notice and name what the writer has done. By contrast, spending time trying to publicly make a weak piece of writing stronger can keep students stuck at their current level of development.

to all their writing. Of course, when we are readers and writers ourselves, "insiders" to what authors do, we understand the authentic contexts that have the potential to make our demonstrations and conversations richer and more effective.

What Successful Writers Do

- Write with an awareness of a reader—engaging lead, voice, humor, satisfying closure, legibility, and presentation.
- Keep the writing flowing in an organized and engaging manner—using paragraphs, transitions, structure, order, organizational devices (including table of contents, headings, and glossary).
- Focus on the language of craft—elaboration and detail, lively vocabulary, precise words, figurative language, literary devices.
- Have a rhythm for how words and sentences sound and go together.
- Slow down the writing to create a vivid setting, character, problem, and so on.
- Aptly use and consider multiple reliable sources, resources, and texts.
- Augment the text with visuals, such as illustrations, drawings, photos, charts, cartoons.
- Incorporate technology and digital tools that increase reader engagement and interest.
- Ensure accuracy of content, resources, spelling, conventions, grammar, and other elements.

Even our youngest students can be taught to notice what authors do, to try/apply it together, to name those qualities and actions, and to apply them to their own writing. The key actions listed here lay the foundation upon which students will build as they mature as writers, and demonstrations featuring read-alouds of outstanding literature can showcase the attributes of successful writing.

Embrace Public Writing Conferences

A public writing conference is a one-on-one conference held in full view of the class. It's the most difficult part of teaching writing because it involves being able, on the spot, to give specific and useful feedback that will propel the writer forward. Holding such a conference requires lots of practice. There is no formula and a "cheat sheet" doesn't work. Teachers get

---

Quick Win

Demonstrate read-alouds and encourage students to read aloud (to themselves or a peer) to improve their writing while in process. For example, hearing writing read aloud can help us pay attention to the rhythm, notice when something doesn't sound right, and realize where we might need a better word choice.

Quick Win

Use the words "revision" and "editing" starting in kindergarten so young writers understand the terms, language, and processes. Many intermediate students are unfamiliar with the terms and therefore get confused in the process.

Quick Win

Reward writers who take risks. Let students know that those who try out something that was discussed, celebrated, or taught that day (conversation, foreshadowing, reworking the ending) will be the first to share in a public conference the next day.

Quick Win

Separate content conferences from editing conferences which saves time in the long run. Once students have made revisions and have a well-organized piece, conferences focused solely on editing can go fairly quickly.

Quick Win

Always have the student do the first reading of his or her piece. Doing so honors and celebrates the writer.

Quick Win

Spend time with a small group of students who are not yet ready to write on their own because they are still unclear about the purpose and specifics of what they are to do. Have additional conversations to scaffold and spark their thinking, and perhaps write together before sending them off to write on their own.

distracted by looking at a page of suggestions for feedback language, and they lose sight, literally, of the person in front of them. To become proficient at these conferences in writing and in reading, we need to see and hear exemplary ones, analyze what we've seen and heard, try them out with support, and have a trusted colleague by our side as we are learning. As previously discussed, we also need to be experienced in providing effective feedback. Particularly in writing, giving encouraging and useful feedback can be transformational for a student's progress.[62]

Put the Writer Before the Writing

A colleague observing a public writing conference recently commented, "It's like you and the student are in silhouette and there's no one else there, even though there is a room full of students and observers."[63] *Putting the writer first is the single most important thing I do in the teaching of writing.* When I am working with a student, I am not thinking about getting that student to improve. My thoughts are "What is this writer trying to say?" "What are this writer's strengths to be celebrated?" "What's most important to say, do, and focus on right now to ensure this writer will want to go on writing?" Putting the writer before the writing means taking a stance that honors a student's best attempts and sees the writer first as a valued person, which ensures that we communicate respectfully.

A student who brings us a coherent paper makes it easier to focus on the writer first because we are not distracted by confusing and disorganized work, and this suggests the important role of frontloading. Preparing our students well before we send them off to write on their own is crucial for an effective and efficient writing conference. Sufficient and excellent demonstrating, providing background knowledge including academic vocabulary, scaffolded conversations, small-group work, shared writing—all or some of these are necessary supports before releasing students to write with little assistance. Nothing is as frustrating and time consuming as reading a large number of papers only to discover that the students were not yet ready for the activity and we need to reteach. Not only do we drain our energy and the students', we lose our excitement about the work. With sufficient frontloading, my experience has been that we can expect at least 90 percent of students to succeed reasonably well on their first attempts.

Read for Enjoyment and Understanding

It's up to us as conscientious educators to instill a love of reading in our students and to do whatever it takes to turn them all into readers. By "readers," I mean those of us who read for pleasure, to satisfy our curiosity, to learn more about a chosen subject, or to seek the peacefulness and joy of being lost in the pages of a wonderful book. I do not mean just being able to read words fluently or move through levels. If we do not deliberately promote a joy of reading, our students' progress and engagement will be limited. So much depends on us, what we know and do, how we spend our reading time, the choices we allow students, and the messages we send to students and their families about reading. Without us educators assuming responsibility for ensuring students become joyful and proficient readers, students' potential for becoming lifelong readers remains limited, even if their test scores are satisfactory.

In far too many classrooms, reading is still drudgery for many students.[64] It's difficult to develop a love or passion for an activity if there is little choice involved and time and emphasis are devoted mainly to exercises and assignments. As previously noted, in most reading blocks in today's schools, scant time—less than 20 percent—is actually spent in continuous reading of text.

All my reading is for pleasure and information, and mostly these two are intertwined. I read the daily *New York Times*, professional journals, current and classic fiction, outstanding nonfiction, recipe books, magazines, blogs, and much more. So far, most of my reading continues to be texts I hold in my hands, but I am doing more online reading, especially to find answers to research questions and for some social media interactions. At the same time, I consciously try to monitor my screen time so it does not take precedence over face-to-face interactions with family and friends or severely limit precious time for reading.

Focus on Reading Joy as Well as Reading Progress

My first goal and most important learning target in any residency is to bring the joy back into reading and writing. If the joy is there, we can teach just about anything to our students. There is little joy without success, engagement, choice, and self-regulation.

In some of my reading residencies, I have been struck by a general lack of enthusiasm for reading on the part of students and teachers. Sufficient

---

Quick Win

Take five minutes at the beginning of a PD meeting to read aloud a great picture book, part of a nonfiction book, or a section from a professional book or article. This activity not only acknowledges for the school that reading is important, but also introduces and builds interest for texts that teachers may not know.

time is set aside for teaching reading every day, but there isn't much pleasure in any of it or much engagement in spite of the fact that students are on task. As well, teachers are often expected to follow a district curriculum or core program with fidelity even though such programs do an inadequate job teaching reading.[65] Often the reading work includes whole-class novels or texts, with every student reading the same page regardless of whether the text is at a reading level all students can read. Also, rarely are students provided that all-important time and choice for accessing appealing texts they want to read and can read. Teaching self-monitoring is not part of most reading instruction, and one-on-one reading conferences—a necessity for checking all aspects of reading, such as fluency, vocabulary, and comprehension—are not commonplace, although they should be.

It's not difficult to bring back or introduce the joy of reading. Simply put, it requires each of us to do the following:

- Be a reading role model who ensures access and choice to interesting books and other texts.
- Ensure support and guidance for everyone's success as an engaged, comprehending reader.
- Provide ample time for students to read books and other texts in multiple genres and forms.
- Value time for book talk, including discussion of significant questions the text and readers raise.

Without our own experience of "being lost in a book," we will remain limited in communicating the joy of reading. Thankfully, it's never too late to become a joyful reader!

Promote book talk

A key to optimal reading comprehension is that students need and benefit from opportunities to talk and interact with each other as well as the teacher.[66] Time and opportunities to talk about books are crucial for increasing reading progress, motivation to read, and reading enjoyment. The social interactions among peers that book clubs and literature conversations promote lead to increased learning, risk taking, collaboration, and openness to other points of view. In fact, literate and meaningful conversations with others are one of the most important skills we can help develop in our students.[67] I use my own experiences as a longtime member of a

Quick Win

Consider implementing weekly oral book reviews, by students, of favorite titles after demonstrating and establishing expectations. This activity gives readers ideas about what to read next, as well as practice in public speaking and summarizing important book elements.

book club (as described in Authentic Book Discussion) to guide book talk in the classroom so that it is an authentic, joyful experience.

Authentic Book Discussion

- Books are carefully selected for their high-quality writing, relevance to our lives and interests, ability to expand our ideas and knowledge, potential to explore big questions, opportunity to spur rich discussion, and potential to challenge our thinking. (Books that we can easily interpret on our own and that don't generate multiple viewpoints are generally not included.)
- Book club members have choice in what they read and discuss; that is, members agree on which books will be read. Often someone who has already read the book or a terrific review of it will do a brief book talk on why the book should be chosen.
- Substantial questions are raised and addressed.
- Facilitator ensures a rich discussion by including background information about the author and reviews of the book from text and web-based sources, and by encouraging each member to participate.
- Members come prepared to discuss the book; close reading of text is expected (this may involve rereading, note taking, selecting key pages for referral, or oral reading of a significant passage), along with opinions and ideas that are supported with evidence from the text and personal experiences.
- Following the book club discussion, an oral or written evaluation is conducted, which may include suggestions for discussing future books.[68]

Maximize engagement

Citing a study by Geoff Kaufman and Lisa Libby, researcher Peter Johnston notes, "When people are fully engaged in a book, they lose their sense of self and take up residence in the characters."[69] That sense of engagement, being "lost in a book," requires sustained time for reading personally relevant books. I recently experienced that feeling when I reread a favorite classic, *Jane Eyre* by Charlotte Bronte. For uninterrupted hours on a weekend, I was transported into another era and into Jane Eyre's life and mind. Mentally and emotionally, time fell away; I happily existed in an altered state. Literature can do that to us, but we have to provide the time that makes deep engagement possible.

It's not just that engagement increases enjoyment; full engagement in any area accelerates progress because the learner fervently seeks to understand and in so doing applies strategic moves and thinks more deeply. This is as true for us as for our students. Here are some ways to increase engagement (in reading, writing, content areas, professional development) and to establish a reading culture:

- Create a "need to know."
- Establish an environment of rich resources with easy access.
- Provide sufficient time and choice.
- Do less but do it in more depth.
- Pause often for "turn-and-talk."
- Promote more small-group work.
- Make thoughtful conversations central to the work.
- Honor all voices.
- Celebrate successes and sincere attempts.

Quick Win

Do small-group work, which allows for maximum interaction and hearing all voices. Apply the OLM to teach groups how to self-evaluate their work and process.

Raise thoughtful questions

Intimately connected to meaningful book talk and student engagement is what we and our students choose to talk about. When discussing literature or any text, the quality of the questions we raise and teach students to raise is crucial for driving students back to the text to think more deeply. Formulating worthwhile questions is a skill that can be taught, and it is a game-changer for raising the quality of talk and for student ownership and enjoyment of the learning process in all subject areas. "The expert in any setting is not just the one who possesses more knowledge—the one capable of giving answers—but also the one who knows *what to ask*."[70] Asking better questions, as is discussed throughout this text, influences every aspect of literacy, learning, and leadership.

For example, applying the Optimal Learning Model (as described in Chapter 2), we can teach students the difference between closed and open questions. Literal-level questions are "closed" questions; they shut down the conversation because once the right answer is given, there's no more to say. Literary-level questions are "open" questions; they expand the conversation because they invite multiple responses. As long as responders can back up their statements with evidence from the text or their life experiences, the response can be considered valid.

Literal or closed questions often begin with *who, where,* and *what,* as in "Where does the story take place?" or "What happened after _____?" Literary or open questions often begin with *why, what do you think, how, discuss, describe,* and they prompt the reader to examine the text more carefully and to consider other points of view. Two examples of literary questions are "Why is the civil rights movement important to the lives of people today?" and "Describe what you learned about [a specific topic, historical period, character]." Researchers have found that when students can answer and respond to higher-level questions, literal-level understanding is assumed. For example, if a student can discuss why a character's actions caused certain behaviors (cause and effect), the student more than likely knows the events that have occurred, where the character lives, and who his friends are.

When students are first learning how to conduct their own book talks or literature conversations and to raise their own questions, a more structured format is needed. Teaching students to respond to one or two thoughtful questions the text raises helps focus their rereading of that text, preparatory note taking, and follow-up discussion. Once students are experienced with asking more significant questions—in literature conversations and in the content areas—we move to a more natural format in which students informally jot down notes related to questions and important insights that arise as they are reading, much as we might do as adult readers preparing for a book club or investigating a topic of inquiry.[71]

Thoughtful questions challenge students' intellect and lead to more active thinking and dialogue. For asking questions related to inquiry and reading informational texts, noted scholars and educators Dorsey Hammond and Denise Nessel recommend prereading and post-reading questions. To increase engagement, interest, and learning before students do informational reading, they suggest asking questions like the following:

• What do we already know about ___ ?
• Why do you think ____?
• What else do we know?
• How is that important?
• What do we want to find out and learn?

To encourage and guide a lively and instructive discussion following the reading, use literary-level questions like the ones on the next page.

- Which of our questions did we answer?
- What questions have we not answered?
- What are some new questions we now have?
- What else did we learn that we didn't talk about or question about?
- What was the most interesting thing we learned?
- What was the most important thing we learned?
- What do we know now that we didn't know before?[72]

Be a Reading Role Model

I always introduce myself to students by enthusiastically sharing favorite books and stories. The stories we tell, read, and write, and the books we share hook our students and leave them wanting more. I include family stories, personal stories, classroom stories, and wonderful fiction and informational books by notable authors—including student authors. Stories make visible the human condition and connect us with one another. Stories are a way into writing and reading.

For all students to find that way in and become engaged readers, we need to be able to demonstrate our own genuine enthusiasm and processes as well as the habits of discerning readers. Perhaps most important, we need to make our thinking and comprehension processes transparent. For that, it's crucial that we who teach reading are also readers. That is, we read across various genres, texts, and formats including multimedia, and we make visible what, why, and how we read. Students benefit when they see how we select texts to read, hear us read fluently, observe us struggle to figure out words and meanings, hear us reread and slow down for clarification, and listen as we think out loud and grapple with challenging concepts.

Demonstrate close reading

Close reading or reading closely (also called "analytic reading") is not just one of the CCSS standards; it has always been a necessary literacy skill for full understanding of genre and analysis of a fiction or informational text, especially one that is difficult or complex. However, for the most part, we haven't asked students to do close reading, largely because many of us haven't been taught how to do so ourselves, that is, how to be metacognitive—thinking about our thinking. Close reading is also a necessity in the content areas, not just for reading informational texts but for effectively writing about what we learn.[73]

Quick Win

Gather as a group of adults to choose an article for close reading. What is the role of interest, engagement, background knowledge, subject matter, genre and form, complexity of the text, bias? What are our reading insights? What strategies and actions do we employ to understand the text? What does this mean for our instruction? Try this activity in a PLC and discuss the instructional insights.

We educators need to model that process as well as how and when to apply it before we can expect students to be proficient. Close reading involves but is not limited to the following:

- Deciding when close reading is necessary, for example, knowing what parts of an article warrant careful reading.
- Knowing when we need to seek more background information to make the text comprehensible.
- Slowing down our reading to pay attention to and understand the writer's intentions and decisions.[74]
- Finding evidence from a text to back up inferences, interpretations, and opinions, and to answer probing questions.
- Questioning and interpreting the text as we read.
- Monitoring our comprehension as we go along.
- Recording of salient points and our thinking through note taking, underlining, highlighting, and so on.
- Rereading to clear up confusion and to seek deeper meaning, as well as to gain fuller appreciation of the text and the author's craft.

Award-winning fiction writer Marilynne Robinson says:

> I tend to think of the reading of any book as preparation for the next reading of it. There are always intervening books or facts or realizations that put a book in another light and make it different and richer the second or the third time.[75]

Value your own reading habits and processes

For the past several years, I have been blogging on "What I'm Reading," which includes my favorite texts over a six-month period, plus commentary about my reading habits with related recommendations for classroom application. (See Blogs at www.regieroutman.org for current and archived books read and reading habits.) I write about my favorite books and why and how they have influenced me. I also blog about keeping a reading log, choosing books to read, rereading, belonging to a book club, and much more. I use my own thoughts, behaviors, actions, strategies, and habits as a reader to guide my instruction and to keep me focused on what's most important.

As with writing, I do not start with a core program or the latest standards (although I keep the anchor CCSS reading standards in mind). To get

---

Quick Win

Read aloud a short selection of text as you display it for all to see. Explain aloud how you think when you do a close reading. Afterward, carefully choose an intact and meaningful excerpt, from a paragraph to a few pages, and give students a copy of it that they can write on (highlight, underline, make notes) to "try out" their own close readings.

The Elliott Bay Book Co., Seattle, Wa., displays staff-written book recommendations.

to know students as readers and to decide how to teach and guide them, I begin with my own reading habits and questions I pose to myself and rephrase them to apply to students. My thinking and questions are along these lines.

- What are students' strengths, interests, backgrounds?
- What authors and series do they like and know?
- What authors, books, and genres can I introduce them to?
- What can I do to make reading joyful and successful for them?
- How can I build their competence, confidence, engagement, and stamina?
- How can I ensure they become self-determining, comprehending readers?

Also, as a reading role model, I let students know that I browse bookstores, peruse book reviews, and search websites, as well as depend on recommendations from librarians, friends, and colleagues to keep me updated on books I might want to read. Bookstore displays and recommendations are always inspiring, and you might consider having students create similar displays for the classroom or hallways (see photos above and on p. 125).

 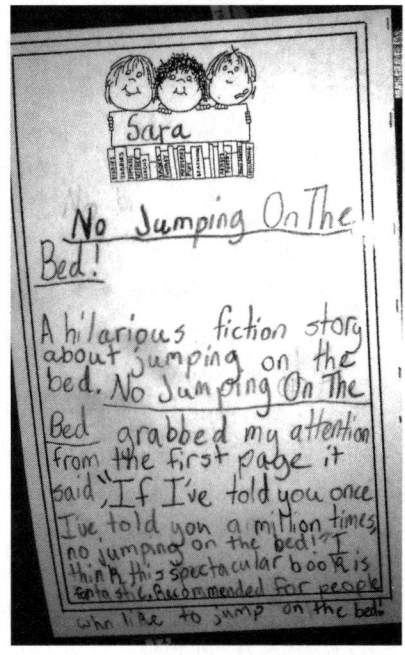

Joyce Hyland's 4th graders use the book store's model to recommend books to other students. Notice the book recommendation for a younger reader. The display is in the school's front hallway.

Read aloud to students

Make reading aloud of excellent texts the cornerstone of the day both in and out of the classroom. Don't leave it out! Reading aloud increases motivation to read, deepens our knowledge, settles our nerves, and expands our horizons. Read aloud first thing in the morning, before or after lunch, and at the end of the day. These read-aloud times need not be long. Consider also beginning professional development meetings by reading aloud—a portion from a professional article, a new children's book, a student's writing.

So much of what we choose to read aloud with expression and enthusiasm can transfer to our students' reading lives. We are not just modeling the actions, fluency, and thinking of proficient readers; we are also modeling the joy of reading and the intellectual and imaginative journey that reading can provide. Students may be inspired to pick up the read-aloud book and other books by that author. They may choose to reread the section we just read. For some students, it is our reading aloud that helps them become avid readers. Reading aloud is an entry into books, texts, genres that our students—and teachers, too—might not find on their own. For students

Quick Win

Have all students present in the classroom during read-alouds. You never know what language, vocabulary, and ideas students will pick up or what connections they will make.

who dislike reading and who struggle as readers, reading aloud can be the catalyst that propels them into reading—even at the high school level.[76] Reading aloud a carefully chosen book that matches the curriculum focus and children's interests and culture is almost always the way I get interesting conversations going with students and teachers in a residency. It's a great way to quickly capture hearts and minds and to bond with a new group.

At workshops and institutes, I have often read aloud a stunning quote or short section from a current issue of *Educational Leadership* or *Phi Delta Kappan*, a newspaper article, or a professional book I am reading. Then I offer the book or journal or newspaper to anyone who would like to borrow it overnight. Someone always does and faithfully returns it to me the next day, often with a comment such as "I'm going to buy this book" or "I'm going to subscribe to this journal now." It's the same for our students. We can arouse their interest in a book or topic by reading aloud a portion and then making the book available as a choice for students to read. With outstanding, high-interest, and high-quality books, I recommend having three to five copies available for small-group reading and discussion.

Not to be minimized, we need to strongly encourage parents and mentor them, when necessary, to read aloud to their children and to talk with them about books. Worldwide, the evidence suggests that parents who read aloud to their young children raised children who are better readers and thinkers.[77]

Rely on Relevant Research

If we are to be excellent teachers of reading, we must know what particular reading research to adopt and what research to ignore. This is a daunting but critical task. So many new resources and programs come into our schools and classrooms with a label that says "evidence-based research" or, more recently, "Common Core aligned." Sometimes these claims come from research or alignment done by the company producing the materials, thereby making the claims questionable. Because so much time, money, professional development, and required commitment accompany these programs, we must as responsible educators ask key questions before purchase, and we must advocate for excellent, reliable, and valid resources. If our efforts fall short, then we must ensure we do everything possible to implement the new resource with fidelity to the student, not fidelity to the program.

> **Quick Win**
>
> *Don't neglect picture books for older readers*—both fiction and nonfiction. The length, concepts, vocabulary, visuals, and text are ideal for engaging readers.

Beware of blindly accepting "research-based," "evidence-based," or "research-validated" material as reliable research. Insist on examining the research being cited and to ask and demand answers to key questions before your school or district commits to a particular program.

In particular, for all research, pay attention to whether or not the evidence is compelling and undeniable. "In order to be considered truly 'scientific,' the evidence from a study must be so convincing that someone with an open mind would be persuaded to reconsider his views."[78] If we are highly knowledgeable and well grounded in our beliefs and practices, we will always be making some adjustments and improvements to our instruction, but we will not overreact and rush headlong into adopting the newest program or latest fad without question. We will apply credible research, our experiences, and common sense to our teaching and advocate with our colleagues for sane and worthy practices and resources.

The inadequate reading-comprehension instruction provided in core reading programs, which the great majority of teachers in the United States rely on, underscores how critical it is that we take responsibility for teaching reading comprehension and knowing how to teach it well. There is no one best program; the highly effective teacher trumps any program or resource every time. At best, a core program is a helpful resource for providing content, methods, and a useful framework, but we have to know how to effectively use and modify any resource so it enhances our instruction without controlling it.[79]

Key Research Questions to Ask
Before Committing to a Program

- Is the research current and relevant to our students, our core beliefs, and our instructional practices?
- Are the researchers themselves objective and credible, and do they broadly represent the available evidence?
- Is the evidence compelling?

Source: From *Reading Essentials* (pp. 195–198), by Regie Routman, 2003, Portsmouth, NH: Heinemann. Copyright 2003 by Regie Routman. Adapted by permission.

A comprehensive review of every lesson in five major core reading programs revealed that the programs recommend too many skills and strategies, provide inadequate teacher modeling of thinking processes, include scant time to practice what is being taught, and offer insufficient comprehension instruction.[80] Very significant, the core reading programs ignore or give little attention to applying the wide research on the benefits of the gradual-release-of-responsibility model.[81] That omission is particularly worrisome for our second language learners and struggling learners who need much more support than what these core programs offer. Additionally, a study of six core reading programs found that "students needed to spend only 15 minutes per day reading. That leaves 75 minutes of every 90-minute reading period for students to engage in something else. Most often, this other activity is skill lessons or workbook page completion."[82] In addition, some schools still rely too much on computerized reading programs whose benefits do not hold up to scrutiny.[83]

Emphasize Comprehension

We need to teach two things at the same time: reading to learn and learning to read. Students must know right from the start that we are always reading text for meaning and understanding. In fact, we can confuse students and stunt their progress when we teach reading by focusing on nonsense words, sounds in isolation, and "sight words" that are disconnected from meaningful texts. A caution: Current early-grade programs for reading texts are designed so students "can learn word identification rather than learning word identification so they can read texts."[84] It becomes our job as knowledgeable educators to keep the focus on comprehension.

A successful reading comprehension program that promotes high achievement includes these research-based elements:

- Large amounts of time for actual reading of continuous, meaningful texts
- Explicit, teacher-directed instruction on all aspects of reading
- Opportunities for students to respond to and talk with their peers, as well as the teacher, about texts
- Ongoing monitoring of reading comprehension through formative assessments
- Time spent in small-group reading
- Time spent in independent reading

- On-the-spot coaching of phonics in the context of reading as well as systematic phonics instruction
- Higher-level questions, which cause students to think deeply and reenter the text
- Effective communication with parents[85]

To independent reading, I would emphasize self-selection of interesting texts. Self-selection makes it more likely that students will choose to read and become engaged readers, essential factors that are needed for the massive amount of reading that students require to gain fluency, vocabulary, new concepts, and self-monitoring skills—all of which enable students to become self-teaching and self-directed learners.

To time spent in small-group reading, I would add two things: that time be geared to "coaching" students so they are better able to read with understanding when they are on their own; and that the small groups be flexible, not fixed—that is, they are convened based on students' actual needs and interests.

Of course, we need to demonstrate all the skills, strategies, and habits we expect students to be able to do, and to apply the OLM so they receive enough support to use those strategies. For example, in both informational texts and fiction, we need to show students how to figure out words and concepts, reread for clarity, consider multiple meanings, approach new information, synthesize information, and raise important questions—to name just a few essential thinking actions of thriving readers. However, it is crucial to recognize that "strategies—absent some level of knowledge, a purpose for engaging in the literate practice, and identification with the domain or the purpose for reading—will not take readers or writers very far."[86]

Also, keep in mind that there is no one best, research-based way to teach reading comprehension.

> [W]e do not possess the research base to establish unassailable a priori learning progressions for reading comprehension; neither cognitive benchmarks nor curricular topics nor text factors can be used alone to determine a sound learning progression for reading comprehension that will lead to college and career success.[87]

Finally, it's also our job as responsible educators to be able to assess just about everything we are asking students to spend time on and that what students spend time on is worthwhile. For example, lots of "management activities" that we assign students may keep them busy and quiet as we meet with a small group, but being on-task is insufficient. We must assess if and what students are learning and if that learning is contributing to their literacy progress. In particular, as teachers, coaches, and leaders, we must be able to answer the question "How do we know *all* our students understand what they read?" The chart below displays some proven ways to check for understanding before, during, and after reading.

How Do We Know Students Understand What They Read?

Some Ways to Check for Understanding

Students can do the following:

- Demonstrate understanding in an informal reading conference.
- Read silently in a guided reading group and write a brief response to a question (allowing us to reteach, as needed).
- Read on independently in a text and respond in writing or orally (which the teacher verifies or checks before having students complete the whole text).
- Cite evidence from text orally or in writing.
- Figure out academic and other vocabulary from surrounding text or other resources.
- Use text evidence to analyze, form conclusions, and defend claims.
- Draw "mind maps" (could be illustrations and graphics) as the teacher reads aloud (the teacher walks around and checks maps; students share with each other).
- Talk with a partner or small group about what they've read; the teacher checks listening and understanding ("Tell me what your partner said." "What did you discuss in your group?" "What did you learn?").
- Put cut-up sentence(s) back in right order (for younger readers).
- Create high-level questions that demonstrate deep understanding of a topic, theme, and content.
- Give an accurate summary to someone who has not read the text.

Provide Adequate Reading Supports

As teachers and leaders, we must advocate for and provide the full support that readers need. Some of the means to do so include push-in models, one-on-one tutoring, small-group reading, buddy reading (older student with younger one), partner reading (in same grade level), and Reading

Recovery (note that Reading Recovery is the only cited program that the What Works Clearinghouse considers a highly effective tutoring intervention). If we teach well—including applying the OLM to ensure sufficient frontloading—only a small proportion of students should need additional support. At least 80 percent of our students should be able to get the full support they need through instruction in the classroom, the universal teaching that is Tier 1 in Response to Intervention.

Do more shared reading

Shared reading, in which students follow along as an expert—usually the teacher—reads the text, is an enjoyable, nonthreatening way to increase reading abilities across the curriculum for younger and older students. Students need to clearly see the text projected in some way or have individual copies of the text in hand. Shared reading works well with the following:

• Class- or student-authored texts
• Required texts in which some passages may be too difficult for students
• Content-area texts
• News reports
• Favorite books, including picture books
• Poetry
• Web-based texts

Shared read-aloud, which combines three elements—reading and thinking aloud, shared reading, and guided reading—all in one lesson, works exceptionally well for students of every age, for teaching all aspects of reading, and for holding students accountable for their thinking. Some high-level strategies that can be effectively and efficiently taught in this context—and in all content areas—include summarizing, rereading a complex passage for specific information, inferring, finding and citing evidence from the text to back up thinking, and figuring out vocabulary.[88]

Shared read-aloud is also highly effective for middle school and high school students, not just in language arts but also in physics, history, and other content-area classes. Using texts in their discipline, content teachers model reading like, for example, a scientist, a historian, or a mathematician. The teacher reads and thinks aloud part of the text; projects a part she wants students to read, reread, or think through together with a partner or small group; checks for understanding; has students revisit the projected

Quick Win

Keep a supply of short informational pieces to give students more access and practice with informational texts. For example, newspaper and magazine articles and well-written blogs are ideal for close reading and discussion.

text to confirm or disconfirm their response; and adjusts instruction as needed. If we expect students to write and be able to cite textual evidence, synthesize information, and interpret meaning, we first need to instruct them about how to do so as readers.

See guided reading as a means to an end

Guided reading—in which the teacher guides one or more students through some aspect of the reading process, building on student strengths and providing support as necessary—can be a highly effective means for supporting students to become proficient so that when they read silently and independently (which is the bulk of all reading in almost every grade and subject area), we and they know they are comprehending. That is, in guided reading, we are consciously working to ensure students can apply what they have learned to reading and problem solving on their own. Guided reading done well—through whole-group instruction, small differentiated groups, and one-on-one—helps students cement a repertoire of strategies, habits, and behaviors that promote self-monitoring and independence as readers. Remember that in guided reading, the student is in charge; the handover of responsibility from teacher to student has occurred. Refer to the OLM chart on page 58 to see where guided reading fits in the learning model.

Guided reading has become *mis*guided and stifling in many settings. As discussed earlier, we need to be cautious about providing too much support, such as spending too much time on prereading activities or giving students all the "answers" so that we wind up doing most of the reading work. As another example of guided reading gone awry, in some middle schools where teachers are not knowledgeable about teaching reading, they rely on leveled readers and direct instruction to the detriment of a majority of the students.[89] There has often been too little thought and practice given to guided reading as a stepping-stone for students becoming independent. Until teachers become expert in teaching reading, guided reading can actually be a waste of students' time.

Part of that reading expertise includes being able to ask ourselves questions that are relevant to the goal of students becoming engaged, self-directed readers. For example, if our main questions are focused on "fitting in all the groups" or "what the rest of the class is doing" or "teaching isolated skills," guided reading will not take students very far. Robin Woods, a highly experienced, excellent 2nd grade teacher, speaks about the gradual shift she made:

Quick Win

Do away with most oral reading in guided-reading groups—it's mostly a waste of time beyond grade 2 except when we need to check for fluency.

I used to spend most of my time preparing materials that I would then need to collect and grade to decide if a child was making progress as a reader. Now I answer the question for myself every day "What is the one thing that this child or group needs to hear from me today that will help carry them forward as readers?"[90]

Following guided reading, more reading is the preferred activity for ensuring that students progress as readers, but the caveat is that students and we must know they are capable of self-monitoring and comprehending as they read. Here the classroom library is crucial. Our end goal is self-determining students who can read, who want to read, and who thrive as competent readers and thinkers. Again, to achieve that goal, our students need daily, sustained time to read while we closely monitor to ensure that they can actually read the words with 95 percent accuracy and can understand the texts that they are choosing and that we are providing with at least 90 percent understanding. Finally, we want students' school reading experiences to extend to meaningful lives fully realized outside of school; that is, being a reader leads students to see possibilities for and beyond themselves, whether it be a job, a hobby, a personal endeavor, or a pathway to college or a chosen career.

Ensure Sustained Time for Independent Reading

Make sustained time for reading, mostly books and other texts that students choose, *the* reading priority, and work backward from there. That is, let other things go, but maintain uninterrupted time to read. The volume of reading students do on their own is significantly related to gains in reading achievement.[91] A serious concern is that in far too many classrooms most of the reading time is devoted to tasks and activities *about* reading and not on the main event—reading continuous, meaningful texts. That unhealthy trend is likely to continue with the call for more complex texts in the latest standards.

We need to be clear in how we define independent reading. In *Reading Essentials*, I differentiated between sustained silent reading and a carefully monitored, independent reading program.[92] The key difference is that with independent reading, as I view it, the teacher is involved in some monitoring of comprehension to ensure students can read and understand the self-selected texts and that includes checking that students are choosing "just right" books. Seek to have multiple daily times for independent reading. Here are some options:

- Daily, whole-class time (20–40 minutes)
- Assigned "reading on" after guided reading (might include partner reading)
- Free-choice reading as main before-school activity; includes rereading of shared reading texts (from shared writing)
- Voluntary reading as main activity when done with required work
- Time at beginning of content-area class for reading texts related to content study

The importance of wide reading for increasing comprehension and enjoyment cannot be overstated. While we want all students to be "college and career ready" and to navigate and understand complex texts with increasing proficiency, my four decades of teaching reading confirm that the best preparation is wide reading of informational books and literary genres at a level where students can read at least 95 percent of the words and understand more than 90 percent of the text. The end goal in reading is always comprehension, and as a field "we cannot convincingly identify learning progressions that reflect the complex nature of higher levels of comprehension needed for college and career success.[93]

Reading scores on NAEP have remained mostly flat for decades. A major factor in lackluster progress is that students don't get to read very much. As previously noted, an analysis of the major core reading programs indicates that students spend on average only 15 minutes a day reading in a typical 90-minute block.[94] According to a wide body of research, large amounts of independent reading lead to more engaged reading and higher levels of reading comprehension and achievement for students of all ages.[95] There is also "a strong rationale for revisiting the role of extended, intensive reading in English language arts classrooms."[96]

Without the practice phase of actually reading coherent, interesting texts, students will not become proficient readers or readers with rich vocabularies. Results from NAEP for grades 4, 8, and 12 indicate that students who score highest in reading proficiency also score highest on the vocabulary component.[97] Therefore, we cannot rely too much on explicit vocabulary teaching. Second language learners and learners who struggle need to undertake massive amounts of reading—of books and other materials they are capable of reading, of course—in order to learn and understand new vocabulary words and concepts.

Finally, as already noted but important enough to restate, we need not rely on levels once students have been taught, guided, and assessed through the process of selecting a text they can read. In fact, we do students a disservice by relegating them to specific levels and limiting their choices.

Instill Daily Reading Conferences

Conducting daily conferences with students on self-selected texts for instruction and assessment—which begins with celebration of what the student is doing well—is crucial for learning and knowing strengths and needs and where more instruction is needed. Research supports the notion that interacting with students around text is especially important for readers who struggle.[98] My own experience is that one-on-one reading conferences are a vital monitoring system for supporting and promoting students' understanding, close reading, and quantity of reading. That in-depth observation with each student allows us to carefully check appropriate text choice, engagement with the text, reading habits, "fix-up" strategies, vocabulary meanings, and so on. Sitting and conversing side by side with a student pays big dividends, not the least of which is ensuring that the student can read and deeply comprehend his or her chosen texts.

I fervently believe that if such conferences were an integral part of our daily reading instruction, far fewer students would need intervention. Too many of our reluctant readers waste precious time by pretending to read or staring at print they don't understand. Through in-depth conferences we ensure that students are actually reading and learning more and are becoming more proficient and self-regulating as readers. We assess how they are doing, teach what's necessary, and set goals for and with the reader. We are also building close and trusting relationships with students who value and look forward to this special time with their teachers.[99]

Written responses to reading are excellent checks for understanding. In *Reading Essentials,* I elaborate on how to employ small notebooks in guided reading, even for our youngest readers.[100] Having them write brief responses to important questions helps us to be certain that we are checking understanding for all students, not just the first one to give a "correct" oral response. As long as it's not overdone—by being too time-consuming or by deterring students' desire to read—having students write their reactions, predictions, and connections is also effective for knowing how and what students are taking away from a text. As well, many students enjoy having their reading reflections as a record of their thinking.

Aim for Self-Determining Readers

A strong marker of a literate person is breadth of reading across disciplines. Wide reading leads to greater knowledge and curiosity of the world, expanded vocabulary, and increased understanding of humanity, concepts, and content in many areas. The Common Core State Standards have it right in wanting struggling readers—as well as those who are more accomplished—to read complex texts, but preparation to do so successfully depends on prior reading and understanding of a large number of substantive texts. That understanding is largely dependent on readers being able to self-monitor and self-regulate their reading behaviors on a wide array of texts in various genres and across disciplines. All of that begins with connecting students with texts they can and want to read and having them do a massive amount of reading for pleasure, information, and discovery.

4

Reducing the Need
for Intervention

The focus in this chapter is on how we can prevent the need for intervention through effective teaching rather than maintaining the current educational climate, which often creates the need for intervention. The number of students who are being referred and identified for special education and support services continues to be staggering and costly both financially and emotionally. The actual numbers of students in our schools who are being identified as needing intervention is close to 20 percent, far higher than it needs to be. We are not talking here about the 1 to 3 percent of the population for whom learning to read is exceptionally challenging. Even for those students, some of whom may be labeled as dyslexic or reading disabled, almost all can successfully learn to read if they receive excellent, intensive instruction.[1]

Kathy is a prime example of a student who illustrates both the perils of intervention gone awry and the promise of eventual success through unwavering advocacy, explicit teaching, sheer grit, and hard work.[2] I first met Kathy when she was a 5th grader in a reading residency at a school where the majority of the population came from low-income households. Unknown to me at the time, Kathy was separated from her classmates daily for literacy instruction because of her special education label. That misidentification in 2nd grade came about because of the school's failure to teach Kathy to read. Her special education status caused her to miss the rich language and learning experiences in her own classroom and negatively affected her behavior and self-esteem. As a result of her inclusion in the residency work, she participated in shared reading and a one-on-one reading conference that revealed strong comprehension but poor decoding skills. Intensive tutoring in the latter for just several months, along with an enormous amount of daily in-school and at-home reading of self-selected books at her "just-right" level, moved her to grade level by the end of the school year. Through her own herculean efforts she was also able to exit special education when she was a high school freshman. As of this writing, she is a full-time college junior with plans to go on to law school to help other students realize their dreams.

Kathy's story is a cautionary tale as she is Hispanic, a second-language learner, and once qualified for free and reduced lunch. A disproportionate number of our students who "need" intervention come from low-income, minority, and immigrant cultures. The sobering fact is that once a language-minority child is referred for testing, that same child is placed in special education about 85 percent of the time. And "once a child is placed in special education, despite a mistaken assessment, it takes them an average of six years to get out."[3] Additionally, special education and Title I programs rarely help struggling readers make sufficient gains so they "catch up" to their higher-achieving peers.[4] A critical point here is that Kathy, rather than becoming a drain on society's resources, is already making a significant contribution. As a high school student, she volunteered in a local public school, tutoring students like herself who had fallen behind and were afraid to speak up in class. Her chosen career path as a lawyer will influence many who have also encountered unequal and inadequate educational opportunities.

I have long been puzzled and disheartened as to why society at large fails to grasp that if we educate all students well, everyone benefits. *It is in our collective self-interest to ensure that every child becomes literate.* Kathy's life was drastically changed by one in-depth reading conference that captured her strengths, pinpointed her needs, and led to short-term, intensive tutoring. Instead of becoming a dropout, pregnant, or a drug user—all of which she confirmed would have been real possibilities and would have cost society untold thousands of dollars—she is on a path to a career that will contribute not only to improving her own life but many others as well. We need to keep in mind that preventing even one high school dropout provides society a net benefit of more than $200,000, according to some estimates.[5] Tragically and foolishly, we still spend more money incarcerating people—and these are mostly people of poverty and color—in large part because we have failed to educate them as literate citizens who can envision and realize a productive future for themselves.

Focus Teaching at the Universal Level

One of the most underreported yet most significant outcomes of excellent first instruction accompanied by raised expectations for *all* students is the fewer numbers of students who need intervention. With excellent first instruction to all, or what is called universal teaching, general education, or sometimes UDL (Universal Design for Learning), all students receive the same challenging concepts, and instruction is differentiated and targeted to ensure all receive and understand the high-level content. Not only is information presented through multiple approaches intended to accommodate and engage all students, but students are encouraged to demonstrate their understanding in various ways to show what they have learned. Effective first teaching at the universal level is a democratic right for all students and is a foundational belief of the Common Core State Standards. The standards emphasize that all students deserve and must have the opportunity to receive the same high-quality instruction before other interventions are considered. Unfortunately, all too often students are referred for extra support before we have done everything possible to provide effective first teaching; the end result is a vast number of students receiving special support services.

A story illustrates this latter point. In a recent teaching residency in a high-needs school, the number of interventionists in the school stunned me. It was typical to have two to four "educational assistants" in a classroom, each assigned to a different student for a whole host of reasons, most of them related to the student's designated label. I'll never forget the conversation I had with the principal in a planning call before the residency. She spent a lot of time preparing me for the "behavior issues of many of our children." As I always do, I requested not to know who those children were and to insist that they all be present. And, as usual, by the end of the week, an observer could not pick out the labeled children. Because of engagement in meaningful work, teaching with a sense of agency and urgency, focusing on students' strengths, being flexible in planning and teaching, and providing students many opportunities for talk and interaction, every child experienced success. The assistant superintendent of schools, who was observing on the last day of the residency, told me he was unaware that this classroom had a number of students who were receiving intervention services.

Increase Teacher Effectiveness

Many research studies conclusively show that teacher effectiveness is the most critical factor for improving student achievement, but questions arise over the most productive ways to improve teacher quality. My lifetime of teaching in diverse schools has taught me that to improve and sustain teacher effectiveness, long-term professional development that is school-based, of the highest quality, and focused around literacy is a necessity. Throughout this book we hear the voices of teachers, coaches, and leaders who have dramatically increased their effectiveness, and in every case it has been excellent, ongoing, intentional professional learning that has been the catalyst for becoming more thoughtful, skillful, and successful. By "successful," I mean that student engagement, learning, and achievement are greatly enhanced and improved—all as a result of higher teacher effectiveness, which is often coupled with strong leadership at the school.

Successful teaching at the universal level—and all excellent teaching—is tied to indispensable qualities and actions, and chief among them are the following:

• A high expectations mindset for all learners
• Ongoing professional learning that leads to teacher expertise and increased student learning
• Deep knowledge of literacy, curriculum, instruction, and assessment
• Excellent management techniques—pacing, urgency, relevant instruction and assignments, grouping, student self-management
• Strong leadership that empowers teachers and learners
• Knowledge of all students' strengths, needs, interests, and cultures, and using those to differentiate instruction and accelerate learning
• Daily formative assessment to improve teaching and learning, including giving useful feedback

Possessing a seamless combination of these essential factors and appropriately putting them into daily instructional and assessment practices requires years of thoughtful preparation, coaching, and practice. For our most vulnerable learners, who typically receive our least qualified teachers, these qualities are even more vital.

Apply the Common Core Standards Wisely

The good news about the Common Core standards is that they focus attention on "what" students need to learn and set a high bar for all students, including struggling learners. During my residencies, I have observed over and over again that when the work is meaningful, engaging, relevant, and challenging—and all students are given the opportunity to participate fully—some students with labels perform similarly to their peers. Many schools have not been challenging large percentages of students for years, with many students reporting that the work is "too easy."[6]

The vision and goals of the standards are commendable and are where we need to keep our focus. In their excellent article "CCSS in ELA: Suggestions and Cautions for Implementing the Reading Standards," esteemed scholars and researchers Sheila Valencia and Karen Wixson provide expert guidance on implementation and where we need to direct our attention. One important caution they offer is that some of the grade-level standards are unsupported by research and are inappropriate. Also, "Sometimes the grade-level standards include so much specificity that it is difficult to identify alignment with a single Anchor Standard."[7] This is vital information because the less knowledgeable we are, the more likely we are to focus on the bits and pieces and continue low-level instruction.

One important suggestion the authors offer is to rely on the anchor standards in reading to guide instruction and to pay attention to the three main areas for comprehension: key ideas and details, craft and structure, and integration of knowledge and ideas. Notice how those three key areas also apply to writing. Just keeping those brief but comprehensive anchor standards in mind for both reading and writing can elevate our planning and instruction and make it more relevant, challenging, and intentional.

Standards can be used as an invaluable guide for what we do as effective teachers if we are knowledgeable. For example, the emphasis on close reading, informational reading and writing, and writing across the curriculum denotes important instructional shifts that schools are taking seriously. However, the troublesome news is that many teachers, coaches, and leaders lack the expertise as teachers of reading and writing across the curriculum to know how to effectively implement challenging standards and to question the ones that are off-base. Lacking that know-how makes it difficult to know where to focus attention and leaves educators vulnerable to relying on

Quick Win

Keep a copy of the CCSS anchor standards handy; these one-pagers provide the big picture of what we need to be teaching and focusing on. See www.corestandards.org/ELA-Literacy/CCRA/R.

prescriptive programs for "answers." Without expertise, we will not succeed in increasing achievement and engagement for most students.

In too many schools, the main emphasis and pressure remain on rapid implementation of the standards rather than thoughtful focus on teaching individual students, meeting them where they are, and considering their unique strengths, needs, and interests. We need to be able to interpret the standards wisely while maintaining our integrity and courage to do what's best for our students. For example, rather than focusing first on teaching complex texts, be thinking, "What supports does this student or group of students need to read this text with understanding?" and "How can I reveal to my students how I engage with and comprehend complex texts?"

Historically, standards come and go rather quickly, so we need to be careful not to make standards the end-all of teaching. At best, standards will raise expectations and possibilities so more students achieve. More likely, using research and history as a guide, the latest standards will have little effect on achievement overall. From 2003 to 2009, states with weak contents standards improved their national math and reading scores at the same rate as states with high standards.[8] As the public and we educators bear witness to a drastic decline in test scores tied to the latest standards and accompanying accountability measures, there will be an outcry, once again, for change. Our best investment remains long-term professional learning that makes us more thoughtful, accomplished literacy teachers and leaders regardless of the programs and standards in place at the moment. What we know for certain is that students learn more when they have expert teachers.

Emphasize Prevention

Valuing prevention is in our best interests in professions such as medicine, law, architecture, and education; yet *undervaluing* prevention seems to be a way of life. From the crumbling infrastructure of deteriorating roads, bridges, and schools to inadequate funding and energy directed to improving major public facilities, we often seem to wait until disaster strikes to fix fundamental problems. In education we have yet to nationally embrace the notion that it's a critically worthwhile investment to put our talents, energies, and dollars into preventing reading and learning problems rather than into the costly cleanup we typically do after allowing millions of our students to fail at literacy.

We know that children of poverty often remain in poverty and that a solid education, right from the start, is the best way to remove class barriers and make a brighter future possible. Yet, nationally only 28 percent of 4-year-olds are enrolled in state-financed preschools.[9] Where early childhood programs adhere to high standards and provide a rich and relevant literacy curriculum taught by highly trained teachers, evidence suggests that these programs do lead to incremental literacy improvements and better lives for students.[10] Moreover, research concludes that such programs—when they are excellent—yield a dollar-value return to society of $7 to $12 for every $1 invested.[11] The fact that nationally we have provided such meager and often substandard literacy support for our most needy preschool learners speaks volumes for how we create a guaranteed crisis that could be averted.

The successful approach to flood control in the Netherlands—as opposed to what happened in New York and other locations struck by Hurricane Sandy in 2012—is a good metaphor for how we might better deal with major educational crises in the United States. They understand in the Netherlands that if things go awry, the invested cost in dollars and energy to "fix" the problem is enormous and goes on for many years, so they focus on prevention of disaster. What we do in education is continuously tread water at best, and at worst completely regroup every time test scores drop. Instead of prevention, we embrace intervention. We are inept as a nation at avoiding those large numbers of students who wind up "under water" (my words). Commenting on Hurricane Sandy, Wim Kuijken, the government official responsible for overall water control policy in the Netherlands, says, "The U.S. is excellent at disaster management, but working to avoid disaster is completely different from working after a disaster."[12]

Sometimes we educators inadvertently "create" the need for intervention through our failure to believe we can take actions that will develop successful learners from the day they enter our schools. Highly skillful teachers who hold a positive-expectations mindset can often prevent intervention for students labeled "at risk," especially in the earliest grades.

Ensure Excellent Literacy Instruction in Kindergarten

In 15 years of reading and writing residencies in the United States and Canada, a key and consistent finding has been that when kindergartners are guided to do meaningful, appropriately challenging, and enjoyable reading and writing all day long, they soar as readers and writers. That is, even in high-challenge schools where students have typically been low performing, almost all students leave kindergarten as readers and writers, and only a small number require intervention. Highly knowledgeable and skillful kindergarten teachers can resolve the reading problems of at-risk students as well as expert tutorial programs; yet most of our schools do not have a plan to provide the classroom instruction that these kindergartners require.[13] Because a kindergarten student's experience with an exemplary teacher can be transformational for that student's later achievement, self-efficacy, and even future earnings, the topic of literacy instruction in kindergarten merits much attention.

Instructional expertise in kindergarten can lead to outstanding results. What follows are the insights, beliefs, and practices of three remarkable kindergarten teachers, expressed in their own voices. Jamie Newman taught full-day kindergarten for many years in an urban Colorado school where more than 90 percent of the students qualify for free and reduced lunch (she now teaches grade 1 in that same school); Lindsay Jacksha teaches two half-day kindergartens—each with a class size above 30—in a small rural school in Oregon where 65 percent of the students qualify for free and reduced lunch; Andrea Lockhart has been teaching for 12 years in Winnipeg, Canada, mainly in full-day kindergarten in a school where 65 percent of the children are from low-income families.

All three schools have sizable minority populations, large numbers of English language learners, and high student transiency rates. All three teachers have a strong sense of urgency and agency, participate in ongoing and school-based Professional *Literacy* Communities, advocate for their students, continually strive to do better, and get superior results with their kindergartners. All of them meet the curriculum requirements of their schools and districts and apply the latest standards to their instruction and assessment. All of them are joyful, effective, and efficient teachers; the kindergartners of all three teachers enter 1st grade as confident readers and writers. It's not just that the students know their letters, sounds, and "sight words." These are students who think and solve problems, see themselves as readers and writers, and use reading and writing to live their lives more fully, in and out of school.

I came to know each of these teachers well through our weeklong collaboration in their classrooms in reading/writing residencies and through follow-up residencies in other classrooms at their schools. Each of these three individuals was already a very good teacher; each one became a remarkable teacher. Their raised expectations and higher results in the earliest elementary grade paved the way for increased expectations and higher results across the grades. Teachers and principals began to ask, "If this is what students can do in kindergarten, what does this mean for 3rd grade and 5th grade and beyond?" Because success in kindergarten is foundational to what's possible in all grades, it's essential we do everything possible to ensure we have excellent kindergarten teachers in all our schools.[14] Also, the story of how each one of these extraordinary teachers has grown can provide instructive learning insights for us all. In the accounts that follow, they express their changes in beliefs and practices in their own confident voices.

Notice how what these thoughtful teachers have to say applies to all grade levels and all content areas: enriching language and literacy experiences, raising expectations for what's possible, embedding needed skills and strategies into meaningful and authentic texts, explicitly demonstrating what we expect students to be able to do, accelerating learning, increasing engagement, making students more accountable for self-checking their work, and—not to be minimized—increasing enthusiasm and joy in learning. Also, these teachers are intensely focused on high-level instruction and learning almost every moment. If we can accomplish these goals in kindergarten in high-challenge schools, surely these are realistic aims for every one of us, no matter where we teach or what we teach.

Jamie's insights

I'm always trying to think bigger. I look beyond the grade level I'm teaching in order to seek perspective into how the content ties into that of other grade levels. Undoubtedly, what happens in kindergarten is foundational for later grades, which means I am not responsible for merely teaching kindergarten curriculum. I am laying the beginning of a foundation of lifelong learners. For example, we use excellent literature to notice and talk about structure, story patterns, author's purpose, and character motivation. By posing questions like "Did [the character] change?" and "Is there really a solution to his problem?" we go from what was merely a noticing task to a thoughtful and meaningful conversation rooted in bigger concepts that strong readers and thinkers use for the rest of their lives.

I'm constantly questioning what I'm teaching and why I'm doing it. I always need to know where I'm headed, and so must my students. My teaching is purposeful. I'm not teaching a bulleted list or a program. By thinking of the big ideas and how the standards fit in with them rather than a set of activities to fit the skills and standards, I am able to better serve my students.

I look at instruction more globally now and do not let myself be bound by a rigid schedule. For example, in my two-hour literacy block, we do lots of instruction in a whole group, small groups, and individually. We are "doing" all that is reading and writing ALL the time. I have found that by eliminating the division between content areas, especially between reading and writing, which has never felt natural to me as a learner or teacher, our conversations, work, thinking, and learning in the classroom can go much deeper. It is so joyous to see a class of 5-year-olds become totally engaged and truly excited about learning.

I tap into kids' curiosity and interests and follow their leads using shared experiences and their own lives as writing topics. I have deviated from a set structure for guided reading that locks teachers into having to see a certain number of groups every day. Instead, we do more independent reading, I have more independent and public conferences, have a longer writing block, and always stop to celebrate all the great thinking that is happening every day in the classroom. When I do put kids in a small group, it's because I've determined that these particular kids need certain skills, and I tailor my instruction to meet that specific need.

Most of our hard work with students happens in school, so I find I have much less work to take home now. I put the work on them, in the classroom, and don't have to spend hours at home planning because I truly use what happened in my classroom today to guide what instruction will look like tomorrow. I take my cues from the kids. It is this kind of responsive teaching and student-centered learning that has enabled us to create such a joyful and productive classroom.[15]

Lindsay's insights

We still have almost two more months of school and the majority of my students have already met the end-of-the-year benchmarks in both reading and writing. I have never had students writing and reading like this before. Their reading scores are higher than I have ever had this time of the year. Almost all are meeting if not exceeding the standards. They are completing at least one full page of their writing, sometimes two or three pages.

I can cover more ground because students are learning at a faster rate because our reading skills and writing skills are embedded in everything we do. My students are making connections from the books we read to their writing. I noticed a huge change when we began using word work from our own writing and texts we created together. The way they are able to play with words and manipulate text is incredible.

In terms of engagement, they take their writing very seriously. People walk in and they are shocked that all my students are engaged in different writing activities—and not just busywork, but authentic writing practices that are important to them! It is incredible to see the difference when a new student walks into the culture of our class. They lack the understanding of why reading and writing are important, and it takes them so much longer to catch up. It is then that I realize just how far we have come and how much more is possible.

The biggest change I have seen in myself is what I believe they are capable of and what I hold them accountable for. I make the kids do all the work now and let them own it. When we are writing, if there is a word we don't have up on our word wall, my kids want me to stop and make a chart for the room! I now look at sharing differently. Most of the time, the public conferences or the celebrations are where most of the teachable moments happen. Real-life examples from their peers! I can't look at a children's book in a store now without thinking of a handful of writing projects we can do with it!

I am excited and exhausted all at the same time. It has been an incredible year![16]

Andrea's insights

I've made dramatic changes in the past two to three years. I'm much more effective and efficient, which is a very big thing. My planning at home has gone down. I used to spend hours planning ahead for days and months. I would overplan the entire day. The focus was more on the lesson than on the students. Now I'm tuned into the students. I have more routines that develop naturally, day by day.

My whole teaching process has changed, the way I scaffold for students. I have internalized the Optimal Learning Model, which perfectly fits the teaching style of kindergarten. I show kids what to do; we do it together; they try it out with my support. Another huge change and an "A-ha" moment for me has been moving to make all my teaching cohesive. It used to be all broken up throughout the day. Now we do shared writing, read-aloud, rhyming words, skills, and everything is connected to an experience, and I'm much more explicit in my teaching. All the skills are embedded in the texts we write and read. I teach more and enjoy it more. I am teaching every moment! I'm exhausted at the end of the day, but when I look back, the day was filled with valuable learning experiences, and I didn't take two hours the night before to plan it all. I plan more week by week, and the reading and writing are more organic and based on where the kids are.

My word work used to be surface, superficial, and taught in isolation. The kids didn't understand the "why." It wasn't until we talked as a staff about what we believe and why we believe it that my thinking started to shift. That shift was huge, and included the way I view kids. I no longer see them as having deficits. I view students as inexperienced rather than struggling, delayed, or unready. They may have had limited literacy experiences, so I immerse them in read-alouds, rich language, and literacy experiences all day long.

The biggest difference is that kids are not reluctant readers and writers. Starting writing on the first day of school is a non-issue. "You're all writers," I tell them. Five years ago I had kids lined up waiting for me to help them. Now they sound out words, apply the OLM, use room resources, and help each other. One of my biggest changes is in how I model. Now, I model what I expect them to be able to do. Before I was just writing without thinking what they would be able to do. A lot of my writing was beyond them. I also emphasize the reading/writing connection a lot more. They read their writing over and over again, and I say, "You're a reader." Reading their own texts and our class books is huge! I don't have a single behavior problem in my room. Kids know they are capable and are not afraid to take a risk. They are happy in their environment and see themselves as capable. Also, very important, in 1st grade very few need intervention. The kids that are behind are the ones who have not been in our kindergarten.[17]

Intervene Early

The earlier we intervene, the greater chance we have to effectively reduce and eliminate the achievement gap in the long run.[18] One reason it is critical to intervene early is because early reading problems often continue through the grades, and beyond the elementary grades many teachers do not teach reading.[19] Also, it's much easier to build on early success than to remediate later failure.

When considering intervention, it's important to distinguish between early-intervention programs that ensure later literacy success and the misplaced intervention that is a first resort, before universal teaching has been given a full effort. Early-intervention programs with proven success records such as Reading Recovery, high-quality preschools, early tutoring, and superior kindergartens focus on excellent first teaching in an intensive and targeted manner so that future literacy problems will be forestalled. In an interview, researcher Richard Allington notes, "We have studies involving multiple school districts and hundreds or thousands of kids demonstrating that, with quality instruction and intervention, 98 percent of all kids can be reading at grade level by the end of 1st or 2nd grade."[20] Early prevention makes it more likely that students "at risk" will benefit from regular classroom instruction and gain content knowledge from reading.[21]

Our continuing residency work focusing on writing and the reading/writing connection in diverse, low-income, high-challenge schools confirms that we can ensure early literacy success. In Winnipeg, Manitoba, where Reading Recovery is firmly in place, kindergartners—even in the lowest-performing schools—who enter 1st grade with a writing vocabulary of at least 12 words have a 100 percent chance of being discontinued from Reading Recovery. "It is the daily authentic writing that has made the biggest difference."[22]

Before these residencies with my colleagues Nancy McLean and Sandra Figueroa, comparable students were exiting kindergarten with a writing vocabulary of fewer than six words and had only a 50 percent chance of being taken out of Reading Recovery. Definitive data from three large school divisions in Canada conclusively show that, in combination with Reading Recovery, focusing on writing early on increases the chances of reading success.[23] An assistant superintendent in Winnipeg had this to say:

> The fact that we could put a number on it challenges kindergarten teachers' expectations to teach writing in kindergarten. Our teachers who are the most successful spend more time with writing with young children.[24]

And again, in a school where the majority of students come from low-income families and where I have been conducting residencies focused on the reading/writing connection with an emphasis on writing, the literacy coach and hard data confirm that since writing has become a daily emphasis in kindergarten, 90 to 93 percent of students are exiting kindergarten as writers and readers.[25] It is the early writing emphasis that has contributed to the accelerated and increased literacy success. The literacy coach says, "We're a year ahead of where we used to be. Kids are getting to exit early intervention in reading because they're writing so well."[26]

If intervention does not occur until later grades—in middle or high school—identifying students for intervention must be done with careful scrutiny. Most often, students have experienced years of failure, and achievement and ability levels can vary widely; variations among students of one to four grade levels are not unusual. With extra personnel at a premium, what often happens is that students who have farthest to go are clumped together and are not always placed with the strongest instructor. Or support is confined to test prep or a narrow focus on a specific standard or set of standards, and gains are very limited. Another common scenario is that students who are deemed to be "close to passing the test" are given priority for support over needier students considered "too low" to make sufficient test gains.

When a school has a high-functioning Professional *Literacy* Community, common formative assessments—not just high-stakes tests—are often used to determine where intervention efforts are most needed, how to form the instructional groups for intervention, who will be providing the intervention, and what the intervention will be. In other words, integrity rules and students' learning needs come first. In those cases, a subset of low performers can reach unanticipated growth through PLC-selected strategies and a strong instructor. "High-level, professional conversations among the PLC members, including an administrator and curriculum specialist/coach, are the tipping point for effecting positive achievement gains."[27]

Avoid Summer Reading Loss

We've all seen it happen. We teach our hearts out to ensure all students make significant reading gains during the school year, but when these same students return to school after summer vacation, we discover many have lost some of those important gains. Students from families and neighborhoods with limited access to books over the summer months may lose a month or more of reading growth. One 1st grade teacher noted that despite the fact that most exiting kindergartners in her high-needs school were reading at the end of kindergarten, a lack of reading practice over the summer meant that it took two full months for the students to return to a similar reading level in grade 1. More sobering is the fact that approximately 80 percent of the reading achievement gap between poor and nonpoor students at age 14 can be explained by summer reading setback.[28]

Although researchers have been drawing public attention to the deleterious effects of summer reading loss on low-income students for many years, little has been done overall to provide easy access to interesting books that lead to an increase in summer reading. Yet it is well documented that providing books to primary-grade students in high-poverty schools increases students' reading achievement.[29] We all need to create and implement solutions that put books into students' hands. When students read six or more books over the summer, they maintain their reading skills and do not slide.[30]

Workable solutions that can help to reverse the disturbing trend of summer reading loss include but are not limited to the following recommendations, almost all of which focus on access to books—with student choice:

- Send hand-picked, appropriate books home with students at the end of the school year and set goals for summer reading.
- Mail books to students over the summer months with a note encouraging them to read.
- Keep school libraries open on designated days for book check-out.
- Enlist community businesses to donate funds earmarked for book purchases for summer reading (books students can keep).
- Use school book fairs to have students choose books specifically for summer reading; set the selected books aside until the end of school.
- During the school year, reach out to the school community and neighboring communities with a summer reading request for donations of new and used books. (A school committee sorts the books.)
- As a staff, brainstorm ways to ensure students have self-selected books on hand for summer reading.
- If possible, pair neighborhood children—an older student with a younger one—and encourage partner reading.[31]

From firsthand experience and discussion with principals and teachers in other schools, I have concluded that summer library participation, whether it be the school or public library, and asking students to keep a

Quick Win

Start teaching reading and writing on the first day of school to help curb the results of summer reading loss. Do not wait for fall testing or other data. A lot of teaching can occur through shared reading, shared writing, and reading aloud.

reading log do not work particularly well. What seems to work best in getting students to read is ensuring they leave school for the summer with a bunch of books in their hands and that these books are ones they have chosen, want to read, and can read with understanding. The expense related to providing these books is minimal, and some publishers offer books at very low cost. (For example, Scholastic periodically offers bundles of popular fiction and nonfiction books for $1 to $2 a book.)

Embrace the Reading/Writing Connection

Most of my work in diverse schools centers on raising reading and writing achievement for all learners, and I depend on the connection between the two to jumpstart engagement, enjoyment, and improvement for both reading and writing. Along with my instructional and assessment plans, I always enter the classroom in a literacy residency armed with one or more excellent nonfiction or fiction texts. I concur with a wise colleague who said, "The best intervention is a good book."[32] Carefully selected, outstanding texts can guide, support, and raise the quality of the work that is possible for all students.

The reading/writing connection has been underused in our schools for decades.[33] In fact, separating reading and writing limits and slows down student achievement, which is especially detrimental for our underperforming, struggling learners. *Writing to Read: Evidence for How Writing Can Improve Reading* is the most comprehensive review and summary report of a large body of research that examines the effects of different writing practices on students' reading performance.[34] The report confirms the significance of applying the reading/writing connection to teaching and learning. Its three main recommendations are the following:

1. **Have students write about the texts they read.** Students' comprehension of science, social studies, and language arts texts is improved when they write about what they read, specifically when they

    • Respond to a text in writing (writing personal reactions, analyzing and interpreting the text).
    • Write summaries of a text.
    • Write notes about a text.
    • Answer questions about a text in writing, or create and answer written questions about a text.

2. **Teach students the writing skills and processes that go into creating text.** Students' reading skills and comprehension are improved by learning the skills and processes that go into creating text, specifically when teachers

- Teach the process of writing, text structures for writing, paragraph or sentence construction skills (*improves reading comprehension*) [emphasis added].
- Teach spelling and sentence construction skills (improves reading fluency).
- Teach spelling skills (improves word reading skills).

3. **Increase how much students write.** Students' reading comprehension is improved by having them increase how often they produce their own texts.[35]

Notice that more writing improves reading comprehension. Yet in schools where writing is not tested, it is often devalued and is barely taught, which negatively affects both writing and reading abilities of students.

We need to begin early and to emphasize more nonfiction writing in classrooms, along with narrative and poetry writing. More informational writing, especially in the primary grades, leads to better readers and writers and higher reading achievement.[36]

In my residency work in schools, I almost always start with a terrific nonfiction book that I read aloud to the class. We use the book not only to do a shared writing, often a summary, but also as a catalyst for getting students excited about nonfiction texts. Most of the schools I work in are high-challenge schools with large populations of English language learners; in such settings we need to teach and expose students to challenging content with regular and academic vocabulary right from the start if they are ever to catch up to their higher-achieving peers.

In Lesley Vermaas's 1st grade classroom, the results of beginning the year emphasizing nonfiction and maintaining that emphasis all year were stunning for her students, many of whom qualified for free and reduced lunch and who entered kindergarten with limited literacy skills. Reading challenging informational texts enhanced their writing, their vocabulary, and their knowledge acquisition, all of which had the effect of decreasing or erasing the typical knowledge gap that ensues when students are fed a diet of "low-level texts of questionable value."[37] In the photos on page 154, see the side-by-side writing samples from an average student at the beginning

> **Quick Win**
>
> *Do not allow dictation to go on too long.* Doing so gives a student a sense of learned helplessness. Also, value illustrations and labeling that require informative detail but less writing.

of the school year and in the spring of the school year, and note the enormous progress in fluency, content, depth, vocabulary, conventions and so on; as well, see the joy on the students' faces from their excitement of wanting to share their published, nonfiction books.

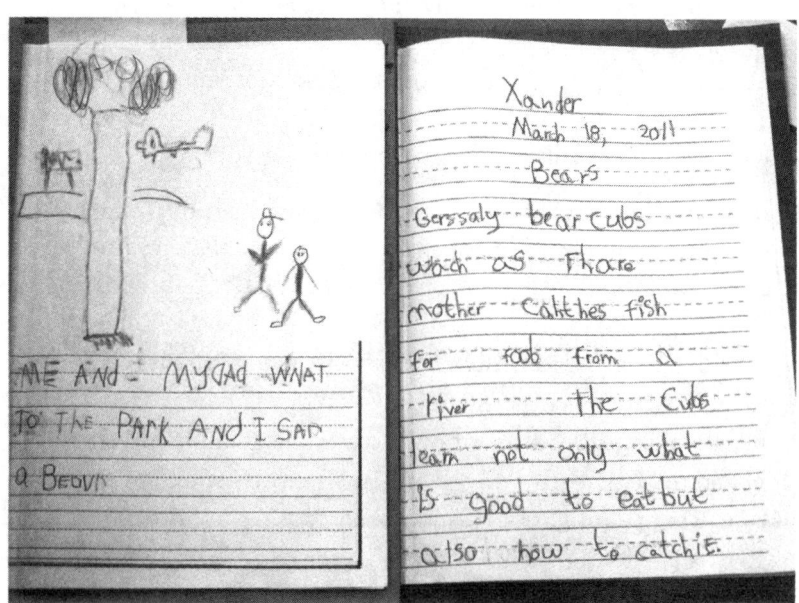

Noticing and celebrating a typical 1st grader's writing growth from fall to spring.

Joy and pride in being accomplished nonfiction writers.

Lesley comments on the remarkable progress that resulted from the daily reading/writing connection and the emphasis on nonfiction:

The biggest change I made was raising the expectations bar for all learners and adding in the "I do it" piece of the OLM model to my teaching. My students learned so much from my demonstrations. We talked a lot about what good authors do so that the reader feels they are right there with the writer. It was amazing how much better and more descriptive their writing became. Also, adding public conferencing was very important. When someone tried something new in their writing, we discussed it, and I would invite others to try it.

Celebration in public conferencing is huge! They all want to be celebrated. I have thirty-four students, but I don't worry about teaching writing. Planning is much easier. Kids are in charge of their own writing and have mostly free choice about 85 percent of the time. We have directed writing about once a month.

While they may not always write a lot, their writing is clear, to the point, and has mostly accurate punctuation and spelling; it's all way beyond what I ever expected from 1st graders. I figured if they used a period at the end of their story, that was great. Now they use periods, exclamation and question marks, commas when listing, and can do quotation marks by the end of the year, and they experiment so much more. They are doing a lot of revising and editing, noticing what's confusing for the reader and fixing it up, lassoing and moving things around.

In terms of nonfiction, kids are always attracted to nonfiction. The key is to find out what they are interested in. "I like planets" leads to getting books, going to the Internet and other sources. Having one or two students publish a book with nonfiction pictures that go with their writing piques other kids' interest, and then they are thinking, "I want to write something too." And they are specific. They say, "I want to write a book about alligators. I want to write something that will wow the reader. Will you help me find books so I can do some research?" Writing for a reader is new. They used to just write for me.

Reading results near the end of the year are much higher because of all the reading they are doing in relation to the authentic writing, all our shared reading, reading their own work over and over again, and reading each other's books. As CCSS goals were rolled out in our district I realized I needed to raise my expectations in reading and writing in order to meet those goals. I was very nervous about the challenge.

By the end of the year the majority of my first grade students not only met, but many exceeded, the CCSS goals. According to a standardized reading assessment, most students are reading at or above a mid–2nd grade level. They are not afraid to pick things up and read them; they are confident![38]

Embracing and applying the reading/writing connection also makes it less likely that students will need intervention. Gloria Heflin has taught an extended-day literacy program for kindergarten students for many years; that is, "at-risk" students receive six additional hours of kindergarten each week beyond their regular half-day kindergarten. Gloria also models for parents the strategies and activities they can incorporate at home to support their children's literacy development. Gloria found that when she shifted her teaching from a phonics-first and skills approach to a balanced literacy approach that focused on the reading/writing connection, her students' literacy learning accelerated. In particular, she credits adding meaningful daily writing to her reading component as the single most important factor for many of her students exiting the program months earlier than in previous years. In addition, students' end-of-year reading scores were much higher and, very significant, her students were more successful as readers and writers in grade 1. Very few required additional intervention.[39] Gloria also notes the enjoyment and pride in learning that resulted:

Remember the boy who wrote the thank you card to his sister for making his bed? Today at parent/teacher conferences, I told his parents what he did. You should have seen their faces beam with joy. And you should have seen him and his twin sister relive the moment. Adorable! Yep! That's what it's all about! They already see themselves as capable and confident, even though they qualified for my intervention class.[40]

Jamie Newman, an outstanding kindergarten teacher in a school where more than 90 percent of the students qualify for free and reduced lunch (and whose experiences are presented in her own voice earlier in this chapter) found that when she looped with her students, that is, took almost all of her kindergartners on to 1st grade and continued her balanced approach focused on authenticity, relevancy, close ties with families, and the reading/writing connection, none of her students—all of whom were limited English proficient (LEPs)—needed intervention in grade 1. "At the end of grade 1, all students left ready for 2nd grade work and above."[41]

Benefits of the Reading/Writing Connection

- *Phonemic Awareness Knowledge and Application*—Most developing readers and writers easily learn phonemic awareness through stretching out the sounds in words in their daily writing. Phonemic awareness is quick and easy to assess: If writers are including beginning and ending consonants and a medial vowel—as they identify and manipulate the corresponding sounds they hear while writing—they have basic phonemic awareness.

- *Teaching Skills in Meaningful Context*—Developing readers also easily learn letters, sounds, and words in the context of a class-authored text they can refer to for their own reading and writing. Pointing to each word as we read a familiar text with students, exposing words gradually, pointing out special features of text, and having students write high-frequency words and self-check their accuracy against the class text all contribute to increased engagement and faster learning.

- *Rereading*—Once rereading of writing has been demonstrated as an integral part of the writing process for deciding what might be revised for clarity and interest for the reader, rereading in writing becomes routine and helps to make the writer a more careful reader as well as a more fluent one. Rereading also improves writing by leading to more thoughtful revision and editing.

- *Increased Reading and Research*—Especially with nonfiction topics that students are interested in, connecting writing with reading raises students' curiosity and desire to learn more and read more. With our encouragement and guidance, they readily seek out books and sources for developing concepts and learning more information.

- *Vocabulary Growth*—Research confirms that learning more vocabulary is tied to higher reading comprehension.[43] Explicit vocabulary teaching is necessary but insufficient for helping students increase their vocabulary. Much of the vocabulary students learn and apply is a result of increased reading and writing.

- *Pride of Authorship*—Texts we write together as a class or small group or that students write on their own for authentic audiences and purposes often become our texts for reading. As well, student-authored texts always become a favorite part of the classroom library, and many students choose these texts.

- *Higher Engagement and Success*—Texts that students write on familiar topics and in words they have chosen to use are always the easiest texts to read, which is especially critical for our second language learners and learners who struggle. Early success in reading and writing forestalls future literacy problems.

- *Joy in Learning*—Not to be minimized are the marvelous effects of enjoyment on both students and teachers for learning more, learning at a faster rate, increasing motivation, and having the learning stick. Students and teachers alike are more engaged, motivated, energized, and willing to do the work.

Also important, be sure not to neglect online reading and writing that are so interrelated that we cannot separate them.[42] Online communications are highly motivating for students and may include blogs, videos, podcasts, texts, social media, and selected websites that invite interaction, to name several. Important to note and contrary to what many believe, writing online has not been found to contribute to poor spelling and grammar; in fact, the increased writing makes students better and more flexible communicators because the audience and purpose are immediately relevant, unlike in many school settings.[44] At the same time, acknowledging the advantages of online literacy does not diminish the critical need for reading full-length books so that students acquire the stamina they will need to complete the massive amount of required reading in high school and, especially, college.

Finally, as much as possible, we need to focus our reading and writing where our students' interests are. If we can reach them, we can teach them. Engagement and relevancy are especially critical for our reluctant readers and writers. Smartly applying the reading/writing connection along with whole-part-whole teaching increases engagement, efficiency, and joy in learning. Engaged readers and writers enjoy reading and writing more, actively participate in discussions about books, are more willing to revise and reread, and are constantly reading and writing for pleasure and information. If we can make that happen for our struggling students, we decrease the need for intervention.

Quick Win

Talk about and model for families how to become reading role models through reading aloud and having reading time at home during which devices are turned off and everyone reads, and taking time to talk about the reading through pleasurable conversation, not interrogation.

Published nonfiction books are featured in a classroom library where they are favorite selections.

Employ Principles of Response to Intervention

Response to Intervention (RTI) is a "comprehensive, systematic approach to teaching and learning designed to address language and literacy problems for all students through increasingly differentiated and intensified language and literacy assessment and instruction."[45] RTI came about as a federal mandate with the goal of decreasing the number of students being placed in special education—many of whom then experienced poor long-term outcomes—by providing struggling readers with early intervention to meet their specific needs and accelerate their progress.

RTI is a multitiered intervention and support system, with Tier 1 being the universal classroom level deemed to meet the needs of approximately 80 percent of our students. That is, if we focus on excellent instruction for all students in regular education as a first resort, that instruction can serve to avoid additional intervention for most students, who will make good progress. As I have previously noted, such expert instruction requires highly skilled teachers and principals who know what to look for, how to assess, how to differentiate instruction, how to provide flexible grouping, how to give productive feedback, and how to move learners forward. "By intervening and supporting struggling students early, we can get most kids to read at grade level within the regular classroom, tier 1."[46] Tier 2 in RTI refers to additional expert instruction the student receives, usually offered daily in a small group by the classroom teacher or support specialist. Tier 3 involves one-on-one tutoring.[47]

Focus on Meaning

As in all federal programs, RTI implementation efforts have varied depending on interpretation of the mandate, choice and use of resources, and, especially, how much expertise the classroom teacher has—in this case, expertise in how to effectively teach reading. Where teachers are highly knowledgeable about literacy—like the kindergarten teachers described earlier in this chapter who constantly adapt and modify their teaching as needed—instruction is meaningful, authentic, and connected to students' lives and cultures as well as the district curriculum and standards. However, continuing pressures to raise test scores tend to have a reductionist effect on teaching and learning; that is, as schools and districts scramble to find and implement the "right" program or resource, meaningful instruction and learning suffer, and many children are not well served.

Response to Intervention works well in principle but less well in practice. Some schools have embraced rigid commercial and scripted programs as RTI solutions and used paraprofessionals to administer these programs. Sadly, fidelity to the program often supersedes fidelity to the child. Many teachers and administrators are unprepared to provide the thoughtful, targeted instruction to students that RTI requires. In too many schools, Tier 1, or the first level of intervention—the universal supports level—is bypassed for Tiers 2 and 3. In making more time for RTI, some of those same schools have actually reduced their instructional time for reading and writing. If we think of RTI as Response to Instruction,[48] then RTI becomes every educator's ongoing mandate to respond to all students in a manner that supports and accelerates early literacy acquisition.

Choose Programs and Resources Carefully: Pay Attention to Research

Proceed with caution. Too many programs being used in the name of research are too costly, are time-consuming, and have only limited or no benefit for increasing literacy. The reading curriculum goals of RTI, like those of No Child Left Behind, continue to focus mostly on skills in phonemic awareness, phonics, fluency, comprehension, and vocabulary, with an overemphasis on lower-order reading skills and a heavy reliance on published reading materials.[49]

The diagnostic assessment and progress monitoring are also restrictive and narrow—relying too much on DIBELS, where, for example, "fluency" means accuracy and rate only.[50] Although I don't have an anti-DIBELS agenda, according to widespread research and data, none of the DIBELS tests are related to improved reading achievement. My best conclusion as to why so many of us continue to ignore that definitive research and persist with DIBELS is that learned helplessness has set in, we don't have enough knowledge to know what else to do, we may be fearful of reprisals, and the numerical data DIBELS provides give us a false sense that we are receiving accurate information when, at best, what we are getting is pseudo-science. DIBELS is just one of many diagnostic assessments that are overly focused on oral reading and low-level skills. A major problem with such assessments is the misuse of valuable time for teachers and students—time that could go toward actually teaching reading and having students read meaningful texts.[51]

The excessive time, energy, and funds that have been squandered on phonics-first programs stagger the imagination. Although, of course, phonics is essential to reading, the highly respected National Reading Panel Report found no positive effects for any phonics program beyond 1st grade.[52] Yet that research, too, continues to be ignored. Research has also confirmed that structured phonics programs work and produce good word readers and decoders but not readers who comprehend, as we painfully learned after investing five years and $6 billion in Reading First.[53]

Finally, as noted in Chapter 3, it's vital to know the research on core reading programs or any program we are thinking of adopting *before* we change our practices. Most important for our low-performing students, none of the most widely used reading programs teach comprehension in a manner that supports struggling readers. Typically, instructional recommendations include

- Too many skills and strategies.
- Too little explicit instruction.
- Too little time for practice of skills and strategies.
- Too little time for comprehension instruction.

Also, the programs rarely follow the gradual-release-of-responsibility model that research recommends for effective teaching and learning.[54] That model, comparable to the Optimal Learning Model, is especially important for our students who need more time and support to learn.

Work with Reading Texts That Lead to Early Success

Although I have already discussed many reading practices in Chapter 3, "Reading and Writing Priorities," here I want to summarize key text practices that are vital for decreasing the need for intervention, especially in reading. Often, we give our lowest-performing students texts that make it difficult for them to accelerate. The "right" text is crucial for ensuring optimal reading progress and success. This statement is true for reading aloud, shared reading, guided reading, and independent reading.

Rely on first-rate texts

I have previously discussed the importance of classroom libraries and easy access to excellent nonfiction and fiction texts that interest students as key to improving students' engagement, motivation, and comprehension.

Quick Win

Employ buddy reading and writing, such as a 5th grader working with a 1st grader, which improves reading and writing abilities for both the tutor and the tutee, according to researchers Hilde Van Keer and Ruben Vanderlinde.

Quick Win

Invest in classroom libraries. Instead of purchasing iPads, e-readers, or the latest technology, first establish extensive collections of high-quality, high-interest books, to be used for in-school and at-home reading. In *The Smartest Kids in the World and How They Got That Way,* Amanda Ripley reports that there is no conclusive research that buying interactive whiteboards or tablets improves achievement.

Many students, like Kathy, whose story is told at the beginning of this chapter, become lifelong readers through extensive, self-selected reading of texts that they can read and interest them.

In the book *Transitions: From Literature to Literacy*, I wrote about how we flooded a 1st grade classroom with a multitude of wonderful children's literature and transformed students' dismal reading achievement in a high-poverty school where failing to successfully learn to read from commercial basal texts had been the norm. Based on the research of Warwick Elley on "book floods" in New Zealand, as well as that of notable educators Don Holdaway, Don Graves, and Brian Cambourne, we set up the conditions for successful literacy learning.[55] We established a well-stocked classroom library; introduced enlarged texts (Big Books) for shared reading; taught almost all skills in the context of the texts we read and wrote together; used predictable, rhythmic, and natural language texts for teaching beginning reading; used daily journal writing by children to capture and celebrate their lives and their stories, teach phonemic awareness, and publish their writing for readers; and incorporated the arts into literacy with songs, illustrations, and drama. The results of moving children from stilted, boring, and too-hard texts to engaging texts that they wanted to read were astounding. Instead of the typical 50 percent of students needing remediation after grade 1, now only 5 percent did, and this turnaround was accomplished in one school year! That transformation was the start of a movement that led the school district to move away from commercial reading programs to teaching reading and writing with the best of children's literature.

We can't teach reading with second-rate texts. If we are to engage our students in content and context that matter to them, the mainstay of any reading program must be excellent fiction and nonfiction texts along with our explicit instruction and guidance and, especially, extended time spent reading self-selected texts. For students who struggle and who are turned off to reading, the "right" text is crucial.

Match students with texts they can and want to read

It's well known that too many of our students who struggle are reading books that are too hard for them. Like Kathy, they regress or stay stagnant rather than progress as readers. Showing students of all ages how to select books they can read and then guiding them to do so is necessary before releasing students to choose books on their own. Even most students who struggle can be taught to self-select appropriate books if an interesting, accessible collection is organized—with students—and we have taken the time to walk them through and practice the selection process.

Take care not to make this self-selection process superficial. In my residency work, it has been common to see impressive-looking classroom charts with criteria for book selection. Students easily recite a mantra of actions for choosing books, but when we check to see if they actually do these things, many do not. Additionally, young readers and struggling readers often rely solely on a stated book level or on a five-finger test or other check focused on word reading. Students don't yet realize that all reading is for understanding and that they also need to read a few pages to be sure they can tell what the text is about. It is rare for students to choose books with comprehension in mind and often that is because teachers have not emphasized that crucial factor.

My experience indicates that explicitly demonstrating, scaffolding, and practicing how to choose books to read—with a focus on understanding—is a necessity, especially for our students who struggle and who come from low-income families. Whereas parents of middle- and upper-class families routinely guide their children to select appropriate books to read from the public library, children from poor neighborhoods are rarely assisted by an adult in a public library.[56] Taking time to slow down and cement the self-selection process early on ensures possibilities for greater understanding and achievement.

In addition to matching texts with readers, choice and interest play a major role in engagement with texts and whether or not students accelerate and read with accuracy and understanding. In fact, many students will make a herculean effort to read a book just beyond their level if their interest in the text or topic is great enough. That is, they will reread, ask for needed help, and stay with the book, all of which is exactly what I do as a curious reader.

Read for understanding from the start

Having students acquire phonemic awareness, decoding, word analysis skills, vocabulary, and fluency skills must always be for the end purpose of making sense of text. Too often readers who struggle are sounding out words without realizing that the skills are a means to an end and the end goal is reading with understanding. I believe we are always reading to learn;

very young children automatically try to make sense of their world through "reading" the signals, the people around them, and what events mean.

I still recall meeting with a guided reading group that included the lowest-performing readers in a 1st grade classroom. Accustomed to a steady diet of decodable texts, phonics drills, and words and skills taught in isolation, they could mostly figure out the words in very simple texts, including the meaningful one I had selected for them, but they had no idea those words were supposed to make sense and that reading was about understanding. When I asked questions such as "What is the problem in the story?" "Where does it say that?" and "How does the story end?" they had no idea what I was talking about. Our reading focus, teaching emphasis, and the questions we ask students can encourage or, inadvertently, deflect thoughtful comprehension. For example, computerized reading programs assess students on literal-level questions almost exclusively; students move through levels with superficial understanding at best.[57]

Depend on partner reading

In the early grades in particular, partner reading is a terrific way to accelerate important aspects of reading progress—fluency, word recognition, comprehension, and enjoyment. Once clear guidelines have been established, understood, and practiced with teacher guidance, partner reading allows for more active participation, excellent practice time, and a cooperative and collaborative learning benefit for all students.

General Guidelines for Partner Reading

- Each participant can see the text clearly (each has a copy or the text is large enough so both can adequately see it with one copy.)
- Taking turns, one person reads a page aloud and tells the partner what the page is about.
- The partners support each other in oral reading, problem solving unknown words and concepts, and in recalling what the page is about.
- Partners reread and rethink together when they have not understood—before moving on to the next page or section.[58]

In my experience and that of many teachers I have worked with, partner reading can be the single most powerful factor for accelerating reading progress for early-grades learners who struggle. Students are often more successful with their writing when they can talk with a partner first.

Incorporate Daily Practices That Deter Failure

After decades of working as a classroom teacher, reading specialist, Reading Recovery teacher, learning disabilities teacher, literacy coach, and mentor teacher, I have found several daily practices that carry especially significant weight for all learners but particularly for our learners who struggle. Let's look at each of these practices more closely.

Daily Practices That Deter Failure

- Make the work more authentic.
- Provide more student choice.
- Make learning intentions clear.
- Celebrate students' strengths.
- Have students do more silent reading.
- Confer with students daily.

Make the Work More Authentic

Although it's not possible for everything we teach to have a real-world context, it is feasible for much of it. Continually asking ourselves "Does this activity or lesson have a real-world application?" helps keep an honest focus on what's most important and gives us "permission" to eliminate practices that don't lead anywhere—for example, isolated vocabulary exercises. Most of our students do well when they find the work relevant and meaningful to their lives—inclusive of their culture, background, interests, and identities; and when we provide lots of time and space for demonstration, practice, discussion, and interaction. Not only that, students—even those who struggle most—develop a sense of agency and possibility for their own lives.

More authenticity in tasks and content and in how we apply required curriculum and standards leads to more engagement and enjoyment, more motivated students, and higher comprehension. In teaching writing, it's the first and most important thing we do—figuring out how to make the writing purposeful for the students. In fact, it's the only way students willingly

> **Quick Win**
>
> *Limit prompt writing to once a month.* This allows more time for authentic writing.

apply their best efforts to their initial drafts and subsequent revision and editing, and this is especially crucial for our low-performing students. For severely struggling readers, their own writing often becomes their first successful reading, so authenticity is not to be minimized. We can also teach, practice, and apply almost all the word work students need to learn and practice through these authentic texts.

For high school students who are labeled at risk, using authenticity, teaching to their strengths, and acknowledging their successes are key.[59] In particular, when students can see how the work is relevant to their lives, they are more likely to invest full effort and sustain interest. Middle school students assigned "fake writing"—for example, writing to a made-up person to persuade them to do something—invested little energy into the work, which held no relevance or interest for them. Not only did they dislike such assignments, a steady diet of inauthentic work led them to dislike writing altogether.[60]

Making the work more authentic and relevant also applies to intervention efforts. When elementary principal Matt Renwick looked at the data from before and after implementation of his school reading intervention programs, he found that participating students who spent their time reading and talking about self-selected texts made greater reading progress than those who participated in a highly structured computer-based reading program.[61] These findings are consistent with those from literacy researchers who have found that more choice and time to read benefit K–12 students by leading them to deeper engagement, giving them a sense of greater agency, resulting in higher test scores, and supporting efforts in their becoming more strategic readers.[62]

Provide More Student Choice

As already discussed in Chapter 2, choice within structure is an essential principle for engaging all students. Here the discussion is more specific and concerns providing more choice to students in selecting books to read. "It may be that what turns too many struggling readers off to reading is the dominant practice of having them read aloud from books someone has selected for them."[63] Allowing students to self-select texts, which in turn relies on their having access to texts they find interesting, is a powerful factor in improving reading comprehension and motivation.[64] When we start with students' preferences and familiar books and authors, we can scaffold for them and guide them find "books that will move them painlessly from where they are to where we would like them to be."[65]

Briefly, choice in writing is also crucial for student engagement and effort—especially for our learners who struggle. Prompts, worksheets, story starters, and test prep do not turn students into writers, although these activities may temporarily and artificially raise scores and give us a false sense that what we are doing is worthwhile.

Make Learning Intentions Clear

The goal of making a learning intention or a learning target public is to accelerate instruction and learning. For that to happen, we need to give directions succinctly and clearly, do sufficient frontloading, and check to be sure students understand and value the intended learning outcome before we have them attempt it on their own.

It's especially important to clearly explain the purpose of the instruction or activity and make the criteria for success transparent with specific and useful language. Here are steps to follow:

- Decide on a worthwhile learning intention.
- Make criteria for achievement visible.
- Explicitly demonstrate.
- Check for understanding.
- Demonstrate and explain further, as needed.
- Provide support and guidance through shared and guided practice.
- Tie everything together with closure.[66]

Being transparent and explicit about the learning target is especially vital for the success of our low-performing students. We cannot assume students understand the learning target and its intention just because we have done what we believe to be an excellent demonstration or explanation and posted the expected target. Be sure to discuss in full with students what the learning objectives mean, how students will use what they are learning, and why it all matters. Then, be certain students understand what they are to do by checking for understanding and reteaching and refining as needed.

The importance of assessing for understanding and making needed adjustments brings to mind an experience during a residency in an intermediate-grades classroom where over 90 percent of the students were from low-income families. Students were working in small heterogeneous

---

Quick Win

Start with photos for students who seem unable to write about a topic—photos the student takes or finds on the Internet. Students can add simple captions, or you can take dictation.

Quick Win

Do more small-group work, which allows for more active participation, collaboration, and discourse from all students.

Quick Win

Check in with struggling students first when students are released to work independently. Provide more guidance before students fail or go off track, thereby saving time and building confidence.

groups on report writing. We already had a carefully constructed chart (a rubric) of everything students were expected to do in writing a short, collaborative research report. However, we had to go back and reteach when it was clear from observing the groups doing their draft writing-in-process that we had not sufficiently checked for understanding of the task beyond "Raise your hand if you understand what your group needs to do." Students raised their hands because they thought they understood. It was only after they started writing that it became clear to us and to them how confused they were.

It wasn't so much that we needed to provide more demonstrations and guided practice. We had devoted enough time and practice to demonstrating and thinking aloud on reading and note taking, organizing notes into a paragraph, and showing how to use our notes to craft an engaging introductory paragraph. Writing a research report is complex, so we had also done a whole-class shared writing before expecting students to write similar reports on related topics they had researched and taken notes on within their small groups of four.

What we neglected to do was to break down the whole writing task into small, manageable, and clearly sequenced steps so all could be successful.

Quick Win

Develop "I Can" statements as one way to make learning targets clear and visible. See Appendix J for some examples.

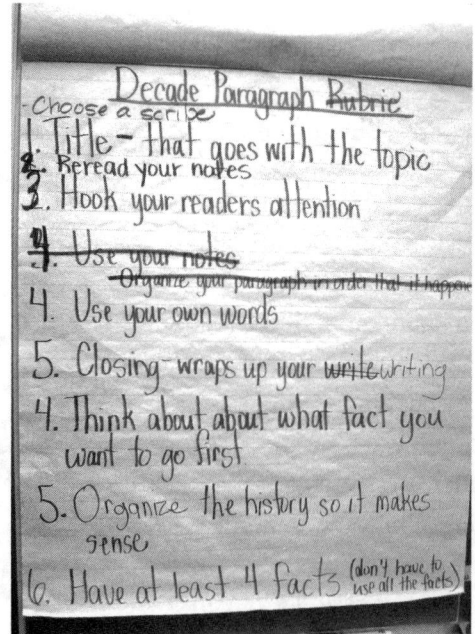

Research Paragraph Guidelines

1. Choose a scribe
2. Write a title that goes with your topic
3. Reread your notes
4. Hook your reader's attention
5. Think about what facts you want to write first (think about what is the main idea)
6. Organize the history so it makes sense
7. Include at least four facts
8. Put facts in your own words
9. Combine two facts to make one good sentence (if you choose)
10. Wrap up your writing (closing)
11. Reread to make sure you have included the most important facts
12. Reread to be sure you have followed all of the guidelines

Learning outcomes that were initially designed to give students guidance for research writing.

Revised and more precise guidelines for research writing.

Because our expectations were high and the work was new, students needed a more detailed framework than what we had provided. Had we done a thorough assessment of their understanding of the task before we released responsibility to the students, we would have saved a lot of time and frustration for all involved. See the photos on the previous page of the first shared writing chart of learning outcomes and of the more detailed revised chart, which led to far better results.

The chart below presents some of the ways to assess and check that students understand the learning intention/target *before* attempting the related task. (Note that this is just a sample of possible options.)

Many students who end up in intervention have only rarely understood the tasks they were expected to do. When we make the learning targets clear, provide exemplary demonstrations and shared experiences, check for understanding before students attempt the task, and then provide the needed supports so they can succeed, we eliminate early failure for many.

Ways to Assess and Check for Understanding

- **Turn and talk**—Tell the partner what the learning expectation/task is.
  Check: Call on either student in the pair to state what was discussed. If one or both cannot state the learning intention/task, have another student-pair state it. Then have the original pair restate it.
- **Create a written rubric with the class**—Lead a shared writing of the expectation once it's been demonstrated, explained, and discussed.
  Check: Call on a student to restate exactly what students are to undertake. Clarify for the class, as needed.
- **Incorporate small-group work**—Have students, in heterogeneous groups of three to four, work together to come up with a shared understanding of the task/learning intention.
  Check: Call on the designated group member to speak for the group or collect one group-written explanation.
- **Put the learning intention in writing**—In their own words, individually or with a partner, or in their small groups, have students write their understanding of the learning target/intention.
  Check: Assess the writing for clarity and understanding of the task.
- **Have a student volunteer demonstrate how to begin the task**—Ask the student to present his or her understanding of what to do, orally or in writing. Classmates listen in.
  Check: Take this opportunity to guide and support the student, if needed.

Celebrate Students' Strengths

As I have said elsewhere, "Celebration is at the heart of my best teaching."[67] By celebration I mean noticing and naming students' strengths and using those strengths to move learning forward. Celebration is not vacuous praise. It is specific to the learner and the task. It is positive and honest feedback that states what the learner has done well and is attempting to do. A prerequisite for celebration requires teachers and leaders to be able to see potential and possibilities for the learner, recognize each learner's talents and build upon them, value what the learner is attempting to do, and personally connect with learners while working with them. In celebration of a learner's efforts, we show kindness and acceptance through our words, actions, tone, and stance. Most important, we use carefully chosen language to boost the learner's competence. Honest celebration promotes confidence, risk taking, stamina, and repetition of a desired action and, very important, puts the learner in the mindset to consider improvements and revisions. Celebration inspires all of us—students, teachers, and leaders.

A touching story that speaks to the power of honoring all learners' thinking took place in a grade 1 classroom the second month of school. Travis was a student who called out and had his hand in the air a lot, but whose responses were often unrelated to the topic at hand. I quickly found that out during a whole-class shared writing activity that was part of a writing residency, with all the school's teachers observing. After several "off task" oral contributions, I said to Travis, "How about if we put what you just said on this chart right here?" The classroom teacher put a sheet of blank chart paper on the wall and wrote down Travis's exact words. We did that twice in the midst of the lesson, and then Travis raised his hand again: "Would you write my name next to my words?" I believe everyone's heart in the room skipped a beat when that happened. What Travis wanted was what we all want—recognition for who we are and what we are trying to do. We never did anything with that chart; it remained on the wall all week. Once Travis's voice and thinking were honored, his "disruptive" behaviors during shared writing disappeared, and he began to contribute in more appropriate ways.

Finally, we teach children to be disabled when we design our lessons or conduct our groups and conferences based on a deficit model. My Reading Recovery training, based on the work of Marie Clay, taught me that a

Quick Win

Say something positive! For students who struggle, acknowledging their efforts can encourage them to keep working.

student's strengths must be used and celebrated, and they serve as the basis for where we begin our instruction.

Have Students Do More Silent Reading

Another crucial factor for reducing the need for intervention is to reexamine and alter our overemphasis on oral reading. A poor oral reading of a text does not benefit struggling readers. Yet it is still commonplace to see a whole class of students, even in the upper grades and high school, taking turns reading out loud from a common text. The practice of oral reading as a dominant strategy is especially routine and egregious for poor readers. They are interrupted more, are more likely to have the teacher figure out the word for them, and get to read fewer words each day than better readers who do more silent reading.[68] All of this is counterproductive when the goal is to become a proficient reader.

Shared reading, guided reading, and independent reading all have the same end goal—that is, for students to silently read and comprehend a large variety of texts for pleasure and information. Once students know how to choose books they can read, students need to spend almost all of their time actually reading, and most of that should be silent reading. In the schools where I have worked, extended time devoted to silent reading is still rare, even where there are well-organized classroom libraries. Let's reconsider Kathy, the severely struggling reader described earlier who had a steady diet of "too hard" books and who became an avid, successful reader. Her tutoring and targeted instruction made it possible for her to read texts for understanding. But it was the massive amount of silent reading on self-selected texts that improved her fluency, motivation, comprehension, vocabulary, and background knowledge, turning her into a lifelong, self-determining reader.

It's important here to note the role of guided reading in promoting more silent reading. If we have matched students with texts they can actually read and understand, during guided reading we are mostly asking them to read silently, and we are observing where they need explicit instruction, scaffolding, or encouragement. I expect readers, even 1st graders by the second semester, to read silently almost all the time. I use oral reading mostly as a check that the book is at the right level; that is, students can read 95 percent of the words so they can focus on meaning. Keep in mind that for most of their time in school, students will be reading independently and that reading will be silent. That's how it is in the world, and that's how it needs to be in school. In fact, if we are to avoid summer reading loss by having students read profusely over the summer months, we need to ensure they already know how to read silently with understanding.

For our youngest readers, along with general classroom instruction, guided reading that is done well can be key for getting students to the point where they can make progress on their own through sustained, self-selected reading, which is mostly silent. This statement is as true for second language learners as it is for readers who struggle. That is, through selecting culturally relevant and interesting books with just a little bit of a challenge, doing a sufficient book introduction, providing necessary background information, explaining and practicing words students might not be able to figure out on their own, and teaching and practicing the skills and strategies students need to read with understanding, students gain the skills and confidence necessary to read on their own.

A vital factor that holds students back from becoming more independent is that we sometimes assume that they need more support than they do. For example, we spend so much time on prereading activities such as explaining vocabulary, previewing every page in the text, and reading pages together that we rob students of the necessary sustained time to read and the opportunity to solve problems and figure out what's happening in the text. While prereading strategies and a text with just the right amount of challenge are necessities for the struggling reader, we have to be careful not to give away the whole story and to be more of the guide-on-the-side. When we assume responsibility for doing all the reading work and thinking, especially when we have done a good job frontloading and they can do "the work," we keep students too dependent on us. That dependency can ultimately limit their confidence and their ability to read and self-monitor.

Confer with Students Daily

As noted in Chapter 3, I depend on one-on-one reading conferences for in-depth assessment and instruction for every reader. Most of these conferences take place during independent reading time, so they are not hard to fit in. For example, our independent reading time usually lasts anywhere from 20 to 50 minutes—depending on the grade level and the students' needs—and while a typical reading conference lasts from 15 to 20 minutes, most students need to be seen only occasionally to ensure they are comprehending. For readers who struggle, consistent reading conferences can change their reading trajectory.

Research confirms that the interactions around text that take place in a reading conference are especially important for readers who struggle and that individual reading conferences can increase independent reading effectiveness.[69] The celebration of the reader's strengths, assessment of comprehension, effective feedback, review, and teaching targeted to the learner's most important needs for moving forward all contribute to the reader's continuing progress and growing confidence.

Perhaps most important of all, we are providing the targeted reading guidance that is especially crucial for our struggling readers. This last statement also holds true for writing. My many years of conducting writing conferences, especially public writing conferences, confirm that these conferences have the power to turn students into writers and, also, readers.[70]

Embrace Whole-Part-Whole Teaching

Teaching and learning are easier and more efficient for us and for our students when we begin with a whole text in reading and writing. The brain is a pattern finder, and when students can't see how or why the pieces fit together in a meaningful whole, they shut down. Moving from a part-to-whole teaching approach to a whole-part-whole teaching emphasis is one of the biggest and most important shifts teachers make on their way to becoming more effective, efficient, and joyful. Essentially, this shift to a more holistic teaching approach results from a shift in beliefs about teaching and learning. Starting with a whole text, even in kindergarten, makes meaning and purpose more apparent.

The underlying premise of whole-part-whole teaching seems counterintuitive. We often think that our most struggling students need and benefit from a part-to-whole approach, which teaches skills in isolation and assumes that all the parts will eventually add up to a complete whole. In fact, just the opposite is true. Students never do see the big picture and have difficulty making meaning. A 1st grade teacher described it this way:

> My students came to me this year with all the skills, but they are not good readers and writers. Most of them came knowing about 75 sight words, but they couldn't read them in context and there was no transfer to their writing. They know all the letter sounds and combinations. When asked what they do when they encounter a tricky word, they can

Quick Win

Put student needs before schedules. There's less need for intervention if we change instruction to meet the needs of all learners.

rattle off strategies, but they are still not able to apply these. They have the hammers, nails, and bricks but don't know how to build a house because they haven't yet had enough exposure to the big and meaningful picture of literacy. Saddest of all, the desire to read, think, and learn is not there. It's been killed with all that skills work.[71]

In fact, skills-in-isolation teaching is one of several factors that low-performing schools have in common.[72] Moving all teachers and administrators to a whole-part-whole approach requires the staff to meet in vertical teams and discuss their beliefs about teaching and learning as part of an ongoing, thoughtful, and intentional Professional *Literacy* Community. The results can be profound. Two teachers' shifts through such professional development changed instruction for their students learning English as a second language and greatly accelerated students' literacy progress, engagement, and enjoyment. Their stories follow.

Put Second Language Learners on a Fast Track to Achievement

Too many second language learners remain stuck at low proficiency, do not acquire the academic language necessary to succeed in school, and become disengaged from school.[73] Once students are teetering on the edge of failure, it's difficult to intervene in a way that accelerates their progress so they catch up with higher-achieving peers. Prevention, truly, is the best intervention.

Sharlline Markwardt, the experienced English language development (ELD) teacher introduced in Chapter 1, had always taught part-to-whole. "As a specialist, I felt I was just supposed to teach the 'parts' and that the classroom teacher was responsible for the 'whole.'"[74] Moving to a whole-part-whole instructional model was a huge shift for her, requiring two years of PLC involvement that led to much rethinking. Not only did Sharlline change how and where she delivered her instruction, her students' achievement in English language proficiency improved so much that she successfully lobbied to have all ELD teachers in her district move to a push-in model. Sharlline reports with excitement:

> You should see our assessment scores! Ever since we implemented the "push-in model" of ELD and we shifted our thinking towards whole-part-whole, our ELD kids have been ROCKING on their ELPA

[English Language Proficiency Assessment]. We met ALL of our ELD goals for this year, yes, even the ones required by the state, and now other schools are coming to observe how we run the program.[75]

Perhaps more important than the high scores is that English language development students now see themselves as an accepted part of the school culture, and all students are benefiting from the push-in model.

> It used to be that the ELD kids felt "different"; they were taken out of the classroom and other kids questioned them about where they were going. Before push-in, one student actually said to me, "Mrs. M., I know why we go with you! It's because I'm Mexican, he's Mexican, and he's Mexican" (he pointed to the other students getting ready to come with us). I could see the look of embarrassment on their faces, the "Oh no, we have to go... again."
>
> The first year we did the push-in model we asked the ELD students, "What did you like about staying in your classrooms?" The answers were consistent and eye-opening: "We don't have to leave our friends." "It's not embarrassing to be ELD" and similar comments. But now? ALL students in the classroom are benefiting from language development strategies, cooperative teaching, and just good old teamwork. Our school culture has changed from one of exclusion to inclusion. All of our students see themselves as language learners for life! It's part of the culture; it's who we are.[76]

Heather Woodroof is a middle school teacher with 15 years of teaching experience who had always relied on daily oral language (DOL) exercises in isolation to teach grammar concepts to all her students, including her large number of English language learners.

> My rationale was that by spending ten minutes editing two sentences each day, my students would have covered up to twenty-five concepts by the end of a week. It just seemed impossible to replicate that in an authentic way.[77]

Heather began to question her beliefs after reading, viewing, and thinking about a whole-part-whole approach to teaching. She took a risk when she and her students created a book for newcomers to the classroom and embedded all the components students typically struggled with into the authentic writing. Heather notes the experience was rewarding for everyone.

I was amazed! Students were so engaged and willing to write. They were so critical of their first draft, revising and editing using so many concepts and skills. The icing on the cake came when on the second day we received a new student! HA! My class thought I had some inside information but I didn't. Now the audience and purpose were real. The new student would actually need to know how to complete reading folder homework and all the things we'd written about. The whole experience was great and also a lot of fun. The risk was worth it! We're now learning grammar concepts very differently.[78]

Heather also notes that her students applied what they'd learned to all writing. Her use of DOL became infrequent and limited to supplemental practice of embedded minilessons for her beginner students.

Finally, another important factor for accelerating second language learners is that based on assumptions or assessments that may be incorrect or incomplete, we may not fully know what second language learners can do—or cannot do—on their own. As with guided reading, too much support when students may be ready to do more on their own or with minimal guidance prevents students from assuming learning responsibilities they can handle and gives students the message that they are not capable.

Write Whole, Meaningful Texts as a Catalyst to Acceleration

> **Quick Win**
>
> *Don't go on too long.* Finish most writing pieces—from draft to publication—within a week or two to maintain energy and enthusiasm for the work.

Embracing whole-part-whole teaching accelerates learning in unexpected ways and can change the learning projection for a struggling student. Owen was a low-performing student who was failing to learn to read and write successfully despite his well-intentioned and caring teachers. When I met him in the fall of 2nd grade, he was subsisting on a diet of skills-in-isolation, worksheets, and story starters. Not much was expected of Owen, and he was fulfilling those low expectations. So when Owen raised his hand and volunteered to have a public, scaffolded conversation as part of our frontloading before students went off to write, the observing teachers let out an audible gasp. One of them later told me they were all thinking, "What's she going to do with Owen? Everyone knows he can't do much." Owen had struggled mightily since kindergarten, but I knew nothing of what he could and couldn't do.

I asked Owen to tell me his "Secrets of 2nd Graders" story, the whole of it. As he told his story, I asked genuine questions—not to interrupt him or make the story longer or to have him add more details—but because I was interested in what this student was trying to say and wanted to help him say it in a way that would do his story justice and appeal to his readers.

Celebration feedback to Owen

In a public conference with the whole class looking on, Owen read his story aloud. Unknown to me at the time, it was the first complete story Owen had ever written in school. But he was prepared. He had witnessed my oral storytelling and demonstration writing on a mischievous secret I had when I was his age; he had had a public scaffolded conversation with me about his story, and he had listened in on two other public scaffolded conversations. I did a second oral reading of his story all the way through so students and I could get a sense of the whole piece.

Watching TV

One night when I was 5 I was watching TV in bed with the lights off. It was past my bedtime. I heard Mom's footsteps in the kitchen. I jumped out of bed. I turned the TV off. She was checking on me. I pretended to be asleep. "Owen, were you watching TV?" I kept pretending to be asleep. Mom went back to the kitchen. Then when I got out of bed, I caught Mom watching TV.

In a third reading, I went line by line and commented on everything Owen had done well. Notice that the comments (on the next page) focus in on the specific language Owen used. The purpose of this feedback here was twofold.

• If the writer has done something well, celebrate it so he is encouraged to "do it" again. He must know what the "it" is, so feedback such as "good beginning" or "I like your ending" are not helpful in that regard, as the listener doesn't know what to replicate.

- Give language specifics—the writer's exact words and techniques—so other writers can "try and apply" what a peer or other author has successfully done well or attempted to do well.

My Feedback to Owen

On the title: "Watching TV." What a great title. In just two words, you've let the reader know what your story is about. And what is really clever, Owen, is that it was not just about you watching TV; it's also about your mom watching TV. Kids, when you go back and reread your story, check to see that you have a title as good as the one Owen has.

First line, content and rhythm, setting: [Reread opening line aloud.] "One night when I was 5, I was watching TV in bed with the lights off." What a great opening, Owen. In this one sentence we know that you were 5, you were watching TV; we know where you are, that it's nighttime and that you're in bed. I love the way that opening sounds. And you put us right there in the setting. So, when all of you go back to your seats and reread your stories, make sure you have an opening as good as Owen's.

Connecting opening line with second line: [Reread first two lines aloud.] "It was past my bed time." I love the way that sounds with your opening. I love the rhythm of the first two lines.

Slowing down the writing: "I heard Mom's footsteps in the kitchen." I can picture that. I love the way you've slowed the writing down and put us in that moment. You're listening for your mom. I can feel suspense building. "I jumped out of bed." I can picture you doing that, and I know what's coming next. "I turned the TV off." And look, kids, [showing paper to class] how Owen put in a caret to add in "I turned the TV off." That also shows you were rereading your story. That's what good writers do to be sure the writing makes sense and to see if they want to change anything or add something.

Elaborating on the moment: "She was checking on me. I pretended to be asleep." I love the way those words sound together [read it aloud again], and I can visualize the scene.

Use of conversation to move story forward: Owen, I think you're one of the first people to use conversation. You wrote, "Owen, were you watching TV?" I can hear your mom's voice right there, and I feel the suspense building.

Effective repetition of wording: "I kept pretending to be asleep." I love the way you've almost repeated an earlier line. Good writers sometimes use repetition to emphasize an action.

Strong sense of effective closure; use of humor: And, then, Owen, your ending was amazing. The reader just knows your story is over. You can just feel that sense of closure. "Mom went back to the kitchen. Then when I got out of bed, I caught Mom watching TV." And you made the audience laugh. It was funny when you wrote, "Then when I got out of bed, I caught Mom watching TV." We call that humor. Good writers deliberately try to do that. Kids, when you reread your stories, check to see your story has a sense of closure and that you've also done some of the good things Owen has done as a writer.

The fascinating part of this celebration feedback to Owen is that it changed his life in and out of school. He stood up taller, became more engaged in his work, grew as a writer and a reader, and behaved with increasing confidence as a learner. He also began to be treated as the capable student he potentially could be. His kind and caring teachers began to expect much more from him and gave him the expert teaching, support, and encouragement he needed to do more meaningful and challenging work.

A troublesome part of this story is that I have shared Owen's draft with thousands of educators. I give the audience Owen's background and ask them what feedback they would give to Owen on his writing—that is, what are the words they would speak to him if they were having a public conference or one-on-one conference with him. Almost without exception, whether the educator is a teacher, a literacy coach, a specialist, an administrator, or a college professor, those that volunteer to give feedback focus on the skills and parts of the writing and on what else Owen needs to do to make his writing better. I have only once had an educator say—and it was a high school teacher—that the writing was good enough because "he has a captivating lead; the piece is sequenced and well organized; he is aware of his audience; the rhythm and length of his sentences are varied and interesting; he used humor; the ending makes the reader feel closure." That secondary school teacher added, "I wish all my high school students could do that."

Acceleration leads to sustainable success: Owen has the last word

I have kept in touch with Owen for more than a decade through letters and e-mail messages. As of this writing, he is an average, happy student in his final year of high school. He still mentions his success in writing as a 2nd grader as a turning point. In an e-mail message written as an 11th grader, he says, "I have been doing good since second grade. Growing up through puberty was a pain though. My grades are good right now. It seems physics is my strong suit at the moment."[79] Owen's most recent e-mail message (February 2014) indicates his intention to attend college.

Owen's story is ultimately a story of how probable intervention for a student who struggled mightily was eventually averted due to raised expectations, meaningful work, the excellent efforts of his teachers supported by a dedicated principal, and whole-part-whole teaching. Not to be minimized, it was ultimately the power of celebration that changed Owen's standing in the classroom and caused his peers, teachers, and Owen himself to see unimagined possibilities. When Owen was a 4th grader, he was asked what had ultimately changed for him and he reflected: "' I can do it' rised up. 'I can't do it' went to its grave."[80]

5

Leadership Priorities

It's not debatable. Effective leadership is essential for excellent schoolwide reading and writing practices across the curriculum, for creating a healthy school culture, and for sustaining achievement. A six-year study reviewing the research on leadership notes: "We have not found a single case of a school improving its student achievement record in the absence of talented leadership."[1] The authors of that research also confirm that the number-one influence on student achievement is effective classroom teaching. Based on my long-term experiences working in diverse schools, I would argue that effectiveness in literacy teaching and effectiveness in leading are inseparable and equally significant when we are talking about whole-school achievement. It's only when we look at achievement of particular teachers that literacy trumps leadership.

If we look at the whole school—and I believe that we must for sustainable gains—then literacy and leadership are equal partners. That is, the quality of teachers and the quality of leaders are the two most important variables in a school.[2] *School leadership matters as much as teacher quality.*[3]

This chapter highlights significant behaviors and actions of effective leaders, which lead to accelerated achievement for both students and teachers. We'll look at the importance of ensuring strong principal and teacher leadership, how to put into practice the qualities of successful leaders, and the role of daily instructional walks by the principal.

Ensure High-Quality Leadership

Outstanding leaders are at the heart and soul of any successful organization. I define a leader as "someone who recognizes what needs to be done for the

When arranging for teacher observation within a school, make the match appropriate. That is, ensure that the difference in effectiveness between the two teachers is not so great that the observing teacher will leave overwhelmed.

good of the organization, initiates ideas, welcomes and seeks others' input and suggestions, and then takes appropriate action to help guide the organization to move forward in a respectful and collaborative manner."[4] These leaders know how and when to innovate, motivate, change direction, listen to learn, collaborate, give clear explanations, and admit mistakes. They make the need for worthwhile change apparent, provide the tools to help people succeed, and support them in a customized, personal, and respectful manner. They are able to do all these things because they have earned the respect and trust of their teachers and community and have established a school culture of collaboration and shared learning.

Foster Principal Success

One of my biggest learning lessons has been that without strong principal leadership, nothing much of significance happens related to improved, schoolwide literacy achievement. More than anyone else, the principal sets the tone, the expectations for student learning, and the trust level in the building. Although strong teacher leadership is also crucial, it must be partnered with steady principal leadership. Among other actions, an effective principal does the following:

- Models high expectations through his or her behaviors—is hands-on and directly involved in improving instruction and learning for all.
- Promotes collegiality and shared learning every day.
- Creates daily opportunities for teachers to collaborate.
- Fosters a culture of trust and risk taking that includes nonjudgmental listening, respect for divergent viewpoints, as well as evidence of caring and honesty.
- Ensures the school's shared vision is actualized.
- Guarantees a challenging and viable content-rich curriculum.
- Exhibits intellectual and emotional intelligence—is an eager learner and is able to "read" people and to cultivate healthy relationships.
- Manages time well, prioritizes, and puts student learning first.
- Values high-quality professional development and works to embed it into the life of the school.
- Makes sure the "distractors" don't outweigh the talented majority.

Vitally important, the principal must be a "leading learner"[5] who possesses personality traits such as curiosity and desire to learn along with humility, respect for others, and "adaptability above all else."[6] In my experience, if principals see themselves as learners first—that is, they value learning, want to learn, and know how to learn—then even if they do not yet know what effective literacy practices look and sound like, they can and do learn those practices. The caveat is the principal must also be flexible and open to new ideas, work extremely well with people, and possess strong leadership skills. *Leadership and literacy must form a tight weave to ensure that achievement gains will not unravel.*

Alonzo Lopez was a successful and esteemed high school principal. He became a leading learner after he was transferred to a failing elementary school in his district as a last resort to save the school before it was to be closed. Because Alonzo saw himself as a learner first, he became equally successful in his new role. Although he knew little about teaching reading and writing to K–5 students, he spent the entire first year building trust—listening carefully to teachers, students, families, and community members; getting a strong infrastructure in place; setting up a leadership team to guide professional development; and visiting classrooms daily and celebrating the positive things he observed. Right from the start, he honestly acknowledged that literacy was not his strong suit, and he sought the support of teachers to learn more. By the end of his second year, the school had become one of the highest-performing Title I schools in the state.

A critical part our job as educators and one that is not much talked about is that we need to support our principals and do our part to help them succeed. The aforementioned school's achievement was not just due to the principal's efforts and leadership. Increasingly, as trust built and teachers in the school felt valued and cared for, many of them—even those who were skeptical at first—rallied to support their new principal to ensure he learned what he needed to know about literacy. Ongoing professional development that was centered around improving literacy practices also played a major role in increased learning across the school. Lasting achievement across a whole school depends on a close working partnership and collaboration between and among the principal, classroom teachers, specialists, coaches, and all members of the school community. Positive teacher leadership makes it more likely that a principal will be successful.

Finally, attention to principal leadership is especially crucial for middle and high schools where expertise and leadership in literacy are more often lacking than at the elementary school level. The structures, relationships,

Quick Win

See the learning and literacy process at K–5, 6–8, 9–12 as connected, with similar goals. What's different are the complexity and length of texts, level and intensity of support needed, and amount of deliberate practice needed for success.

and history of the principal as an authority figure all contribute to maintenance of the status quo. Typically, principals in middle and high schools do not have frequent and direct contact with teachers in their classrooms. In fact, teachers report that it is rare for an administrator to be in their classrooms. For larger schools with high-poverty populations, it is also the norm that principal leadership is more likely to be weak compared with the leadership in high-achieving schools.[7] All these factors point to the imperative for improving and supporting principal leadership.

Promote Teacher Leadership

Although the principal's leadership is crucial for schoolwide achievement, teacher-leaders are also essential to the highly functioning school. Because the role of principal as instructional leader is often not adequately defined, supported, and protected, we must depend on teacher-leaders to take the lead in improving instructional practices across a school. Yet, although teachers as leaders constitute a growing movement in schools, in my experience the concept is still atypical. Because research suggests that "collective leadership has a stronger influence on student achievement than individual leadership,"[8] we need to promote and mentor shared leadership for optimal learning across a school and district. In fact, "when a school has one or two good teachers, it is usually a matter of individual initiative. But when a school has many good teachers, it is a result of leadership."[9]

Quick Win

Capitalize on the special talents of individual teachers— such as pacing, engaging students, questioning strategies, assessing while teaching, managing the classroom— and free up other teachers (regardless of grade level) to observe that colleague's techniques.

The same qualities that make principals highly effective also apply to teacher-leaders. Teacher-leaders can be classroom teachers, literacy coaches, specialist teachers, content-area teachers, special education teachers, librarians, staff developers, or interventionist teachers. Highly functioning teacher-leaders are the conscience of the school. They are willing to ask the hard questions, to stand up for what they believe, to reach out and nudge their colleagues on important issues, and to listen with an open mind to the concerns of others.[10] Teacher-leaders actively work to support and inform the principal in ways that benefit the whole school community.

Effective principals and experienced teacher-leaders can be highly successful in encouraging and mentoring the teacher-as-leader process. Just as with our students, progress in becoming teacher-leaders can be modest and uneven. Along with the principal, teacher-leaders commit to long-term, thoughtful, schoolwide improvement, which includes professional deliberation and debate about beliefs and practices in Professional *Literacy*

Communities. The most prominent role of the teacher-leader is often as a member of a school's leadership team or what some call a learning team or literacy leadership team. (See Chapter 6 for more on this topic.)

Take on the Qualities of Effective Leaders

Foremost among all leadership qualities is the ability to form, nurture, and sustain trusting and respectful relationships. Without those trusting relationships, not much of significance will happen for schoolwide achievement and a healthy school culture. Other necessary competences are the ability to communicate effectively in oral and written form, to hold and act upon high expectations, to establish a strong infrastructure, to be highly knowledgeable about literacy and curriculum, to give and receive effective feedback, and to monitor achievement using various forms of data. Additionally, acting with courage, humility, integrity, fairness, kindness, and equity is essential for successful leadership. Although the roles of principals and teacher-leaders are different, the essential qualities for being an effective leader are similar and apply to all leaders at all levels. As noted, because instructional leadership is less common at the secondary school level, high school principals need to be deliberate about creating and fostering trusting relationships if they expect to have a worthy instructional impact.

Build Trusting Relationships

Although many essential leadership skills are transparent and have been well documented, here I want to discuss the vital leadership traits that may be less heralded, partly because they are less transparent or less common in practice. These are qualities and actions that are relationship builders; that is, they are potential game-changers for a leader's success. These are qualities that are at the heart of a thriving and achieving school culture. Finally these are qualities that foster the development of a healthy infrastructure, which is essential for ensuring the optimal learning conditions that promote opportunity to learn for all students.

The hard truth is we can have clear and measurable goals, a focus on important and challenging work, effective data teams, and a great mission statement; but without a culture of high trust and healthy relationships, none of those factors matter much. We simply won't have people who want to be at the school, and we won't get best performances from teachers, staff, or students. A culture that lets people know we are their partners and will support them, even when the going gets rough, is a culture that attracts and keeps the "right" kind of people and motivates them to do the work we have set out to do. Yet, although a positive and nurturing school culture is foundational for continuous improvement in a school, principals typically receive little training or preparation in this area. When leaders understand how crucial trusting relationships are to the school's climate and culture, they seek to intentionally build such relationships. Principals who establish a trusting school culture seem also to have a greater influence on academic achievement.[11] As well, trusting cultures experience less teacher turnover, which also makes whole-school achievement more likely.

Celebrate teachers

Celebration is at the heart of all effective teaching and leading. That is, we honestly let the learner know, whether it's a teacher or student, exactly what he or she has done well or attempted to do. "Celebration is not just the actions we take or the words we use; it's a mindset and demeanor that propel us to primarily see, observe, and value strengths."[12] Starting with genuine celebration is a necessity for creating a school culture in which raising and sustaining student achievement is possible. Celebration must come before evaluation if teachers are to value and benefit from formal evaluations, which compel some teachers into a rigid teaching mold due to fear and pressure to excel.[13]

Even a short, simple note can affirm and encourage. A 2nd grade teacher who attended an Urgency and School Change Conference in Seattle in 2013 comments on taking on the role of leader and beginning with celebration:

> My mind has been very focused since leaving the conference. That night I decided to identify the teachers in our school that will work for positive change, both professionally and urgently, and get in their rooms. The following day, I asked one of our kindergarten teachers if I could visit. She opened her doors and the experience was wonderful. I wrote her a note on a post-it and she beamed. I then went to a 5th grade teacher (same day) and she said she heard I was leaving sticky notes in teachers' classrooms and said she'd like to be a part of all this. Hurray!![14]

Here are some suggestions for celebration:

- *Develop a celebratory school culture.* Such a culture means affirming principals, too. Principals typically don't get celebrated enough. As one teacher said, "I don't verbally give my principal enough positives."
- *Begin all conferences with celebration.* That is, adopt a mindset of noticing and naming strengths, and begin there.
- *Include celebration—of teacher work and of student work—in PLC or PD meetings.*
- *Celebrate efforts and risk taking.* Success often comes after lots of trial and error. We need to demonstrate that small failures can lead to moments of learning and eventual success. By publicly acknowledging a colleague's or student's effort, we make it safe to take a risk and try again.

Let yourself be known

Although our colleagues and staff may respect us, to earn their full trust they have to see and know our human side. A highly knowledgeable principal that I worked with for many years had the admiration and respect of all her staff, but she never gained their full trust. Deliberately, to guard her privacy, she shared almost nothing about her personal life—not even small details. That made it hard for some to fully trust her, which made it challenging for her to lead the whole staff where she wanted them to go. Although she led with integrity and fairness, she never became a highly successful principal in the eyes of her teachers. The truth is we trust the people we come to know and understand at their core, and for that to happen we have to see their human and personal side.

Bringing our own personalities, interests, and backgrounds into our schools makes the work more meaningful and authentic. Here are some ways to do that:

- *Share stories.* Personal stories humanize us. Tell stories and anecdotes you are comfortable publicly sharing. They don't have to be intensely personal, just honest accounts that allow staff, students, and families to know you a little better.
- *Promote a caring and more humane school culture.* As leaders we set the culture, or climate, of the school, which determines how well people can work together and succeed—teachers, students, and their families. Much

of what binds people together are the stories we know about each other's lives.

With my work in schools, whenever possible we try to schedule an after-school potluck or dinner out together as a staff. It's a deliberate attempt for all of us to get to know each other beyond our classrooms. Learning about each other's hobbies, families, dreams, and concerns in a social setting increases trust levels and makes it easier to work together.

Listen without judgment

Listening is often cited as necessary to leadership, but it's not enough to set aside time to listen. As leaders, we need to try to understand the needs of the person who is talking to us and to create a caring listening environment. Here are some things to keep in mind to become a better listener:

• *Be engaged.* Do not do anything else but listen with an open mind. Be thinking, "What is this person trying to say?" "How might I be able to help?" Do not let your own agenda take over the conversation.
• *Make no assumptions.* Sometimes someone just wants to be heard and is not seeking conversation, advice, or a solution. Ask something like, "Do you want me to respond in any way?"
• *Be open to feedback.* Be willing to rely on others in your work environment to help examine your own behaviors.

Tolerate ambiguity and uncertainty

Successful leaders recognize that they must project a confident outlook that includes an openness to changing direction based on new evidence and experiences.

• *Be willing to change course when it's warranted.* Flexibility is required for any successful venture. Rarely do things go exactly as planned.
• *Recognize that we're on a journey; we're not in a race.* It's going to take time, false starts, and team effort to approach the finish line.
• *Welcome divergent thinking wherever possible,* even when you disagree.
• *Let teachers know that while you don't know for certain at this time, based on your knowledge, facts, and data, this recommended action makes the most sense.* Most teachers will be on board if you have earned their trust.

• *Don't be afraid to challenge the status quo and propose reasonable alternatives* when district initiatives seem to be in conflict with beneficial instructional practices.

Nurture resilience

Successful leaders create a culture of resilience. "Resilience is defined as remaining steadfast in the face of destabilizing conditions. Resilience can also be defined as having more protective factors than risk factors."[15] Some protective factors that schools can provide to increase educational success include fostering caring relationships, conveying high expectations, and promoting opportunities for meaning participation.[16] "The evidence suggests that with the right supports, many young people can reach levels of success that neither they nor most adults around them thought possible."[17] Research confirms that one person can make a difference in helping students defy the odds.[18] Research also tells us that high-quality relationships are especially important, and that for children who have faced "higher levels of risk," a supportive school environment matters a lot.[19]

Resilience makes it possible to rebound from difficulties and to maintain hope even in the midst of adversity. Here are some specific actions that can help create resilience:

• *Reduce vulnerability factors.* Providing meals, clothing, after-school activities, counseling, free books to keep, and whatever else is possible to keep students safe, warm, comfortable, and well cared for will make it easier for them to learn. Some schools now offer free breakfasts in classrooms for all students so students from backgrounds of poverty are not further stigmatized.
• *Mentor students and teachers who are floundering.* Such mentoring might include counseling or acting as an older brother or sister.
• *Share the research on resilience with teachers and students,* and let them know what you and others are doing to help them become resilient.
• *Work to change learners' mindsets.* Students' mindsets about learning predict what they can and will accomplish.[20] If students think failure or low performance is likely—or that they're not smart enough—they probably won't bother to try or their effort will be limited.[21] I believe this to be true for teachers as well.

- *Remain hopeful.* Overcoming the hard realities of poverty is a "tumultuous and uncertain task, but it can be done.... It's worth remembering that sheer grit, and a helping hand, can sometimes blaze trails where none seem possible."[22]
- *Help learners develop grit.* That is, through encouragement, supportive actions, and sharing our own experiences, let them know hard-earned success requires drive, a will to win, and a spirit that doesn't quit.

Fostering resilience is also important for our high-achieving students, some of whom are less likely to take on a challenge if they fear failure or a lower grade. We need to help them recognize and value that persistent efforts, accompanied by setbacks, are part of the journey to worthwhile accomplishments.

Demonstrate fairness

Fair-mindedness and impartiality are critical attributes for successful leadership and the willingness of the entire group to work together and to follow their leader. One principal I greatly admired had terrific interpersonal skills with parents and community members, so I was surprised to learn that some teachers referred to peers as "being on the A team" while they were only on the B team or the C team. Their feelings of hurt ran deep and appeared to be unknown by the principal, who carried on with her usual cheerful, confident manner without ever gaining the trust of about one-third of her staff. Without fairness to all, we limit possibilities for whole-school achievement, which depends on collaboration and cooperation. It can be helpful to keep these points in mind:

- Work hard not to show favoritism.
- Give feedback with evidence, not judgment.
- Know the research on pay-for-performance. Performance pay does not work any better than just paying people fairly. Most people want fairness, not incentives that promote unhealthy competition. "When we think we are somehow being manipulated or controlled by rewards and punishments, our sense of autonomy is threatened, and then we rebel (albeit subconsciously) by refusing to do, or by doing the opposite of, what is desired."[23]

Rethink use of time

One of the most important gifts we can give to colleagues is time to work together. A survey report from the National Center for Literacy Education revealed that the professional learning that educators across all grade levels and content areas value most is coplanning with colleagues.[24] New requirements for evaluations and implementation of standards, for example, can exhaust us, as rarely is anything taken away when a new mandate is added to our load. Collaboration, on the other hand, can lighten our workload. How and where we spend our time says a lot about what we value.

Here are some ways to allocate time to promote collaboration:

- *Build in time for coplanning and collaboration.* After staff members have a shared understanding of what collaboration is, intentionally build time for planning and collaborating. (Note that often there is confusion between *collaborating* and *cooperating*; collaboration goes beyond cooperation and collegiality to increase a person's sense of efficacy, confidence, and openness to new ideas.) Time to collaborate and learn together increases the flow and exchange of ideas, as well as efficiency and enjoyment in our practices, and it leads to greater learning for us adults. Shared learning by educators also leads to deeper learning for students.[25]
- *Spend more time with teachers who can mentor others.* As one principal lamented, "I'm spending most of my time watering the rocks instead of the flowers." Although we need to do what we can to support teachers who are struggling, that effort should not supersede empowering strong teachers who can then teach others and thereby raise the level of teaching and collaboration schoolwide, as well as lighten our load.
- *Extend professional development meetings.* Many schools allow scant time for professional development. Many of us have found that when we extend worthwhile professional development meetings on a voluntary basis and "trade time"—for example, allow teachers to leave early on a Friday in exchange for staying longer on another day—most teachers choose to stay and participate.
- *Create flexible time structures.* Enlist teacher-leaders to work on a school schedule that makes common planning time possible, puts students' needs ahead of specialists' schedules, and promotes such in-school ventures as

> ### *Quick Win*
>
> *Take something away in one area if you are asking more from teachers in another area—for example, let teachers leave early when they have voluntarily stayed longer at a PLC or PD meeting. Or hire a few roving substitutes (if funds permit) to give teachers uninterrupted time to write report cards, score writing samples, plan, or collaborate.*

peer tutoring across grade levels. Be sure to also arrange the schedule so teachers and leaders can come together on a regular basis.

Communicate differently with families

Effective teachers and leaders view families as valuable resources that have the potential to make our work with their children more productive. Our mindset toward students' families and how we communicate with them is vital for maximizing student achievement.

- *Use social media.* You are more likely to get the attention of busy families through e-mail and social media sites such as Twitter and Facebook. Traditional printed newsletters are often ignored—even when successfully delivered.
- *Assume best intentions* of parents and caregivers, as you don't know what challenges they may be facing. A comment such as "I know you wanted to be at your son's conference. Let's talk about when we can reschedule" (instead of "You missed your son's conference, and it's going to be difficult to find a time to reschedule") makes it more likely parents will be willing to partner with you.
- *Include welcoming messages* as the first communications families see upon entering the school. These might include brochures on helping with homework, a listing of upcoming events for families, or information about how to read to and with their child. Information might be in the form of a pamphlet but could also be a website or video or interactive medium.
- *Spend more time with parents and families.* Families are educators' best public relations tool. Promote family nights, game and movie nights, and special events unrelated to academics to bring families to the school. When parents feel welcome and supported in and by the school, they are more likely to trust us and work cooperatively. If they feel satisfied with their child's teachers and education, they are our biggest boosters.
- *Ensure messages are easy to understand.* Keep messages concise and clear, and have communications available in English and in the other languages spoken by families in your school.

Take on the role of coach

Effective leaders are excellent coaches—and coaches who are excellent at their jobs are also leaders. Coaches take the lead to ensure that learning

---

Quick Win

Send home positive notes stating and describing something the student is doing well; include kind acts and effort as well as academic achievement.

Quick Win

Call families early in the school year with compliments so when you need to call with a concern, the family is more likely to be receptive.

occurs. I define a coach as a side-by-side teacher-learner—someone who is not just handing out resources and giving advice and suggestions, but is also teaching and mentoring, as well as supporting and giving useful feedback. What follows are some key actions of expert coaches:

- *Assume the role of mentor.* It's difficult to help a person move forward until that person has some self-awareness. Here are five useful questions to pose when mentoring:

    1. What is it that you really want to be and do?
    2. What are you doing really well that is helping you get there?
    3. What are you not doing well that is preventing you from getting there?
    4. What will you do differently tomorrow to meet those challenges?
    5. How can I help, and where do you need the most help?[26]
       Have the person restate what was said in this conversation.

- *Apply the Optimal Learning Model.* That is, demonstrate and make explicit the purpose and actions of exactly what you want the teacher or student to do. Then—and this is the crucial step that is often omitted from coaching—do side-by-side teaching (the "we do it") before expecting the teacher to try out the lesson.

- *Give effective feedback.* Initially, lead the debrief following a teacher's lesson that you have observed by stating what went well and, perhaps, making one or more suggestions. However, as the teacher demonstrates readiness, move to having the teacher—with your encouraging support and guidance—increasingly take on the role of self-evaluation and goal setting.

Demonstrate thoughtful reflection

Successful leaders in any field deliberately strive to gain insights from their own words and actions. Demonstrating a willingness to be open and reflective models a behavior we want from all team members and from our students as well. Even when we have been mostly successful, it is useful to think and speak aloud our responses to inner questions such as these:

- What have I learned?
- What might I do differently next time?
- Did I hear all the voices? Who did most of the talking?

Quick Win

Provide professional development stipends for teachers who attend and participate in PD. Stipends are for teachers who come before school, stay after school, or attend a Saturday session. Often districts have a per-hour stipend, or half-day/full-day stipends that can be earned over a period of time—for example, $100 for four one-hour sessions completed on the third Wednesdays in September, October, November, and January.

- Have my words and actions empowered others?
- Are my words and actions helping to build a culture of trust, risk taking, and shared learning?
- Have I requested feedback from others and acted upon that feedback?

Such inner questioning also demonstrates our curiosity and desire to learn more and do better.

Show gratitude

Effective leaders let the people they work with know their contributions are integral to realizing a school's vision, goals, and higher achievement. Give the message through words and deeds: "You're important. We couldn't do this job without you."

- *Begin staff meetings by celebrating something going well.* It could be celebrating teachers for applying what you've been focusing on in PD meetings or something nonacademic such as having students enter the school in an orderly fashion. We are all more likely to be open to suggestions once we've been acknowledged for our positive actions.
- *Thank people for their efforts.* This includes peers, custodians, secretaries, students, families, teachers, principals, and administrators. It takes only a moment or a minute or two to express sincere gratitude, but that may be enough to propel the person on the receiving end to continue to invest in the work.

Practice attentiveness

Being able to successfully lead in a school and a district depends on emotional and social intelligence that makes us wholly present in the moment. Although full attentiveness depends on active listening, the kind of attentiveness that makes us more effective leaders goes beyond that. United States Supreme Court Justice Sonia Sotomayor says it this way:

> Leveraging emotional intelligence in the courtroom, as in life, depends on being attentive; the key is always to watch and listen.... What holds a jury's attention, essentially, is the quality of one's own attention. If you are palpably present in the moment, continuously mindful of and responsive to your listeners, they will follow where you lead. If, however, you are reading from a script, droning on as though they weren't

there, soon enough they won't be, irrespective of how unassailable your argument.[27]

That attentiveness includes being physically and emotionally available and removing possible barriers. Keeping an office door mostly closed, sitting behind a large desk, being unwilling to listen in a moment of fatigue, or multitasking while "listening" to a teacher may be all that it takes to lose momentum. When teachers and colleagues sense we are available, they are more likely to share with us a celebration, a concern, new thinking, or what they are processing in that exact moment. In fact, sometimes all it takes for people to advance their thinking and solve a problem on their own is to listen attentively and respectfully and to convey through words and body language that we have confidence in them to figure it out.

Display a sense of humor

Without some humor and a good laugh once in a while, it's hard to give our all to the serious work ahead of us each day—ensuring our students learn. Although it is difficult to find humor in tough circumstances, a good dose of humor goes a long way toward tackling overwhelming problems. In fact, our most effective leaders deploy humor and laughter more often than average leaders.[28] Myriad standards, cumbersome evaluation systems, the politics of education, and rigid rules can make it difficult to cope with the job of daily teaching and leading without feeling disheartened. We need to strive to instill a sense of humor into teaching and learning and to consider humor as essential to our emotional and intellectual health—and that of our students—as instructional expertise. Here are some ways to make this element part of day-to-day life:

- *Smile more.* Smiling and laughing don't just make us physically feel better, more relaxed, energetic, and hopeful; humor and mirth also increase our creativity and cognitive functioning.[29]
- *Apply the benefits of humor to the school and classroom.* Include comic books, joke books, and riddles in classroom libraries. Have a student joke or funny story of the day (preview with the student before the student shares it). Occasionally, begin professional development meetings with a funny story. (If we look hard—especially days, weeks, or even months later—we educators can often find some humor in a situation that initially seemed dismal.) Apply humor to demonstration writing and storytelling.

Include humorous read-alouds. Support teachers and students to be appropriately funny in their spoken and written words.

• *Use in-house closed-circuit TV* if classrooms have TVs or specially equipped LCD projectors or other technology tools to publicly share a humorous story or piece of writing.

Apply common sense

Not to be minimized, one of the most powerful tools strong leaders possess and use is common sense. That is, regardless of the current mandates, standards, and latest programs, assertive leaders provide the clarity, wisdom, and sense making that enable a school to move forward in a way that preserves the dignity of teachers and families and promotes the learning of students.

• *Put students before standards.* Instead of "Common Core Aligned" (the label often seen on the plethora of "new" materials from publishers), think "Common Sense Aligned."

• *Use the parts of core programs and resources that make sense; ignore what's not worth the time.* Effective leaders do not have teachers marching in lock-step or with everyone literally on the same page.

• *Minimize test-preparation time.* There is no research that indicates that test prep increases learning or achievement. In fact, students who take part in excessive drilling may actually do worse—and, surely, they enjoy school and learning less. If we are expert teachers, the students do fine on the tests.

• *Advocate for sane and sensible practices.* Sometimes it becomes necessary to lobby for changing an unfair, disruptive, or unsound practice that does not serve our students or us well. In Seattle, where I live, high school teachers are no longer required to give what used to be a mandated test—all because of strong teacher advocacy.

Link audacity with humility

Strong leaders are bold. They are risk takers who will go out on a limb for a worthy goal. At the same time they are modest, not boastful or prideful, in their demeanor and actions. The following quote from a highly successful business leader says it well:

You've got to be audacious enough to set goals that make you stretch and give you clarity of vision and purpose. But you have to have the humility to know that this work is hard, and that you might not get there. If you start off talking about all the reasons that you're not going to get there, you're not going to get there. And so it's holding that balance of not being reckless, but also having a huge element of fearlessness.[30]

Display a spirit of generosity

Through mentorship and encouragement, strong leaders help others succeed. Such leaders become "multipliers." That is, they "recognize the intelligence in others, provoke it, and cultivate it to its fullest."[31] Make it possible and easy for others to contribute by allowing some choice, providing needed emotional space, leaving room for others to make their ideas known, encouraging divergent thinking, and not dominating the discussion. "Share the leader's views last, after hearing other people's views."[32] One of Nelson Mandela's greatest talents was his practice of leading from behind by encouraging the views of others before summarizing those opinions and guiding people toward action.[33] Generosity of spirit is also indicated by what we do to support colleagues when no one is looking and we're not expecting or deserving of personal recognition. One example is privately reassuring and praising colleagues for their efforts through comments, gestures, and notes.

> **Quick Win**
>
> *Offer to cover a class for an exhausted teacher* so he or she can visit another class or just take a needed break.

Make Daily Instructional Walks Integral to Higher Achievement

As previously mentioned but important enough to restate, principals have to know literacy if we are to raise and sustain schoolwide achievement. Recognizing this pivotal point from my work in diverse schools, I now spend half of my time in school residencies mentoring principals, and the major part of that mentorship involves demonstrating and coaching principals in what I call *instructional walks*. On an instructional walk, the principal is an actively engaged participant, interacting with the teacher and students in the classroom, with the sole goal of moving teaching and learning forward.[34] Positive feedback and celebration, as well as instruction and coaching, are part of these essential walks.

Very crucial, the growing trust that results from instructional walks allows principals to balance affirmative feedback and support with suggestions delivered in a positive manner. Teachers welcome this celebratory and informal school routine and come to separate it from formal teacher evaluations. Formal evaluations can be fraught with anxiety, especially where principals are mandated to evaluate teachers on dozens of indicators and those evaluations carry undue weight in judging teacher competency. Instructional walks always strive to validate the teacher in a nonthreatening and supportive manner.

Defining Instructional Walks

Classroom instructional walks are a conceptually different concept from "walk-throughs" and "instructional rounds." Traditional walk-throughs are brief walks that typically last a few minutes and are often based on using a checklist of "look-fors" to collect data. The frequency of specific behaviors—related to literacy and other matters—is often tallied to assess where the staff is instructionally. It's often a hit-and-miss approach, with the principal hoping to find the teacher engaged in instruction on this quick visit. Typically, if the principal is spending about 30 minutes a day on walk-throughs, a teacher is seen once a week.

In instructional rounds, a group of educators (often a group of leaders from the school and the district) try to determine what a school's next steps should be when achievement is declining or stagnating and the school is not sure what instructional steps to take next to improve teaching and learning. By observing some teachers in their classrooms and analyzing their instructional practices along with student performance data, the group's goal is to support instructional improvement across a school.[35] During instructional rounds, the goal is not to improve the observed teacher's instruction or to give any comments to the teacher. Feedback to the teacher is reserved for formal observations and evaluations.

In an instructional walk we are looking first for the teacher's strengths, noticing where support is needed, and also discerning instructional patterns across a school. We are not just quietly observing and writing notes the teacher may or may not see, checking off look-fors, or collecting numerical data through a clicker. It is a process that respects both teacher and students. We are in the classroom to celebrate and support teachers, give positive feedback, move instruction forward, and increase the trust level between administrator and teachers across a school. On an instructional walk, the principal does the following:

- Notices what's going well in the classroom (environment, management, engagement, level of student independence, lesson content, grouping arrangements, quality of student work, level of discussion, and so on).
- Takes brief, nonjudgmental notes on what he or she observes going well and what needs attention.
- Comments orally or in writing (or both) on what's going well, making at least several positive comments to the teacher or students (or both).
- Suggests a strategy or an idea on the spot, if appropriate (and if the teacher is receptive and the relationship between the principal and teacher is a trusting one).
- Does not leave the classroom without letting the teacher know what he or she has observed.
- Revisits observational notes for whole-school patterns of strengths and needs.
- Uses those observations to determine and share schoolwide strengths and weaknesses (without naming a particular teacher or grade level).
- Leads the staff to determine next steps and actions.[36]

Even when, occasionally, the instructional walk is only five minutes long, time in the classroom is always an intentional learning visit, not a pop-in, pat-on-the-back stop. Every instructional walk is made with the eventual end goal of raising student achievement, which is especially crucial for our underperforming students in high-challenge schools. In addition, every visit is intended to support the teacher. Based on a history of principal-as-evaluator, teachers are often initially wary of this new role, but where principals go in with a respectful stance and a positive viewing lens— and as trust develops—teachers come to welcome their principal as coach, coteacher, and colleague. *Leaders need to first take on the role of supportive coach before taking on the role of evaluator.*

Trena Speirs is a superb example of an active principal-as-instructional-leader. She currently serves as a principal in a school where more than 90 percent of the students qualify for free and reduced lunch. She makes it her first priority to spend up to 50 percent of each day in classrooms. Teachers welcome her visits, and both she and the staff see firsthand the value of these instructional walks. Trena reflects on instructional walks.

Quick Win

Go with a leadership team member or two when you are trying on the process of instructional coach— for example, go with the literacy coach or a trusted teacher or colleague. The team member can repeat back to the principal (from notes taken) what was said to the teacher. Revisiting feedback language and actions can help build the role of principal-as-supportive-coach, thereby increasing the likelihood of developing positive communication and trust between the teacher and principal.

The time I spend in classrooms and with teachers and students is invaluable! As an instructional leader, it's imperative that I have a clear understanding of what is being taught and learned, schoolwide. This provides a catalyst for meaningful professional development and conversations, schoolwide. Additionally, spending time in classrooms further strengthens the relationships with teachers and students. It also sends a strong message to the community that learning is the heart of the work that goes on at our school each and every day.[37]

Once trust levels are established and teachers get used to seeing their principals in their classrooms, they welcome and request these visits. Fourth grade teacher Ann Thomson commented on the impact of a visit from the principal, literacy coach, and me: "It felt so affirming to have you, Kate, and Kim come in and give specific positive feedback on what the students and I were working on! I'm growing so much as a writing and reading teacher."[38]

Find the Time

Although it can be challenging to find the time for daily instructional walks, given all the ongoing demands of a principal's job, if we plan for these to happen and put them on the calendar for one hour each day, follow-through is more likely. We must, at least, try, because the payoff is huge. In my firsthand experience with instructional walks, I have seen a number of important advantages and outcomes. Of primary importance, instructional walks

- *Build trust and respect between the principal and teachers.* The principal is in the role of a supportive coach, not an evaluator, at this time.
- *Provide frequent opportunities for positive feedback.*
- *Offer a possible opportunity for teaching and coaching.*
- *Focus on collaboration and support*, not competition or "gotcha."
- *Encourage risk taking by teachers.*
- *Accelerate learning for students and the teacher.*
- *Highlight schoolwide trends*—both strengths and needs.
- *Improve the culture of the school* and help to build a "climate of change," with interdependence among and between all teachers and the principal.
- *Increase credibility with teachers.*
- *Reduce staff turnover.* It's rare for a teacher to choose to leave.

- *Give the principal a break.* Being with students in classrooms is where the joy is!
- *Put the role of principal-as-evaluator in perspective.* Because the principal's ongoing time in classrooms as coach and colleague is the major focus, the less frequent role of evaluator becomes less threatening to teachers.

Another big benefit is that instructional walks make it possible for the principal to encourage and support the strongest practitioners, who can then become even stronger and can mentor others—a win-win situation. Too often, conscientious principals spend most of their time with the weakest teachers, which can be draining and does not necessarily lead to substantial change.

Even where there is no assistant principal in the building, investigate if a teacher-leader, coach, secretary, or other staff member is willing to handle some of the inevitable crisis situations and unexpected demands that are part of any leadership job. From my experiences working closely with principals for many years, I have found that they are, as a whole, very kind-hearted and generous and often take on tasks that others could also do, if the principal would only let them. Conscientious principals look after their teachers, and conscientious teacher-leaders look after their principals and pitch in to help when they can.

For those who have difficulty "detaching," I recommend leaving the cell phone in the office and letting the secretary know not to disturb you unless there is a catastrophe, such as a missing child or a fire. Although this may sound extreme, there will always be something else that needs attention and pulls us away from being in classrooms. If we keep reminding ourselves that increased student learning is the true essence of the work we do, we will find the time and the will. It really is all about priorities.

Know What to Look For

Because the primary purpose of the instructional walk is always improved student learning through affirming and augmenting teachers' expertise, it's critical we know what to look for, what to say, and what to do. Knowing what to look for and what to say when we go into classrooms to support teachers and move learning forward—whether we're principals, coaches, or peers—is pivotal for any worthwhile change or improvement to occur. Well-intentioned people can waste a lot of time, for example, by

Quick Win

Do not interrupt instructional walks. In schools where administrators *must* carry emergency radios for security reasons, wear an earpiece so that radio calls do not disrupt visits to classrooms.

looking at student work when they lack foundational literacy knowledge accompanied by excellent relationship skills to make useful comments.

Knowing what to look for goes beyond literacy and the curriculum and includes taking a deliberate emotional and physical stance that will yield positive interactions with the teacher. It's a delicate dance, with the principal leading while carefully attending to, following, and anticipating the teacher's moves. Slowing down is essential for more enjoyment, better observations, and sufficient time to provide teacher support.

Keep key questions in mind

What follows are some key questions to keep in mind while observing in the classroom. This inner questioning is necessary for maximizing impact. These questions are not just for principals and leaders but also serve as self-reflection questions for classroom teachers, coaches, and literacy specialists.

- Who's doing most of the talking? Are all students' voices being heard?
- Are the language and conversations moving student learning forward?
- How are choices being provided for students?
- Are students spending most of their time reading and writing connected, meaningful texts?
- How do we know students are reading with understanding?
- Is assessment for learning, by teachers and students, taking place daily? (self-monitoring, self-checking, conferring)
- What are the expectations for writing in terms of topics, choice, frequency, correct conventions and spelling?
- Are students clear about the purpose of the lesson/activity? How do we know?
- Are there effective and sufficient demonstrations and shared experiences before moving to guided and independent practice?
- Is time being provided for sustained and deliberate practice?
- How are students being guided to be more independent and self-directed?
- Are the students' activities authentic—with an audience and purpose that matter—and with assessment that moves learning forward?
- How and when are students being celebrated?
- Are resources such as word walls and charts being used by students for self-checking?
- How are testing demands influencing instruction? For example, are writing prompts being overused and overemphasized?

- How are the beliefs of teachers and administrators influencing practices and achievement?
- Are students enjoying learning? How do we know?

Focus on the big picture of literacy

Deliberately, I focus on the whole of literacy in an instructional walk. As in the poetry writing lesson described in Chapter 2 and the writing lesson with Owen in Chapter 4, the whole really is greater than the sum of its parts. As knowledgeable educators, we can glean more when we take in the teaching, behaviors, and student learning all at once and then focus on the parts, as needed. While observing and taking notes, we keep in mind key questions about literacy and learning as well as the priorities to look for in the reading-writing classroom. (See Appendix D.)

At first, some principals—and teachers, too—prefer a checklist of descriptors to guide them. Checklists provide a beginning framework until the big picture of literacy has been internalized. However, eventually the goal is to move beyond the checklist; if we concentrate our focus on the list, we lose sight of the teacher and students in front of us.

Here are the "big 10" areas I keep in mind during the instructional walk and use for my note taking:

- Environment
- Engagement
- Focused instruction
- Ongoing assessment
- OLM application
- Student interaction
- Quality of student work
- Authenticity
- Level of discussion
- Self-directed learners

I put these 10 major topics at the top of a blank note-taking form (see an example of my note taking on p. 208). Until this whole-part-whole note taking feels comfortable, try note taking using the same "big 10," with descriptors for each heading, to guide you (see Appendix H).

Another way to observe during an instructional walk is to keep Richard Allington's 6 T's in mind:

- *Time* is spent on meaningful reading and writing.
- *Texts* include a wide range that students can access and read accurately with understanding.
- *Teaching* is responsive to students' needs, includes explicit demonstrations of excellent literacy actions, and fosters independence.

- *Talk* promotes thoughtful conversations and purposeful dialogue between and among students as well as the teacher.
- *Tasks* are relevant and challenging with some choice provided.
- *Testing* and assessing are one measurement of achievement; effort and growth also matter.[39]

If you are not yet highly knowledgeable about literacy, think about beginning with looking at some areas that are pretty straightforward to observe and assess:

- Classroom libraries
- Word walls and what's posted
- Writing that is organized, dated, and kept in an easy-to-access collection
- Legibility and spelling
- Who's doing the talking
- Use of technology
- Usefulness of independent and practice work
- Pacing of lesson
- Support students are receiving in the classroom

Give Immediate Feedback

Instructional walks that lead to improved student learning depend on many interrelated factors. Chief among them is being able to give timely and effective feedback. It is still uncommon for principals to give teachers regular and specific feedback on how to improve instruction.[40] In my experience, principals have not been taught or mentored to do so. Principals who are able to give effective feedback are in a positive mindset, able to notice and choose what they comment on (depending on their level of knowledge and beliefs), and are able to be responsive to their teachers. Giving productive feedback is a learned behavior that takes lots of coaching and practice to do well. (See Chapter 2 for much more on feedback.)

If you keep in mind five essential questions, you are more likely to be relevant and effective when giving feedback—even if you are new to this process.

My strongest recommendation in an instructional walk is not to leave the classroom without letting the teacher know what you saw, heard, and admired. That feedback can be oral, written, or both. Each of us has to find a style and method we're comfortable with. Some principals feel

---

Quick Win

Talk directly to the teacher when giving feedback at the end of an instructional walk. If the students are doing things well, it's most likely because of the teacher's instruction. Publicly celebrating their teachers also makes students proud.

uncomfortable interrupting a lesson. I see it differently. First, feedback is most effective the closer it occurs to the event. Second, we just don't have time to add to our workload. For example, although it may be admirable to revisit notes and give feedback through e-mails or another written form, I worry that the extra time needed to write those adds pressure to an already too-stressful job.

A Self-Evaluation Checklist for Giving Feedback

- Is it necessary?
- Is it useful?
- Is it kind and respectful?
- Is it timely?
- Does it move the learner forward?

One principal told me she sent e-mail messages at the end of the day because she could never "interrupt" a teacher's lesson, but she shifted her thinking after seeing the positive effect on one of her teachers. It was late in the afternoon, close to the end of our instructional walks, and I had been giving demonstrations and coaching the principal. We had only about five minutes left when we walked into a French class. It was quickly clear from the teacher's tone of voice, gestures, actions, and total student engagement and participation that her lesson was highly effective. I said something like the following to the teacher when there was a very brief pause, before she was about to move on in her lesson:

> I'm so sorry to interrupt, but I don't want to leave without letting you
> know some of the terrific things we have observed about your teach-
> ing. Would that be OK? (The teacher smiles and gives her assent.)
> Well, I don't speak or understand French, but just from the few min-
> utes we've been in your classroom, it seems like every student is totally
> engaged. They didn't even look up when we came in; their attention
> was totally focused on you and the lesson. I liked the way you checked
> for understanding through questioning before moving on. Many kids'
> hands were in the air, eager to respond, and you were pointing to
> things you'd written on the board to affirm them. Also, your lesson

Quick Win

Partner with another principal or two and, without judgment, write down everything the other principal says and does in giving feedback to his or her teachers. Swap schools and repeat. This activity encourages self-reflection and goal setting.

Quick Win

Do give the teacher a quick verbal affirmation before leaving the classroom. Even if the principal immediately sends an e-mail message, the teacher may not see it until the end of the day.

pacing is very good, and the kids seem very excited about what they're learning, as evidenced by their smiles, enthusiasm in their voices, and eagerness to participate.[41]

I make it a point to never leave a teacher's classroom without giving some positive feedback. The payoff is huge. First, the teacher feels affirmed for what she is attempting to do or is doing. She is more likely, then, to be open to suggestions and to another visit. Second, the students see and hear their teacher being celebrated, and they are justly proud. Third, the teacher doesn't have to worry: "I wonder what she was thinking about my lesson?" This is no small matter, because the stress of not knowing what we think makes some teachers highly anxious. And, not to be minimized, giving immediate feedback is efficient. In the scenario just described, because we had so little time and I didn't want to split my attention between observing the teacher and taking notes, I only observed. Because what I'd just seen was so fresh in my mind, I could comment on all of it. By the end of the day, after other events had intervened, it would be unlikely my recall of detail would be as complete.

The teacher in the story and I did not know each other, as it was this school's first residency. Adding to that, she had been so quiet throughout the first day of the residency that when I entered her classroom the following day, I didn't know anything about her. After she was celebrated in her classroom, we began to hear her voice in our after-school professional development meetings. The principal, Sue Marlatt, comments on how the observational experience affected her:

> While visiting classrooms, I witnessed the pride on students' faces when what their teacher was doing—that was so good for the students' learning—was highlighted right in front of them. This celebration was powerful. One of my goals when I now visit is to not leave a room without commenting on great teaching and learning.[42]

To ensure a similarly positive outcome, keep in mind the following key actions for productive instructional walks:

• *Adopt a positive mindset.*
• *Be respectful of the teacher and students.*
• *Focus first on what's going well,* which could be something the teacher is *attempting* to do.

- *Take nonjudgmental notes.* Write down actions and language, as they occur.
- *Talk directly to the teacher.* If the students are doing things well, it's likely it's because of the teacher's actions.
- *Make at least several positive comments about what you see and hear.*
- *Read the body language.* Is this teacher ready for a suggestion?
- *Offer a suggestion or two* if the teacher appears open to it.
- *Be intentional.* Know what you're looking for.
- *Go with another educator* at first—a literacy coach, an assistant principal, or a trusted teacher so the "other" can say back what the principal has said to the teacher.
- *Comment on what's most important* for the teacher at that time.
- *Leave the teacher with the will and energy to teach.*
- *Revisit observational notes for school trends.*

Take Nonjudgmental Notes

Whatever note-taking form and format you adopt for most of your visits, keep it simple, nonjudgmental, and informal. Some teachers feel intimidated by seeing someone take notes on a clipboard, an iPad, or other device. As previously noted, I handwrite all my notes on a blank sheet of paper with the 10 key areas posted at the top as a guide and framework for thinking. I am consciously aware that if I inadvertently left the paper in the classroom, anyone could pick it up and read it and not feel judged. That is, I write down what I see and hear, just the facts, with the areas I consider most important. Also, it works well to jot down the time you enter and leave the room on the observation sheet, and also to keep track of which classrooms are visited to ensure fairness in how time is allocated. Although an occasional brief visit is fine, aim for 15 to 20 minutes on average or a long enough time frame to get a sense of the whole lesson.

Depending on the purposes and how much time is available, the feedback and note taking (not just from principals but also from coaches, teachers, and other leaders who work in classrooms) can take various forms and actions, such as the following:

- Sticky notes
- Short handwritten note on a card
- Oral comments only (occasionally), especially after a very brief visit

- Informal jottings on a blank piece of paper
- Hand-off of observational notes to the teacher before leaving the class-room (see partial example, below)
- Notes of several visits all on one sheet, listing observations by grade levels without teacher names, especially when looking for school trends
- Written record of the teacher's exact language and actions
- Use of a mobile device

INSTRUCTIONAL WALKS

Observations: Environment, Engagement, Focused Instruction, Ongoing Assessment, OLM Application, Student Interaction, Quality of Student Work, Authenticity, Level of Discussion, Self-Directed Learners

Notes: Ann, grade 4, 10-3-12, 12 min.
Working on precise language (using Haiku as vehicle to teach it)
Doing a shared writing about a dog.
"Let's think of one characteristic. Picture in your mind a dog doing something active." Kids offer "jumping," "fetching."
"Okay, picture a dog playing fetch. Think of those characteristics— everything you see and hear."
Kids offer "slobber, playful, fast, rowdy, pouncing, jumping, ripping, speeding, tearing, sniffing."
"Okay, look at our chart. Who has a first line for our Haiku?"
Took all language from students as they gave it.
"Let's reread. How are we on our precise language?"
"That's a possibility. What else can we do? What do you think?"
Took suggestions, then gave direction, and helped shape their language.

Capturing the teacher's language allows her to revisit the experience and feel affirmed by her expert instruction and assessment.

The use of a mobile device brings up the issue of trust. My recommendation is that unless trust levels are high, make the physical note-taking process easily transparent. That said, using a stylus with a tablet re-creates handwritten feedback and provides digital storage for later use. Principal Matt Renwick takes all notes using a stylus on his iPad and sends the teacher immediate feedback through e-mail as he is leaving the classroom.[43]

Exemplary principal Kim Ball varies her feedback. Sometimes her goal is schoolwide trends (strengths and needs). Therefore, she compiles notes from multiple classrooms with the grade levels noted on a page without teachers' names. Sometimes—about once a month—she carefully scripts what the teacher does and says, adds some positive and personal feedback, and hands that sheet to the teacher before leaving the room. She writes these notes on light purple copy paper, and teachers save and treasure their "purple sheets." Other times the feedback may be oral, especially for a very short visit. Kim comments on the impact of her note taking and feedback:

> The writing is a mirror of their instruction. It's become such an important tool for supporting teachers in best practices and valuing what they are doing. I write down teachers' words and actions along with global observations. With the purple sheets, they're like little kids at Christmas. They read and save them and have come to expect them. Teachers often stop me in the hall saying, "Come into my room and see what we're doing."[44]

Give Suggestions Carefully

Each of us can always improve in some aspect of the work we do. Sometimes we can see what we need to do without another's insight and support, but often improvement depends on effective feedback from a person we trust. Especially for teachers who are new, reluctant, or struggling, that feedback also needs to be specific and explicit, limited to one or two doable actions, and applied within a short and reasonable time frame—for example, within a day or several days. For stronger and more confident teachers, feedback might be wider and applicable within a longer time frame, such as a week or more.

Keep trust at the forefront

The language we use with teachers and peers needs to be a model for the way we want teachers to talk with other teachers and their students—as well as for how we want students to give feedback to each other.[45] Our language, stance, and any suggestions we give need to convey an attitude of "I'm here to support you." Offering earnest support builds trust, and that pays big dividends.

There have been occasions when a teacher, for various reasons, has been so fearful of another person in the classroom that I begin with "How can I help you?" and then suggest we sit down at a table and talk (while students are given a task to do independently, often free-choice reading). Where there is fear, trust is crowded out, so we begin gently. For example, I might say, "We have about 20 minutes. What would be most useful to you? We can talk, look at student work, or do anything that would be helpful to you." Once trust is steadily built, the teacher is almost always open to suggestions for improvement. One principal noted that when she began asking her teachers, "How can I help you with what you're doing?" the impact was enormous. "I have teachers who now come to me with questions, seeking resources and guidance."[46]

Once trust levels are high, much of the feedback does center on suggestions. Effective teachers are always eager to do better and truly want to know how they can improve. What follows are my exact notes during instructional walks in March 2011 in two classrooms during the first year of a writing residency at Sandy Grade School in rural Oregon. The informal notes were originally handwritten, and although I did not give them to the teachers, they served as my talking points to them. Both teachers embraced and followed through on all suggestions. Not only that, with ongoing learning through infused Professional *Literacy* Communities in their school, they went on to become strong teacher-leaders and to mentor many others.

Laurie Espenel, grade 5 teacher

Kids love writing, have lots of choice, are very enthusiastic and highly engaged, great poem by low-performing student who hated writing

Suggestions:

• comment sheet at back of published books does not reflect quality of book; students' handwritten comments are sloppy with poor handwriting and spelling; comments are not useful; need to use OLM to model that
• many excellent published books—get those into a wider audience, other classroom libraries
• publish less, but publish 2 editions, one for student, one for another library

Lesley, grade 1

Kids love writing, lots of publishing of mostly nonfiction

Suggestions:

- showcase published books, hard to notice them in the classroom
- compare journals, note progress (followed up with phone call)
- standardize 1st grade paper; put lines on both sides
- take your time to tell your story when demo. writing—had great pacing

Know what to do and say when teachers need improvement

Keeping essential feedback behaviors in mind can be especially import-ant when working with a teacher who needs improvement but may not yet be open to suggestions. In such cases, as principals, coaches, teacher-leaders, and peers, we need to be especially mindful of our words, tone of voice, and actions. Sometimes the best we can do at the moment is to script every word and action, and in giving feedback make comments such as these:

- *"I noticed ___"* or *"This is what I saw ___."* For example, "Your room is more organized; there are fewer students walking around looking for materials, and more are getting to work right away." (Starting with an affirmation.)
- *"You said ___"* or *"This is the language I heard ___."* For example, "I'm wait-ing for Daryl to join us. Daryl, you're holding up the whole class." (High-lighting the teacher's comment that led to inappropriate student behavior.)
- *"You did ___"* or *"This is what I saw you do ___."* For example, asking a student to leave the group. "How do you think that worked? Would you do anything differently next time?" (Assessing and encouraging the teacher's ability to self-evaluate.)

Through your questioning, check to determine if a teacher is ready for suggestions. See the following brief notes I made after being in a kinder-garten teacher's classroom for just five minutes and looking at her students' writing:

Lindsay, kindergarten teacher
Lots of enthusiasm, knows her expectations aren't high enough after seeing first grade lesson in residency

Suggestions:
I ask her, "What do you think of the level of your kids' writing?" She responds, "Not good enough." Very open to seeing what we expect. I show her K samples from another school, which reflect higher

expectations. She responds, "My kids are going to be able to do that. I'm going to get them there."

That instructional walk and feedback took place during the first year of our residency. Through her own initiative, relentless pursuit of excellence, and full participation in schoolwide Professional *Literacy* Communities, she became an outstanding teacher. Almost all students in both morning and afternoon kindergarten in her Title I school ended the school year as readers and writers who met or exceeded the standards, and this trend has continued and accelerated.

When I asked Lindsay how she accounted for her students reading and writing so well, she replied, "They read and write all day long."[47] There's nothing simplistic about that statement. Adopting a whole-part-whole teaching philosophy and a sense of urgency, she embedded explicit skills work and authenticity into every reading and writing text. The director of curriculum and instruction for the district commented, "You get what you expect. It's amazing to watch Lindsay now and remember where she was three years ago."[48]

It takes time and practice to become effective at doing instructional walks. Getting together with a small group of principals is one effective way to put instructional walks into operation. Here's how it might work:

• Meet monthly at one of the schools (rotate schools each month).
• Observe each other during instructional walks and give feedback.
• Coach each other.

Another way is to go on instructional walks, at least at first, with a literacy coach or trusted teacher-leader. Have that observer note and script the exact feedback language used. Debrief together and discuss successes and ways to improve.

Guide Teachers to Align Beliefs with Practices

As noted in Chapter 3 regarding the importance of developing and establishing shared beliefs, the principal as well as teacher-leaders must ensure that schoolwide practices stem from common beliefs that reflect credible research and best practices. Through instructional walks, we can "see" how beliefs are being translated into practice. Whether we are principals, coaches, or teachers working with peers, our leadership role needs to extend to having ongoing conversations that begin something like this: "Let's talk about what we saw and how it relates to our beliefs." Otherwise, schoolwide progress will remain limited and transient. Therefore, not only do we establish schoolwide beliefs, we visit them a couple of times a year and prominently post them in the school.

As I have noted elsewhere, teachers' *awareness* of how their beliefs drive their practices is absolutely crucial for highly effective teaching.[49] "When old beliefs are gone, there's an open space for new possibilities and new results to pour in. While thinking outside the box is a first step, *acting* outside the box becomes a daring act of courage."[50] Charity Haviland is a competent and dedicated 1st grade teacher who displayed that courage, although it wasn't easy or comfortable to do so. Through an honest and respectful conversation and her own self-reflection, she was able to recognize that her beliefs and practices were not aligned, which was limiting what she and her students could achieve.

Charity and I have a trusting relationship based on past work together. She knows I admire her as a teacher and see her as highly capable. During an instructional walk where I was mentoring her principal, when I saw a mismatch between Charity's core beliefs and her practices, I asked her about it. But first I commented on what I saw going well. It was mid-October, and her 1st graders had written a meaningful and engaging letter to an important visitor coming to the classroom that day. The impressive letter, created together through shared writing on chart paper, was a full page and a half. I observed Charity lead a spirited shared reading of it. Second, I commented on the "morning reading notebooks" all the children had. (I saw these while walking around the room.) These notebooks included all the classroom-authored, shared writing pieces produced since the beginning of the school year—letters, narratives, poems, news. When students came in each morning, they read in their notebooks, independently or with a partner. Finally, I made some positive comments related to the well-organized and well-equipped classroom library.

Instructional walks can provide teachers an opportunity to extend their thinking, try out an alternative practice, and reflect on their teaching. So when I observed Charity doing a word-study exercise in which each student cut up sentences that were phonetically regular but made no sense (decodable texts), I interceded. I had already affirmed her instruction; I knew almost everything she did in her classroom was connected to meaningful purpose; yet here, she and her students were struggling mightily to engage in a nonsense activity. The activity came from a new, district-mandated reading program, and Charity was dutifully implementing it. Based on our mutual respect and trust, I now made a suggestion:

> Why not use the first two sentences from your terrific class letter as cut-up sentences instead? All the phonics sounds you need to teach the kids will be in the authentic daily writing you are doing with them. Not only that, using the letter you wrote together will be a lot more enjoyable and efficient for you and the kids. Keep track of what you're teaching, and check off the phonics sounds that are required in the reading program as you teach them.

Charity began to refocus her practice in light of her beliefs and her students. She comments:

> That suggestion certainly caused me to rethink my practice that day, and it lingered in my mind as I planned the next few weeks. What was it that I truly believed would be the most meaningful to the students? I began thinking and acting more critically, using common experiences and writing as ways to teach students what they needed, when they needed it, and in a meaningful context. This interaction did more than refocus my practice for that small moment; it helped me gain back the confidence that I had let go and got me back to where I was making instructional decisions I believed in.[51]

Charity was struggling with a common problem in schools and districts where multiple belief systems and practices coexist without alignment at the school and district levels. An assigned program or resource may be a mismatch with a school's, or even a district's, stated beliefs about teaching and learning. The selected program or resource determines the teaching focus rather than giving first priority to the school or district beliefs and desired practices, and then looking for resources and programs that support those. Once Charity took a step back and realized she was allowing a program to drive her teaching, she was able to use the program as a useful framework and resource to support her core beliefs and strong literacy knowledge. She also reembraced the critical concept of fidelity to the child, not fidelity to the program.

Go Beyond Analysis of Results to Improving Instruction

Too often analysis of assessment results and data does not then proceed to the most important next step, which is using the results for "developing instructional responses to specific learning needs."[52] One of the ways we seek to improve instruction is by directly addressing school patterns, strengths, and needs that we have observed and documented from instructional walks, environmental walks, interim assessments, student work samples, and more.

For instance, in taking notes during instructional walks, we note schoolwide trends, organize them into a list we share with staff (see the example on this page), and use those as the focus of some of the PLC work. We always begin with naming and discussing what's going well in the school, followed by what needs attention. It's an honest look at the state of literacy and learning at the school with the sole focus on increasing both. In vertical teams, we determine, together, what the first priorities are that we need to address. Note that these indicators can apply across the curriculum.

Instructional Walks

Some Examples of Schoolwide Strengths

- High student engagement
- Classroom libraries
- Authentic writing
- Reading conferences
- Collaboration among staff
- Self-checking by students

Some Examples of Schoolwide Issues

- Postings as artifacts—hallways and bulletin boards
- Spelling, handwriting, and editing
- Word walls
- Management during guided reading
- Need for common language
- Coherence and consistency at and across grade levels

Quick Win

Focus on improving handwriting schoolwide. With a full-school effort and plan, improvement happens quickly, is easy to see and celebrate, and is a public relations win—all of which gives teachers and students energy and confidence to do the hard work of writing. Not only that—writing fluency improves.

Quick Win

Teach handwriting every day, beginning in kindergarten, formally and informally in authentic writing and in small-group work where you are available to quickly show and practice correct letter formation. This is an easy way to increase fluency and stamina. Even by grade 1, it's hard to alter "bad" habits in holding the pencil and forming letters.

As an example, in one school focused on improving writing, the staff took ownership for poor handwriting at every grade level when they realized that not formally teaching handwriting, starting in kindergarten, was handicapping students with letter formation, legibility, writing fluency, and writing stamina. As part of their work, the whole school took part in reviewing and discussing key research on handwriting, which led to agreeing on the type of paper and lines to use at each grade level, identifying and valuing handwriting as an essential skill, and committing to teach it at every grade level. A year later, handwriting had significantly improved schoolwide, accompanied by teachers' and students' pride in legibility and increased writing fluency. Students came to value the idea that we write for readers and that readers have to be able to read our work to appreciate it. In and out of our schools, not all writing is done on a computer or a handheld device.

Learn from Highly Effective School Leaders

Sometimes we learn the most from others who have walked in our shoes. The following wise voices are those of leaders who are principals, literacy coaches, and teacher-leaders who have sometimes taken uncommon or courageous actions to build trust and increase learning throughout the learning community.

Elementary (K–6) principal Mike Henderson took on the role of coteacher:

> It is important that the school principal clearly communicate priorities for the school. I like to think that I have taken my level of transparency one step further by modeling beliefs, expectations, and non-negotiables. I hold great value in not only observing classrooms but also modeling strong instructional practices. One avenue I have found to be impactful and gratifying is mentoring teachers as a member of the classroom community.
>
> This past school year, I embarked on a team teaching model with Ms. Sirianni's 6th grade class during her writing workshop. On a weekly basis, I joined the teacher and her 6th graders as we studied mentor texts, developed our craft as writers, identified authentic topics to argue through our writing, conferred with one another about our writing, and celebrated our successes as a writing community. I am confident that those 6th graders taught me as much as I taught them. It was a truly rewarding experience that allowed me to model, grow, and

Quick Win

Ensure legible writing when using special unlined paper. Place lined paper (with lines in bold so they show through) behind blank paper, which supports students to write legibly on unique paper being used for publication.

be part of a learning community in a different way than in my role as principal.[53]

Teacher-leader Kate Gordon took the initiative to house all specialists together as part of promoting a schoolwide "push-in" model:

As a classroom teacher I remember feeling frustrated with the "revolving door" education that some of my students experienced. They were pulled away daily from our classroom culture and instruction for testing, for speech, for ELD group, for Special Education services, for Title I interventions. I remember thinking, "This student is one of my most likely to be confused by new learning and they are never in one place long enough to master any of the fragmented lessons they are receiving. Even my highest learner would struggle to achieve in these circumstances."

When I became a Title I teacher I was determined to provide a consistent and quality educational program for these struggling learners. Teaming with the courageous and dedicated specialists at my school we combined our services and increased our communication by moving, with our instructional assistants, into one centrally located room. We then worked to morph our interventions to a primarily push-in model to minimize the time individual students spend out of their classrooms.

While teachers were initially nervous about having support services in their rooms, they now look forward to this time. Teaming for instruction with our ELL teacher or talking with a Title I support person about what they have both observed about a particular student has provided an opportunity for professional growth, as well as student growth.

The teachers love being able to come to one room to discuss a particular child rather than experiencing multiple, unrelated conversations in a variety of rooms. Students appreciate being able to spend time in their own classroom with a "team" that supports their (and their peers') learning.[54]

Experienced leader Marilyn Jerde, who has been both an elementary principal and a K–5 director of elementary education, took on the role of "leading learner":

As an effective school leader, I need to have lots of credibility. If I want my teachers to be on the cutting edge of instruction and research, I need to be able to clearly articulate my own beliefs system and the reasons we are moving in a different direction.

I have always felt very responsible for developing teachers and helping them reach a higher level in their instructional practice. As a principal and district leader, it was critical to stay informed about current trends, research, and policies in education. I can't lead my school or district in a meaningful direction unless I am well informed. I found it essential to spend sustained time reading and learning about effective practices. I always want to speak with knowledge and confidence to my community. It is critically important that teachers have confidence in the person leading the way.[55]

Leadership greatly matters, and leadership styles vary. However we lead, like the actions of each of the aforementioned leaders, our leadership must contribute to supporting our schools to become thriving cultures focused on improving instruction.

As leaders we also need to look at indicators beyond test scores and other assessments to evaluate our schools. How do we know our schools are becoming healthy, thriving environments for learning? In one school working to become self-sustaining, a good indicator of progress is that parent turnout has greatly increased at all evening and school events. Now that the school is more welcoming and the staff is more cohesive, teachers are more positive when talking about students. Whereas previously just a few teachers were having lunch together in the teachers' lounge, now most teachers are choosing to eat together, and the talk is about teaching and learning, not gripes. Another indicator is that the numbers of students being sent to the office for problems of one sort or another have steeply declined. Also, attendance is up for students, and staff turnover is down.

A healthy school culture breeds a learning culture. Ultimately, of course, it is increased and sustained achievement that lets us know we are moving in the right direction and that we have gone beyond a focus on analyzing data to improving instruction and learning for all our students.

Quick Win

Seek anonymous feedback from staff surveys to ensure a healthy school culture; act upon that feedback without applying it to teacher evaluations.

6

Professional *Literacy* Communities

In this chapter and throughout this book, the abbreviation *PLC*—which has traditionally meant professional learning community[1]—stands for Professional *Literacy* Community. This term emphasizes and denotes that the work we do is always connected to literacy; that is, if students are to learn more, we educators have to know how to expertly teach reading and writing, adjust instruction to meet the needs of all students, and guide application of those effective literacy practices in the classroom, regardless of the grade level, the subject matter we teach, or the position we hold. That know-how is developed with strong leadership in a highly functioning PLC that offers a continuous, school-based cycle not just of collaboration but of rich conversations around literacy and learning at and across grade levels and content areas. That know-how is the missing piece we educators must supply in order to implement the latest standards (including CCSS), provincial curricula, or international guidelines.

The best professional development is professional learning that leads to new insights, confirmations, expanded thinking, improved and enhanced teaching and leading, and—most of all—increased student learning. In communities of professional learning, groups of teachers and administrators come together regularly to share what's working, to read and discuss research and literacy practices across the curriculum, to observe and analyze best practices, to apply those practices to their classrooms and schools, to assess what's working, to celebrate learning, and to responsively adjust to do better.

The principal, with the support of teacher-leaders, ensures that high-level, professional learning becomes the school norm, not as an end in itself but as a means to greater student learning. *The Professional Literacy*

Community becomes the daily culture and foundation of the highly effective school. That is, the PLC becomes the school's heart and soul and operating system. Teachers become wholly focused individually and collectively on improving instruction and accelerating student learning all day long, not just during designated meeting times. Perhaps most crucial, the principal is a learner alongside teachers.

> In terms of the link between a principal's action and student learning, there is one finding that stands out in time as more powerful than any other, and it is this: the degree to which the principal participates as a learner in helping teachers figure out how to get classroom and school-wide improvement.[2]

When professional learning through ongoing collaboration, conversations, coaching at and between grade levels, sharing of student work and ideas, and reflection permeates the school, a school is transformed. So how does this happen? Before we move to a detailed discussion of creating Professional *Literacy* Communities led by a school's leadership team, let's look at a successful PLC school and its culture, as well as what research says about professional development, especially as it relates to successful professional growth that translates to improved student learning.

Embed a PLC Culture into Schools

A whole-day, everyday focus on improving teaching and learning is atypical in the daily routine of schools.[3] So is principal as literacy expert and teacher as leader. However, both scenarios play out daily in schools where a PLC culture permeates, where PLC meetings are embedded into the life of the school, and where those meetings align with the aforementioned research. Although a PLC culture is uncommon, it is doable, possible, and necessary if all students are to thrive as learners.

Expand the PLC Definition and Vision

For many years, the work of successful schools has been seen as forming a professional learning community, focusing on student work (through assessment), and changing instructional practice accordingly to get better results.[4] As well, the most instructionally helpful leadership practices, according to teachers and principals, have been seen as including a whole-school focus on achievement, meeting teachers' professional development needs, and creating opportunities and structures for teacher collaboration.[5]

Although there has been much research and writing about professional learning communities as an agent for successful school change, much of the emphasis has been on the structure of a professional learning community, in particular the time needed to work together with colleagues. As well, often professional learning communities have been overly focused on examining data and achievement gains.[6] Without ongoing and embedded emphasis on the focus of a Professional *Literacy* Community as knowing, understanding, and applying exemplary reading and writing practices, schoolwide literacy achievement is not likely or sustainable.

First, teachers and principals have to be knowledgeable about literacy to know what's most important to look for and focus on when examining and interpreting student work. Second, data must be used and analyzed in ways that improve and customize instructional practices, not just dutifully document progress or lack of it. *Focus on data must not trump focus on the student.* Data must inform our work, not dictate it. The end result must be that our students are continuously getting better and learning more as listeners, speakers, readers, writers, thinkers, and learners in all disciplines. Achieving that result depends on expanding the definition, aims, and reach of PLCs to include improving literacy practices across the curriculum.

Based on more than four decades of teaching, coaching, and leading, I respectfully suggest that we modify and enhance those expectations to include the following elements in a whole-school Professional *Literacy* Community focus:

- *Infuse* a structure for collaboration that includes reflection, goal setting, reading, observation, discussion, planning for application, and shared learning throughout the life of the school.
- *Improve* teaching and learning by focusing on appraising student work, at grade level and across the grades—continually examining, discussing, and analyzing the work to assess growth over time, strengths, needs, and next instructional steps.
- *Increase* student learning and accelerate improvement through teachers' and principals' ongoing shared learning, mutual accountability, and commitment to the application of best practices to the classroom.

• *Support* application of best practices through timely teacher feedback, peer coaching, mentoring, opportunities to revisit the PLC learning structure, such as observing or reviewing video lessons, and analyzing and planning at the grade level or in content-area teams.

Without the all-important application piece, there is no real or strong transfer of knowledge or practices to the classroom. With application and consistent implementation, effective transfer can rise to 95 percent.[7]

To ensure better results in the classroom, it is important to *make professional learning a daily school norm.* Components of the daily, ongoing PLC school culture (at and between grade levels) that make it more likely that every teacher and student improves and succeeds include the following:

• Mentoring and coaching
• Professional dialogue
• Discussion centered on student work
• Instructional walks
• Timely and specific feedback
• Collaborative planning

Although the residencies described in this book serve as a catalyst for change, it is the professional conversations that take place daily and at regularly scheduled meetings that determine whether or not teachers and students apply new learning.

Without exception, I have only seen long-lasting change leading to higher student achievement in schools with strong principal leadership, ongoing collaboration including peer coaching, and in-depth professional study and conversations. Almost always, these professional conversations take place weekly, in a formalized way, and daily in informal and planned structures. As teachers and leaders become expert, they are able to responsively teach and innovate. That is, sufficient deep knowledge of the structure and craft of reading and writing instruction allows them, on the spot, to make and support responsible instructional decisions and adjust their teaching to increase student learning.

Learn from a Professional *Literacy* Community School

Sandy Grade School is a K–5 elementary school in rural Oregon, an hour's drive from Portland. Sixty-five percent of the students qualify for free and reduced lunch, 15 percent are English language learners, and the transiency rate each year is over 50 percent. A few years ago, the school was the lowest performing of the seven elementary schools in the district, with students routinely two years below grade level in writing, according to district and statewide assessments. Teachers did not work well together; grievances to the union were the highest of any school in the district; and there was no shared vision, shared beliefs, or well-coordinated and effective professional development.

The director of curriculum and instruction, whose ongoing support to the school was essential to its improvement, described the school as it was before we began our residency work together and how the school began to change:

> The staff didn't talk about expectations for students, curriculum, or student growth. They had no idea about what writing looked like across grade levels. When the culture shifted to kids first, the finger pointing which put everyone on the defensive stopped. That started to happen when we met in PLCs and looked at writing samples across grade levels. The change was transformational. It was like something turned a light switch on—someone actually said, "The problem is not the children; it's us." There was a call-to-action response, and everyone owned up to the responsibility.[8]

Two years after embracing a schoolwide PLC culture, the school was designated a Model School by the state of Oregon for performing in the top 5 percent of Title I schools for successful student outcomes, according to state tests. The number of students meeting the standards in reading moved from 50 percent to 70 percent. In writing, only 40 percent were initially meeting the standard. We estimate that 70 percent also met the standard in writing, based on our interim standardized assessments (the statewide assessment in writing had been dropped).

The principal, the literacy coach, the leadership team, the teachers at the school, and the director of curriculum and instruction credit the following for the improvement:

- *Getting a solid infrastructure in place*—Schoolwide assessment through teacher interviews and review of data was led by Taffy Raphael, a leader in the school change process, and included assessing the school's culture and getting needed structures in place, such as creating and following norms and defining roles and responsibilities of school members.[9]

- *Improving the culture of the school*—Foremost was strong principal leadership that focused on building trusting relationships, improving literacy and learning conditions, and mentoring and supporting emerging teacher-leaders; a knowledgeable and generous literacy coach; kindness and respect toward all; and a relentless effort to become better teachers of reading and writing and to have all students succeed.
- *Focusing on continuous improvement*—Strategies included weekly PLCs (whole school or grade level), weekly leadership team meetings, instructional walks, interim writing assessments (twice yearly), professional reading, writing residencies, viewing videos of effective writing and reading practices with expectation of classroom application, joint analysis of data and student work, connecting CCSS to "the work," and ongoing daily collaboration, coaching, and professional conversations at and across grade levels.
- *Assuming responsibility for all students*—Doing so was accomplished by meeting in vertical teams and grade-level teams, raising expectations at every grade level, looking at student work with the whole-school staff knowing what writing looks like from kindergarteners to exiting 5th grade writers, and ensuring steps between grade levels are steep enough.

Develop a PLC culture

In particular, it is the focus on improving teaching and learning throughout every day that has been the most striking and significant change at Sandy Grade School. As one teacher noted, "It's the way we operate." *A PLC culture is the daily routine of the school.* It has to be. That's the only way we gain enough time to do the persistent thinking, dialoguing, wrestling with ideas, planning, analyzing, and doing the trial and error necessary to apply newly learned instructional strategies and actions that result in improved student learning.

But there's more. Without a PLC school culture it's difficult to rise to the level of inner questioning and inner conversations discussed in chapters 2 and 5. When we don't have enough knowledge to know what our questions are—or what the most important questions might be for improving instruction and learning—our questions remain at the procedural level, and little of substance improves. Early on, teachers at Sandy Grade School didn't know what they didn't know. Also, they had experienced so much fragmented professional development, they didn't know what they believed.

As their knowledge grew and their shared beliefs developed, their main question changed from "What are the steps I need to know to teach writing well?" to "How can I teach writing and reading in a way that all learners understand and can apply?"

The schoolwide focus shifted not just to more meaningful content and better instructional strategies but also to greater student learning. That shift also included a mental shift from "These are my students" to "These are our students." Teachers assumed collective responsibility for all students at the school.

Another enormous change that visitors often comment on in PLC schools is the "joy factor." Teachers have never worked harder, but they are working smarter and having a good time teaching and learning together. Smiles and laughter fill classrooms and hallways. It's not an artificial, "feel good" attitude displayed by chanting or charting success goals. It's the joy and satisfaction that come from knowing what we're doing and that we're doing it well and seeing improved results. Learning and laughing together is a real sign of a true collaborative, safe, and trusting learning environment for teachers and students. Joy in learning for all students, teachers, and leaders is the ultimate triumph.

Reflective teacher Ann Thomson sums up what's it like to collaborate schoolwide:

> What has been wonderful is that our whole staff meets once a week, and we work together with common goals and common language across the grades. There is camaraderie now that has pulled people together. We talk more; we know each other better. We're all struggling and learning together at the same time. It's been great![10]

Goals of an effective Professional *Literacy* Community

Where PLCs raise performance levels for students, teachers, and leaders, teams of teachers and leaders continuously commit to sustained time for high-level professional conversations, collaboration, reflection, study, and shared learning in order to do the following:

- Establish common norms, goals, purposes, shared values, and shared beliefs.
- Align shared beliefs with worthwhile practices and resources.
- Set priorities for the long term (3–5 years) and the short term (1 year).

> **Quick Win**
>
> *Think and say "our students"* as much as possible. When we hear teachers beginning to shift their thinking from "my students" to "our students," we have evidence of true, schoolwide collaboration and a win-win situation for all.

- Engage in rich professional conversations around literacy and learning, including wrestling with key questions, ideas, concerns.
- Increase collective knowledge of relevant research and *coherent* instructional and assessment practices.
- Apply those effective literacy and content-specific practices in the classroom, at and across grade levels and in all subject areas.
- Focus on student learning.
- Collect evidence of student (adults and children) learning and share the evidence with all learners.
- Analyze samples of student work and other relevant data.
- Use data to celebrate strengths, monitor progress, identify needs, set new goals, and modify instruction for what's most important to move student learning forward.
- Celebrate daily successes.
- Strive to do better.

Take a look at the professional learning environment where you work and ensure that this precious learning time is being well spent. Negotiate time for shared learning, create common norms for how the team will work together and when the team will meet, and identify the focus for instruction based on the whole school's greatest instructional needs. (This is the essence of a data team, which is the analytical arm of a PLC.) Too often, PLCs become just another set of required meetings where not much changes in terms of student learning results.

Put in Place Effective Learning Structures

To maximize learning and increase results, we need to have a structural foundation in place that supports acceleration, shared learning, efficiency, and enjoyment for doing the work. If we examine what makes a school such as Sandy Grade School a successful PLC school, we see that putting the necessary learning structures in place, in addition to the operating system infrastructure, is a huge part. Ensuring that optimal learning structures are in place depends on a strong principal and leadership team working closely with the staff to keep the focus on student learning.

"School structures need to be built around the work, not the other way around."[11] Highly effective teachers are a by-product of having the supportive structures in place that promote and enhance ongoing professional learning and student learning, and these structures are created and sustained through strong leadership.

Many of these essential structures, as well as the need for a strong infrastructure, have already been discussed in this book. These include but are not restricted to the following:

- Strong principal leadership
- Collaborative and trusting school culture
- Establishment of a vision, mission, and goals for the school
- Curriculum expectations and guidelines
- Professional *Literacy* Communities
- Effective leadership team
- Schoolwide shared beliefs
- Application of an optimal learning model
- Successful coaching experiences
- Adequate support systems[12]

Include an effective data team

Another essential element for improving student learning is providing time for looking at data in school teams for the purpose of noticing areas of strength, student growth, and needs, and determining how to use these data to improve performance. Data teams are a necessary progress-monitoring, "keeping-track" structure for any schoolwide sustainable change process. It is essential that teachers be given guidance to learn how to disaggregate data that are meaningful and relevant to their own teaching and students' learning. A data team headed by the principal can lead much of this work and continue to monitor it. Ideally, teacher-leaders who become expert in the data team process can eventually take over this responsibility.

The data team is actually an extension of the PLC. The data team's job is to examine student work from common assessments, determine the strategies and interventions that will be used to monitor progress, decide where and what particular resources and specialists will be deployed to make the largest impact on improving student learning, and then keep track of students' progress and note where instructional adjustments are needed. With a highly functioning PLC, all teachers assume responsibility to be part of the data team process. The process involves the following steps:

- Collect and chart/display the data.
- Analyze data and prioritize needs.
- Set, review, and revise incremental SMART goals: *s*pecific, *m*easurable, *a*chievable, *r*elevant, and *t*imely.
- Select common instructional strategies to be employed to address the learning challenges discovered when analyzing data and prioritizing needs.
- Determine results indicators: "When this strategy is implemented, we expect to see the following evidence of its effectiveness."[13]

Data teams have the potential to positively affect student outcomes. For example, without excellent instruction early on, some students never catch up. Based on a school's data, the team might recommend putting most of its resources into tutoring, after-school programs, or a new resource.

Two specific examples come to mind. When the data team at a high-poverty school determined that a high proportion of students were entering grade 3 as struggling readers, the school's PLC decided to focus most of their resources on grade 1 reading. A year later, the majority of students were leaving 1st grade as readers, which was a major change and one that affected the whole school's achievement. In another school, looking carefully at student writing across the grades through a data team process caused teachers to raise their expectations and make effective writing the PLC focus for several years. The end result was a dramatic increase in teachers' effectiveness and students' writing achievement.

The caution with any data team is to ensure that analysis of data leads to action that improves student learning. That end result requires leadership in the data team process, time for data-driven conversations around pertinent questions, applying knowledge and informed judgment to the data, and not overgeneralizing or overrelying on data, such as making important decisions about students based solely on tests. Sometimes teachers and leaders lack the confidence and know-how to recognize, let alone examine, data that are not scores, numbers, or levels.

Data-driven decision making must be balanced and tempered with recognizing data's limitations—for example, making clear that we are not just "measuring" quantity or "moving up levels." We must also be valuing student work and thinking through such formative assessments as class-authored texts, charts, and rubrics; the depth of questions students are asking; responses in discussion; and the everyday reading and writing of a literacy classroom. The bottom line is that any use of data must lead to improved student outcomes and greater effectiveness in instruction.

Apply the Research on Professional Development

To form an effective Professional *Literacy* Community, we need to know and apply the research on professional development. Although professional development can be costly and time-consuming, it is a necessity for providing high-quality instruction to all students in the school. Studies show that teachers who are effective with students and who successfully respond to their needs are part of a strong professional learning community that meets often and provides ongoing PD support.[14]

Without strong PLCs wrestling with crucial literacy issues and applying best practices in the classroom, change and professional growth remain superficial and temporary. The end result is that many teachers remain instructionally ineffective with students.

Specifically, to be successful and positively affect student learning, professional development must have the following attributes:

- Be job-embedded, ongoing, coherent, and intense
- Involve 30–100 hours over six months to a year
- Be connected to teachers' classroom practice; that is, focused on content and effective teaching
- Align with school improvement goals
- Be designed to foster staff collaboration
- Include significant amounts of structured and sustained follow-up and support after the main professional development activities[15]

In my experience, the above-cited research on professional development is largely ignored; that is, most professional development is not job-embedded, long term, and meaningfully connected to improving classroom practices. Despite billions spent on professional development, not much has changed.[16]

Support Continuous Principal and Teacher Learning

Evidence suggests that ongoing, school-based professional development must be considered a necessary condition of the opportunity to learn.[17] Not only that, in order for teachers to articulate and implement effective and coherent instructional practices across the grades with sufficiently high

Quick Win

Make time to hear all teachers' voices. For example, take the time at a PD session to honor all teachers: "What's going well? What's one question you have?" After one such PD session, a teacher commented how rare it was for all teachers' voices to be heard and how that models what we hope will happen in all PD and in our classrooms.

expectations for students, they need years of support for collaborating and learning in professional learning communities.[18]

Evidence also suggests that collective learning of new practices is more likely in a professional learning community when there is principal leadership and when the *focus is on the quality of student learning*.[19] This last point is very important: what and how students learn greatly matters. Here is where principal leadership becomes paramount. The principal must ensure PLCs are all about implementing effective literacy practices so students learn more. That is, for teachers to become highly effective, the principal must not just know what excellent reading and writing practices look like and sound like in classrooms, but also must be able to move teachers forward through effective demonstrations, coaching, and feedback.

When principals lack the know-how for expert instruction, they "are likely to rely exclusively on data because they have so little understanding of teaching."[20] Such principals (and teachers, too) rely too much on pre-established systems—standards, programs, tests, and evaluation procedures—and rely too little on responsive teaching and assessment driven by the needs and interests of students as well as required curriculum and standards. Equally critical, without sufficient knowledge and beliefs that align with worthwhile practices, the questions we ask about teaching and learning remain superficial and limit what's possible for our students and us.

Seek Professional Learning, Not Just Professional Development

Too few of us observe viable and expert alternatives to our usual practices, so we persist in a culture of doing what we've always done. As one example, administrators and districts persist in using assessments that are either unreliable, are not supported by credible research, or yield too little useful information relative to the time and costs for implementation.[21] I believe at least part of why we persist in adopting materials and skills that do little good in terms of increased student learning—and sometimes do harm—is because our collective knowledge is so limited. Being able to show data instantly through graphs, numbers, and levels is seductive; it satisfies some stakeholders because the results look impressive. However, what those results show may be mostly a simplistic achievement mirage.

Professional development is big business, especially in the age of the Common Core State Standards. "Common Core aligned" is the new mantra. If we're not knowledgeable about effective literacy practices, however, we can't determine which resources, workshops, seminars, and conferences are actually going to help us improve our practices and student learning. Those resources and workshops may be labeled and "aligned" for professional development, but professional *learning* is quite another matter.

A principal I know well and highly respect shared with me the following statement one of her teachers made after being part of her school's Professional *Literacy* Community: "I've had lots of professional development, but this is the first time I've ever had professional learning." By that the teacher meant that it was the first time in her teaching career that she had the continuing opportunity, over many months, to do the following:

- *Dialogue professionally with the principal and teachers* on literacy matters of substance.
- *Observe, discuss, and apply exemplary reading and writing practices* with the support of the principal, teachers, and experts.
- *Concentrate on whole-school literacy improvement* through shared learning.

Consider using those bulleted items as a self-assessment for whether or not your school is carrying out professional learning. We need to advocate for and do our part in ensuring top-notch professional learning. Professional development that consists of sending teachers to conferences and workshops, bringing experts in to work with a staff, or learning how to implement a new program can be useful, but such PD is insufficient without continuous and embedded schoolwide professional learning.

Set Up a Highly Functioning School Leadership Team

Before an effective and self-sustaining PLC culture can be established in a school, a leadership team needs to be formed and functioning. Because little has been written about leadership teams—member selection and guidelines, roles and responsibilities, and potential for raising school expectations and results—I am covering the topic here in considerable detail. None of the work related to leadership teams is beyond what any committed school can do, but it does take a firm belief that the work is essential to lasting schoolwide achievement. I have not yet seen a school with highly effective PLCs or schoolwide achievement that does not have a strong leadership team (or a group that performs similar functions) in place.

> **Quick Win**
>
> Designate a "knowledge sifter" for the school—that is, a teacher who reads professionally, is knowledgeable, and is willing to keep the staff abreast of the latest research and excellent professional articles and books.

Looking at student work as knowledgeable teachers.

The primary role of the leadership team is to determine, organize, and facilitate the ongoing professional learning for the school. The leadership team is in charge of the Professional *Literacy* Communities—the actual meetings and the PLC culture of the school. A highly functioning leadership team is essential for sharing schoolwide leadership responsibilities with the principal, for coleading ongoing professional development, and for improving the culture of the school.

Professional development is based on information gathered from reviewing and analyzing assessment data, agreed-upon goals, teachers' needs and interests, conversations with colleagues, instructional walks, coaching visits, and other sources of input. The focus of all professional development is ultimately on student learning: that is, "What will be happening in the PLC that will increase and enhance students' competency, engagement, and independence as readers, writers, thinkers, and learners?"

Separate the discussion of matters related to the daily operations of the school from the professional learning work. To ensure clear coordination and communication of school matters such as parent night, report cards, scheduling issues, and similar matters, create a committee with grade-level representatives to meet monthly with the principal. The committee communicates the key information to teachers in a timely, effective manner—for example, during a designated monthly time for grade-level meetings.

(Note that the work of a committee is usually procedural and informative; the work of a collaborative team and PLC is visionary and centered around teaching, learning, and leading.)

To underscore the importance of a leadership team to successful PD, Kim Ball, principal of the Professional *Literacy* Community school discussed earlier in this chapter, had this to say:

> I see other schools struggling with embracing their PD. The critical difference is the leadership team. If you have a leadership team, then PD isn't *done* to you. It's an important collaborative process, and every teacher has a voice. The leadership team provides teachers not only voice and a clear vision, but also a very sharp focus for where we're going. Wednesday afternoon is sacred time; it's literacy PD only. We're dedicated to that schoolwide. Contractually, it's an hour, but we go one and one-half hours. It's now part of our changed culture. Most teachers choose to stay beyond contract time because we have a professional learning environment. Everyone is giving 100 percent, and it wasn't like that previously.[22]

Develop a Selection Process for Membership

Before a school's PLC can be up and running well, a leadership team needs to be carefully selected. The ongoing success of a PLC depends on a strong, knowledgeable team to effectively plan, organize, and lead the PLC sessions and to keep between-session work and conversations going throughout the school. In some schools, the principal or literacy coach (or both) assumes all responsibility for planning and carrying out the PD work. In my experience, that scenario can work, but distributed leadership is more effective and does not leave the principal and coach overwhelmed and exhausted. That said, the principal must be part of all the PLC sessions—the planning, participating, and debriefing—if student achievement is to improve schoolwide.

Keep selection process fair, balanced, and open

Strive to create a fair and balanced selection process for team membership. Having been involved with this course of action with various schools, teams, and principals over a number of years, I strongly recommend that selection be an open process with any teacher eligible to apply. The principal can quietly encourage strong potential team members to apply if they have not done so. Six to eight members on the leadership team is ideal, and the principal is always one of the team members. (In a small school, one representative per grade level is not advisable as having half of the staff on the team is not advantageous.) I further recommend that the principal make the final decision for team selection and that members serve for two years. It also works well to have half the team members rotate off every two years, so there are always experienced members to mentor the newcomers.

An exception to the two-year membership is the recommendation that, along with the principal, one leadership team member be designated a permanent member. (The team, with strong principal input, decides on that member, someone who is well organized and respected as a strong literacy leader by staff.) That way, if a principal leaves or a key literacy leader leaves, there is someone in place who has more than two years of background knowledge and understanding of the team's process, decision making, and history as to why things were decided as they were. That same team member can also be the archivist, the keeper of records of all the hard work the staff has done over the years, so the evidence of growth in student and teacher learning is apparent in a variety of ways beyond test scores. Literacy leader and team member Kate Gordon notes the importance of keeping and examining work over time:

> We see the growth in complexity and reflective thinking in the evaluations we've done as educators at the end of each residency, in the student writing samples that we are now archiving, in the staff beliefs that have grown and changed over time. These documents are important visible proof that our work is paying off, we are more reflective, ask better questions, and are focusing more on the whole of writing. For example, we no longer view conventions and editing as our main indicators for strong writing. We value those, of course, but also emphasize audience and purpose, craft, revision, and a whole lot more.[23]

For the first year, it is recommended that the principal select team members to apply for membership based on established criteria (e.g., ability to lead the school's shared vision, knowledge of the focus curriculum area, respect from all colleagues). For the second year and beyond, I suggest that grade-level colleagues recommend coworkers based on the established set of characteristics or qualities being sought in a leadership team member.

Usually the leadership team is composed of the principal, one representative from each grade level, and the literacy coach, reading specialist, or instructional specialist (if the school has one or more of these positions). For middle and high schools, content-area representatives are included.

This selection process works well as long as there is a healthy, collaborative culture using agreed-upon criteria that are available in writing to all. (If the culture is not yet collegial, have the principal invite applicants who are strong teachers and respected by their peers.) The principal has a conversation with each nominee before making final selections. Final composition of the team is geared to whole-school cohesion and goals—and is balanced, for example, among primary and intermediate and support specialists—but might not include every grade level or content area.

Use a structured application/interview process

What follows is an application and interview process with some suggested procedures that have worked well at other schools. You will want to tailor any application process to suit your school's needs.

- *Have teachers apply for membership* on the leadership team. It can be as simple as letting the principal or existing team know they are interested or as formal as submitting a written application. Encourage teachers who you think would be strong members to apply.
- *Set a time frame and expectations for the interview process*—when, where, what (content), who does the interviewing.
- *Have the principal conduct the interview.* Although the leadership team can conduct the interview, I strongly recommend the principal do it. The discussion with the individual teacher can then be used as an excellent opportunity for professional growth, trust building, and goal setting.
- *Let applicants know to come prepared to discuss their strengths* in the following areas: beliefs, teaching and assessing expertise, coaching skills, relationship skills, content expertise, and leadership skills. (A week or so before the interview, give applicants a copy of the "Essential Characteristics of a Highly Effective Teacher-Leader" [see Appendix I]. The form is organized into three main areas of expertise that encompass these areas: Relationships, Beliefs, and Teaching and Assessing.)
- *Conduct an interview with each applicant.* What follows are some thoughtful questions created by Trena Speirs, a principal in Thornton, Colorado, who notes, "I intentionally didn't ask a specific question about

student achievement or learning, as it was a good assessment for me to see who would connect the work to student achievement on their own."

- *After examining the roles for the PD/Leadership Team, why do you want to be part of the team? Use specific examples of how you have demonstrated or will demonstrate your commitment to professional learning for the school.*
- *Describe your strengths in each of the areas, providing specific examples. In addition, which areas do you most want to grow in? Why?* (Both applicant and interviewer are looking at a copy of the information from "Essential Characteristics of a Highly Effective Teacher-Leader.")
- *Talk about a time when there has been professional conflict within your work environment. How did you respond? What happened as a result of your response?*
- *We are undergoing a big transition, schoolwide, in how we work and learn together. How do you see yourself supporting our school's vision?*
- *What is your greatest hope for our school over the next two years? Talk about what's possible for students and teachers.*[24]

Organize Team Structures for the PLC

The two main structures for implementing professional development by the leadership team are vertical teams and grade-level teams. A PLC meeting often includes both groupings in one session. As an example, grade-level teams might first look at writing samples for strengths and needs at the grade level. Then, vertical teams might look at those same samples across the school to note trends, strengths, expectations, needs, and goals for the entire school.

Vertical teams

Whole-school PLC meetings are often organized as vertical teams; that is, teachers from different grade levels and specialists sit and work together as a group. A typical vertical team comprises a representative from each grade level or content area and one or more support specialists. For example, if there are three teachers at a grade level, there will be three vertical teams. Vertical teams are employed during whole-school PLC meetings so that effective practices and issues around reading, writing, assessment, working with struggling readers, reading a professional article, and other matters are discussed, debated, and understood through a whole-school lens.

As an example, vertical teams might start by reading, reflecting, discussing, and analyzing current research, an article, or a video-based lesson. The conversations become rich as team members from all grade levels and content areas learn from each other and make connections to their instruction and students' learning.

Grade-level teams

The grade-level team consists of teachers of the same grade level and specialists who support students at that grade level. In a small elementary school, a grade-level team might include all primary teachers or all intermediate grade teachers. Although vertical teams are usually the norm for at least part of the PLC meeting, it is also essential to provide time for grade-level planning for application of new learning during the whole-group session. Vertical teams are asked to break at this time and regroup themselves into grade-level or content-area teams. Teams use this time to *begin* to plan together and identify their focus for instruction and how they will apply what they have just learned or attempted to learn.

Typically, in between whole-group sessions, grade-level teams continue to plan during their common planning time and agree to meet at least one day a week as a team. They plan together and apply the work and goals from the whole-school PLC. Whenever possible, the principal participates in grade-level meetings or instructional team meetings, not to oversee but to show respect and support for the time teachers devote to collaborative planning.

It is recommended that notes from grade-level meetings be taken and given to the principal so a record of all work and discussion across a school is visible and preserved. The principal is then aware of where more support might be needed, even if he or she is unable to attend. As an alternative, depending on needs, adjacent grade levels might also work together, such as kindergarten and grade 1, grades 2–3, and so on. Or partner teams of two or three colleagues might plan together following the PLC meeting.

Getting started and getting organized

Two lists that follow provide guidelines and organizational tips that can help create and support the optimal functioning of the leadership team, which is essential for the success of effective and ongoing Professional *Literacy* Communities.

Keep the leadership team going

- *Plan for the leadership team to meet every other week or weekly, if possible,* and when necessary. Consider meeting after school for 45 minutes to an hour (and granting a small, annual stipend for team members' additional time, if possible).
- *Plan to use school release times* (when the school calendar permits) for whole-school professional development, at least once a month.
- *Ensure that PD meetings include vertical teams*, at least some of the time. (It's crucial that PLCs sit and discuss as cross-grade-level teams, at least part of the time, to get a whole-school picture of literacy and learning.)
- *Determine future selection process for the leadership team.* (Most often the principal has put together the initial team.)
- *Help establish PD structures in the school*, for example, how and when grade-level planning takes place and what the expectations are for things such as taking notes on the meeting, planning for application of what was discussed and demonstrated in schoolwide PD, and providing support, as needed.
- *Select two or three team members to lead/facilitate PD* (once the principal and school have built a climate of collaboration and trust). Members can vary. The principal needs to be an active participant who delegates responsibility to various team members, taking leadership as appropriate but encouraging distributed leadership and responsibility among the group members. Although the principal can and does facilitate the PD, that responsibility is often shared.

Attend to ongoing nut-and-bolts responsibilities

- *Use time wisely.* It's easy to let one issue take priority. Stay focused on the end goal—enhanced student learning through high-level professional learning. It is essential that the session's goals be both measurable and observable and that the goals for the session drive the conversation. This is the facilitator's greatest responsibility—to keep the session focused on the learning and on-task with the session's goals.
- *Plan, prepare for, and carry out professional development*, including sharing an agenda with time frames and related professional reading for

discussion, in advance of the PD meeting. (Distribute general ideas of agenda content to the whole staff a month ahead of time so staff members are aware of specific focus.)

• *Get all needed materials ready*—for example, photocopying and distributing articles for professional reading and copies of student work for examination.

• *Review and act upon evaluations from every PD session.* Celebrate participants' learning. Address participants' concerns. Typical evaluation forms are open-ended and include such questions as these:

  ◦ What was most helpful in today's session?
  ◦ What did you learn (or confirm) that would be most useful to your teaching?
  ◦ What evidence do you have that students are learning more and becoming more independent as learners?
  ◦ What questions or suggestions do you have?

• *Set up a coaching protocol* so team members (including the principal) practice modeling exemplary literacy practices for each other, with guided feedback.

• *Provide common planning time* in master school schedule for collaboration among colleagues, application of learning, and observation.

Set Up a Coaching Protocol for the Team

Coaching one another within the leadership team is a vital but rare team activity that pays big dividends. Within the safety and trust of the team, members try out what they will be asking teachers to do, and they coach each other. That practice time with feedback is vital for ensuring that team members become expert in demonstrating, supporting, and applying exemplary literacy practices so they can expertly offer meaningful support to teachers. One powerful example is writing and thinking aloud in front of the team in order to get better at teaching writing.

A leadership team that I was coaching and collaborating with included the principal, a literacy coach, the K–12 director of teaching and learning, a reading coach, and two classroom teachers. Initially, all expressed feeling vulnerable, hesitant, and anxious about the coaching activity, although they were willing to try and believed it could be useful. We had agreed that each of us would do a demonstration writing lesson on a topic close to our hearts.

Just as we often do in an instructional walk with teachers, we observed what the demonstrating writer did, scripted what she said, and focused on the writer's strengths in giving feedback. When it was the principal's turn, she "wrote aloud" about how much it meant to be so fully welcomed by the staff to her new school and about her determination to ensure that all students in the school learn. She was visibly emotional as she wrote about how deeply she cares about staff and students, and we were all very moved by her passion and commitment.

Afterward, using our notes, we each spoke aloud our feedback and handed over our papers to her. She later said, "That was the best professional development experience I've had in the last 15 years." Having the words she said recorded and read back to her made a powerful and lasting impression. Although the principal still does instructional walks four to five days every week, she now ensures that about once a month she hands over her notes to the teacher, and that action has had an enormous, positive impact on teachers.

Because literacy excellence is the focus of the PLC and the school, leadership team members—who guide large- and small-group discussion and support teachers between sessions—must know literacy and teaching. If the principal or literacy coach is not able to understand the stresses of teaching, to notice what's most important about what's happening in the classroom, to offer realistic suggestions, to demonstrate effective practices, and to support teachers in a way that increases instructional expertise, teachers may find that person's presence a distraction and an annoyance.

Establishing a coaching model within the team makes it more likely the team will be successful coaching others in the school. Therefore, make it a priority to schedule some leadership team meetings for the purpose of becoming more expert at applying excellent literacy practices. Establishing a coaching model within the team and noticing what works helps with the set-up of a whole-school coaching model later on, which is essential to whole-school change and achievement.

Establish Roles and Responsibilities

A well-functioning leadership team optimizes the learning work of the school by successfully leading and guiding the ongoing professional development and supporting all staff to extend and apply the learning from PD sessions. The team develops and helps create the interaction, structures,

---

Quick Win

Share responsibilities for PLC meetings. Consider having the leadership team members assume such roles as keeping teams on task and on time, recording and distributing minutes from the meeting, creating charts to document thinking and data, and ensuring all staff receive related professional reading.

and expertise needed to guide, support, and sustain the work. The following sections provide detailed guidance.

Provide ongoing leadership and support

- *Use the various strengths of team members and all staff,* especially in planning professional development. Often team members and other teachers have different areas of strength and interest. Highlighting this expertise creates enormous potential for growing capacity within the school.
- *Set the tone for PD as schoolwide, crucial, thoughtful, shared learning* that is relevant and enjoyable, so that learning by and from all becomes a cultural norm.
- *Demonstrate willingness and ability to talk about your own literacy practices* and how these apply to the whole school.
- *Help facilitate communication between and among all staff members*—for example, noticing and bringing back to the team ideas from staff for PD, next steps, concerns to be considered. Very important, work to ensure voices of all staff members are respectfully heard.
- *Support literacy specialists and coaches on classroom visits*; share positives you have noticed in the building with them so successes and progress can be made public and available to others.
- *Support grade-level teams* and ensure grade levels have regularly scheduled time to meet (e.g., once a month during Wednesday release time devoted to grade-level meetings, plus common, weekly planning times, if possible).
- *Set up grade-level and cross-grade-level coaching opportunities* (after establishing norms for the school coaching process). Work toward school-wide coaching.
- *Act as a clearinghouse for building issues that need resolution*—for example, poor spelling across the grades, teachers needing to collaborate more effectively, raising literacy expectations.
- *Do whatever is necessary to support the literacy work*—infrastructure, writing/reading process, and effective monitoring—and move it forward, including using the shared knowledge in the school to best advantage.[25]

Implement key processes for PLC meetings

- *Lead a process for establishing ground rules for how the PLC will operate.* Discuss ground rules that everyone agrees to follow. (See the National

School Reform Faculty at www.nsrfharmony.org for excellent procedures for "Forming Ground Rules," as well as for many other useful protocols.)

- *Follow established school norms,* including acknowledging when things aren't going well and taking responsibility for ensuring norms are followed. When necessary, review norms at the start of every meeting, emphasizing each individual's commitment to and responsibility for maintaining these norms in professional interactions.

- *Initiate and facilitate the crucial conversations around developing school-wide, shared beliefs as a first priority* for successful PD and curriculum alignment and ensure that beliefs are revisited in vertical and grade-level teams, formally and informally, during the school year. (Appendix C on reading beliefs can be helpful for providing a protocol.)

- *Create a sense of urgency and shared mission* by regularly anchoring conversations around the shared beliefs, connecting the beliefs to classroom practices that are consistent with them, and setting priorities for PD that reflect what is most crucial for developing the shared knowledge that will move instruction and learning forward.

- *Help lead the staff in establishing a vision of the graduating reader and writer* and making the vision public throughout the school and with the students and their families. (Post the vision; share it in newsletters.)

- *Come to agreement on the decision-making process*—what decisions are made by consensus, by majority vote, or by the principal.

- *Begin every PD meeting with an authentic celebration* (new learning or something you've noticed that a staff member or student has done well), the more specific the better. When we notice and name best practices, it increases the potential for those practices to spread.

Additional thoughts regarding organizing effective PLCs come from a classic resource on how to establish a learning community within a school as well as how to sustain change: *Professional Learning Communities at Work* by Richard DuFour and Robert Eaker:

- Access multiple sources of data (summative and formative assessments) to note trends over time. Use analysis of these data to drive the PLC's curriculum focus.

- To sustain and ensure continuity of the school's PLC, create a yearlong schedule that includes regular time for both vertical and grade level teams to meet. (Vertical teams are especially useful for discourse around school-wide data.)

Quick Win

Facilitate bragging. Teachers are often reluctant to voluntarily speak publicly about their successes. Notice something a teacher has done well and ask him to bring the work sample to share at the PLC. Introduce the person by saying, "I've asked Michael to share _____." The teacher is often more comfortable sharing when someone else initiates that sharing.

- Provide funds that allow teachers to be released to observe and work in their peers' classrooms.
- Make parents part of the PLC process by including them in the school's vision and goals through clear communication, for example, through curriculum nights and sharing the school's achievements.[26]

Establish a consistent PLC agenda

What follows is a typical and consistent agenda for a schoolwide PLC that has worked well in many schools. Think about including celebration, demonstration, discussion, analysis, application, and evaluation in some form in every session. Depending on the time available for PD, the agenda might be spread over three meetings. The leadership team facilitator guides the group to do the following:

- *Engage, reflect, assess.* Colleagues share in vertical teams the results from the previous session and reflect on what they tried and applied in their own practice. Almost always, teachers bring samples of student work, and the session begins with one or more celebrations related to a student's or teacher's efforts or progress.
- *Discuss professional reading.* Colleagues come prepared to discuss the reading of an article, a chapter, or research that is most often connected to the focus of the previous PLC session.
- *Set goals.* The facilitator shares/posts the measurable and observable goals to meet by the end of the session.
- *Focus on the session's literacy emphasis.* Identify an area or an issue that requires staff's change or increase of knowledge and skills. Decide what to learn and how to learn it, and engage in the learning.[27] Often we introduce a video on effective instruction, view the video, and take notes—all with the end goal of learning more and getting better at teaching reading and writing. Following a video, a demonstration, or an explanation, teachers reflect and share their observations.
- *Achieve a deeper understanding.* The goal here is to begin to move from the procedural level (that is, following steps) to greater understanding by teaching at the application level (adjusting one's planning, teaching, and assessment by responding to what students know, need, and can and want to do).[28]
- *Try it/apply it in the classroom.* Participants begin to plan to apply some aspect of the lesson in their classroom. (Without this commitment to

application of learning, teachers are unlikely to use the content of the PLC to increase learning for their students.) Planning, trying, applying, and conferring on the processes, strategies, and actions continue beyond the whole-group PLC by grade levels over the following two to three weeks.

- *Wrap up.* Highlight the learning from the session. Collect feedback on the session and debrief with colleagues on how the PLC went. Use evaluations to guide ongoing work. Encourage grade-level teams to meet weekly in between sessions to revisit videos, notes, and observations from the PLC, and to plan together and try out new learning. Team members also commit to share lessons, student work, and samples of their new learning at the next PLC session.[29]

Lead a productive PLC

Essentially, successful PLCs increase student learning, schoolwide, through high-level, shared professional learning. In summary, key actions include the following:

- *Make a commitment to meet regularly* for at least 30 minutes (weekly is best) and follow agreed-upon norms. From a practical standpoint, it works well to have whole-school PLC sessions every three to four weeks. Some schools are fortunate enough to have built-in release time for PD, but any time structure that is at least 30 minutes long can be made to work.
- *Focus on schoolwide collaboration and shared learning* with the goal of increased student learning and greater teacher effectiveness and collegiality. Move from grade-level focus to whole-school focus on literacy achievement across the curriculum.
- *Post an agenda* in advance that meets the groups' needs.
- *Begin and end on time.*
- *Share and celebrate success stories* at every meeting.
- *Have a volunteer take notes* on the content of the PLC meeting; distribute these to all staff, including those not in attendance.
- *Encourage everyone's respectful voice to be heard*, without judgment.
- *Demonstrate yourselves as learners.*
- *Seek to build trust* between and among participants.
- *Develop a schoolwide shared vision and beliefs system*; post it; revisit it often and revise it so that it is always refining and evolving.

Quick Win

When possible, include food. Having coffee, cookies, fruit, or other snacks at a PLC meeting, which is often at the end of the day, gives people energy and makes them feel valued. Also, conversations often become richer and more open when we extend hospitality.

Quick Win

Use Title I funds, when applicable, to provide PD stipends when teachers must meet outside of contracted time.

- *View, share, discuss, and apply excellent literacy practices.* This is the heart of the PLC.
- *Continually examine student work and data* across the grades (without blame); focus first on schoolwide strengths; then note schoolwide weaknesses; develop and implement a plan and process for improvement and raising schoolwide achievement. Worthwhile change occurs slowly, but we do see evolving positive patterns over time.
- *Work to develop a collective responsibility for finding solutions* that implement innovative, proven practices, and for raising student achievement.
- *Provide helpful and relevant professional articles* to read to promote thinking and discussion about research, theory, and practice.
- *Provide opportunities for teacher-leaders to facilitate PLCs,* as well as the principal.
- *Keep the focus on authenticity and matters of substance* that have the potential to lead to increased student learning and more effective teacher practices.[30]

Sandra Figueroa comments on how implementing PLCs as the foundation for all professional development empowered her as a first-year principal in a failing school:

> Our Professional LITERACY Communities were the single most important factor in our increased student achievement after the first year. While sustained improvement takes several years we were able to create a culture of collaboration and improve student learning even with all the challenges that come with being a novice principal in a high-poverty underperforming school.[31]

Ensure Successful PLCs and Accelerated Learning for All

When the Professional *Literacy* Community is effective, it becomes the life-giving force of the school. That is, everyone is striving to work well together, to collaborate to learn more so that daily instruction, assessment, and response to students propel them forward as astute readers, writers, speakers, listeners, and thinkers. Several additional structures and qualities that have not yet been fully discussed are crucial for optimizing and increasing schoolwide learning: asking deeper questions, using time astutely, and simplifying the work.

Quick Win

Begin your Professional Literacy *Community meetings in small groups* and ask teachers to voluntarily share what's working well in their classrooms. Afterward, when gathering as a whole group, ask members to nominate specific teachers to share their stories. The nomination honors the teacher.

Ask Deeper Questions About Teaching and Learning, Schoolwide

In schools that are working to become self-sustaining, the questions we ask contain bigger ideas as well as smaller ones, and our questions are more clearly focused than at schools that are marching in place or barely moving.

In science, too, the right questions often come from having both the big and the small pictures in mind. There are grand questions that we all want to answer, and there are small problems that we believe to be tractable. Identifying the big questions is rarely sufficient, since it's often the solutions to the smaller ones that lead to progress....

An almost indispensable skill for any creative person is the ability to pose the right questions. Creative people identify promising, exciting, and most important, accessible routes to progress—and eventually formulate the questions correctly.... Many of the creative people I know also have the ability to hold a number of questions and ideas in their heads at the same time.[32]

Asking questions that challenge us and our students to think in expanded ways becomes possible because, largely through the PLC work and ongoing shared learning, teachers and leaders have gained a foundation of knowledge and experience and are able to use informed judgment and insights to go beyond pat answers and data. Much of that knowledge comes from professional reading and related discussion, which help drive higher-level thinking. We also apply common sense, interpret research and data sources to inform decision making without driving it, and constantly reassess what we are doing so students learn more.

The leadership team of a school can guide the posing of questions that will lead to more productive PLCs and more focused dialogue. Working with the principal, have teachers "identify five or six crucial questions that get at the heart of what they need to know."[33] Examples of crucial questions appear on p. 247.

Asking deeper questions profoundly changes teaching and learning. April Waters is an excellent elementary school teacher in Winnipeg, Manitoba. When I first met her in a writing residency, she was teaching 1st grade, and we were focusing on writing free-verse poetry as a way to engage students in this high-challenge school. A majority of the school's students came from low-income families; there was a substantial Aboriginal population; the transiency rate was high; and by 4th grade, reading and writing achievement lagged two years below grade level, on average.

My big, whole-school question after planning with primary and intermediate teachers before the residency and listening to their concerns was "Why do we have so many reluctant writers?" which led to "How can I best engage their hearts and minds?" The big question teachers were asking was "How can we teach all the skills students need to become better writers?" which had led to "How do we teach kids to revise and edit their work?" Although the teachers' questions were important, they didn't address the larger issues, which would first need to be tackled if writing was to improve. Without engagement, we can't teach much that will resonate for students or that they will consistently apply.

Examples of Crucial Questions to Ask as a School

- Where and why are students meeting success in reading and writing, and what are we doing that's causing that success?
- Where and why are students failing to thrive as readers and writers, and what must we do as a school to reverse that outcome?
- What kind of instructional support—and how much—do teachers need to raise achievement for students who are below grade level?
- Where is intervention working well and what can we learn from that success? Where and what changes do we need to make in our intervention programs?
- What steps do we need to take so that we have literacy alignment and cohesion at and across grade levels?
- How are we using the latest standards in a way that supports effective instruction but does not dictate or dominate our teaching?
- What else do we need to be thinking about and addressing that we have not yet considered?

The 1st graders embraced the poetry reading and writing, as did the teachers. Following the Optimal Learning Model, before my visit and during it, we immersed kids in reading published poems written by students,[34] as well as by adults; noticed what poets did and charted those attributes; and spent lots of time with demonstration writing and shared experiences before expecting students to write poems on their own. During a public scaffolded conversation with Dennis, April whispered to me, "This is taking so long and is hard to do—getting the language out of him. Should we just send him back to his seat?" My inner question was "What do we need to do to ensure this child leaves this scaffolded conversation feeling successful?" My belief was—and is—that the extra time it would take is worth it, both for this child and for his observing classmates.

I didn't know anything about Dennis at the time. April later wrote to me that Dennis had an educational assistant assigned to him due to serious speech issues, which were improving this year. She also noted:

> As a student, he's fairly average but was a habitual crier every time he had to write something. He's a BIG perfectionist, terrified to make a mistake when he's writing, and as a result will shut down when it's time to write. When I saw his hand go up to write a poem with us, I chose him immediately because I wanted him to have success with this. I wasn't surprised in the least when we had to work our tails off with him (very typical with Dennis), but he was so excited with the result, and it was way easier for him to start today on his Father's Day poem.[35]

April is a highly reflective teacher, and with ongoing professional dialogue through PLCs in her school, she and many of her colleagues began to shift their beliefs and practices from the teaching of isolated skills to embedded teaching of skills in meaningful texts (moving to a whole-part-whole approach). Asking deeper questions drove much of that mental and material change that led to raised expectations and higher achievement. Asking deeper questions and looking for resolutions also ensured that the concrete, smaller but important questions she and other teachers wanted answers to were addressed, but these issues were now grounded in an authentic purpose and context that made sense for the learner.

As of this writing, two years since that first residency, April successfully teaches a combined grade 4/5 classroom. She notes, "Moving to a higher grade level was no big deal. I knew the process for teaching reading and writing and could easily apply it."[36] Recently she was asked to represent her school in giving a presentation to leaders in her province. Her poise, confidence, and connection of her beliefs to her practices impressed everyone in the audience. Today she is one of the teacher-leaders in her school who continue to drive the professional learning. Her ability to ask more important questions—not just for her own teaching but for the whole school's achievement—has played a pivotal role in her effectiveness as a teacher and a teacher-leader.

Asking deeper questions is the hallmark of thoughtful, creative individuals who are always curious to learn more. When we teach student and adult learners to formulate their own important questions, they are more engaged and energized, and they learn more. The end result is higher-quality thinking.[37]

Use Time Astutely

In successful schools, we consciously spend time on what we value most and then make sure that time investment is yielding worthwhile results. If not, we make adjustments. Such structures as specialist and classroom schedules, PLCs and other meetings, instructional walks, field trips, and special programs all need to use time in a way that maximizes learning. The purpose and content of what we do must remain focused on improved student learning. That time also includes taking time for ourselves so we come to school refreshed and energized each day.

Embrace time enhancers

The work can be exhausting, so it needs to also be exhilarating. I say that in all sincerity. At the end of a residency, I am exhausted from all the hard work and thinking, but I have a sense of satisfaction and exhilaration that comes from seeing what students, teachers, and principals are capable of and willing to do. As a school, we have made our infused PLC work the highest priority and made everything else secondary. We have put our time and energy where we believe we can make the greatest impact, and that includes people, resources, and teaching/learning activities. Using our time well also makes it more likely we experience joy in teaching and learning.

Spend time in ways that add energy and efficiency to your days and that can save you time in the long run. This can involve things such as the following:

• PLCs that are meaningful, well organized, and connected to improving and enhancing classroom literacy practices
• Coteaching/coaching with a trusted peer
• Debriefing and giving feedback as part of the event
• Whole-part-whole teaching
• Writing for an audience and purpose that matters
• Explicit skills teaching that is embedded in reading and writing texts

- Distributed leadership
- Well-thought-out plans
- Special times to socialize with staff
- Celebration of strengths—student, teacher, principal, school, families

Avoid time wasters

Negative people, divisiveness, and inadequate resources exhaust us. So do constant complaining, overly complicated processes and activities, and perpetual naysayers (whose input is different from healthy skepticism). To maintain cohesion and optimism, and to carry out the shared vision and beliefs of the staff, find ways to minimize or eliminate the following:

- Staff meetings around "stuff" and PD that is not meaningful
- Whole-school interruptions
- Programs that don't support the school's shared beliefs and goals
- Research that does not meet rigorous standards
- Isolated-skills instruction
- Mandated programs that must be followed in lock-step
- Unnecessary paperwork and nonessential e-mail and text messages
- Discussion of problems that others can solve on their own
- Debates about the "small stuff"
- Homework that doesn't contribute to successful practice
- Technology tools that do not increase student learning
- PLCs where the emphasis is not on improving literacy and learning
- Excuses for why students are not learning
- Long staff meetings (communicate by e-mail when possible)
- Excessive test prep
- Nonessential initiatives

Simplify the Work

By "simplify" I mean making the work more manageable, more focused, less complicated, and even elegant. "Elegance is the subtraction of weight so you end up with the essence of the issue.... the search and use of ideas that have maximum impact with concise effort."[38] I do not mean dumbing down the content or making the work simplistic. In fact, simplifying the work allows us to raise expectations and results because we get to the heart of the work—that is, the precise learning habits, concepts, and strategies that are most important to teach and have students learn. Simplifying the work so all participants understand it ultimately makes it possible for students to read complex texts, understand and apply learning goals, self-evaluate, and set their own goals.

Steve Jobs, who was a genius in getting to the essence of the work, believed "Simplicity is the ultimate sophistication" and made it Apple's design mantra.[39] The chief designer at Apple, Jony Ives, elaborates: "Simplicity... involves digging through the depth of the complexity. To be truly simple, you have to go really deep.... You have to deeply understand the essence of a product in order to be able to get rid of the parts that are not essential."[40] That last sentence gets to the core of the work. We educators can't simplify until we thoroughly understand all the intricacies of the work as a whole, how the parts fit together, what we can leave out, and what is an absolute priority. That is, simplifying well requires our highest levels of knowledge and understanding.

Teaching and leading in today's schools can be so challenging that in order to stay hopeful and not become cynical, teachers have to believe that the work is doable. Without making the work manageable and comprehensible, we just go through the motions of following procedures and top-down mandates; we never get to the vital essentials of our work, and nothing much changes.

Implementation of the Common Core State Standards is one example of a situation in which we need to simplify the work and figure out the instructional core in order to determine where to best exert our time and energies. Also, as one principal noted, "With the CCSS, we have to be intentional of also taking things off teachers' plates. In efforts to make every minute count, we often try to do too much, and we wind up focusing on parts, instead of on meaningful literacy."[41] Some other examples of the need to simplify are teacher evaluation systems and other accountability measures, report cards, lesson plans, written learning targets, use of resources, and interpretation and application of research. Often, these issues and mandates are outside our control. However, when possible, visionary and organized principals who are supported by teacher-leaders do find concrete ways to make the work more manageable and meaningful and give teachers more time and energy for instruction. Some actions we can take include but are not limited to the following:

- Eliminate almost all staff meetings except for well-planned professional development where teachers are notified well in advance of the date and agenda.
- Find ways to free teachers from before- and after-school duties.
- Ensure teacher planning time is scheduled with grade-level/content-area teammates so they can collaborate and plan together.
- Give teachers additional time to prepare report cards.
- Provide excellent professional articles that are not lengthy, that teachers can choose to read (perhaps one article a month), and that support the ongoing work of the PLC.
- Have instructional materials organized by a support staff member.
- Discourage elaborate centers and projects that drain energy.
- Create more avenues for teacher collaboration, PLCs, and time together, all of which reduce the isolation of teaching and the work load.
- Keep the focus on writing priorities and reading priorities as discussed in Chapter 3.

One way we can simplify is to "slow down the teaching so we can hurry up the learning."[42] For learning to stick, we have to understand the concepts, and that takes time. Because time is in such short supply, we attempt to cover a lot of material instead of choosing the most important concepts, teaching them deeply, and guiding students to apply their learning to all aspects of school and their lives. It takes the courage and stamina of a visionary leader to make that harder choice, to do less but do it well, to prioritize and focus on what's most important, and to not get crazed and derailed by the latest set of standards and tests or the newest crisis.

Another way we simplify is through whole-part-whole teaching, a major premise of this book. We have made teaching so much more complex than it needs to be. Literacy coach Kate Gordon put it this way:

> Teachers think everything is too hard, too big, and then it all doesn't seem manageable. For example, teachers are afraid to write in front of their kids. We think we have to write about something big. The simplest, true story will entrance kids. We think what we have to say isn't good enough. Kids love us, so they love our simple stories, and then they can do it.[43]

Finally, efficient classroom management is essential for being able to stay focused on the heart of the work. Effective teachers do not spend time with elaborate management systems, which can sometimes take more time to explain and set up than the work itself. Choice within a carefully defined and practiced structure can greatly simplify the work—for example, classroom libraries set up with students for free-choice reading, writing topics that have been successfully demonstrated, and students generating their own worthwhile questions. Also, as part of effective management, we apply the Optimal Learning Model. That is, we teach students how to take increasing responsibility for self-checking and self-monitoring their work, setting their own worthwhile goals and learning targets, and communicating their progress to their peers and families—all of which simplifies our work.

One principal who has kept her focus on getting to the essence of the work says this:

> Our focused professional development around literacy is continuing this year, a bright spot in the midst of one of the most difficult years in memory due to the steep budget challenges in the district. The elegance of our focused professional development is that it has a core of simplicity that teachers instantly recognize for its authentic quality. It gets to the meat of what students need with great economy and power. This is always welcome, but especially compelling in times when teachers are more taxed than usual in terms of time and workload. It is not a quick process, but there is a slow and deep transformation underway. Very exciting.[44]

Simplifying the work has been a personal lifetime goal for me, both in teaching and living. When I first began writing for educators, I didn't know what to leave out, and while I included a great amount of detail, sometimes it was so much it became overwhelming for readers, especially for those who were struggling. I have learned that simplifying the work—not making it simple but making it significant, manageable, and easy to understand and apply—is a necessity if we are to commit to doing better for our students and to find joy and optimism in our work. Finally, it is the authentic literacy experience that works best. As one teacher noted, "If we want our students to be good readers, we must give them time to read! Such a simple concept, but so often overlooked!"[45]

7

Sustaining the Work:
We Can Do It!

When a school becomes self-sustaining, teachers and leaders are able to successfully carry on the literacy and learning work even if some key people leave. Almost all the teachers and leaders at the school have become highly effective, and they collaboratively work together for the common good of the school. That work includes maximizing student learning and achievement, maintaining the positive school culture, and mentoring newcomers and quickly bringing them on board. Answers to the questions "What do we value?" "What's the purpose? and "How will we get there?" are clear to all.

Sustainable, worthwhile change is uncommon in our schools because such change depends on an unwavering commitment to developing excellence in leadership and literacy practices at all levels. The realities of poverty, politics, funding inequalities, curriculum mandates, rigid evaluation systems, staff changes, and many other factors outside our control can wreak havoc on our best efforts. Time and time again, things fall apart in a school because a few outstanding teachers retire, a principal leaves, or an ineffective teacher transfers into the school. And yet, we can and must do better.

It is possible to create and maintain a school of highly effective teachers and leaders—a necessity for positively altering and accelerating students' literacy trajectory and especially crucial for our low-performing students. It is possible to have a trusting and joyful school culture where people love coming to work and learning together. And it is possible to have almost all students reading and writing well, setting their own purposes and self-monitoring and self-directing their learning. Although the process of becoming a self-sustaining school is not quick, easy, or educationally fashionable, it is essential that we at least attempt the journey. There's no other way to provide all students equal and ongoing opportunity to learn, which is their birthright in a democratic society. This chapter builds on all the other sections of the book and focuses on the behaviors, mindsets, and actions that have the potential to lead to sustainable and worthwhile school change.

Focus Relentlessly on What's Most Important

One of the most vexing problems in becoming self-sustaining as a school is that it takes courage, patience, resilience, steady leadership, and persistence to stay on a sometimes rocky course over time. A school's chances for becoming self-sustaining hinge on full commitment to an unrelenting pursuit of excellence, high expectations for all learners, a sense of urgency, and a PLC culture of optimal learning for all.

Expect Commitment

Commitment undergirds the sturdy foundation of worthwhile change; without it, change stalls every time. Commitment embodies the unrelenting resolve and obligation to do whatever it takes to increase engagement, enjoyment, and achievement in reading and writing across the curriculum for all—students, teachers, and leaders. Commitment is more likely to occur when leaders we trust don't just give us facts and data, but also emotionally appeal to us so we feel the necessity and obligation to act.

Commitment means that just about every teacher and leader at the school willingly invests sustained time and energy to stay focused on improving literacy and learning practices for all. "And when I say focused, I mean single-mindedly, can't-help-but-think-about-it, intently-concentrated-on-our work focused."[1] Commitment means the principal makes it a priority to get into classrooms daily to celebrate teachers and to support their efforts to improve and enhance their instructional and assessment practices. Commitment further means looking at the data with students in mind and "putting faces on the data,"[2] not "chasing the data" and focusing too much on numbers.

Where deep commitment and knowledge coexist, educators increasingly look to themselves to make the best literacy and learning decisions, and they do not let outside factors veer them off course. How educators get to that place where they are willing to take a leap of faith and assume responsibility for the change is usually a long process of trial and error that is influenced by factors such as a history of disappointment with top-down programs, inadequate student progress, and a school culture that has worked against collaboration and trust. Commitment is for robust educators who invest their time and energies in high-level, schoolwide professional development because they have learned that there is no other solution that works in the long run. Many of those committed educators' voices are part of the fabric of this book.

In my experience, when teachers do not move along as expected and fail to improve despite much support, it's often because they have not made the commitment to do whatever is necessary so students learn at higher levels. There is no sense of urgency or energy to do better and not much self-reflection. These are most often kind teachers who care about their students, but they do not feel a compelling need to alter their literacy and learning lives.

Quick Win

Post only high-quality work. Ensure bulletin boards in hallways and classrooms reflect exemplary work and a literacy focus. Doing so sends a message about expectations and what we value.

Here are some things to do to make commitment more likely:

- Expect teachers to participate in PLCs; make every teacher feel valued and celebrated; let teachers know every voice is important and respected.
- Require a teacher's commitment to read a professional book designated for school study before giving the book as a gift.
- Offer reasonable and ongoing mentoring support with the caveat that the teacher is expected to "try and apply" the instructional moves.
- Provide a reasonable time frame, along with support, for an agreed-upon action to be put in place.
- Demonstrate your own commitment to doing whatever it takes to improve student learning.

Commitment also means there is always room for improvement in some aspect of our teaching and leading. Complacency is the enemy of continuing progress. When Sandy Grade School moved from being the lowest-performing school in the district to one of the highest-performing Title I schools in Oregon, teachers and the principal acknowledged they had more work to do. The principal noted:

> It is not just the school's level of achievement I am proud of. It is the fact that we have stronger academic outcomes for students that makes my heart happy. We clearly have farther to go, but wow, it feels so good to see the staff energized for what we are going to help students accomplish this year.[3]

Become solution oriented; don't just complain

Connected to our long-term commitment to optimal learning for all is doing our part to address troublesome issues. Complaining about our problems is common; less common but more productive is offering possible solutions along with the complaint. In high-success cultures—such as schools in the process of becoming self-sustaining—effective leaders and teachers complain but also bring ideas for a solution. For example, they might say, "Here's a big problem, and here are a couple of ideas for what we can do to solve it."

Complaining without accompanying constructive action can make us feel victimized and powerless. In fact, constant complaining can adversely affect our health, our interactions with others, and our job success. However, when our complaint leads to a successful resolution, we feel a sense of empowerment and achievement.[4] Choosing when to complain and complaining well are hard to do.

Literacy specialist Lori Johnson came to the realization that to have a positive impact in her school and district, she had to go beyond advocacy efforts. She had to alter her mindset from complaint and dismay regarding a districtwide mandated implementation of a questionable reading assessment to a mindset focused on the question "What can I do to make a worthy, positive change?" She wrote to me after attending our 2013 Urgency and School Change Conference.

> When your speakers met with me on the last day, they kept pushing me to think about how I might be able to create change in my school. I kept coming back to the mandated reading assessment, explaining that we were being forced to use this and... They listened and then they said, "Now, how are you going to create change in your school?" After repeating this cycle several times, I finally understood what all of you had been saying the whole time. Standards and mandates will come and go, but we have to be effective literacy teachers in spite of them.[5]

Lori went on to use her renewed spirit and courage to respectfully and knowledgeably speak up, which ultimately led to being able to use the assessment in question in a sensible manner.

If a complaint seems to be in order, do it with a positive purpose. As a guide, follow these tips:

- Start with a positive comment about something that is working well.
- Speak directly and without rancor to the person or group who is able to support or sanction a change.
- Complain without whining. Do it in as neutral a way as possible.
- Offer workable solutions along with the complaint.
- Override an initial defeatist attitude and the inner voice that says, "Why bother? There's no point."[6]
- Be willing to be part of the solution.
- Respect the listener's time. Make an appointment and be concise.

As you are working to constructively shift from complaining or compliance to working for constructive change, consider how to teach your students in a parallel fashion. Being solution oriented about problems is a great life lesson for our students, not just our colleagues. Teaching students how to use persuasion, reasoning, research, debate, and facts to make a worthy difference will serve them well in all aspects of their lives.

Instill a Culture of Collaboration, Learning, and Empowerment

Quick Win

Make coteaching and coaching a reality, especially when roving substitutes cannot be afforded. When teachers have good management skills and trust levels are high, two teachers and two classrooms can occasionally work together for coaching or coteaching opportunities.

Particularly important, a self-sustaining school is relationship oriented in a unique manner. Members of the school become a large extended family. Returning to a school where I have bonded with teachers and students always feels like coming home. I care about the people I work with, I am happy to see them, and I look forward to our shared conversations and learning. In our schools, caring relationships make trust and successful collaboration more likely. Just as it is in our personal lives, most of our happiness stems from relationships with others.

Teachers and leaders in a self-sustaining school come to depend on each other and share responsibility for students' learning. Because trusting relationships are the bedrock of the school, teachers work together effectively, seek each other out, have ongoing spontaneous conversations about teaching beyond PLCs, and encourage one another to take risks. Such whole-school trust also allows for honesty and authentic dissent, which not only invigorates everyone but sparks creativity of thinking and taking new action.

A school moving toward sustainability makes the shift from an individual- and a grade-level focus to a focus on all students in the school. That is, the school's notion of family extends to caring for and taking responsibility for all students in the school. That shift greatly changes the focus of professional learning in PLCs and makes learning and dialoging together throughout the day a cultural norm. Making the choice to stay optimistic and to take a risk is easier to do when we have the support of a whole and caring community led by a visionary principal supported by teachers and teacher-leaders.

In a school that is becoming self-sustaining, joy in teaching and learning is evident. The school is a happy place to be! Enjoyment comes from the confidence of knowing how to do something well, from working with colleagues we respect and admire, and from assuming joint responsibility for ongoing learning—for our students and for ourselves. It is rare for someone to choose to leave such a school. Those who do leave usually do so because they are unable or unwilling to rise to the level of excellence that is required and to become fully present in the collaborative culture.

Empower teachers and students

In self-sustaining schools, constructive empowerment is everywhere. By creating relationships and trust throughout a school, teachers and students are empowered to be risk-takers, advocates, and self-determining thinkers, readers, and writers. "In education systems that are high in international rankings, teachers feel they are empowered by their leaders and their fellow teachers."[7] That is, teachers know and value that great results depend on whole-school effectiveness, which is achieved by working together as a team. The mindset of the school shifts from "me" and "my" to "us" and "we." A teacher put it this way: "My thinking changed. I came to rely on the whole school as a great team for improving literacy."[8]

Teacher empowerment is most evident on the leadership team, where the principal mentors and encourages teacher leadership. While the principal heads the team, a highly functioning leadership team proposes solutions to issues, tackles PD needs, and does whatever is necessary to support increased student learning at the school. For example, members of one leadership team proposed to the principal that more time was needed for collaborating and colearning with colleagues during the day, and the team suggested possible ways this could happen.

As an example of student empowerment, let's revisit the 5th graders who turned their reading and writing work on bullying (see Chapter 2) into whole-school and district advocacy for a bully-free zone and for performing acts of kindness. We can predict that at least some of them will continue to empower and influence others—not only in school but also in their lives outside school. The important lesson they learned—that through their own efforts they could work toward resolution of a problematic issue and positively influence future behaviors of children and adults—was as important as any literacy lesson.

Fifth grader Abigail Pinard, who went on to independently write and publish many books, including *A Million Acts of Kindness*, plans to "go to college to be a teacher and children's author." Speaking about how the year-long focus on writing and kindness empowered her, she says:

> I never liked writing until the fifth grade when we wrote about topics that mattered, and I had lots of choice. I learned how to write better in all different ways. After that, I was writing like there was no tomorrow! I wrote seven books that year and continue to write more! I especially enjoyed the fishbowl experience when I learned how to write better in a group. I still read during the summer. I read the first *Harry Potter* in two days (the first day I read nine hours straight!). I am working on the second book of the series. I continue to write during the summer. Mrs. Espenel and Mrs. Routman have helped my writing incredibly![9]

Several other examples of student empowerment include students taking over the bulletin boards with the knowledge that what's posted must be authentic, meaningful, and readable; creating booklets on school safety; guiding visitors around the building; volunteering to work with younger students who may be struggling to learn to read and write; creating posters that teach the rules or expectations of the school. (See the photo on p. 261 for an example of a poster created by a kindergarten class.)

Perhaps one of the most reliable measures of student empowerment is what happens when the teacher or another adult is not in the room or the school. Students who are empowered know what to do and how to act, and they accept that responsibility in a respectful manner so that the learning work goes on. Working collaboratively, they ensure that class rules, procedures, and the literacy and content work go forward in the usual manner. Positive empowerment at all levels of the school community is not only an indication of a healthy school culture and climate. Such empowerment positively affects achievement. In fact, a multitude of studies indicate that "when school climate measures go up, students' performance on statewide tests in reading, mathematics, and writing also goes up."[10]

Kindergartners create a chart to post in the hallway to help reduce bullying.

Empower the principal

Not only do we want to empower teachers and students, principals also need to be empowered. District constraints, personnel issues, constant demands, and nonnegotiable responsibilities often make such empowerment difficult. If a new principal or a principal new to a school is to carry on the work of a school in an intentional, trusting, and forward-looking manner, that principal needs the full support of teacher-leaders who have been empowered by their former principal. Together they work out a process to maintain the school's commitment to the literacy and learning work.

All of this is not as easy as it sounds. Sometimes schools deliberately work against the success of a principal who is new to the school. The former principal or teachers fiercely loyal to that person can behave in ways that undermine the new principal. In such cases, it is up to mature and responsible teachers and the former principal to take the lead by publicly backing and supporting the new person. For example, they publicly show support for the principal, keep the principal in the loop on school issues that need attention that the newcomer may not be aware of, identify inconsistent messages he or she may inadvertently be giving, refuse to engage in gossip, and let the principal know through kind words and good deeds that they are supportive. Such support can make the difference in giving a principal the courage and stamina needed to tackle a tough job and stay the course. All principals need that kind of support—not just new ones.

Develop a Model for Short-Term Gains and Long-Term Improvement

The majority of schools show little enthusiasm for implementation of long-term strategies that will transform learning. Rather, efforts most often go toward short-term improvements, which are popular but rarely lead to sustainable change.[11] My residency work confirms that most schools feel great pressure to show results as quickly as possible, and they have little time to reflect on their practices. I still demonstrate sure-fire, easy-to-implement strategies so teachers experience immediate success. However, I also teach a combination of the habits, actions, and strategies that require the deeper thought and practice that lead to long-term results. Teachers are willing to do more reflective thinking and develop a culture of inquiry if their confidence is built with winnable strategies right from the start. Especially when an initiative or proposed change requires new learning, rethinking, and an enormous effort, quick wins and short-term gains provide the immediate and continuing reinforcement needed to stay the course.

The last statement applies to all aspects of our lives, not just work. Our school cultures reflect our society, which favors short-term fixes over long-term, sustainable results. Even where the culture of the school is collaborative and professional learning opportunities are rich, short-term thinking

Quick Win

Invite middle and high school principals to spend time in kindergarten, especially in a high-needs district where students are unexpectedly achieving at high levels as readers and writers because of excellent, accelerated instruction in kindergarten. Such an experience can be eye-opening and quickly raise expectations in upper grades.

and perspectives are most often the norm because people are desperate to see some immediate improvement—especially in schools where students are failing to learn to read and write well.

The reality is that the pressures of teaching and leading are so great that it's difficult for most of us to subscribe to and envision long-term solutions to complex educational issues. Teachers are exhausted from spending so much time dealing with the demands of paperwork, regulations, standards, and high-stakes testing, and so thinking about and enjoying teaching often become secondary.[12] As well, teachers feel pulled in so many directions and are often overwhelmed with guilt because they cannot "do it all." And yet, *while it is the harder choice in the short run to commit time and resources to long-term results, it's the only investment that will pay lasting dividends.*

We can learn a lot about taking the long view from Nelson Mandela, who became the first black and democratically elected president of South Africa. Twenty-seven years in prison shifted the direction of his thinking and actions. He became a "long-distance thinker" who came to believe that "a rushed, short-term mistake might have long-term consequences." He learned that one could be bold and still be cautious and that sometimes it was necessary to change long-held beliefs. "Look, you might be right for a few days, weeks, and months and years, but in the long run, you will reap something more valuable if you take a longer view."[13]

Celebrate short-term gains

Given that the time frame around the pressure to get results is always "now," it's important to balance the need for immediate gains with gains that last. We can help students improve their test scores, yet those higher scores can be elusive—that is, they may only indicate short-term learning that isn't sustained.

Sustaining literacy achievement gains is a bit like maintaining a hard-fought loss of weight. If the weight loss is a result of a highly prescriptive or regimented program, pounds are often shed quickly, and the dieter initially feels satisfied with the results. However, most often those results prove temporary unless a long-term commitment is made to applying the knowledge and healthy eating habits that bring about long-term weight loss. The same holds true for us educators. A scripted program, a quick fix, excessive attention to the high-stakes test will yield some gains, but they are likely to be fleeting without a deep and knowledgeable commitment to sustainability.

With long-term strategies, positive results may take longer but they are more likely to be permanent. There may also be an implementation dip as teachers are trying out new practices.[14] We need to allow for that dip as a predictable part of the change process.

> The implementation dip is literally a dip in performance and confidence as one encounters an innovation that requires new skills and new understandings…. Leaders who understand the implementation dip know that people are experiencing two kinds of problems when they are in the dip—the social-psychological fear of change, and the lack of technical know-how or skills to make the change work.[15]

The goal is to provide a balance of quick wins and early successes to support people in committing to do the work for the long run. The goal is also not to lose heart when things are not going as well as expected—for example, adjusting to multiple staff changes in a school—and to realize that worthwhile school change is always a flexible work in progress. Temporary setbacks are a normal part of the sustainable school change process.

Assess continuously

In schools that are continuously improving, assessment is built into the daily fabric of the school. That is, teaching and assessment responsively work together, and we are constantly checking if, how, when, and what students are learning. The teacher is always thinking and acting—before, during, and after the instruction, guided practice, and independent work—with these questions in mind:

- What do the students know?
- What do they need to know?
- What demonstrations, support, and guidance do they need to move forward?
- How will they and we know when they have learned it?

Assessment *is* the school culture; that is, we are always checking to see how and what students are learning and how they and we can do better. Work and results from data teams are put into action. Reading and writing conferences are the norm in every classroom. Formative assessments, small-group work, thoughtful questioning and dialogue, and student self-evaluations continuously inform and improve instruction and learning across the curriculum. In these classrooms we see the following:

- Self-directed groups collaborating in reading, writing, and researching
- Students creating and answering their own high-level questions
- Students—even our youngest ones—comparing and discussing samples of their work in terms of strengths, needs, growth over time, and goals (see photo p. 154)
- Teachers doing less talking and more listening to students' ideas, explanations, and attempts to solve problems
- Students becoming self-determining learners

Aim for Self-Determining Readers and Writers

Self-determining learners are readers, writers, and thinkers who can use what they know and apply it to different contexts (e.g., applying the qualities of effective writing to all genres and forms) for their own meaningful purposes. Becoming a self-determining learner begins in kindergarten when we teach students how to self-check spelling, find and use resources, connect what authors do with their own writing, and reread and revise their own work to make it easier for the reader to follow along and understand.

> **Quick Win**
>
> *Use short texts or excerpts* that stand on their own for reading and writing. These texts allow us to teach everything we want students to know and do, including critical thinking.

Becoming a self-determining learner goes beyond working independently. Students can be successfully working on their own on tasks that are not worth their time. Self-determining theory, as described by Daniel Pink, means that we work with

- *Autonomy*—the desire and ability to self-direct our lives and activities; involves choice over the task, time, and technique.
- *Mastery*—the urge to get better at something that matters; requires engagement and a mindset that "requires the capacity to see your abilities not as finite, but as infinitely improvable."
- *Purpose*—setting meaningful goals that often go beyond self-interest.[16]

It becomes possible for our students and us to become self-determining learners once we become more knowledgeable and our understanding and confidence grow. When that happens, the work becomes easier and more satisfying, which opens up space and energy for us to ask deeper questions, solve problems more thoughtfully, and seek more meaningful purposes for the work we do.

In today's jobs and in the future, our students will be expected to be able to work out the answers to questions others raise. To do so, they will require greater skills in more areas, curiosity and flexibility, resilience, ability to solve problems individually and collaboratively, and excellent communication skills. Those qualities require us to graduate students who are self-determining learners—that is, to have them leave school as learners equipped to handle the challenges and opportunities their future offers and demands. These statements are as true for us educators as they are for our students. Self-determining learners do not just learn on their own; they are determined to go on learning.

Seek to Have Learners Self-Monitor and Set Their Own Goals

It is mid-June in Laurie Espenel's 5th grade class, and the students are on fire with a passion for writing, determination to do better, and a belief that they can make a difference in their own lives and others' lives as well. These are the students from Chapter 2, who used writing to decrease bullying and increase kindness in their school and district. "The engagement of the kids is huge. The kids are taking over and are revising on their own for everything we do."[17] Laurie further comments:

> They were writing, writing, writing until the last possible minute. I went through several reams of my own paper this last week because we ran out of paper at school and then ran out of ink. I was amazed that they were all writing on the next-to-last day of school. I'm exhausted but also exhilarated.[18]

Because of the firm foundation that Laurie has established for teaching writing well, along with the authenticity of the writing work and the sustained time to do it, writing has moved beyond a school subject to a way of life for these students. They are choosing their own worthwhile topics, self-directing and self-improving their writing, self-publishing for authentic audiences and purposes, and continuing to stretch themselves. The students are confident; they believe they have something important to say, that their voice matters, and that people are listening to them with respect and interest. They have become self-determining learners.

In fact, most of the students are settling for no less than excellence. During the fall residency, in talking with teachers who were observing in Laurie's classroom, I remarked—and students overheard—that sometimes "good is good enough." We don't always need to be asking for more length, better words, or required revision—all of which can sometimes destroy a writer's spirit. But by the end of the school year, when Laurie conferred with students and proclaimed a piece of writing "good," they wanted more. All year they had been hearing and talking about what authors do; they had been reading like writers; they recognized the qualities of excellent writing, and they demanded more from themselves without anyone telling them what they needed to do. These students are secure as writers and their voices are strong, and this is true even for the most low-performing students.

Develop Benchmarks and "I Can" Statements

In schools working to become self-sustaining, teachers and leaders establish benchmarks for what a successful exiting reader and writer looks like and can do at each grade level. That is, they and students agree on criteria and show and identify what those criteria look like in an actual piece of writing or a text that a student would be expected to read. Choosing benchmarks that are appropriate and rigorous enough and that align at and across grade levels depends on discussion, analysis, and deep teacher and leader knowledge—plus the belief that an all-school focus is necessary.

Here is where the Common Core State Standards can be helpful. The exemplars the standards provide in reading and writing can be a useful guide, especially if we are knowledgeable enough to determine which exemplars are valid and which are off the mark and should be ignored. For example, the range of reading texts provided gives a sense of the text complexity that students are expected to read at a grade level. But with the writing exemplars, caution is urged because we don't know how much help and what kind of help a student got on the writing exemplar provided.

In my experience, it takes up to three years in a PLC-infused school culture for teachers and principals to have gained enough literacy knowledge across the grades to know what's most important to focus on, what and how to expertly teach, and how to apply responsive teaching and assessing to increase student learning. Establishing worthwhile benchmarks also depends on literacy coherence, which yields higher aspirations and achievement schoolwide. As my esteemed colleague Judy Wallis has often stated, "You can't have rigor without coherence." In addition, we're not likely to reach schoolwide coherence without being part of an infused PLC culture. Coherence around instructional practices requires shared beliefs, vision, and solid knowledge of learning and teaching—all of which have been developed and refined collaboratively through deliberative conversations and constant reflection upon how curriculum, beliefs, and practices can intersect in consistent and complementary ways, at and across grade levels. Scholar and former IRA president Kathy Au states:

> The idea of the staircase curriculum is often referred to as curriculum coherence. In a staircase or coherent curriculum, teachers at each grade level systematically build on what students learned in the grades before.[19]

Even with coherence, determining benchmarks can be overwhelming and scary for teachers. Some have found that starting with "I Can" statements in place of formal benchmarks takes the fear and worry out of the process. Using language that is easy for everyone to understand is far less daunting than writing benchmarks in academic language. As one apprehensive teacher said after the benchmark work: "This wasn't hard to do, and I actually enjoyed the process."

See the "I Can" statements with accompanying work samples from Sandy Grade School for kindergarten and grade 5 in Appendix J. The samples shown are typical writing samples from a standardized, interim writing assessment in a Title I school that has greatly improved student achievement. The kindergarten statements were written by teachers with student input, and the 5th grade statements were written by the students with teacher input. (See the photo on p. 269 showing two teachers reviewing a draft of "I Can" statements.) A specialist teacher who works in many of those classrooms reported that students "are using the 'I Can' statements 24/7, whenever they're writing and revising."[20]

A huge advantage of making the benchmarks public is that everyone in the school community—administrators, families, teachers, students—knows what the literacy expectations are because they are visible, public, comprehensible, and easy to talk about. To that end, we post these "I Can" statements in the classroom and school.

Once students know, understand, and value what the goals and learning targets are—including having some say in constructing them—and they also receive expert instruction in a school where the work has meaning and purpose, it's not a big leap to move to self-evaluation of the highest order. That is, students are confident and competent enough to use "I Can" to encompass their full literacy achievement.

Almost two decades ago, in *Literacy at the Crossroads*, I wrote about what can happen in schools when expert teaching empowers learners

Kindergarten teacher Lindsay Jacksha and literacy coach Kate Gordon are reviewing "I Can" statements.

to take charge of their own learning—that is, they initiate, monitor, and self-evaluate across the curriculum. We had students, starting in kindergarten, making intentional choices, advocating for what they needed, writing persuasive letters to attempt to solve real-world problems, conducting student-led conferences during which they shared portfolios of their work and their progress with their families, and writing their own narrative report cards that accompanied the formal ones prepared by teachers.[21] Reviewing those outcomes in high-challenge schools so many years ago is a reminder of what's still possible.

Mentor Other Teachers, Leaders, and Schools

Dream big! Lasting change is possible, and it depends on continual mentoring and coaching. All teachers and leaders are mentors, coaches, and catalysts for worthwhile change. We don't just model literacy practices; we also model an environment and a culture where teachers and students can thrive as learners. Students are also mentors through peer coaching and partnering with younger students. Public conferences can also be mentoring experiences as students are expected to learn from what another student has done well or is encouraged to try.

Embed Whole-School Coaching

Quick Win

*Pair isolated or
new teachers with
a knowledgeable
teacher* who is a good
personality match and
who works well with
adults; grade-level
pairing doesn't matter
as much. More flexible
partnering is usually
easy to do and can be
a game-changer for
some teachers.

Schools that are high achieving have a culture of "each one, teach one." It's a given that the level of teaching expertise in a school varies due to a mix of teachers that can range from highly experienced to novice. However, school members subscribe to the belief that everyone in the community needs to excel, and that requires doing what we can to support each other every day to improve teaching and learning for all.

Where whole-school coaching is a goal or is in place, principals and teachers find ways to make it possible for teachers to be in each other's classrooms. In one school, when a specialist teacher is absent and a substitute is called in, the principal sometimes bends the rules to maximize the presence of the substitute. In cases where the substitute's role would be mostly that of a placeholder, perhaps due to the specificity of the specialist's job, the substitute is occasionally used to free up classroom teachers to be in each other's classrooms. In other cases, where funds allow, roving substitutes are specifically hired to encourage teachers to observe, coteach, and coach each other. Some principals use discretionary professional development funds to pay substitute teachers to accommodate the observation rotation. A teacher comments:

> Sharing substitutes among teachers has opened up possibilities. It's been amazing. Our closed-door atmosphere is gone! Teachers are in and out of each other's classrooms all the time. Teachers are talking positively about each other, which is boosting everyone's confidence. Just about all teachers are now open to coteaching and coaching.[22]

Schoolwide coaching, where teaching becomes transparent for all to see, only works if teachers have high trust levels. One highly skillful teacher I admire admitted that some of her previous actions had led some staff members to distrust her. She spent an entire year trying to change that perception. When she went into teachers' rooms she made a deliberate and sincere effort to comment on what she saw and heard that was positive. Although some teachers were wary of her presence, her continuous affirmation and good will toward them led to growing trust. Until that trust was established, other teachers would not be able to learn from her.

Although coaching is a role that all successful educators take on in one form or another, it requires great skill. A successful literacy coach must possess all three of the following crucial qualities:

- *Respectful and trusting relationships with colleagues.* We also have to trust the people we mentor and lead. They'll make mistakes, as we all do, but they need to know we're behind them.
- *Ability to work well with adult learners.* This includes knowing what kind of feedback is most useful, delivering it in a kind and compassionate way, and being honest.
- *Deep knowledge of literacy and learning.* Such knowledge is crucial, but without the previous two factors, it won't matter much.[23]

Nancy McLean, a highly experienced and expert literacy coach, comments further on what makes coaching work:

> When I think of the coaching situations that are nearest and dearest to my heart, I realize that the teacher and I joyfully shared the journey of learning together and that the students were the beneficiaries. How did that happen?
>
> Coaching is certainly not an "I've come to fix you" endeavor. It's a positive partnership centered on the question "What can you and I, teacher and coach, learn and do together to enhance student learning?" This partnership must be approached with a sincere respect for the teacher with whom I'm working, with genuine appreciation for the strengths and expertise that the teacher brings to our collaboration. However, to ensure that our coaching partnership has been productive, there must be a continual focus on student work, ongoing planning and debriefing conversations, as well as a gradual release of responsibility.
>
> Sometimes I've done too much of the work, without giving the teacher the opportunity to "solo," if you will. Once I realized that, I slowed down the coaching, and that has paid big dividends. A novice teacher with whom I recently worked provided the following feedback: "You showed me 'how' by modeling, but you also expected me to try it myself, with you as observer and supporter. I would not have learned as much if you had simply demonstrated and moved on quickly to another coaching situation."[24]

For more information and tips on all-school coaching see Routman, 2008, *Teaching Essentials*, pp. 122–125.

Transform Teaching Through Peer Coaching

Peer coaching is a necessity for new skills to transfer from professional development and PLCs into the classroom.[25] Without that transfer, there is no sustainable learning. Tracey Johnson is a great example of the transformational potential of excellent peer coaching. Tracey was an experienced teacher who transferred within her district to a grade 5 classroom after teaching a grade 2–3 class for five years. Of her former school she says:

> It was a comfortable place. I was used to it, but I was on my own. People stayed in their rooms and did their own thing. We wrote for ourselves. It was like, if you're happy with it, it's good enough, even if it had mistakes in it.[26]

She confesses to being "shocked" by the raised expectations at her new school, especially after the first interim writing assessment, when she saw the difference between her students' writing and that of her colleagues' students. She quickly admitted that her previous expectations were too low and that she had been publishing writing that wasn't "good enough."

To Tracey's credit, she worked closely each day with colleague Laurie Espenel as her peer coach, and Tracey also embraced the school's PLC culture. By the end of the school year, the quality of Tracey's students' writing was similar to that of Laurie's students. Tracey comments on the change:

> I was surprised at what 5th graders can do—the content, stamina, and fluency—and how much they like to write. The culture of this school has made a huge difference—the collaboration, the higher expectations. You feel like you need to live up to those expectations.

Adopt a Residency Model

My impetus for creating a residency model in the late 1990s arose from a need I saw as I worked in classrooms and schools. Teachers and principals were expected to implement new or improved practices, but frequently the professional development provided was limited to learning how to use a new program or resource. Even when there had been a book study on a targeted area, teachers had difficulty implementing what they had read about because they needed to see and hear the "what" and "how," and then, with support and guidance, "try and apply" those practices in their classrooms. Without deepening of literacy knowledge and knowing how and when to apply selected and effective practices, little of importance changes for students or teachers.

In the residency model, we make the thinking and the decision-making process visible so it can be replicated—the instructional moves, the teaching points, the language of feedback, the formative assessment that is interwoven with responsive teaching, and the implementation of required standards and curriculum. Teachers and principals can be taught how to get better at noticing what students are attempting to do, using the language of effective feedback, and teaching responsively. A residency model has the potential to work well because principals, teachers, leaders, coaches, curriculum directors, and specialists all get to observe, discuss, analyze, and "try out" what they have seen and heard in the classrooms in their own school or a school similar to their own.

Benefits of a Residency Model

Using a residency model, educators do the following:

- Examine their current beliefs and practices and achievement data schoolwide.
- View exemplary reading and writing practices in diverse classrooms and schools.
- Continue to talk about what has been seen and heard in host classrooms and apply learning to their classrooms and school.
- Read and discuss professional articles that provide the research, theory, and practices that support and expand the work.
- Try out practices with support of colleagues and coaches.
- Gain an understanding of what literacy practices look like at every grade level.
- See student progress over time.
- Extend the experiences or residency through an ongoing schoolwide PLC model, which applies the principles of an Optimal Learning Model.
- Elevate their school culture to one of high trust, collaboration, professional learning, and high achievement.

What follows is the story of successful school change in a large district/division. The story is very much in process, with lots of work still to be done, but early results are promising and provide much hope to students, teachers, coaches, administrators, and families.

A journey to improve writing in many schools

In 2009 I began a partnership and literacy project in Winnipeg, Manitoba, schools led by Allyson Matczuk, the professional development liaison for Winnipeg and the trainer/coordinator of the Canadian Institute for Reading Recovery (Western Division) in Manitoba. The purpose of our multiyear collaboration with three large urban school divisions was to raise expectations and results in many schools where literacy achievement levels were low and languishing. In addition to literacy challenges, the schools that joined the project faced the challenges that often accompany populations with high mobility, low socioeconomic status, limited preschool experiences, and large numbers of second language learners.

Our main project goal was to improve writing instruction for teachers and writing expertise and engagement for students. Most of the teachers and administrators in the participating schools lacked sufficient knowledge and experience to effectively teach writing and to lead the effort toward more effective teaching. The Manitoba curriculum offered more global guidance, and teachers and students demonstrated little enthusiasm or writing expertise, as noted in classroom observations, teacher interviews, interim writing assessments, and student writing samples.

Our major instrument of change for increasing teachers' and principals' knowledge and effectiveness in both literacy and leadership was creating ongoing Professional *Literacy* Communities committed to shared learning. The focus of the schoolwide PLCs would be on increased student learning through extending teachers' knowledge, cultivating a deep commitment to a worthy change process, examining student work over time to assess progress and move learning forward, and ongoing collaboration.

Schools that participated in the project had to agree to commit to a multiyear professional growth plan focused on improving writing instruction. The schools first demonstrated that commitment by implementing schoolwide PLCs with the continuing support of a video-based literacy series.[27] Our initial plan included a launch day with teams from 37 schools, followed by a half-day for principals and leaders; creation of three "hub" schools to demonstrate excellent teaching of writing through an in-school residency model; and identification of satellite schools in each division to observe the residency and apply the learning to their respective sites.

Creating hub schools

In each of the three divisions, a hub school was selected to host a four-day residency; each residency was led by either my esteemed colleagues

Sandy Figueroa and Nancy McLean or myself. In each hub-school residency, we followed the Optimal Learning Model with principals, teachers, specialists, and students. We demonstrated, provided shared and guided experiences, and facilitated professional conversations throughout the day as we coached and mentored teachers, principals, and students.

Each hub school was selected for its strong principal leadership, high trust level with and within staff, Reading Recovery teacher on-site, and agreement of just about every teacher to fully participate in the project. One ultimate goal of the residency was for the hub school to eventually become an ongoing center of writing excellence where educators from other schools in the various divisions—as well as other visitors—could come to observe excellent literacy practices.

During each residency, teachers at the school were released to observe the demonstration teaching in two host classrooms. Small teams—which always included the principal—from satellite schools came to observe the full residency and participate in the ongoing professional conversations sparked by the residency, and then to apply that learning in their own schools. After the residency, to support the writing work in classrooms, all participating schools were expected to regularly meet in their own school's PLC to study, discuss, and apply learning from the residency and the virtual residencies in the *Regie Routman in Residence: Transforming Our Teaching Through Reading/Writing Connections* series.[28] Sometimes principals at satellite schools got together to support and guide each other—for example, by giving each other feedback on instructional walks. By the second year, the assistant superintendents from the three divisions began meeting regularly to support each other and to expand the vision beyond their individual division to the larger provincial area.

Assessment in all three divisions was designed to note strengths and needs, customize the work, plan for future residencies, and document ongoing progress. Careful documentation has included surveys, questionnaires, observations, focus groups, teacher-administered writing assessments, interim standardized writing assessments, everyday student writing, analysis of student writing samples, and self-evaluations and reflections from principals, teachers, and students. (Note: Self-evaluations took place on a consistent basis only at the hub schools.) Some of our key findings appear on the next page.

- High level of commitment and enthusiasm for the project[29]
- More students leaving kindergarten as writers and readers (note evidence stated on pp. 149–150).
- Raised writing expectations for what students at all grade levels can do
- Teachers identifying students first as readers and writers and not by labels or family background
- Increased writing for an authentic audience and purpose (Partial evidence of that outcome is visible in what is posted in hallways; most of that writing is clearly meant to engage and inform readers.)
- Greater alignment of beliefs and practices at and across grade levels and use of common language with understanding
- Students assuming much more responsibility for producing richer writing content and for revising and editing
- Writing infused across the curriculum
- Greater writing competence, confidence, engagement, and enjoyment by principals, teachers, and students in all aspects of teaching writing

Margaret Fair, an excellent principal who has continued to successfully lead one of the hub schools and has completed three years of a residency with Nancy McLean, comments on the effect on her staff and herself:

> Our writing work is progressing very well and has ignited a huge interest in writing in our division. I am very proud of our school! The students and teachers here have been amazing! Also what has become more and more evident is that the parents are noticing the writing and how proud their children are and are often mentioning it or complimenting the teachers now to me.[30]

Jason Drysdale, the assistant superintendent in the same division, has led the effort to bring the project model into middle school, with plans to also take it to the high school. Jason comments:

> As we have worked on the project over the last several years, excitement has built across all of our early-years schools in the division. Recognizing the power of the initiative, the impact on student performance and the awareness of how good teaching practices in early years can transfer to middle years, the middle schools in our division were eager to engage in similar residency work. Building on this eagerness, a middle-years residency and ongoing professional learning was put in

place. Simultaneously, as the impact on student learning and achievement became clear, our senior years [high school] began to apply this important work to their level. As a division we are excited to be working across all grade levels, kindergarten to grade 12, on the reading/writing connections.[31]

Project coordinator Allyson Matczuk comments on the ongoing work:

As the project has evolved and matured, it is clear that our initial goals are being met. While it is encouraging to see principals and teachers excited with a sense of empowerment, the key indicator has been the changes in the students who see themselves as writers and who easily connect reading and writing. The energy, time, and commitment on the part of educators to bring about a change in beliefs, pedagogy, and expectations have been worthwhile. All children in the hub and satellite schools, from kindergarten onward, have built their confidence, have found their voice, and view themselves as writers working to improve their craft. Equally remarkable has been the collaborative, collegial, and cohesive tone within schools, within school divisions, and amongst the three urban school divisions. A positive outcome for learners is the result when there is an investment in high quality professional development. The journey is worth every minute of effort.[32]

Finally—and this is unusual because of the intense commitment required—we have a waiting list of schools wanting to join the project. Word is out that students and teachers are growing significantly as writers and teachers of writing and that joy is an integral by-product of the work.

Protect the School

Sustainable change is possible, but many factors need to be in place, not least of which is protecting a school in the process of becoming self-sustaining. That is, teachers, principals, administrators, and families need to do everything possible to positively confront and ameliorate the expected and unexpected challenging factors that arise in any organization. In schools, some of those challenges can be attrition of teachers and principals, implementation of new standards, district mandates that do not align with a school's beliefs, massive paperwork, cumbersome evaluation systems, severe budget cuts, families in crisis, and unbendable rules. It's easy to experience a perpetual state of being overwhelmed. Continuing to prioritize what is absolutely essential to focus on for the short term and the long haul is a necessity.

Advocate for excellent principals

Finding, supporting, and keeping excellent principals is a daunting task that requires all of us to do what we can to ensure outstanding leadership at our schools. As one former middle school principal notes:

> Until the job description of a principal is better defined and protected as an instructional leader, we MUST rely on our ability to identify, encourage, and support the strongest practitioners who will lead the improved instructional strategies.[33]

In a school that was close to becoming self-sustaining, the superintendent replaced an outstanding principal who was retiring with a promising first-year principal. At the same time, the superintendent also moved a poor teacher in the district to the same school. The novice principal was too new to the district to realize what was happening and to question the superintendent's move. The new principal showed great courage and fortitude by conscientiously spending much of the first half of the school year meticulously documenting the poor teacher's instruction while trying to help her to improve. Because of those efforts by the principal, which were supported by the teachers union, the teacher was removed from the school, but at a great cost. The principal had little time to focus on professional learning, instructional walks, and close bonding with the staff. It took another six months to gain momentum in the school.

Shortly after the incompetent teacher left, the principal and I met with the superintendent to request that he "protect the school" and not place inept teachers there. The school had become a literacy hub—in effect, a lab school where he proudly sent other teachers and leaders from inside and outside the district to observe successful literacy practices. (The "literacy hub" reputation had been gained over six years with two previous principals who embraced a residency and PLC model with their dedicated staff.) The superintendent heard us out, agreed to our request, and kept his word.

Another example confirms the need for advocacy. In a previously failing school that was in the process of becoming self-sustaining, the outstanding principal who was largely responsible for the school's success was being moved to another school after just two years. Recognizing the fragility of

the school's achievement gains, the reading specialist and special education teacher—who were on the school's strong leadership team—insisted
on being part of the district's selection committee for the new principal.
Because the school had become a beacon of hope for literacy possibilities in
a low-performing district, their request to the superintendent was granted.
The two teachers' continuing advocacy and actions in seeking an excellent principal and their refusal to accept the rigid hiring time line when no
"acceptable" candidates appeared were instrumental in the eventual hiring
of a very strong candidate, making it likely that the school's gains would be
maintained and advanced.

 Finally, we need to use our collective professional trust, energies, and
resolve to stop the practice of shifting poor teachers from one school to
another. Doing so would send a strong message to staff that we value their
work and understand the importance of students progressing to each grade
level as well prepared as possible. More principals need to be supported by
other administrators and teachers unions to do the necessary, courageous,
time-consuming work to document a teacher who has proven, despite
much support, to be insufficient.

 Just one or two dismal teachers can adversely affect schoolwide achievement. In addition, other teachers in the school, especially those at the next
grade level, are forced to pick up the slack and try to make up for a whole
year of inadequate teaching. Through relentless efforts and deep commitment to their students, some teachers do manage to close that education
gap. However, out of respect and a sense of fairness to all, we need to protect those teachers by ensuring—as best we can—that everyone is competent and assumes equal responsibility.

Take action

 Protecting a school that is beginning to achieve more or is already high
achieving is a necessity because gains can be fleeting. It doesn't take much
to derail a school's progress. We must all do our part in the following ways:

- *Hire leaders and teachers who are relationship oriented and show
  potential for excellence.* If they don't work well with people, they won't
  do well. We can teach them what they need to know about literacy if they
  show commitment, curiosity, and desire to learn.
- *Keep excellent principals and teachers in a school for a minimum of
  three to five years.* We need that much time to create a hub school and

the potential for self-sustainment. School cultures are fragile, and a move too soon can tip the balance in a negative way. Very important, it takes at least three years for most teachers and principals to become excellent. Too much turnover in a school negatively affects schoolwide achievement.

• ***Make mentorship a given for new teachers and for teachers and principals new to the school.*** For principals, do include the former principal if that person's loyalty is first to the success of the school and to the new principal. The leadership team might take the lead in providing mentorship to teachers and to a new principal as well. Mentorship for principals is still far too rare. For new teachers, focus on teacher mentoring by expert teachers (who need not be at the same grade level). Teachers who feel supported, valued, and professional are more likely to improve quickly and to stay in the profession.

• ***Provide more human resources***, especially in high-poverty schools. Qualified educators need to come before technology when prioritizing school needs. Work to ensure, whenever possible, that excellent librarians, literacy coaches, counselors, and curriculum leaders are part of the school's staff.

• ***Be smart about technology investment and use.*** Although the potential for improving teaching and learning through technology is evident, technology is often used in ways that do not advance learning or change the nature of schooling. For example, in middle and high school math, computers are largely used for basic drills. "Schools frequently acquire digital devices without discrete learning goals and ultimately use these devices in ways that fail to adequately serve students, schools, or taxpayers."[34] Important to note, the highest-performing systems internationally "place their efforts primarily on pedagogical practice rather than digital gadgets." [35]

• ***Publicize successes.*** The best public relations boosters for the work we do are our families and students. Keep the lines of communication open and make schools welcome places where families are eager to talk up the good work of the principal, teachers, and students.

• ***Schedule visitors for classroom observations.*** Once a school begins to become known for increased student achievement, an improved school culture, and a collaborative and joyful workplace, requests for educators to visit can become overwhelming, especially from within the same district. At the same time, having visitors is an opportunity for teachers in a school to continue growing and to acknowledge every teacher's contribution. Be sure to work out a manageable and equitable process that is not exhausting for the principal and teachers and that also benefits the school. See Appendix K for detailed visitor guidelines that have worked well for many schools.

Live a full life

Finally, it may be that the best way we protect our schools is to be wholly present and enthusiastic when we come to work, not just knowledgeable about the content we teach and skilled in effective practices. The environments many of us work in are pressure cookers that drain our energy without restoring it. We need to set some reasonable limits on when we are professionally available and when our time is our own. We must do our best to take care of ourselves emotionally and physically if we are to have the energy and will to make a long-term, positive difference with and for our students.

We educators are caregivers. We need to also ensure we nurture ourselves and enjoy the lives we are living. It is important that we take the time to do things that give us pleasure, energy, and feed our curiosity; many of these activities are often unrelated to our work in schools. For me it's going to farmers markets, cooking for family and friends, making preserves every summer, spending time with my husband, Frank, enjoying my granddaughters, Katie and Brooke, reading great fiction and nonfiction, learning more about a topic I'm interested in, walking, gardening, writing poetry, arranging flowers, eating a meal out, visiting with friends, traveling, and going to the theater.

For example, in the course of writing this book, spending a couple of hours in the kitchen creating a wonderful soup, a fruit tart, or a dish made from appealing choices at the local farmers market grounded me and restored my energy. When I cook or bake, I forget about everything else and just immerse myself in the fun of creating something familiar or new, but always delicious and beautiful. Usually I am cooking for Frank, and part of the pleasure derives from knowing that he will appreciate and enjoy my efforts.

Reading transports me in a similar way. It takes me to another place where I lose myself and forget about the outside world, and all the while my mind is being enriched and, often, stretched. At the time I was writing this passage, I was reading Alice Munro's latest short story collection, *Dear*

Life.[36] Munro is one of my favorite writers, and I am transported into other lives through her brilliantly crafted narratives. In late afternoon or before going to bed, reading settles me down and relaxes me.

Taking quiet time for myself is essential for feeling renewed and re-energized. It is not enough that our students and we are living; we want to be living and leading fulfilling lives. My commitment is to literacy, but it is foremost to living a worthwhile life. When we bring our interesting lives into our classrooms and schools, we are giving more than literacy to our students. We are showing them, through our own example, what a well-lived life can be. And, as one group of intermediate-grade students with whom I bonded recently wrote to me, "We enjoyed learning about you and getting to know you as a person." It is always all about relationships, in school and in life. When those relationships are genuine, caring, and trusting, all things are possible.

We Can Do It!

My hope is you will use the questions raised, research, voices, issues, strategies, and success stories in this book to lead the way in your own school. You can be successful, too! Commit to a PLC culture of excellence, engagement, and high achievement for all! You *can* get your school on board and focus on improving literacy. You *can* get better results. You *can* have joy in learning. Preserve your dreams for students and teachers, but make the work manageable and the end goals possible. Strive to simplify teaching, leading, and learning.

I leave you with three touchstone questions to keep in mind in moving forward with any plan, activity, assignment, demonstration, strategy, vision, assessment, program, meeting, grouping, or resource:

• Does it have compelling value?
• Will it advance student learning?
• Will it increase engagement, enjoyment, and competence?

Keep your focus on what's most important, and do not allow yourself to be diverted. Use your knowledge, expertise, common sense, and courage to make your voice heard and your actions positive on behalf of everyone—students, teachers, and leaders. We can make a positive, lasting difference and help students excel. Our students and their families are counting on us.

Postscript

Most of the time, we never learn about the lifelong impact our efforts have made on our students. Once in a while, often many decades later, we may hear from a grateful student who reaches out to us. I had just completed the final review of this book when two former students "found me" on Facebook. One let me know she had been a student in my classroom my very first year of teaching. She wrote, "I love learning and reading so much.... You are a very inspiring teacher." The other student, who noted we had worked together on her reading, wrote "I am still a fast reader and love to read.... Everything you did was a foundation for my success, and I thank you."

I don't remember these particular students, mostly because I taught them so long ago and so many other students came after them. But here's what's important. Our students remember us. When they know we believe in them and see them as capable, and when we do everything in our power to support them to become successful learners, we remain a vital part of their lives—even if we don't know it. For these students, even if it's just a small number of them, our influence can be life changing and affect their future success and well-being. That is a gift that matters.

READ WRITE LEAD

APPENDIXES

Appendixes may be photocopied or downloaded, for your individual use at www.ascd.org/ASCD /pdf/books/Routman2014figures.pdf. Use the password Routman 2014113016 to unlock the files. Additional examples and guidance, including a study guide, may be found at that website.

Change Process Worksheet

Under each heading, write ideas to share with colleagues during the planning process.

• Prepare people for change process.

• Infuse optimism.

• Build in ongoing support and collaboration.

• Establish a schoolwide culture that promotes trust and risk taking.

• Lead the change effort.

• How do we know we're learning more and getting better?

• How do we know students are learning more?

Planning Instruction with the Optimal Learning Model

Who Holds Book/Pen	Degree of Explicitness/Support		Planning Notes
How will I assess the learners? How will I celebrate the learners?			
Teacher/Student	Demonstration	Teaching/ Learning Context	
I DO IT	• Explains • Shows how to do it (demonstrates) • Tells	• Reading aloud • Writing aloud • Thinking aloud	
Teacher/Student	Shared Demonstration	Teaching/ Learning Context	
WE DO IT	• Invites student participation • Scaffolds • Negotiates • Shapes thinking • Supports	• Shared reading • Shared writing • Shared read-aloud • Shared experiences • Scaffolded conversations	
Gradual Handover of Responsibility			
Student/Teacher	Guided Practice	Teaching/ Learning Context	
YOU DO IT/ WE DO IT	• Scaffolds • Coaches • Negotiates • Focuses instruction • Observes • Demonstrates as needed	• Guided reading • Guided experiences • Small-group work • Partner work • Informal conferences	
Student/Teacher	Independent Practice	Teaching/ Learning Context	
YOU DO IT	• Assists as needed • Coaches • Evaluates	• Independent reading • Independent writing • Independent problem-solving • Small-group work • Partner work • Informal conferences	

Source: Regie Routman in Residence: Transforming Our Teaching Through Reading to Understand (Session 2) by Regie Routman, Portsmouth, NH: Heinemann. © 2009 Regie Routman. Reprinted by permission.

From *Read, Write, Lead: Breakthrough Strategies for Schoolwide Literacy Success.* © 2014 Regie Routman. **ASCD**

Examining Beliefs About Reading

Agree or Disagree? Read, think about, and discuss the following statements with your colleagues. (There are no right or wrong answers.) Use these beliefs to start conversations in your school and to begin to develop a common belief system about reading.

- Reading is always about making meaning.

- Students need to learn to read before they can read to learn.

- The responsibility for teaching struggling readers belongs primarily to the classroom teacher.

- Leveling books in the classroom library is a good idea.

- Moving through designated levels is an accurate way to assess a student's reading progress.

- Almost all the reading students do should be silent.

- Choice in what students read and how much they read influences motivation and achievement.

- The easiest texts for second language learners to understand are those in which the concepts and vocabulary are familiar.

- Having adequate background knowledge is a prerequisite for understanding text.

- Homogenous grouping in the intermediate grades is beneficial to student achievement and self-esteem.

- Competition and outside rewards motivate students to read more.

- Texts need to have a small challenge in order for students to problem-solve and apply new learning.

- Students who do not read well orally are poor at comprehension.

- Pull-in models work better than pull-out models when providing additional reading support.

- Rereading is an excellent strategy when comprehension breaks down.

- Students need to do lots of independent reading of self-selected texts.

- Easy access to books students can and want to read is crucial to readers' success.

- For students to progress as readers, meeting in a guided reading group is a necessity.

- Writing about reading enhances enjoyment and understanding.

- Students need to be taught how to choose "just right" books.

- Kindergarten students are capable of inferring meaning from text.

- All students need to be matched with appropriate texts they can read.

- To assess for deep understanding, sitting side-by-side with a student is necessary.

- Most vocabulary is learned through widespread reading.

- Students who read more nonfiction texts have higher levels of reading comprehension.

- Students who constantly read books that are too hard for them regress as readers.

- In guided reading, the student does most of the work.

- Students who read easy books most of the time continue to progress as readers.

Source: From *Regie Routman in Residence: Transforming Our Teaching Through Reading to Understand* by Regie Routman, Portsmouth, NH: Heinemann. Copyright 2009 by Regie Routman. Adapted by permission.

What to Look for in the Highly Effective Reading and Writing Classroom

Reading and writing are reciprocal processes. Research demonstrates that competence in one discipline positively influences the other.

READING PROGRAM

- **Well-stocked and organized classroom library** and reading corner with at least 50 percent nonfiction/informational texts (70 percent for high school) and student input in terms of organization and content
- **Reading aloud** daily of excellent nonfiction, fiction, or poetry, with opportunities for rich discussion
- **Sustained time daily (20–40 minutes) for free choice, independent reading** with appropriate book match (with evidence that students read fluently and ways to monitor their understanding of the texts they are reading)
- **Reading records** kept by students: titles, authors, genres
- **One-on-one conferences** with anecdotal notes noting strengths and needs—to ensure students are selecting and reading texts they can read and understand, applying strategies to solve problems, and self-monitoring and self-correcting
- **Teacher applying OLM** and thinking aloud and demonstrating his or her own reading process, including book selection, record keeping, strategy use, fluency, comprehension, monitoring for understanding, discussion of ideas
- **Shared reading experiences**—teacher reading and thinking aloud while students follow along in the text (some of these texts will come from shared writing)
- **Many opportunities for productive student talk** and student-led talk about texts (partner reading, small groups, shared read-aloud with "turn-and-talk," heterogeneous literature conversations, reciprocal teaching)
- **Small-group, guided silent reading** (daily for grades 1 and 2; as needed in grades 3–5; heterogeneous grouping once kids read well)
- **Vocabulary, word work, and explicit skills and strategy instruction** (mostly in meaningful literacy contexts) with opportunities for authentic application
- **Evidence of students applying new vocabulary, strategies, and word work**
- **Most time spent reading** (not responding to reading or doing exercises)
- **Indications of increasing self-monitoring and self-assessing**

WRITING PROGRAM

- **Writing for authentic purposes and audiences**
- **Organized, student-managed system** for housing and dating writing
- **Celebration and sharing of writing**: focus on writer first, the writing second
- **Teachers-as-writers**; teacher thinking and writing aloud
- **Connecting writing to reading** (good writers are good readers)
- **Noticing what authors do**, including student authors, and applying to writing
- **Shared writing**—composing collaboratively with the teacher or within small group (with many of these texts becoming published reading texts)
- **Daily sustained time to write** (20–30 minutes minimum)
- **Some choice involved in most writing topics**; limited use of prompts
- **Opportunities for students to talk about texts** before, during, and after writing (partner sharing, peer conferencing, whole-class share) in scaffolded conversations
- **Writing records** kept by students
- **"Skills" and strategies taught primarily in the context of meaningful writing** and as needed—topic focus, detail, organization, revision, editing, and so on
- **Spelling lessons**—connected to writing; common patterns, high-frequency words, prefixes and suffixes, and so on; high expectations for application
- **Revising and editing taken seriously** because students are writing for readers
- **Editing/proofreading expectations defined and demonstrated**—with students at grade 2 and above assuming most of the responsibility
- **Writing in various genres and forms**—across the curriculum—with clear and explicit demonstrations and expectations before students write
- **Writing fluency and stamina**, including legible handwriting
- **Daily conferences**—public, one-on-one, roving—with accompanying teacher and student record keeping; focus on content conferences before editing
- **Writing mostly short pieces**; some writing going to publication monthly (beginning in grade 2). More focus on informational writing
- **Accuracy** in facts, genres, formats, conventions, spelling
- **Most time spent writing**, not on lessons or exercises about writing (for example, not going overboard on planning before writing)
- **Indications of increasing self-monitoring and self-assessing**

Look also for joy and engagement, high expectations for *all*, productive and efficient use of time, students assuming increasing responsibility, whole-to-part instruction, ongoing teaching and assessment, and clear communication to parents. Encourage grade-level and across-grade-level conversations and classroom observations related to reading and writing.

Recommended Technology Tools and Uses

Online learning communities—Teams of educators can create digital spaces using **Google+** and **wikis** to facilitate dialogue around educational topics and student learning. And these spaces are not just for adults. Learning management systems (LMSs) such as **Edmodo** and **Schoology** enable students to interact with content and peers. Of course, a teacher's modeling and guidance are essential. Just as in face-to-face interactions, online collaborations rely on trust and relationships for success.

Audio recording—When students record themselves while sharing their learning, their work goes "live," and the entire world is the potential audience. This access brings an increased level of purpose and importance to what is documented. Examples of work suitable for recording include book talks, peer tutorials, and summaries of learning. Applications such as **Audioboo** and **Educreations** are free and accessible to use on both desktop and mobile computing devices.

Google apps for educators—Google offers a number of apps suitable for school environments. **Google Drive** is a file storage and synchronization service that allows learners to collaboratively create documents in real time and asynchronously, which can be helpful for modeling how to take notes, for example. **Google Sites** can serve as a student's or teacher's own website, populated with multimedia products that represent one's learning. A Site could also serve as a school's hub for student data and important web resources. **Blogger** is Google's blogging platform. It is simple to use for anyone looking to post their ideas and reflections for access by a broader audience. Google offers other helpful tools in addition to these three.

Blogging—Teachers and administrators K–12 have seen the impact—in terms of authenticity, voice, and volume of words produced—of having students post their writing online. Sharing ideas on a web log (blog), provides that authentic audience for emerging and proficient writers. **Edublogs** and **Kidblog** are two of the most popular blogging platforms for students because of the safe privacy settings and ease of use. Blogs are also an excellent tool to teach students how to give feedback in the comments section. As well, family members can see their child grow in writing skills throughout the school year, which makes blogging an excellent tool for developing digital portfolios.

iMovie—If I had to select only one classroom application for the iPad, iMovie would be it. Despite the name, its potential is not limited to just making movies. For example, visual podcasts can be developed with photos and narration about a topic important to the learner. Students can become the teacher by creating visual tutorials for essential concepts. Once these tutorials have been uploaded to **YouTube** or **Vimeo**, classmates and students from around the world can watch them again and again. Many educators know how effective it is when peers teach peers. This type of technology can put students in the teacher's seat and help them take charge of their own learning.

Evernote—This productivity tool offers highly integrated technology that is free for basic use. Learners can embed text, images, and audio into one note, which can then be shared with others or stored into a digital notebook for later retrieval. Students can use Evernote to hear themselves read a text—including their own writing—and to easily reflect on their learning, as well as share their progress with their family.

Twitter—Twitter has become one of the most powerful tools for connecting beyond the school walls. Besides the ability to follow and connect with educators from anywhere in the world, teachers can share their students' learning with families and other classrooms. Many have created classroom accounts to post daily activities, such as an image of student work. Because of the 140-character limit per tweet, Twitter is also an excellent tool for teaching summarization and making wise word choices. On Friday, curate all the tweets from the last five days in one document using a tool such as **Storify** and you have a foundation for your weekly newsletter to send home.

Digital texts—Whether they are web-based, on a tablet, or on an eReader, digital texts allow readers to interact with the words others have written in new ways. Applications such as **Skitch** and **Goodreader** allow learners to highlight and annotate texts and then share them with the teacher and others via e-mail or a web-based storage tool such as **Dropbox**. To create an interactive library of resources about specific topics, services such as **Diigo** allow many readers to add texts to a group. The learners' highlights and annotations show up with every addition.

Digital publishing—In today's connected world, anyone can be an author and potentially reach a huge audience. Software such as **Book Creator** and **Storybird** address multiple areas of literacy in exciting and engaging ways. Reading, writing, speaking, listening, and usage all come into play when students develop narratives and informational text. Original artwork and digital images can be embedded in these types of tools.

Digital note taking—Using a tablet and a stylus, handwriting apps such as **Notability** and **Penultimate** give the student or educator several ways to document learning. The ability to embed photos taken with the mobile device into the current page allows for a visual summary of instruction. For students who struggle to remember or record important information, digital note-taking applications can be a game-changer.

Staff input—Asking for feedback on schoolwide decisions can make a positive difference when implementing a new initiative. Digital response tools like **Google Forms** and **SurveyMonkey** can provide that information in a quick and timely fashion. The data collected are aggregated in a visually appealing way so leadership teams can spend their limited time making informed decisions instead of collecting paper surveys.

This list was compiled and written by Matt Renwick, a veteran teacher and elementary school principal. Renwick writes for *EdTech* magazine, blogs at www.readingbyexample.com, and is the author of *Digital Student Portfolios: A Whole School Approach to Connected Learning and Continuous Assessment* (Powerful Learning Press, 2014).

Schoolwide On-Demand Writing Assessment

To ensure the assessment is standardized across schools, follow directions exactly.

Setting Purpose: (To be read aloud by teacher prior to the writing by students.)
"This writing will show parents, teachers, and the principal how we are doing as readers and writers at our school. Use everything you know about what good writers do so we can celebrate our school's writers and also learn what we need to do improve as a school.

Preparing for On-Demand Writing Assessment: Procedures

- Decide with your grade level team what the writing prompt will be.
- Determine with your grade-level team what type of paper will be used for the assignment. (Use a consistent and appropriate paper type for each grade level.)
- The prompt needs to be pre-written and placed on the top of each student's paper.
- Also, on each student's paper, include at the top, filled out by teacher or student:
  - The student's name, school, and date(s) of prompt
  - Names of student's teacher and school the previous school year
  - The very first grade that the student attended in this school
- Read the prompt immediately before the first session and tell students how much time they will have to write. Allow students 5 or 10 minutes for a turn and talk discussion with a partner. Then ask students to start writing independently.
- Students in K and grade 1 should complete their writing in one 20-minute session.
- Students in grades 2–8 should complete their writing in two 30-minute sessions or three 20-minute sessions. (Sessions can be spread out over two days.) The teacher should read the prompt aloud to the students before they begin writing each day.
- Tell students they are to write without assistance and to make any changes by crossing out (no erasures.)

After the Writing Session

- As a grade-level team, meet, review samples, and select one *typical* writing sample for the grade level. (Each grade level will submit only one sample, not one per teacher.)
- As a grade-level team, note the typical "strengths" and the typical "needs" from the agreed-upon sample. (Write these on a separate sheet with the grade level and prompt at the top; attach sheet to the selected sample.)
- Collect and save ALL students' papers.
- Depending on your purpose(s), you may want to do a strategic random sampling from each classroom; for example, pull 3–4 papers from every classroom written by students who have been in the school for the whole year and/or whole school career. Use these papers for assessment by classroom and for teacher self-evaluations, to show maximum effect of the writing professional development and instruction.

Source: Regie Routman with Sheila Valencia, along with input from Sandy Grade School, Sandy, OR

Analyzing Schoolwide Writing Samples

On-Demand, Interim Writing Assessment

1. Getting started (10 min.)

- Have staff sit in vertical teams. Have large blank charts at the front of room with headings "Typical Writing Samples: Strengths and Needs" and "Priorities/Next Steps."
- Open the meeting with the leader describing the purpose of the exercise: To notice strengths and needs schoolwide and prioritize and carry out next steps for improving instruction.
- Have each team choose a facilitator and a note taker.
- Distribute a packet of typical writing samples, one from each grade level—with strengths and needs noted—to each member of the vertical team.
- Allow participants to observe/read the work in silence, perhaps making brief notes about aspects of the work that they notice, at and across grade levels.

2. Describing the work (15 min.)

- Work in groups and have the facilitator of each vertical team ask, "What have you noticed?"
- Share observations within the group *without judgment*. Group members support their statements with evidence from the writing samples. Note taker records observations.
- Prompt the group with questions as needed. The facilitator may ask, "What do you notice about writer's craft? Conventions? Legibility?" "Are the steps steep enough between grade levels; that is, does there seem to be a full year's growth from one grade level to the next in each typical writing sample?" (It helps to lay out the samples side by side to view grade-level continuum in student writing.)
  - What do you notice about the teachers' language used to name strengths/needs?
  - What major strengths do you see, schoolwide? Needs? Trends?

3. Gather as a whole group to share ideas (35 min.)

- The PD leader (principal and/or leadership team member) invites each group, one grade level at a time, to share their findings.
- Record ideas by having the leader write the most important observations on the chart(s) by grade level.

4. Discussing schoolwide implications for teaching and learning (15 min.)

- Leader facilitates whole group discussion on implications of observations for schoolwide growth and achievement: "What are our writing strengths as a school?" "Where do we need to grow?" (Alternatively, do this step in small groups and then report to the whole group.)

5. Determining next steps (15 min.)

- Reflect as a group on most the important writing priorities.
- Reach consensus on the most important schoolwide priorities and next steps for improving writing instruction—and chart these.

Teaching Points Related to "Six Traits +1" of Writing

Trait	Teaching Points

Ideas/Content	• Write with your audience in mind.
	• Use literature as a resource.
	• Pick a meaningful topic so writing is purposeful and enjoyable.
	  ○ Select a memory about something that happened in the past.
	  ○ Narrow the focus.
	  ○ Use list to help plan.
	• Get ideas from other writers including peers and published authors.

Organization	• Tell the story (oral rehearsal) before writing.
	• Include a beginning (lead) that hooks the reader.
	• Craft a satisfying ending that ties everything together.
	  ○ Reflect on why memory is important to the writer.
	• Use paragraphs.
	  ○ Group similar ideas/topics.
	  ○ Give the eye a break.
	• Choose an original title that frames the writing for the reader.
	• Include a descriptive setting.

Sentence Fluency	• Reread to be sure sentences flow, sound right, and have a pleasing rhythm. • Vary beginnings of sentences.
Voice	• Incorporate meaningful dialogue. • Write with unique style. • Write so it "sounds like you." • Show, don't tell.
Word Choice	• Use words that convey emotion. • Choose words carefully to express exactly what you want to say. • Add details to breathe life into the text—embellish meaning.

Revision	• Reread to decide what to write next.
	• Reread to make sure text makes sense to the reader.
	• Reread to make changes:
	  ○ Attend to word choice (cross out old, write new word above).
	  ○ Add missing words (use carets ^).
	  ○ Move sentences (use arrows).
	  ○ Add more detail (cut-and-paste strategy).

Conventions	• Writer has final responsibility of editing for the reader:
	  ○ Spelling ○ Grammar
	  ○ Punctuation ○ Paragraphing
	  ○ Capitalization ○ Legibility

Source: From *Professional Development Notebook* for *Regie Routman in Residence: Transforming Our Teaching Through Writing for Audience and Purpose* (Session 7, p. 6) by Regie Routman, Portsmouth, NH: Heinemann. © 2008 Regie Routman. Adapted by permission.

From *Read, Write, Lead: Breakthrough Strategies for Schoolwide Literacy Success.* © 2014 Regie Routman.

Observation Framework for Instructional Walks

+ **Environment**

Excellent classroom libraries, access to resources and charts, desks clustered, peacefulness, joy, safety, risk taking, established routines

+ **Engagement**

Students motivated and on-task with worthwhile work; students managing own behaviors

+ **Focused Instruction**

Teacher prepared and instruction well planned; clear directions to students; appropriateness of lesson content and sequence for students' needs, interests, and culture; appropriate challenge and pacing; quality texts used; responsive teaching

+ **Ongoing Assessment**

Formative assessments; constant checking for understanding; whole group, small group, and self-assessments; adjustments as needed to increase student learning

+ **OLM Application**

Sufficient frontloading—demonstrations; shared and guided experiences; checking for understanding before students do "the work"

+ **Student Interaction**

Opportunities for peer and small-group work and collaboration; various groupings to promote learning; students clear on what to do and how to do it

+ **Quality of Student Work**

Connections to instruction; relevancy to curriculum; use of resources; students able to state purpose of work; clear about what to do and ready to do it; technology used to enhance teaching and learning; pride in work

+ **Authenticity**

Writing and reading for real-world audience and purpose; choice within structure; use of highest-quality texts across the curriculum

+ **Level of Discussion**

Level of questions being asked (open or closed); who's posing the questions; conversations versus interrogations; quality of the conversations

+ **Self-Directed Learners**

Self-checking, students setting own worthwhile goals, learning for own purposes, joy in learning

Essential Characteristics of a Highly Effective Teacher-Leader

Relationships with colleagues, students, and community are strong.

- Seeks to develop respectful and trusting relationships.
- Effectively collaborates and communicates with all members of the school community—principal, administrators, teachers, students, families.
- Is responsive to students' and teachers' cultures, interests, and needs.
- Holds high expectations for all learners—self, students, peers, principal—and continually strives to make high expectations a reality.
- Celebrates each learner's strengths and builds upon them.
- Fully participates in ongoing, school-based, professional learning experiences.
- Willingly shares own knowledge and practices with others.
- Demonstrates openness to useful feedback and to others' ideas.
- Sees self as a leader as well as a teacher and a learner.

Beliefs align with best practices.

- Articulates core beliefs about teaching, literacy, and learning.
- Daily practices match stated beliefs.
- Reflects on how beliefs drive practices.
- Seeks to improve and adjust beliefs and practices in light of new information and experiences.
- Is open to productive change.

Teaching and assessing are expert.

- Is highly knowledgeable about literacy, learning, and leadership.
- Implements challenging and relevant curriculum and standards in a productive and meaningful manner.
- Provides appropriate and sufficient demonstrations, shared experiences, and guided practice before releasing learners to work independently.
- Embraces authenticity—audience and purpose, literature, content, resources.
- Reads and discusses professional texts, reflects on that reading/research, and makes relevant application to teaching and assessing practices.
- Relies on daily, formative assessment to differentiate and improve instruction.
- Uses multiple sources of data to improve instruction and learning.
- Uses effective and efficient management techniques in a kind and fair manner.
- Makes instruction and learning engaging, enjoyable, and relevant.

From *Read, Write, Lead: Breakthrough Strategies for Schoolwide Literacy Success.* © 2014 Regie Routman.

Benchmarks for Writing

Kindergarten

Sample of typical, year-end kindergarten writing

Note the craft, organization/flow, accuracy, responding to writing-in-process, presentation

Title present and matches story.

Picture matches words.

Beginning of sentence capitalized.

Applies (or attempts) beginning, middle, and ending sounds.

Evidence of rereading and revision.

Elaboration and detail.

Ending punctuation in place.

"No excuse" words spelled correctly.

Handwriting neat and legible.

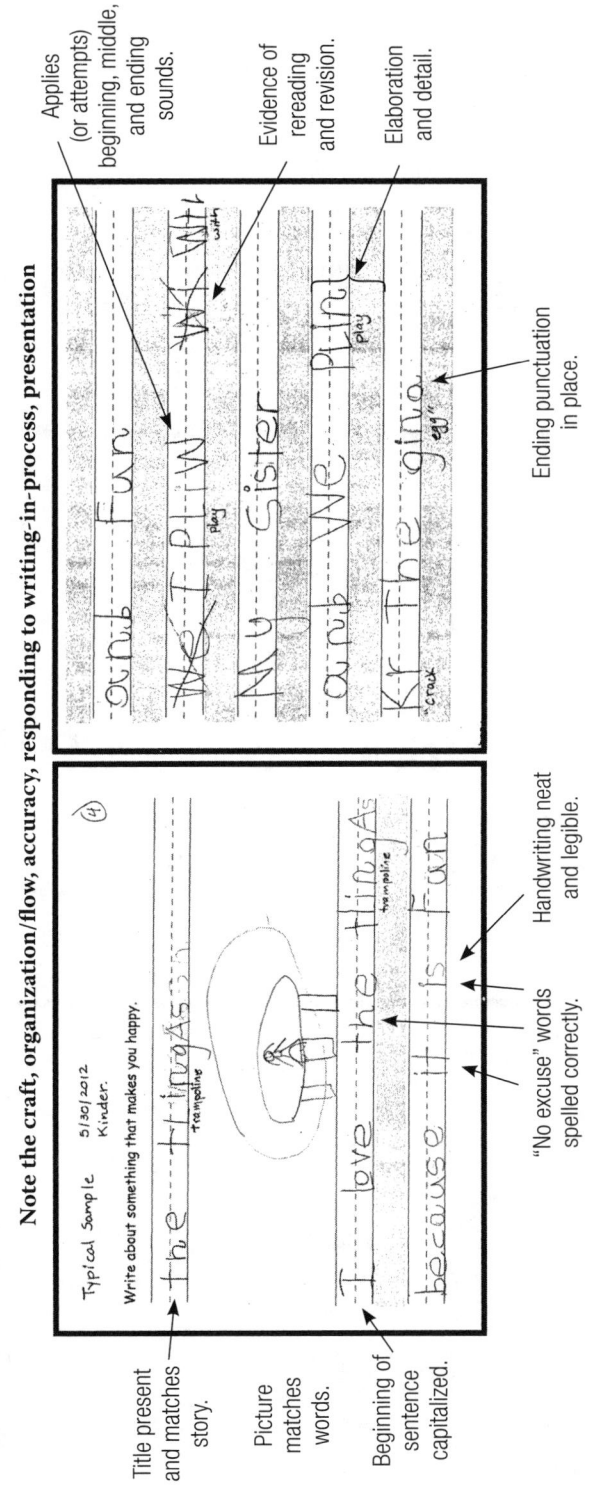

Kindergarten "I Can" Statements

- I can write a title that tells what my story is about.
- I can reread to fix up my story so it makes sense.
- I can spell "no excuse" words correctly and sound out words.
- I can make my writing easy to read.
- I can make my picture match my words.
- I can make my writing fun to read.

Source: Sandy Grade School, 2013, developed in cooperation with Regie Routman.

APPENDIX J

Benchmarks for Writing—*(continued)*

Fifth Grade
Sample of typical, year-end 5th grade writing

Note the craft, organization/flow, accuracy, responding to writing-in-process, presentation

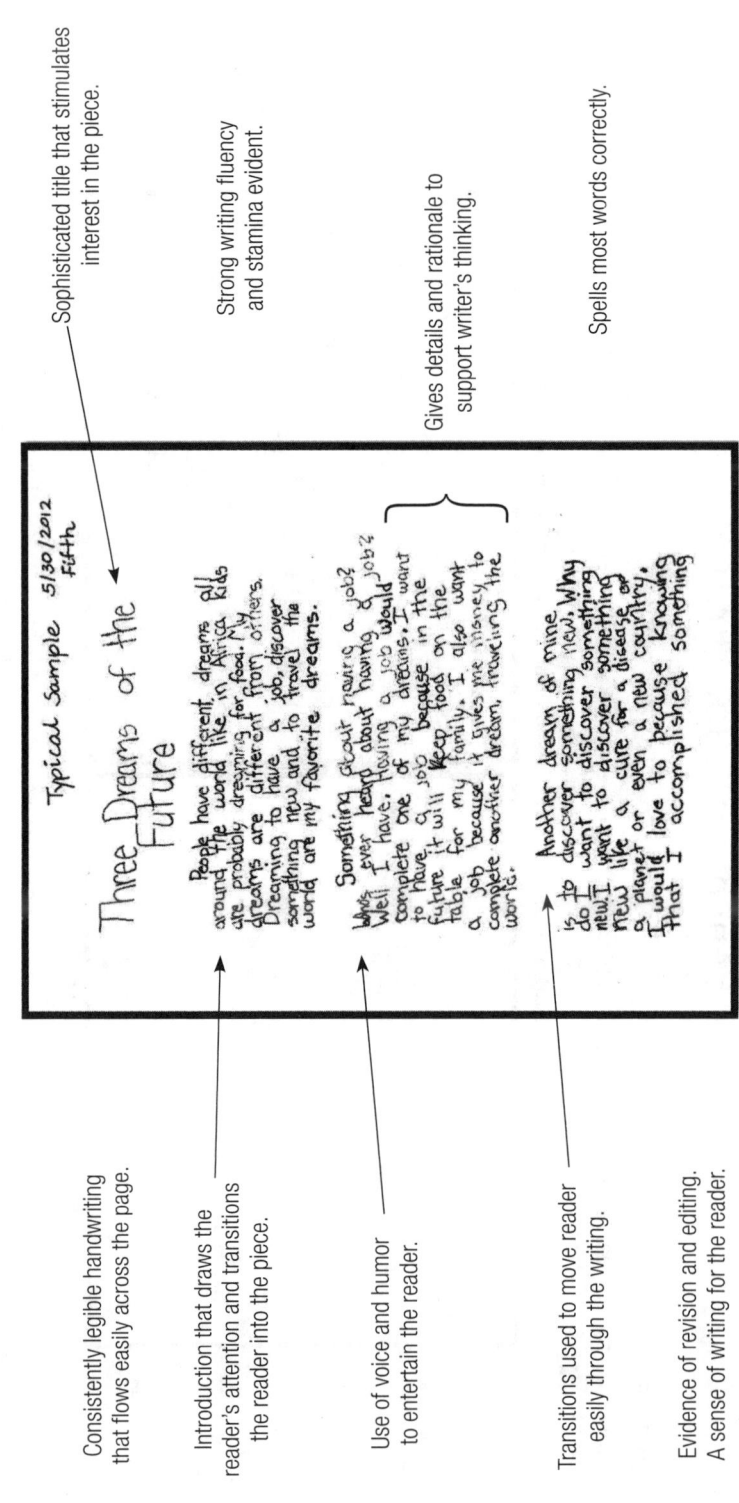

Sophisticated title that stimulates interest in the piece.

Strong writing fluency and stamina evident.

Gives details and rationale to support writer's thinking.

Spells most words correctly.

Consistently legible handwriting that flows easily across the page.

Introduction that draws the reader's attention and transitions the reader into the piece.

Use of voice and humor to entertain the reader.

Transitions used to move reader easily through the writing.

Evidence of revision and editing. A sense of writing for the reader.

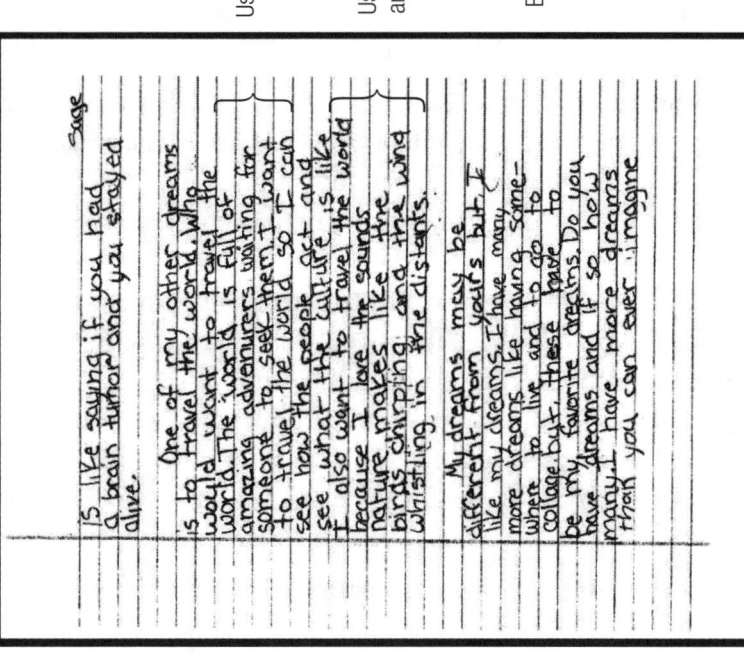

Capitalization and punctuation used correctly.

Use of precise language and word choice.

Use of figurative language and other literary devices.

Ending provides satisfactory closure that ties whole piece together.

5th Grade "I Can" Statements

- I can write a title that sets the stage for the reader.
- I can write an introduction that captures the reader and leads the reader into the story.
- I can organize and paragraph the information (or tell a story) in a logical order to make it easy for the reader to understand.
- I can enhance my writing with details and precise words.
- I can embellish my writing with literary elements and sophisticated transitions that make it easier for the reader to follow.
- I can reread my writing for accuracy, interest for the reader, revision, spelling, and editing.
- I can give several reasons to support my opinion (expository: or back up my statement with facts).
- I write accurate facts from a variety of sources with accurate details to support them. (expository)
- I can write an ending that connects all my main points, adds new information/ideas, and leaves the reader satisfied.
- I can cite my sources clearly. (expository)

Source: Sandy Grade School, 2013, developed in cooperation with Regie Routman.

Visitor Guidelines for Classroom Observations

The following guidelines have worked well for successful schools when they receive requests for visitors. Of course, any guidelines need to be modified to fit the particular school and context.

We use visitations as an opportunity for growth for all teachers. Even for a teacher who is not yet expert, with support and guidance from the principal and other teachers, that teacher could take the opportunity to get better at something important—for example, shared writing or shared reading. With input from peers and the principal, the teacher could be encouraged to write a plan; revise the plan with input; practice the activity with coaching from another teacher; and be prepared to have her classroom open for just 30 minutes to visitors. Just as we do with students, we celebrate small victories and continue to encourage and value all learners.

Limit days and times and number of visitors. Make it clear that established visitation times are the only available times for the current school year. Hold firm! A plan that has worked well is to schedule visitors one morning a month for five or six months during the school year—for example, October, November, January, February, April, and May. Decide as a leadership team or school what months, days, and times work best and the maximum number of educators per visit—for example, 20. Often schools decide to begin open visitations in October or November, after routines are well established.

Create a record book dedicated to scheduling visitors, and have the secretary handle requests by taking down the name, school, and contact information of confirmed visitors. Once all the spots for a month are filled, the request is moved to the next available month. Once all spots are taken for the school year, no more visitors are permitted for that school year.

Invite all teachers to have their classroom open to visitors. It's important not to select "best" teachers but to give all teachers the opportunity to host visitors. Teachers who are open to visitors create a written plan based on the Optimal Learning Model, letting observers know the learning intention, lesson objective, literacy/curriculum content, assessment, and time frame for when their classroom will be open. For example, a teacher might choose to have her classroom open just from 10:00 to 10:30 a.m. for a shared-writing lesson. Or a teacher might choose to participate for the whole morning or not at all. Some schools decide on a limited number of classrooms that will be open for the visitation so that not every teacher feels the need to participate every visitation day.

From Read, Write, Lead: Breakthrough Strategies for Schoolwide Literacy Success. © 2014 Regie Routman.

Set expectations for teachers. The teacher's plan and time frame are reviewed for approval (and possible discussion and revision) by the principal or leadership team at least several days before the visit. Teachers or students (or both) may, if they choose, publicly explain the what, why, and how of their lesson and also to be open to answer questions to visitors at an agreed-upon time. Teachers and students also may ask the visitors questions.

Set expectations for the visitors. Prepare a school guide for visitors, and include the school's literacy beliefs, demographics, and ongoing professional development plan. (In some schools, students write part of the guide—for example, how their classroom works, including schedules, routines, and rituals.) Include a map of the school and a schedule for the morning that lists classrooms that are open with corresponding grade levels and teachers' names along with what visitors can expect to see. Visitors are asked to only go into open classrooms, to stay for at least 20 minutes to get a feel for the lesson, to quietly observe, to refrain from interrupting the teacher, and not to take any photos without permission. They are also expected to give feedback on what they have observed before leaving the school.

Meet with all visitors before and after the classroom visitations. When visitors sign up, the secretary indicates the time to arrive and depart. It's important that visitors commit to staying for the full morning so they see the big picture of teaching and learning and so we are clear about what they take away from their visits, including instructional strengths and other impressions. As a public relations matter, we will want to clear up any questions, concerns, or misperceptions before visitors leave our school.

Have all visitors meet in a designated room, welcome them, make introductions, give them the school guide for that day, and explain visitation procedures. Let visitors know we will be reconvening at the end of the morning for a post-observation debriefing and evaluation (oral or written.) The principal usually conducts these meetings, but the literacy coach or members of the leadership team can also lead and participate. These before and after meetings can also become a learning opportunity for us as hosts; we can ask and learn about issues other educators are facing and how they are dealing with them.

Glossary

Agreement on definitions of important terms, strategies, and approaches is a necessity for a whole school whose staff members are learning together to move students forward in learning.

Academic language—The oral and written vocabulary and terminology of academic disciplines (such as social studies and science) that facilitate communication and thinking in the specific content area.[1]

Agency—The belief that we can intentionally influence our own functioning and life circumstances through our own actions and personal efficacy, even in the face of difficulties. Includes a "core belief that one has the power to effect changes by one's actions."[2] Extends to the belief that teachers have agency to make a difference in students' lives. See also ***Self-determining learners***.

Assessment, educational—The act of determining what and how well someone knows something and what that person can do with that knowledge. In schools, assessment is often a systematic, ongoing process to monitor and determine what students are learning and what needs improvement. Assessments may take many forms; they may be formal, such as summative and interim assessments, or informal, such as formative assessments. (See also ***summative assessment***, ***interim assessment***, and ***formative assessment***.)

Benchmark—An expectation, often an end-of-year learning target, that all students are expected to meet. Often established across grade levels to ensure consistency, cohesion, and increasing and appropriate difficulty between the grades. Benchmark texts, in writing and reading, are chosen by and with teachers and leaders after discussion and analysis; those tangible representations of goals are evident to students and their families.

Common Core State Standards—A set of standards in K–12 language arts and math that have been adopted in almost all states in the United States for the purpose of raising expectations for *all* students, providing a framework for "what" we need to be teaching, and ensuring all high school graduates are prepared for college or a career. Focus is on core ideas, with each grade level continuing to build on concepts and knowledge of previous grades. In both the reading and writing standards, emphasis is on close reading and analysis, with recommendations for more reading and writing of informational texts. See http://www.corestandards.org/ for complete CCSS information and the actual standards with exemplars.

Fluency (in oral reading)—Reading with accurate word recognition and appropriate rate, phrasing, expression, and comprehension. Some assessments of oral reading fluency measure only accuracy and rate (e.g., words correct per minute); others include prosody (phrasing, expression), and others also include comprehension. High scores in accuracy and rate (based on grade-level norms) are not always correlated with good comprehension.

Formative assessment—Day-to-day and moment-to-moment classroom assessment used to inform, guide, and adjust instruction and learning to fit students' needs and interests and to propel them to further competency and independence. Often takes the form of probing questions and observation but also includes such assessments as anecdotal records, on-demand writing, student work samples, paper-and-pencil activities, one-on-one conferences, and self-assessments. Goal is always to improve and advance student learning.

Frontloading—The preparation we do and background we build before expecting students to try out a task or strategy. May include immersion in a genre, hearing stories read aloud, demonstrations and thinking aloud, shared experiences, or scaffolded conversations—all of which make it more likely that most students will know how and what to do and achieve success.

Genre—The type or form of reading or writing, such as poetry, literary analysis, or research report. Each type conforms to specific expected rules and, often, a unique format.

Guided reading—Any learning context (but most often a small group) in which the teacher guides one or more students through some aspect of the reading process. The teacher builds on students' strengths and supports and demonstrates whatever is necessary to move the learner toward independence. The teacher provides a text with just enough challenge so the learner is able to do most of the reading work.[3]

Infrastructure—The necessary physical and emotional structures that are in place for the smooth running of the school or organization. A solid infrastructure must be in place for a school to successfully focus on instruction and learning.

Instructional walk—An intentional, informal visit (not an evaluation) by the principal to a teacher's classroom to notice, record, and affirm strengths, build trust, offer possible suggestions, or coach—all for the purpose of increasing student literacy and learning across the curriculum. Feedback to the teacher is given immediately or as close to the visit as possible and focuses mostly on celebrating the teacher's strengths. Principal also notices and records schoolwide trends—strengths and needs—to be shared with the Professional *Literacy* Community for the purpose of improving instruction schoolwide.

Interim assessment—A periodic assessment, often uniformly administered, meant to examine and analyze how a system or teaching/learning approach is working over time for individual students or groups of students. It is designed to measure the same broad goals as summative assessment or predict performance on high-stakes summative assessments given at the end of the school year. See in Appendix F as one example.

Lexile—A lexile level measures the complexity of a text based primarily on word frequency and sentence length.

Optimal Learning Model—A cyclical learning model that begins with demonstration (showing the learner how to do it), includes shared experiences (doing it together with the expert in charge), and moves to guided practice of the specific strategy or activity (with the student in charge with expert support available) before releasing responsibility to students to "try and apply it" independently. Sometimes referred to as the "I do it, we do it, we do it, you do it" model. Cycle also includes celebrations and ongoing assessment.

Phonemic awareness—The ability to hear, identify, and manipulate individual sounds (phonemes) in spoken words. Phonemic awareness—for example, oral awareness—contributes to a student's ability to write words, as does knowledge of letter-sound relationships.

Phonics—In reading and writing, the relationship between phonemes (the sounds of spoken language) and graphemes (the letters) that spell words; also called *decoding*, which is necessary but insufficient for understanding text.

Professional *Literacy* Communities—Teams of teachers and leaders who come together on a regular basis to influence and improve teaching effectiveness and student learning. Highly effective PLCs are school based, ongoing, and literacy focused. Shared learning goes beyond scrutiny of data to analysis of successful literacy practices across the curriculum. Participants collaboratively view, discuss, read, study, analyze, reflect, plan, and apply effective reading and writing practices to their own classrooms.

Public conference—A one-on-one conference, usually in writing, held in full view and listening range of the entire classroom so all students bene-fit. Begins with celebration of writer's strengths before moving to possible teaching points based on most pressing need(s). Provides opportunities for careful listening and speaking for the student as well as the teacher. Observing students are expected to apply what they learn to their own writing.

Rubrics—A list of criteria (such as organized paragraphs, interesting and precise word choice) for determining and improving the quality of specific writing products. Rubrics are also used to determine what's to be included in the writing (e.g., an introduction and at least three important facts); rubrics are sometimes employed as scoring guides. The most useful rubrics are created with learners and shared with them and their families before being used in evaluative ways.

Scaffolded conversation—Instructional, focused conversation in which the learner is led by an expert—through specific questioning, encourage-ment, and modeling—to expand and clarify her or his thinking about story, text, concept, and so on. Scaffolds are meant to be temporary and may increase or decrease based upon the needs of the learner.

Self-determining learners—Readers, writers, and thinkers who can use what they know and apply it to different contexts (e.g., applying qualities of effective writing to all genres and forms) for their own meaningful purposes.[4]

Self-sustaining school—A school that is continuously improving in a trusting, collaborative culture of ongoing deep, professional learning. Includes a single-minded focus on high expectations and excellent literacy results for all learners at the school—students, teachers, and leaders. Even if some key people leave, the school's strong leadership team, highly knowledgeable, effective staff, and support at the district level make it likely that staff members new to the school become part of its learning and achievement culture.

Shared read-aloud—A combination of reading aloud and thinking aloud, along with shared reading. That is, even though the teacher begins by reading aloud and doing all the reading, demonstrating, and thinking, once she feels students are ready to do so, she shares that responsibility on one or more pages of the text. That is, with the pages visible in front of them, students read and think aloud with a partner or within a small group, attempting to think through a text and apply the strategies that have just been demonstrated.[5]

Shared reading—Activity in which students and teacher read a meaningful text together, which all can easily see and most can readily read, with the teacher taking the lead and guiding the student(s) with her voice and, at times, exposing the text word by word and line by line. The focus is always first on reading the text together; then letters and sounds, word work, grammar, and conventions can be taught and practiced within the text; but the main focus remains on enjoyment, fluency, and having learners feel competent.

Shared writing—An activity in which students and teacher collaboratively compose a coherent text with the teacher doing the writing while scaffolding students' language and ideas; often these texts become shared reading texts as well as published texts for guided and personal reading.

Skills—Automatic, learned responses that are the same for each situation—for example, knowing that a letter makes a particular sound. Skills are strategies under automatic versus deliberate control.[6]

Strategies—In-the-head mental thinking that learners construct for each unique learning situation in order to read, write, solve problems, and so on. Strategies are deliberate, effortful, purposeful, and carefully selected to accomplish a task, such as decoding, understanding words, and constructing meaning. Once strategies become automatic, they take the form of skilled performance.[7]

Summative assessment—Periodic assessments such as state tests, district tests, interim assessments, end-of-unit tests, and scores used for accountability that yield information on how well programs, curriculum, and school improvement goals are working in a classroom, school, district, state. Typically used after instruction to evaluate student proficiency. Needs to be accompanied by interim and formative assessments to get a balanced picture of how students are progressing.

Vertical team—A group of teachers from different grade levels and specialties who work and learn together doing specific tasks—for example, looking at student work for the purpose of improving instruction and learning. Professional *Literacy* Communities focused on whole-school achievement are organized, at least part of the time, in vertical teams.

Endnotes for Glossary

[1] Adapted from a definition in William Nagy and Dianna Townsend, "Words as Tools: Learning Academic Vocabulary as Language Acquisition," *Reading Research Quarterly,* January/February/March 2012, p. 92.

[2] Albert Bandura, "Toward a Psychology of Human Agency," *Perspectives on Psychological Science,* June 2006, pp. 164, 170.

[3] Adapted from Regie Routman, *Reading Essentials: The Specifics You Need to Teach Reading Well* (Portsmouth, NH: Heinemann, 2003), p. 151.

[4] This definition is based on self-determining theory, as explained in Daniel Pink, *Drive: The Surprising Truth About What Motivates Us* (New York: Riverhead Books, 2009).

[5] See Session 9 of *Regie Routman in Residence: Transforming Our Teaching,* video-based series (Portsmouth, NH: Heinemann, 2009).

[6] Peter Afflerbach, P. David Pearson, and Scott G. Paris, "Clarifying Differences Between Reading Skills and Reading Strategies," *The Reading Teacher*, February 2008, p. 368.

[7] Afflerbach, Pearson, and Paris 2008, pp. 368–373.

Endnotes

Introduction

[1] This communication took place on August 25, 2013, in the airport in Tucson, Arizona. I was working on this book when the parent, looking over my shoulder, said she felt compelled to talk with me. I don't know her name. I just listened.

[2] Principal Kim Ball made this observation during an interview on January 28, 2013.

Chapter 1

[1] Jonathan Kozol, *Fire in the Ashes: Twenty-five Years Among the Poorest Children in America* (New York: Crown, 2012); Linda Darling-Hammond, "Restoring Our Schools," *The Nation*, May 29, 2010; Erica Frankenberg and Gary Orfield, eds., *The Resegregation of Suburban Schools: A Hidden Crisis in American Education* (Cambridge, MA: Harvard Education Press, 2012); Kimberly Shannon, "Researchers Say Nation's Schools Undergo More Resegregation," *Education Week*, September 28, 2012, p. 5.

[2] Jason DeParle, "For Poor, Leap to College Often Ends in a Hard Fall," *The New York Times*, December 23, 2012; Lesli A. Maxwell, "Growing Gaps Bring Focus on Poverty's Role in Schooling," *Education Week*, March 6, 2012.

[3] Richard Innes, "Commentary Misleading on NAEP, Dropouts," Letter to the Editor, *Education Week*, October 24, 2012, p. 26; Nick Pandolfo, "New Report: Dropout Rate Five Times Higher for Poor Students," blog post, October 19, 2011.

[4] John Dewey, *The School and Society* (Chicago: University of Chicago Press, 1907), p. 19.

[5] Arthur Miller quoted in Bob Herbert, "The Public Thinker," *The New York Times*, Op-Ed, February 14, 2005, p. A23.

[6] Kathy Au, "Creating a Staircase Curriculum," *Reading Today*, August/September 2009, p. 15; Taffy Raphael participated in a residency collaboration with me, 2010–13, as coleader in the school's change process.

[7] See Regie Routman, *Regie Routman in Residence: Transforming Our Teaching*, video-based literacy series (Portsmouth, NH: Heinemann, 2008, 2009, 2013).

Chapter 1 Endnotes, *continued*

[8] The principal is Barb Ide, who was offering a personal response on June 6, 2013, to reading the entry titled "Observe a Great Kindergarten Teacher" in my book *Literacy and Learning Lessons from a Longtime Teacher* (Newark, DE: International Reading Association, 2012).

[9] Amanda Ripley, *The Smartest Kids in the World and How They Got That Way* (New York: Simon & Schuster, 2013).

[10] Michael Fullan, *Leadership and Sustainability: System Thinkers in Action* (Thousand Oaks, CA: Corwin, 2005), p. 72.

[11] Trena Speirs, a principal in Westminster, CO, made this statement during a presentation at a Literacy and Leadership Institute in Oshkosh, WI, in June 2011.

[12] Atul Gawande, *Better: A Surgeon's Notes on Performance* (New York: Henry Holt, 2007). The author uses the term "urgency killers" in the context of medicine, not education, but it's applicable in many fields.

[13] Richard Elmore, "Institutions, Improvement, and Practice," in *Change Wars* (pp. 221–235), ed. Andy Hargreaves and Michael Fullan (Bloomington, IN: Solution Tree, 2009).

[14] Brian Dennis, Kirby Larson, and Mary Nethery, *Nubs: The True Story of a Mutt, a Marine and a Miracle* (New York: Little, Brown, 2009).

[15] Elmore, in Hargreaves and Fullan, 2009, pp. 224–225.

[16] This observation came from principal Matt Renwick via e-mail on November 4, 2012.

[17] Kozol, 2012, p. 204.

[18] Sharlline Markwardt shared her thoughts in an e-mail on June 30, 2013.

[19] Laurie Espenel made these comments during a telephone interview on June 3, 2013.

[20] Barb Ide shared this account in a personal communication in July 2013.

Chapter 2

[1] Regie Routman, *Reading Essentials: The Specifics You Need to Teach Reading Well* (Portsmouth, NH: Heinemann, 2003).

[2] Linda Darling-Hammond, Brigid Barron, P. David Pearson, Alan H. Schoenfeld, Elizabeth K. Stage, Timothy D. Zimmerman, Gina N. Cervett, and Jennifer L. Tilson, *Powerful Learning: What We Know About Teaching for Understanding* (San Francisco: Jossey-Bass, 2008). A summary of the findings presented in the book is available on the Edutopia website at http://www.edutopia.org/inquiry-project-learning-research.

[3] Nell K. Duke, "Some Key Findings from Research on Reading Comprehension and What They Mean for Classroom Practice," presentation for the Texas Reading First Higher Education Collaborative (Austin, TX, October 2008).

[4] Victoria Purcell-Gates, Nell K. Duke, and Joseph A. Martineau, "Learning to Read and Write Genre-Specific Text: Roles of Authentic Experience and Explicit Teaching," *Reading Research Quarterly*, January–March 2007, pp. 8–45, as quoted in Beth Maloch and Randy Bomer, "Research and Policy: Teaching About and with Informational Texts: What Does Research Teach Us?" *Language Arts*, July 2013, p. 443.

[5] Milton Chen, *Education Nation: Six Leading Edges of Innovation in Our Schools* (San Francisco: Jossey-Bass, 2010), p. 79.

Chapter 2 Endnotes, *continued*

[6] Nell K. Duke, Victoria Purcell-Gates, Leigh A. Hall, and Cathy Tower, "Authentic Literacy Activities for Developing Comprehension and Writing," *The Reading Teacher*, December 2006/January 2007, pp. 344–355.

[7] Teacher Sherri Steuart offered her comments in an e-mail on July 16, 2013.

[8] Contrary to what many believe, our highest-achieving students learn as much as our low achievers when placed in small heterogeneous groups.

[9] Adapted from Regie Routman, "Literature Conversations" (pp. 171–204), in *Conversations: Strategies for Teaching, Learning, and Evaluating* (Portsmouth, NH: Heinemann, 2000).

[10] Peter Johnston and Gay Ivey, *Reading Research Quarterly*, July/August/September 2013; Nancy Atwell, *The Reading Zone: How to Help Kids Become Skillful, Passionate, Habitual, Critical Readers* (New York: Scholastic, 2007); Kelly Gallagher, *Readicide: How Schools Are Killing Reading and What You Can do About It* (Portland, ME: Stenhouse); Nancy Allison, *Middle School Readers: Helping Them Read Widely, Helping Them Read Well* (Portsmouth, NH: Heinemann 2009); Donalyn Miller, *The Book Whisperer: Awakening the Inner Reader in Every Child* (San Francisco: Jossey-Bass, 2008); Penny Kittle, *Book Love: Developing Depth, Passion, and Stamina in Adolescent Readers* (Portsmouth, NH: Heinemann, 2013).

[11] Thomas Newkirk and Penny Kittle, eds., *Children Want to Write: Donald Graves and the Revolution in Children's Writing* (Portsmouth, NH: Heinemann, 2013); Don Murray, *Shoptalk: Learning to Write with Writers* (Portsmouth, NH: Heinemann, 1990); Lucy Calkins, *The Art of Teaching Writing* (2nd ed.) (Portsmouth, NH: Heinemann, 1994); Regie Routman, *Writing Essentials: Raising Expectations and Results While Simplifying Teaching* (Portsmouth, NH: Heinemann, 2005); Regie Routman, *Teaching Essentials: Expecting the Most and Getting the Best from Every Learner, K–8* (Portsmouth, NH: Heinemann, 2008).

[12] Laurie Espenel's 5th grade students shared their excitement in a personal letter, June 10, 2013.

[13] Emily Bazelon, *Sticks and Stones: Defeating the Culture of Bullying and Rediscovering the Power of Character and Empathy* (New York: Random House, 2013), p. 56.

[14] Joan Richardson, "Highlighted and Underlined: A Notebook of Short but Worthy Items," *Phi Delta Kappan*, May 2013, pp. 6–7, citing a study by researchers William E. Copeland, E. Jane Costello, Adrian Angold, and Dieter Wolke, based on 20 years of data and 1,420 children.

[15] Sheila W. Valencia, "Using Assessment to Improve Teaching and Learning," in *What Research Has to Say About Reading Instruction* (4th ed., pp. 379–405), ed. S. J. Samuels and A. E. Farstrup (Newark, DE: International Reading Association, 2011).

[16] Routman, 2003.

[17] P. David Pearson and Margaret C. Gallagher, "The Instruction of Reading Comprehension," *Contemporary Educational Psychology*, October 1983, pp. 317–344.

[18] In her response to a draft of the manuscript in July 2013, Judy Wallis provided insights that shaped my writing of this paragraph.

[19] The power and potential of the OLM can be felt and seen in a feeling of "I can do it" on the part of the learner. See "We can do it!" an original and inspiring musical video by Ryan Miller and students available at http://www.youtube.com/watch?v=B3CPEGkedas.

[20] Richard Elmore, "Institutions, Improvement, and Practice," in *Change Wars* (pp. 221–235), ed. Andy Hargreaves and Michael Fullan (Bloomington, IN: Solution Tree, 2009), p. 225.

[21] Routman, 2008.

Chapter 2 Endnotes, *continued*

[22] Kay Sprader provided this account in an e-mail on June 20, 2013.

[23] Danica Lewis included this information in an e-mail on July 2, 2013.

[24] For much more on what demonstrations look and sound like (teaching actions and language), see *Regie Routman in Residence: Transforming Our Teaching*, video-based literacy series (Portsmouth, NH: Heinemann, 2008, 2009, 2013).

[25] Gerald G. Duffy, Laura R. Roehler, and Beth Ann Herrmann, "Modeling Mental Processes Helps Poor Readers Become Strategic Readers," *The Reading Teacher*, April 1988, p. 765.

[26] Regie Routman, "Mapping a Pathway to Schoolwide Highly Effective Teaching," *Phi Delta Kappan*, February 2012, p. 59.

[27] Melissa Kirkland wrote this in her evaluation of the writing residency in Winnipeg, Manitoba, Canada, on February 28, 2013.

[28] Melissa's comments are from an e-mail on June 26, 2013.

[29] Tamara Van Gog, K. Anders Ericsson, Remy N. J. P. Rikers, and Fred Paas, "Instructional Design for Advanced Learners: Establishing Connections Between the Theoretical Frameworks of Cognitive Load and Deliberate Practice," *Educational Technology, Research and Development*, 2005, p. 75.

[30] Interview. In *Regie Routman in Residence: Transforming Our Teaching Through Writing for Audience and Purpose* (Routman, 2008, sessions 9, 10, and 11), see Debbie Fowler's growth from observing demonstrations of the editing conferences, to viewing her own competency and high expectations with students expected to "do the work," to hearing her describe how her beliefs and practices have changed over time.

[31] Marilyn Robbins made these comments in a personal communication in June 2011.

[32] John Hattie, *Visible Learning: A Synthesis of over 800 Meta-analyses Relating to Achievement* (New York: Routledge, 2009), p. 174.

[33] Grant Wiggins, "Seven Keys to Effective Feedback," *Educational Leadership*, September 2012, p. 16; emphasis in original.

[34] Graham Nuthall, *The Hidden Lives of Learners* (Wellington, NZ: New Zealand Council for Educational Research Press, 2007).

Chapter 3

[1] Commission on the Humanities and Social Sciences, *The Heart of the Matter: A Report of the American Academy's Commission on the Humanities and Social Sciences* (Cambridge, MA: American Academy of Arts & Sciences, 2013), p. 25.

[2] Richard L. Allington, *What Really Matters for Struggling Readers: Designing Research-Based Programs*, (3rd ed.) (Boston: Pearson, 2012).

[3] Principal Kim Ball shared her thoughts during an interview on January 28, 2013.

[4] Judy Wallis provided this succinct definition in a presentation at a Literacy and Leadership Institute in Madison, WI, in June 2012.

[5] First grade teacher Eliana Santos made these comments in an e-mail in January 2013.

[6] Judy Wallis's observations were part of her response in July 2013 to a draft of this book.

[7] Kate Gordon's account emerged during an interview on January 28, 2013.

[8] Ann Thomson related her experience in an interview on January 28, 2013.

Chapter 3 Endnotes, *continued*

[9] Mike Henderson is a former principal at Galveston Elementary School, a K–6 school in Chandler, AZ. He was recognized in 2013 as an exemplary principal by the Rodel Foundation for Outstanding Leadership in Education. His description came in an e-mail on June 26, 2013.

[10] National Center for Education Statistics, *Writing 2011: National Assessment of Educational Progress at Grades 8 and 12* (2011). Washington, DC: U.S. Department of Education.

[11] Grant Wiggins, "Real-World Writing: Making Purpose and Audience Matter," *English Journal*, May 2009, pp. 35–36.

[12] Kate Gordon made this observation during a conversation on October 21, 2012.

[13] Margaret Fair's comments were included in an e-mail on August 19, 2013.

[14] For more on classroom libraries and organizing them with students, see Regie Routman, *Reading Essentials: The Specifics You Need to Teach Reading Well* (Portsmouth, NH: Heinemann, 2003), pp. 66–80, and Session 4 in *Regie Routman in Residence: Transforming Our Teaching Through Reading/Writing Connections* (Portsmouth, NH: Heinemann, 2008, 2009, 2013).

[15] Michael Fullan, ed., *Motion Leadership: The Skinny on Becoming Change Savvy* (Thousand Oaks, CA: Corwin, 2010), p. 25.

[16] Machel Lucas's middle school was using *Regie Routman in Residence: Transforming Our Teaching Through Writing for Audience and Purpose* (Heinemann, 2008). She shared her experience in a personal letter dated February 12, 2009.

[17] See the *Teaching Essentials* website for research on DIBELS: http://www.regieroutman.com/teachingessentials/DIBELS.asp

[18] Joanne Ujiie and Steven D. Krashen, "Comic Book Reading, Reading Enjoyment, and Pleasure Reading Among Middle Class and Chapter I Middle School Students," *Reading Improvement*, Spring 1996, pp. 51–54.

[19] Richard L. Allington and Anne McGill-Franzen, eds., *Summer Reading: Closing the Rich/Poor Reading Achievement Gap* (New York: Teachers College Press, 2013); Susan B. Neuman and Donna Celano, "Access to Print in Low-Income and Middle-Income Communities," *Reading Research Quarterly*, January–March 2001, pp. 8–26.

[20] Kathleen T. Horning, Merri V. Lindgren, and Megan Schliesman, *A Few Observations on Publishing in 2012* (Madison, WI: University of Wisconsin–Madison, Cooperative Children's Book Center, 2013).

[21] Allington and McGill-Franzen, 2013; Jeff McQuillan, *The Literacy Crisis: False Claims, Real Solutions* (Portsmouth, NH: Heinemann, 1998); National Institute of Child Health and Human Development, *Report of the National Reading Panel: Teaching Children to Read: An Evidence-Based Assessment of the Scientific Research Literature on Reading and Its Implications for Reading Instruction* (2000), p. 12; Routman, 2003, pp. A22, A23.

[22] Scholastic, *Kids and Family Reading Report* (4th ed.), study by Scholastic in conjunction with Harrison Group, (New York: Author, 2013) pp. 10, 12.

[23] Some outstanding titles used in our bullying lesson that students continued to pick up and read throughout the school year include *Confessions of a Former Bully, Trouble Talk, Sorry,* and *Just Kidding,* all by Trudy Ludwig; *Bullying and Me: Schoolyard Stories,* by Ouisie Shapiro, photographs by Steven Vote; *Each Kindness,* by Jacqueline Woodson; *Bully,* by Patricia Polacco; *The Juice Box Bully,* by Bob Sornson and Maria Dismondy; and *Wonder,* by R. J. Palacio. Some of these books include useful websites. For excellent background information on bullying, see also the video and TED talk *To This Day,* by Shane Koyczan, February 2013,

Chapter 3 Endnotes, *continued*

and *Sticks and Stones: Defeating the Culture of Bullying and Rediscovering the Power of Character and Empathy*, by Emily Bazelon.

[24] Steven Krashen and Jeff McQuillan, "The Case for Late Intervention," *Educational Leadership*, October 2007, p. 68.

[25] Gay Ivey and Peter Johnston, "Engagement with Young Adult Literature: Outcomes and Processes," *Reading Research Quarterly*, July/August/September 2013, pp. 355–375.

[26] Mark Bauerlien and Sandra Stotsky. "New Study Suggests Remedies for Common Core's Literature Deficit," Pioneer Institute Public Policy Research, [press release] 2012.

[27] Routman, 2012, *Literacy and Learning Lessons from a Longtime Teacher*, pp. 152–153.

[28] A long-standing, highly respected body of research definitively shows that students who read more, read better, and have higher reading achievement: Richard C. Anderson, Paul T. Wilson, and Linda G. Fielding, "Growth in Reading and How Children Spend Their Time Outside of School," *Reading Research Quarterly*, Summer 1988, pp. 285–303; National Center for Education Statistics, *Executive Summary: NAEP 1998 Reading Report Card for the Nation and the States* (Washington, DC: National Center for Education Statistics, 1999), p. 134; Jim Trelease, *The Read-Aloud Handbook* (5th ed.) (New York: Penguin, 2001); U.S. Department of Education, *National Assessment of Educational Progress (NAEP) Trends in Academic Progress Report* (Washington, DC: U.S. Department of Education, 1997); Stephen Krashen, "Free Voluntary Reading: Still a Very Good Idea," in *Selected Papers from the Tenth International Symposium on English Teaching*, held by the English Teachers' Association in the Republic of China, November 16–18, 2001; Barbara M. Taylor, P. David Pearson, Kathleen F. Clark, and Sharon Walpole, *Beating the Odds in Teaching all Children to Read*, CIERA Report #2-006 (Ann Arbor, MI: Center for the Improvement of Early Reading Achievement, September 1999), one of the findings of this report is that the most effective teachers of students in grades 1–3 devote more time to independent reading.

The value of free independent reading in classrooms was called into question: *Report of the National Reading Panel. Teaching Children to Read: An Evidence-Based Assessment of the Scientific Research Literature on Reading and Its Implications for Reading Instruction (NRP)* (Washington, DC: National Institute of Child Health and Human Development, 2000); S. Jay Samuels, "Reading Fluency: Its Development and Assessment," in *What Research Has to Say About Reading Instruction* (3rd ed., p. 174), edited by Alan E. Farstrup and S. Jay Samuels (Newark, DE: International Reading Association, 2002).

Research linking independent reading with achievement to share with administrators and parents: In particular, see Stephen Krashen, "More Smoke and Mirrors: A Critique of the National Reading Panel Report," *Phi Delta Kappan*, October 2001, pp. 118–21. Krashen reports that in his review of the research on voluntary reading programs in school, in 51 out of 54 comparisons, students (both traditional language arts students and second language learners) participating in voluntary reading programs did as well or better on tests of reading comprehension as students who did not participate in such programs. The longer the program lasted, the better the results. Krashen explains, "The National Reading Panel report included only studies of sustained silent reading, included no long-term programs, contained only a dozen comparisons, and misinterpreted and misreported some of the studies they did include."

[29] E. Blair, *Listen to the Story: As Demographics Shift, Kids' Books Stay Stubbornly White*, June 25, 2013, available at http://wkar.org/post/demographics-shift-kids-books-stay-stubbornly-white, story as reported on *Morning Edition* on NPR, citing Census Bureau data. Census

Chapter 3 Endnotes, *continued*

Bureau data are available: http://www.census.gov/newsroom/releases/archives/population/cb13-112.html

[30] See *Reading Essentials* (Routman, 2003) and *Regie Routman in Residence: Transforming Our Teaching Through Reading/Writing Connections*, Session 4 (Routman, 2008), for specifics on how to set up the classroom library so students have ownership, choice, and easy access.

[31] Temple University College of Education professor Michael Smith, quoted in Jessica Calefati, "N.J. Educators Unsure How to Improve 4th-Grade Boys' Reading Scores on State Test," *The* [Newark] *Star-Ledger*, December 9, 2012.

[32] Ivey and Johnston, 2013; Regie Routman, *Transitions: From Literature to Literacy* (Portsmouth, NH: Heinemann, 1988).

[33] For a demonstration of how to teach children to choose books they can read and understand, see Session 5 in the *Reading to Understand* video in *Regie Routman in Residence*, 2009.

[34] The bulleted list and this paragraph are adapted from the author's post on a blog with Larry Ferlazzo. "Response from Regie Routman" as invited by Larry Ferlazzo, who wrote "Response: More Ways to Help Our Students Become Better Readers—Chance and Access," February 21, 2012.

[35] Heidi Anne Mesmer, James W. Cunningham, and Elfrieda H. Hiebert, "Toward a Theoretical Model of Text Complexity for the Early Grades: Learning from the Past, Anticipating the Future," *Reading Research Quarterly*, July/August/September 2012, p. 236.

[36] Elfrieda H. Hiebert, "The Common Core's Staircase of Text Complexity: Getting the Size of the First Step Right," *Reading Today,* December 2011/January 2012, pp. 26–27.

[37] Allington and McGill-Franzen, 2013.

[38] For detailed information on understanding and applying text complexity to teaching reading, see Elfrieda H. Hiebert, "Supporting Students' Movement Up the Staircase of Text Complexity," *The Reading Teacher*, March 2013, pp. 459–468.

[39] See Routman, 1988, for that story and information on a leveled book collection.

[40] Mesmer, Cunningham, and Hiebert, 2012.

[41] Elfrieda H. Hiebert, "Text Matters in Learning to Read," *The Reading Teacher*, December 1999, pp. 552–569.

[42] Steven Krashen, "The Lexile Framework: Unnecessary and Potentially Harmful," *CSLA* [California School Library Association] *Journal*, Fall 2001, pp. 25–26.

[43] Mesmer, Cunningham, and Hiebert, 2012. Additionally, Elfrieda Hiebert recommends two other references that support caution in using Lexiles. The first is more accessible to practitioners; the second one provides the research evidence: E. H. Hiebert, "Supporting Students' Movement on the Staircase of Text Complexity," *The Reading Teacher, 66*(6), 459–468. E. H. Heibert and K. Van Sluys, "Standard 10 of the Common Core State Standards: Examining Three Assumptions About Text Complexity," in *Whose Knowledge Counts in Government Literacy Policies? Why Expertise Matters* (pp. 144–160) K. Goodman, R. C. Calfee, & Y. Goodman, eds. (New York: Routledge, 2014).

[44] Jeffrey D. Wilhelm, "CODA: Proactivity Versus Reactivity: Preparing Students for Success with the CCSS," *Voices from the Middle*, September 2012, p. 68.

[45] Julie E. Learned, Darin Stockdill, and Elizabeth Birr Moje, "Integrating Reading Strategies and Knowledge Building in Adolescent Literacy Instruction," in *What Research Has to Say About Reading Instruction* (4th ed., pp. 159–185), ed. S. Jay Samuels and Alan Farstrup (Newark, DE: International Reading Association, 2011), p. 181.

Chapter 3 Endnotes, *continued*

[46] Matt Renwick, "How Should Social Media Etiquette Be Taught in Schools?" *EdTech*, February 10, 2013.

[47] Clive Thompson, "Clive Thompson on the New Literacy," *Wired Magazine*, September 2009. In his article, Thompson quotes and cites a Stanford University study by Andrea Lunsford, who looked at almost 15,000 student writing samples on multiple topics and in multiple forms and found students to be very skillful at adapting their tone and technique for their particular audience.

[48] Kristen Purcell, Judy Buchanan, and Linda Friedrich, *The Impact of Digital Tools on Student Writing and How Writing Is Taught in Schools* (Washington, DC: National Writing Project and Pew Research Center, July 16, 2013), p. 24.

[49] Lorna Collier, "Changes in Writing Instruction—The Challenge and the Promise," *Council Chronicle* [National Council of Teachers of English], March 2013, citing research by Arthur Applebee and Judith Langer; Michael C. McKenna, Kristin Conradi, Camille Lawrence, Bong Gee Jang, and Patrick Meyer, "Reading Attitudes of Middle School Students: Results of a U.S. Survey," *Reading Research Quarterly*, July/August/September 2012, pp. 283–306.

[50] Amanda Ripley, *The Smartest Kids in the World and How They Got That Way* (New York: Simon & Schuster, 2013), pp. 214–215.

[51] Student Nancy Garcia shared her feelings in a letter in May 2011.

[52] Alfred Tatum, *Fearless Voices: Engaging a New Generation of African American Adolescent Male Writers* (New York: Scholastic, 2013), p. 6.

[53] For a multitude of authentic writing ideas, see Regie Routman, *Writing Essentials: Raising Expectations and Results While Simplifying Teaching* (Portsmouth, NH: Heinemann, 2005).

[54] For information on characteristics of specific genres, see Routman, 2005, *Writing Essentials*, p. A-13, and www.Heinemann. com/writing essentials.

[55] Teacher Machel Lucas described her reaction in a December 31, 2011, letter. For directions and a video demonstration on snapshot writing, see Routman, 2008, *Regie Routman in Residence: Transforming Our Teaching Through Writing for Audience and Purpose*, Session 4.

[56] You can see the writing demonstration in Routman, 2008, 2013, *Regie Routman in Residence: Transforming Our Teaching Through Writing for Audience and Purpose*, Session 7.

[57] Kelly Gallaher, *Write Like This: Teaching Real-World Writing Through Modeling and Mentor Texts* (Portland, ME: Stenhouse, 2011), p. 15.

[58] For examples of how to establish editing expectations with students and hold them accountable, see Routman, 2005, *Writing Essentials* and accompanying DVD, and Routman, 2008, *Regie Routman in Residence: Transforming Our Teaching Through Writing for Audience and Purpose*.

[59] Steve Graham and Michael Hebert, *Writing to Read: Evidence for How Writing Can Improve; Carnegie Corporation Time to Act Report* (Washington, DC: Alliance for Excellent Education, 2010).

[60] Stephen King, *On Writing: A Memoir of the Craft* (New York: Scribner, 2000).

[61] Walter Dean Myers, *Just Write: Here's How!* (New York: HarperCollins, 2012).

[62] For more on public conferences in diverse classrooms, see Routman, 2005, *Writing Essentials*, pp. 205–237 and accompanying DVD; and Routman, 2008, *Regie Routman in Residence: Transforming Our Teaching Through Writing for Audience and Purpose* and *Regie Routman in Residence: Transforming Our Teaching Through Reading/Writing Connections*.

[63] This comment came from Kate Gordon during a conversation in February 2013.

Chapter 3 Endnotes, *continued*

[64] Kelly Gallagher, *Readicide: How Schools Are Killing Reading and What You Can Do About It* (Portland, ME: Stenhouse, 2009).

[65] P. Dewitz, J. Jones, & S. Leahy, "Comprehension Strategy Instruction in Core Reading Programs, *"Reading Research Quarterly, 44*(2), 102–126.

[66] Linda G. Fielding and P. David Pearson, "Synthesis of Research/Reading Comprehension: What Works," *Educational Leadership*, February 1994, pp. 62–68.

[67] W. Dorsey Hammond and Denise D. Nessel, *The Comprehension Experience: Engaging Readers Through Effective Inquiry and Discussion* (Portsmouth, NH: Heinemann, 2011). This superb book provides excellent ideas and guidelines for productive conversations and teaching comprehension K–12, across the curriculum.

[68] For detailed information and guidelines on literature conversations and book clubs in the classroom, see "Literature Conversations," pp. 171–204, in Routman, 2000, *Conversations: Strategies for Teaching, Learning, and Evaluating*, and Harvey Daniels, *Literature Circles: Voice and Choice in Book Clubs and Reading Groups* (Portland, ME: Stenhouse, 2002).

[69] Peter H. Johnston, "Reducing Instruction, Increasing Engagement," blog post, July 23, 2012, Stenhouse.com.

[70] Dan Rothstein and Luz Santana, *Make Just One Change: Teach Students to Ask Their Own Questions* (Cambridge, MA: Harvard Education Press, 2011), p. 45, emphasis in original.

[71] For more on asking thoughtful and deeper questions that lead to high-level discussion, see Jim Burke, *What's the Big Idea? Question-Driven Units to Motivate Reading, Writing, and Thinking* (Portsmouth, NH: Heinemann, 2010); Regie Routman, "Asking Literary Questions" (pp. 183–186) in *Conversations: Strategies for Teaching, Learning, and Evaluating* (Portsmouth, NH: Heinemann, 2000); and W. Dorsey Hammond and Denise D. Nessel, *The Comprehension Experience: Engaging Readers Through Effective Inquiry and Discussion* (Portsmouth, NH: Heinemann, 2011).

[72] Hammond & Nessel 2011, pp. 58–62.

[73] For guidelines on teaching close reading to adolescents, see Douglas Fisher and Nancy Frey, "Engaging the Adolescent Learner: Text Complexity and Close Reading," *IRA E-ssentials* (Newark, DE: International Reading Association, 2013).

[74] Thomas Newkirk, *The Art of Slow Reading* (Portsmouth, NH: Heinemann, 2012).

[75] Marilynne Robinson, "By the Book," *The New York Times Sunday Book Review*, interview, March 7, 2013, p. 9.

[76] Penny Kittle, *Book Love: Developing Depth, Passion, and Stamina in Adolescent Readers* (Portsmouth, NH: Heinemann, 2013).

[77] Ripley, 2013, pp. 110–111.

[78] Routman, 2003, p. 197, citing J. Cunningham, *Reading Research Quarterly*, 2001.

[79] One excellent resource that includes what the research says about teaching reading, along with recommended effective practices, is Peter Dewitz and Jonni Wolskee's *Making the Most of Your Core Reading Program: Research-Based Essentials* (Portsmouth, NH: Heinemann, 2012).

[80] Peter Dewitz, Jennifer Jones, and Susan Leahy, "Comprehension Strategy Instruction in Core Reading Programs," *Reading Research Quarterly*, April/May/June 2009, pp. 102–126.

[81] P. David Pearson and Margaret C. Gallagher, "The Instruction of Reading Comprehension," *Contemporary Educational Psychology*, October 1983, pp. 317–344; Routman, 2003, *Reading Essentials*.

Chapter 3 Endnotes, *continued*

[82] Richard L. Allington, "What At-Risk Readers Need," *Educational Leadership*, March 2011, pp. 40–45. Allington is referring to the study by Brenner and Hiebert (2010).

[83] Routman, 2003.

[84] Mesmer, Cunningham, and Hiebert, 2012, p. 251.

[85] For first four bullets, Linda G. Fielding and P. David Pearson, "Synthesis of Research/Reading Comprehension: What Works," *Educational Leadership*, February 1994, pp. 62–68; for last five bullets, Barbara M. Taylor, P. David Pearson, Kathleen F. Clark, and Sharon Walpole, "Effective Schools, Accomplished Teachers," *The Reading Teacher*, October 1999, pp. 156–159.

[86] Elizabeth B. Moje, "Developing Disciplinary Discourses, Literacies, and Identities: What's Knowledge Got to Do with It?" in *Discourses and Identities in Contexts of Educational Change* (pp. 49–74), ed. M. G. L Bonilla and K. England (New York: Peter Lang, 2011), p. 52.

[87] Sheila W. Valencia, P. David Pearson, and Karen K. Wixson, *Assessing and Tracking Progress in Reading Comprehension: The Search for Keystone Elements in College and Career Readiness* (Princeton, NJ: Center for K–12 Assessment & Performance Management at ETS, 2011), p. 32.

[88] See Routman, 2009, *Reading to Understand* virtual residency, Session 9 video for a grade 5–6 class applying shared read-aloud to understanding an informational picture book.

[89] Former middle school principal Barbara Ide included this example of "guided reading gone awry" in a personal e-mail in fall 2012.

[90] Robin Woods shared her thoughts on how her teaching shifted in an e-mail on May 29, 2009.

[91] Emily A. Swan, Cassandra S. Coddington, and John T. Guthrie, "Engaged Silent Reading," in *Revisiting Silent Reading: New Directions for Teachers and Researchers* (pp. 95–111), ed. Elfrieda H. Hiebert and D. Ray Reutzel (Newark, DE: International Reading Association, 2010).

[92] See Routman, 2003, *Reading Essentials*, p. 85, for a chart defining differences.

[93] Valencia, Pearson, and Wixson, 2011, p. 35.

[94] Devon Brenner and Elfrieda H. Hiebert, "If I Follow the Teachers' Editions, Isn't That Enough? Analyzing Reading Volume in Six Core Reading Programs," *Elementary School Journal*, March 2010, pp. 347–363; Peter Dewitz, Jenifer Jones, and Susan Leahy, "Comprehension Strategy Instruction in Core Reading Programs," *Reading Research Quarterly*, April/May/June 2009, pp. 102–126.

[95] John T. Guthrie, Alan Wigfield, and Wei You, "Instructional Contexts for Engagement and Achievement in Reading," in *Handbook of Research on Student Engagement* (pp. 601–634), S. L. Christenson, A. L. Reschly, and C. Wylie, eds. (New York: Springer, 2012); Krashen and McQuillan, 2007; Linda B. Gambrell, Barbara A. Marihak, Heather R. Brooker, and Heather J. McCrea-Andrews, "The Importance of Independent Reading," in *What Research Has to Say About Reading Instruction*, 4th ed., pp. 143–158, S. J. Samuels and Alan E. Farstrup, eds. (Newark: DE: International Reading Association, 2011).

[96] Ivey and Johnston, 2013, p. 272.

[97] U.S. Department of Education, National Center for Education Statistics, *Vocabulary Results from the 2009 and 2011 NAEP Reading Assessments*, December 6, 2012.

[98] D. Ray Reutzel, Cindy D. Jones, and Terry H. Newman, "Scaffolded Silent Reading: Improving the Conditions of Silent Reading Practice in Classrooms," in *Revisiting Silent*

Chapter 3 Endnotes, *continued*

Reading: New Directions for Teachers and Researchers (pp. 129–150), ed. Elfrieda H. Hiebert and D. Ray Reutzel (Newark, DE: International Reading Association, 2010).

[99] For examples of reading conferences, see Routman, 2003, *Reading Essentials*; and Routman, 2000, *Conversations: Strategies for Teaching, Learning, and Evaluating.* For more examples, including videos of students, see Routman, 2009, 2013, *Regie Routman in Residence: Transforming Our Teaching Through Reading to Understand.*

[100] See Routman, 2003, pp. 179–181.

Chapter 4

[1] Richard L. Allington, *What Really Matters in Response to Intervention: Research-Based Designs* (Boston: Pearson, 2008).

[2] I previously wrote about Kathy in *Teaching Essentials* (Routman, 2008, pp. 6–9), and I showcased her clear, intelligent voice in my video-based literacy series (*Regie Routman in Residence: Transforming Our Teaching Though Reading to Understand*, 2009); see "View Success Story" for part of an interview with Kathy at http://www.regieroutman.com/inresidence /overview.aspx.

[3] Evangeline Harris Stefanakis, "Assessing Young Immigrant Students: Are We Finding Their Strengths? *Harvard Education Letter,* May/June 2004, p. 7.

[4] Allington, 2008.

[5] Henry M. Levin, Clive Belfield, Peter Muennig, and Cecilia Rouse, *The Costs and Benefits of an Excellent Education for All of America's Children* (New York: Teachers College Press, 2007).

[6] Ulrich Boser and Lindsay Rosenthal, *Do Schools Challenge Our Students? What Student Surveys Tell Us About the State of Education in the United States* (Washington, DC: Center for American Progress, 2012). This report is derived from student surveys that are part of the National Assessment of Educational Progress.

[7] Sheila W. Valencia and Karen K. Wixson, "CCSS in ELA: Suggestions and Cautions for Implementing the Reading Standards," *The Reading Teacher,* November 2013, p. 183.

[8] Tom Loveless, *How Well Are American Students Learning? With Sections on Predicting the Effect of the Common Core State Standards, Achievement Gaps on the Two NAEP Tests, and Misinterpreting International Test Scores,* Brown Center Report on American Education (Washington, DC: Brookings Institution, 2012), p. 11.

[9] W. S. Barnett, M. E. Carolan, J. Fitzgerald, and J. H. Squires, 2012 *The State of Preschool 2012: State Preschool Yearbook* (New Brunswick, NJ: National Institute for Early Education Research, 2012).

[10] David Brooks, "When Families Fail," Op-Ed, *The New York Times,* February 15, 2013, p. A23; Cynthia Lamy, "How Preschool Fights Poverty," *Educational Leadership,* May 2013, pp. 32–36.

[11] "Getting Preschool Education Right," editorial, *The New York Times,* February 16, 2013, p. A16.

[12] Andrew Higgins, "Lessons for U.S. from a Flood-Prone Land," *The New York Times,* November 14, 2012, p. A5.

[13] Richard L. Allington, "What At-Risk Readers Need," *Educational Leadership,* March 2011, pp. 40–45.

Chapter 4 Endnotes, *continued*

[14] Regie Routman, *Literacy and Learning Lessons from a Longtime Teacher* (Newark, DE: International Reading Association, 2012).

[15] Jamie Newman provided her story in a phone interview on January 21, 2013.

[16] Lindsay Jacksha's account came via e-mail, April 26, 2012.

[17] Andrea Lockhart told her story in a phone interview on January 10, 2013.

[18] Sean F. Reardon, "The Widening Income Achievement Gap," *Educational Leadership*, May 2013, pp. 10–16.

[19] Richard L. Allington, "Reading Intervention in the Middle Grades," *Voices from the Middle*, December 2011, pp. 10–16.

[20] Anthony Rebora, "Responding to RTI," *Education Week, Teacher PD Sourcebook*, interview of Richard Allington, April 9, 2010.

[21] Jennifer K. Gilbert, Donald L. Compton, Douglas Fuchs, Lynn S. Fuchs, Bobette Bouton, Laura A. Barquero, and Eunsoo Cho, "Efficacy of a First-Grade Responsiveness-to-Intervention Prevention Model for Struggling Readers," *Reading Research Quarterly*, April/May/June 2013, pp. 135–154.

[22] This observation comes from a conversation in March 2012 with Allyson Matczuk, an early literacy consultant with Reading Recovery in the Western Division in Winnipeg, Manitoba.

[23] Reading Recovery Executive Summary, Winnipeg, 2012.

[24] Assistant Superintendent Jason Drysdale made his comments during a conversation in March 2013.

[25] The percentages, accurate as of July 2013, come from literacy coach and reading specialist Kate Gordon, who documented that students achieved a Developmental Reading Assessment (DRA) score of 3 or above and a Smarter Balance score of 2 or above.

[26] Kate Gordon made this statement during a conversation on October 15, 2012.

[27] This observation, and many of the ideas in this paragraph, came from Barb Ide, school improvement coach, in an e-mail in July 2013.

[28] Karl L. Alexander, Doris R. Entwisle, and Linda Steffel Olson, "Lasting Consequences of the Summer Learning Gap," *American Sociological Review*, April 2007, pp. 167–180.

[29] Richard L. Allington and Anne McGill-Franzen, "Why So Much Oral Reading?" in *Revisiting Silent Reading: New Directions for Teachers and Researchers* (pp. 45–56), ed. Elfrieda H. Hiebert and D. Ray Reutzel (Newark, DE: International Reading Association, 2010); Anne McGill-Franzen and Richard L. Allington, "Got Books?" *Educational Leadership*, April 2008, pp. 20–23; Susan B. Neuman, Donna C. Celano, Albert N. Greco, and Pamela Shue, *Access for All: Closing the Book Gap for Children in Early Education* (Newark, DE: International Reading Association, 2001).

[30] McGill-Franzen and Allington, 2008.

[31] The list of solutions is based on information and recommendations included in McGill-Franzen & Allington, 2008; Allington & McGill-Franzen, 2013; and James S. Kim, "Effects of a Voluntary Summer Reading Intervention on Reading Achievement: Results from a Randomized Field Trial," *Educational Evaluation and Policy Analysis*, 2006, pp. 335–355.

[32] Lois Bridges, *RTI: The Best Intervention Is a Good Book*, white paper (New York: Scholastic, 2010).

[33] Routman, 2008, *Teaching Essentials*.

Chapter 4 Endnotes, *continued*

[34] Steve Graham and Michael Hebert, *Writing to Read: Evidence for How Writing Can Improve Reading, Carnegie Corporation Time to Act Report* (Washington, DC: Alliance for Excellent Education, 2010).

[35] Graham and Hebert, 2010, p. 11.

[36] David K. Dickinson and Lori Lyman DiGisi, "The Many Rewards of a Literacy-Rich Classroom," *Educational Leadership*, March 1998, pp. 23–26; Nell K. Duke and Susan Bennett-Armistead, *Reading and Writing Informational Text in the Primary Grades* (New York: Scholastic, 2003); see also Routman, 2005, *Writing Essentials*, Notes, pp. A-28, A-29, A30 for research on how writing improves reading.

[37] Susan B. Neuman, "The American Dream: Slipping Away?" *Educational Leadership*, May 2013, p. 21.

[38] Lesley Vermaas provided this account of her experience in an interview on February 20, 2013. The standardized assessment she refers to is the DRA2 (Developmental Reading Assessment) by Joetta Beaver. Students' reading scores on the DRA2 used to be levels 12–16, on average, which equate to about mid to end of 1st grade; now levels 24–28 are the average reading scores, which equates to mid to end of 2nd grade. In other words, the students are a full year ahead of where a similar cohort used to be. Two examples of texts almost all students can read by the end of grade 1 are *The Littles* series by John Peterson and the *Flat Stanley* series by Jeff Brown. It is important to note that according to the publishers' guidelines on the DRA2, former 1st graders at this school were already meeting recommended expectations. However, the school district raised those expectations—but not only to meet CCSS guidelines. As teachers were becoming more knowledgeable through a PLC-infused school culture, it became evident that students could achieve much more.

[39] Gloria Heflin wrote to me about her results with students, including verifying student test data, on January 15 and 21, 2013.

[40] Gloria shared this anecdote in an e-mail message on October 14, 2011.

[41] Jamie Newman reported this success during a phone conversation on January 21, 2013.

[42] Elfrieda H. Hiebert and D. Ray Reutzel, eds., *Revisiting Silent Reading: New Directions for Teachers and Researchers* (Newark, DE: International Reading Association, 2010). The authors also cite other researchers.

[43] National Center for Education Statistics, "Vocabulary Results from the 2009 and 2011 NAEP Reading Assessments," Executive Summary, December 6, 2012.

[44] Clive Thompson, "Clive Thompson on the New Literacy," *Wired Magazine*, September 2009.

[45] Marjorie Y. Lipson and Karen K. Wixson, eds., *Successful Approaches to RTI: Collaborative Practices for Improving K–12 Literacy* (Newark, DE: International Reading Association, 2010), p. 2.

[46] Mary Howard, *RTI from All Sides: What Every Teacher Needs to Know* (Portsmouth, NH: Heinemann, 2009), p. 3.

[47] Allington, March 2011.

[48] Allington, 2008.

[49] Christina E. Van Kraayenoord, "Response to Intervention: New Ways and Wariness," *Reading Research Quarterly*, July/August/September 2010, pp. 363–376.

[50] Van Kraayenoord, 2010.

[51] See the *Teaching Essentials* website for multiple research studies on DIBELS: www.regieroutman.com/teachingessentials/print.asp.

Chapter 4 Endnotes, *continued*

[52] National Reading Panel, Report of the National Reading Panel. *Teaching Children to Read: An Evidence-Based Assessment of the Scientific Literature on Reading and Its Implications for Reading Instruction* (Washington, DC: National Institute of Child Health and Human Development, 2000).

[53] See Routman, 2009, *Reading to Understand*, video excerpt at http://www.regieroutman .com/inresidence/rdg/samples.aspx, which shows how a group of low-performing 1st graders, whose reading emphasis has been decoding and decodable texts, struggle to make meaning in a simple text.

[54] Peter Dewitz, Jennifer Jones, and Susan Leahy, "Comprehension Strategy Instruction in Core Reading Programs, *Reading Research Quarterly*, April/May/June 2009, pp. 102–126.

[55] Warwick Elley, "Acquiring Literacy in a Second Language: The Effect of Book-Based Programs, *Language Learning*, September 1991, pp. 375–411; Don Holdaway, *The Foundations of Literacy* (Portsmouth, NH: Heineman, 1979); Don Graves, *Writing: Teachers and Children at Work* (Portsmouth, NH: Heinemann, 1983); Brian Cambourne, *The Whole Story: Natural Learning and the Acquisition of Literacy in the Classroom* (Richmond Hill, Ontario, Canada: Scholastic, 1988).

[56] Neuman, May 2013, pp. 18–22.

[57] Routman, *Reading Essentials*, 2003.

[58] For more extensive guidelines on partner reading, see Routman, 2003, *Reading Essentials*, pp. 91–93.

[59] David O'Brien and Deborah Dillon, "Engaging 'At-Risk' High School Students: Perspectives from an Innovative Program," *Reading Today: Research Updates from the National Reading Research Center*, April/May 1996, p. 18.

[60] The point about "fake writing" comes from a conversation with a group of middle school students in Seattle, WA, in February 2013.

[61] Matt Renwick, "Increasing Engagement: A School Revamps Its Reading Intervention Program," blog post, January 22, 2013.

[62] Richard L. Allington and Patricia M. Cunningham, *Schools That Work: Where All Children Read and Write,* 3rd ed. (Boston: Pearson, 2006); Kelly Gallagher, *Readicide: How Schools Are Killing Reading and What You Can Do About It* (Portland, ME: Stenhouse, 2009); Gay Ivey and Peter Johnston, "Reading Engagement, Achievement, and Moral Development in Adolescence," paper presented at the annual meeting of the National Reading Conference/ Literacy Research Association (Fort Worth, TX, December 2010); Penny Kittle, *Book Love: Developing Depth, Passion, and Stamina in Adolescent Readers* (Portsmouth, NH: Heinemann, 2013); Nancy Allison, *Middle School Readers: Helping Them Read Widely, Helping Them Read Well* (Portsmouth, NH: Heinemann, 2009).

[63] Allington and McGill-Franzen, 2010, p. 48.

[64] Johnston and Ivey (2013), Kittle (2013), Miller (2008), Routman (2003).

[65] Teri S. Lesesne, *Reading Ladders: Leading Students from Where They Are to Where We'd Like Them to Be* (Portsmouth, NH: Heinemann, 2010, p. 48). See also, especially for middle and high school students, Chapter 2, endnote 10, for recommended titles by the following researchers: Atwell, Allison, Gallagher, Kittle, and Miller. These authors also provide excellent guidance on matching students with books, providing more choice, reading conferences, and independent reading.

[66] The list is slightly adapted from John Hattie, *Visible Learning: A Synthesis of Over 800 Meta-Analyses Relating to Achievement* (New York: Routledge, 2009), p. 206.

Chapter 4 Endnotes, *continued*

[67] Regie Routman, *Literacy and Learning Lessons from a Longtime Teacher* (Newark, DE: International Reading Association, 2012), p. 111.

[68] Allington and McGill-Franzen, 2010.

[69] D. Ray Reutzel, Cindy D. Jones, and Terry H. Newman, "Scaffolded Silent Reading: Improving the Conditions of Silent Reading Practice in Classrooms," in *Revisiting Silent Reading: New Directions for Teachers and Researchers* (pp. 129–150), ed. Elfrieda H. Hiebert and D. Ray Reutzel (Newark, DE: International Reading Association, 2010); Regie Routman, *Writing Essentials: Raising Expectations and Results While Simplifying Teaching* (Portsmouth, NH: Heinemann, 2005).

[70] For more specifics, examples, and videos of students, see Routman, 2003, *Reading Essentials*; Routman, 2000, *Conversations: Strategies for Teaching, Learning, and Evaluating*; and Routman, 2009, *Regie Routman in Residence: Transforming Our Teaching* (video-based series), "Reading to Understand." See also Routman, 2005, *Writing Essentials* and Routman, 2008, *Writing for Audience and Purpose.*

[71] Jamie Newman shared her experience in a conversation on January 21, 2013.

[72] Richard Elmore, "Institutions, Improvement, and Practice," in *Change Wars* (pp. 221–235), ed. Andy Hargreaves and Michael Fullan (Bloomington, IN: Solution Tree, 2009). Elmore uses the term "high levels of atomization," which I have interpreted as skills in isolation. The other factors are low expectations and low sense of efficacy and agency on the part of the adults.

[73] Lesli A. Maxwell, "Calif. Poised to Spotlight ELLs Stalled in Schools," *Education Week*, September 19, 2012, pp. 1, 18. Maxwell is reporting on a study that found that 59 percent of second-language learners in grades 6–12 had failed to achieve English language proficiency despite being enrolled in American schools for more than six years.

[74] Sharlline Markwardt's comment is from an e-mail sent on July 13, 2013.

[75] Sharlline Markwardt's report came in an e-mail dated May 28, 2012.

[76] This account is from an e-mail from Sharlline Markwardt on July 13, 2013.

[77] Heather Woodroof included these comments in a letter on January 4, 2009.

[78] Heather Woodroof shared her experience in a letter on January 4, 2009.

[79] Owen sent the e-mail message on November 16, 2012.

[80] See Routman, 2005, *Writing Essentials*, p. 22, for more about Owen as a writer and how celebration of his writing transformed him as a learner. In the same text, see a lesson plan for "Secrets of Second Graders," pp. 292–304. See also Routman, 2008, *Teaching Essentials*, pp. 17–18. View Owen's "I can do it!" video interview on the *Teaching Essentials* companion website, Video Resources, Chapter 2, "An Interview with Owen," at http://www.regieroutman.com/teachingessentials/chapter2.asp.

Chapter 5

[1] Karen Seashore Louis, Kenneth Leithwood, Kyla L. Wahlstrom, and Stephen E. Anderson, *Learning from Leadership: Investigating the Links to Improved Student Learning* (St. Paul, MN: Center for Applied Research and Educational Improvement, University of Minnesota; and Toronto: Ontario Institute for Studies in Education, University of Toronto, 2010), p. 9.

Chapter 5 Endnotes, *continued*

[2] Douglas B. Reeves, *Leading Change in Your School: How to Conquer Myths, Build Commitment, and Get Results* (Alexandria, VA: ASCD, 2009), p. 67.

[3] Pasi Sahlberg, "What If Finland's Great Teachers Taught in U.S. Schools?" in "The Answer Sheet" blog by Valerie Strauss, *The Washington Post*, May 15, 2013. Sahlberg is a Finnish education expert and author of *Finnish Lessons: What Can the World Learn About Educational Change in Finland?*

[4] Regie Routman, *Literacy and Learning Lessons from a Longtime Teacher* (Newark, DE: International Reading Association, 2012), p. 22.

[5] Susan M. Brookhart and Connie M. Moss, "Leading by Learning," *Phi Delta Kappan*, May 2013, pp. 13–17.

[6] Barbara Markle and Stephanie VanKoevering, "Reviving Edward Bell," *Phi Delta Kappan*, May 2013, p. 9.

[7] Louis et al., 2010. The information in this paragraph is synthesized from this entire report, which is based on interview data from teachers and principals from a random sampling of districts across the United States.

[8] Louis et al., 2010, p. 19.

[9] Michael Fullan and Andy Hargreaves, *What's Worth Fighting For in Your School?* (rev. ed.), (New York: Teachers College Press, 1996), p. 112.

[10] Richard Ackerman and Sarah V. Mackenzie, "Uncovering Teacher Leadership," *Educational Leadership*, May 2006, pp. 66–70.

[11] Sarah D. Sparks, "Principals Lack Training in Shaping School Climate," *Education Week*, March 6, 2013, p. 8.

[12] Routman, 2012, *Literacy and Learning Lessons from a Longtime Teacher*, p. 111.

[13] Regie Routman, "To Raise Achievement, Let's Celebrate Teachers Before We Evaluate Them," *Reading Today*, June/July 2013, pp. 10–12.

[14] Teacher Shana Bowens shared her experience in an e-mail on March 25, 2013.

[15] Alfred Tatum, *Fearless Voices: Engaging a New Generation of African American Adolescent Male Writers* (New York: Scholastic, 2013), p. 37.

[16] Sarah Truebridge. "Resilience, Research, and Education Reform." ASCD Whole Child Blog, Nov. 29, 2010. Accessed: www.wholechildeducation.org/blog/resilience-research-and-educational-reform.

[17] Ben Levin, "The One-Legged High Jumper and the Perils of Prediction," *Phi Delta Kappan*, October 2012, p. 75.

[18] Levin, 2012, cites the research of Emmy Werner and Ruth Smith, as presented in *Overcoming the Odds: High Risk Children from Birth to Adulthood* (Ithaca, NY: Cornell University Press, 1992).

[19] Jan Moore, "Research Alert: The Research on Resilience," *Educational Leadership*, September 2013, p. 8.

[20] Carol S. Dweck, *Mindset: The New Psychology of Success* (New York: Random House, 2006).

[21] Eric Jensen, "How Poverty Affects Classroom Engagement," *Educational Leadership*, May 2013, pp. 24–30.

[22] Nicholas Kristof, "Sewing Her Way Out of Poverty," *The New York Times*, September 13, 2011.

Chapter 5 Endnotes, *continued*

[23] Yochai Benkler, *The Penguin and the Leviathan: How Cooperation Triumphs over Self-Interest* (New York: Crown Business, 2011), p. 179. Additionally, pay for performance does not raise test scores or student outcomes. See http://news.vanderbilt.edu/2010/09/teacher-performance-pay/.

[24] Kent Williamson, "Teachers Should Receive More Time to Collaborate," Letter to the Editor, *Education Week*, May 8, 2013, p. 29. Williamson is director of the National Center for Literacy Education and executive director of the National Council of Teachers of English.

[25] Williamson, 2013.

[26] The five questions were mentioned in an interview in the *New York Times* with business executive Tony Tjan, who credited his business partner, Mats Lederhausan, with developing them as part of a framework for mentoring. See Adam Bryant, "A Good Mentor Never Tramples on Big Dreams," *The New York Times*, December 8, 2012, p. B2.

[27] Sonia Sotomayor, *My Beloved World* (New York: Alfred A. Knopf, 2012), p. 210.

[28] Daniel Pink, *A Whole New Mind: Why Right-Brainers Will Rule the Future* (New York: Riverhead, 2006).

[29] PBS Online, *This Emotional Life*, 2009. Available: http://www.pbs.org/thisemotionallife/topic/humor/benefits-humor.

[30] Jacqueline Novogratz, chief executive of a nonprofit organization in New York City, made this observation in an interview with Adam Bryant. See Adam Bryant, "When Humility and Audacity Go Hand in Hand, *The New York Times*, September 29, 2012, p. B2.

[31] Liz Wiseman, Lois N. Allen, and Elise Foster, *The Multiplier Effect: Tapping the Genius Inside Our Schools* (Thousand Oaks, CA: Corwin, 2013), p. 10.

[32] Wiseman et al., 2013, p. 101.

[33] Richard Stengel, *Mandela's Way: Fifteen Lessons on Life, Love, and Courage.* (New York: Random House, 2009), p. 81.

[34] Regie Routman, "Mapping a Pathway to Schoolwide Highly Effective Teaching," *Phi Delta Kappan*, February 2012, pp. 56–61.

[35] Elizabeth A. City, Richard Elmore, Sarah E. Fiarman, and Lee Teitel, *Instructional Rounds in Education: A Network Approach to Improving Teaching and Learning* (Cambridge, MA: Harvard Education Press, 2009), pp. 1–6.

[36] Routman, February 2012, p. 57.

[37] Trena Speirs shared her comments at a Literacy and Learning Institute session in Madison, WI, in June 2012.

[38] Ann Thomson made these comments during a conversation in October 2012.

[39] Richard L. Allington, "What I've Learned About Effective Reading Instruction from a Decade of Studying Exemplary Elementary Classroom Teachers," *Phi Delta Kappan*, June 2002, pp. 740–747.

[40] Louis et al., 2010.

[41] The interaction with the French teacher occurred during a residency in Winnipeg, Manitoba, in February 2013.

[42] Sue Marlatt is a K–5 principal in Winnipeg, Manitoba. Her comments were part of the reflection she completed in February 2013 for the evaluation of the residency.

[43] Matt Renwick shared his method during a phone conversation on August 21, 2013.

[44] Kim Ball provided her comments during an interview on January 28, 2013.

Chapter 5 Endnotes, *continued*

[45] Helpful books on effective language use and feedback include *Choice Words: How Our Language Affects Children's Learning* and *Opening Minds: Using Language to Change Lives*, both by Peter H. Johnston; and *Visible Learning* by John Hattie. The last title is also exemplary for extensive research and practices connected to optimal instruction and assessment.

[46] Principal Leah Whitford included this comment in a personal note on March 16, 2013.

[47] Lindsay is the remarkable kindergarten teacher whose voice we hear in Chapter 4. She made this comment during an interview in January 2013.

[48] This comment came from Debbie Johnson in an interview on January 28, 2013.

[49] Routman, February 2012, p. 58.

[50] Karla J. Reiss, *Leadership Coaching for Educators: Bringing Out the Best in School Administrators* (Thousand Oaks, CA: Corwin, 2007).

[51] Charity's comments came from an e-mail message on June 25, 2010.

[52] Ronald Gallimore and Bradley A. Ermeling, "Why Durable Teaching Changes Are Elusive and What We Might Do About It," *Journal of Reading Recovery*, Spring 2012, p. 44.

[53] Mike Henderson shared his experience in an e-mail on June 26, 2013.

[54] Kate Gordon offered her reflections in an e-mail in August 2013.

[55] Marilyn Jerde expressed her beliefs in an e-mail in August 2013.

Chapter 6

[1] Richard DuFour and Robert Eaker, *Professional Learning Communities at Work: Best Practices for Enhancing Student Achievement* (Bloomington, IN: Solution Tree, 1998); Shirley M. Hord and William A. Sommers, *Leading Professional Learning Communities: Voices from Research and Practice* (Thousand Oaks, CA: Corwin, 2008).

[2] Michael Fullan, ed., *Motion Leadership: The Skinny on Becoming Change Savvy* (Thousand Oaks, CA: Corwin, 2010), p. 36. In making this statement, Fullan is citing research presented in "The Impact of Leadership on Student Outcomes," by Viviane M. J. Robinson, Claire A. Lloyd, and Kenneth J. Rowe, *Educational Administration Quarterly*, December 2008, pp. 635–674.

[3] Ronald Gallimore and Bradley A. Ermeling, "Why Durable Teaching Changes Are Elusive and What We Might Do About It," *Journal of Reading Recovery*, Spring 2012, p. 43.

[4] Michael Fullan, "The Three Stories of Education Reform," *Phi Delta Kappan*, April 2000, pp. 581–584.

[5] Karen Seashore Louis, Kenneth Leithwood, Kyla L. Wahlstrom, and Stephen E. Anderson, *Learning from Leadership: Investigating the Links to Improved Student Learning* (St. Paul, MN: Center for Applied Research and Educational Improvement, University of Minnesota; and Toronto: Ontario Institute for Studies in Education, University of Toronto, 2010), p. 66.

[6] Andy Hargreaves and Dennis Shirley, *The Fourth Way: The Inspiring Future for Educational Change* (Thousand Oaks, CA: Corwin, 2009).

[7] Bruce R. Joyce and Beverly Showers, *Student Achievement Through Staff Development*, 3rd ed. (Alexandria, VA: ASCD, 2002).

[8] Debbie Johnson, director of teaching and learning K–12, offered this account in a January 28, 2013, interview.

Chapter 6 Endnotes, *continued*

[9] Taffy Raphael and I collaborated in the Sandy Grade School Residency from 2010 through 2013. Her initial needs assessment with Cindy Brock and her follow-up support—based on the principles of SchoolRise and its standards-based change process— ensured the development of a solid operating system. Establishing a working infrastructure as well as an understanding of a cohesive benchmark process was foundational to our moving forward in improving literacy instruction and learning schoolwide.

[10] Ann Thomson shared her thoughts in a conversation on January 29, 2013.

[11] Principal Trena Speirs made this statement during a session titled "Creating a Self-Sustaining School: The Journey of One School" at a Literacy and Leadership Institute in June 2011, in Milwaukee, WI.

[12] This list is adapted from Regie Routman, "Mapping a Pathway to Schoolwide Highly Effective Teaching," *Phi Delta Kappan*, February 2012, pp. 56–61.

[13] All the data-team process steps are from Angela Peery, *The Data Team Experience: A Guide for Effective Meetings* (Englewood, CO: Lead and Learn Press, 2011).

[14] Linda Darling-Hammond, Ruth Chung Wei, Alethea Andree, Nikole Richardson, and Stelios Orphanos, *Professional Learning in the Learning Profession: A Status Report on Teacher Development in the United States and Abroad* (Palo Alto, CA: School Redesign Network at Stanford University; and Oxford, OH: National Staff Development Council, 2009); Cerylle A. Moffett, "Sustaining Change: The Answers Are Blowing in the Wind," *Educational Leadership*, April 2000, pp. 35–38.

[15] Linda Darling-Hammond and Nikole Richardson, "Teacher Learning: What Matters?" *Educational Leadership*, February 2009, pp. 46–53; Thomas R. Guskey and Kwang Suk Yoon, "What Works in Professional Development?" *Phi Delta Kappan*, March 2009, pp. 495–500.

[16] Gallimore and Ermeling, Spring 2012, p. 42.

[17] Linda Darling-Hammond, "Keeping Good Teachers: Why It Matters, What Leaders Can Do," *Educational Leadership*, May 2003, pp. 6–13.

[18] Kathryn H. Au, Taffy E. Raphael, and Kathleen C. Mooney, "What We Have Learned About Teacher Education to Improve Literacy Achievement in Urban Schools," in *Improving Literacy Achievement in Urban Schools: Critical Elements in Teacher Preparation* (pp. 159–184), Louise C. Wilkinson, Lesley Mendel Morrow, & Victoria Chou, eds. (Newark, DE: International Reading Association, 2008); Linda Darling-Hammond, May 2003; Barbara Taylor, Debra Peterson, P. David Pearson, and Michael Rodrigues "Looking Inside Classrooms: Reflecting on the 'How' as Well as the 'What' in Effective Reading Instruction," *The Reading Teacher*, November 2002, pp. 270-279.

[19] Louis et al., 2010, p. 42.

[20] Diane Ravitch, *The Death and Life of the Great American School System: How Testing and Choice Are Undermining Education* (New York: Basic Books, 2010), p. 192.

[21] Two reading assessments that fit those criteria are DIBELS and mClass. See *Teaching Essentials* website for research on DIBELS: www.regieroutman.com/teachingessentials /DIBELS.asp

[22] Kim Ball made her comments during an interview on January 28, 2013.

[23] Kate Gordon included these comments in an e-mail on August 7, 2013, and she is also the source of the ideas in the previous paragraph.

[24] Routman, 2012, "Mapping a Pathway," with special thanks to principal Trena Speirs for her contributions to this description of the application/interview process.

Chapter 6 Endnotes, *continued*

[25] Regie Routman, "To Raise Achievement, Let's Celebrate Teachers Before We Evaluate Them," *Reading Today*, June/July 2013, pp. 10–12. The list was created with input from Nancy McLean, Judy Wallis, Kate Gordon, Taffy Raphael, Sandra Figueroa, and Trena Speirs.

[26] Richard DuFour and Robert Eaker, *Professional Learning Communities at Work: Best Practices for Enhancing Student Achievement* (Bloomington, IN: Solution Tree Press, 1998).

[27] Hord and Sommers, 2008.

[28] For examples and analysis of deeper understanding of video lessons from diverse classrooms—that is, the explicit teaching points, ongoing assessment, questions/reflections, and learning outcomes—see *Regie Routman in Residence: Professional Development Notebook*, (2008 & 2009).

[29] Adapted from Regie Routman, 2008, *Regie Routman in Residence: Getting Started Guide*. For a more detailed agenda outline with suggestions for PLC sessions, see the *Getting Started Guide*, pp. 36–41.

[30] I developed this synthesis of key actions with colleagues Judy Wallis, Nancy McLean, Greta Salmi, Marilyn Jerde, and Sandra Figueroa.

[31] Sandra Figueroa included her comments in an e-mail on June 25, 2013. For information on the impact of that PD on achievement, see http://www.regieroutman.com/inresidence/samples/AZCaseStudy.pdf.

[32] Lisa Randall, *Knocking on Heaven's Door: How Physics and Scientific Thinking Illuminate the Universe and the Modern World* (New York: HarperCollins, 2011), pp. 402–403.

[33] David Ronka, Mary Ann Lachat, Rachel Slaughter, and Julie Meltzer, "Answering the Questions That Count," *Educational Leadership*, December 2008/January 2009.

[34] Regie Routman, *Kids' Poems: Teaching First Graders to Love Writing Poetry* (New York: Scholastic, 2000). Other books in this series are for kindergarten, grade 2, and grades 3–4.

[35] April Waters provided this account in an e-mail on June 2, 2011.

[36] April made this comment to me in a conversation on February 28, 2013.

[37] A helpful book for teaching how to ask better questions is *Make Just One Change: Teach Students to Ask Their Own Questions* by Dan Rothstein and Luz Santana (Cambridge, MA: Harvard Education Press, 2013).

[38] Fullan, 2010, p. 16.

[39] Walter Isaacson, *Steve Jobs* (New York: Simon & Schuster, 2012), pp. 127, 143.

[40] Isaacson, p. 343.

[41] Kim Ball made these comments in January 2013.

[42] Routman, February 2012, p. 59.

[43] Kate Gordon expressed her thoughts in a conversation on January 28, 2013.

[44] Susan Rodriguez, a K–5 principal in Beaverton, OR, conveyed her thoughts about professional development in an e-mail on December 20, 2012.

[45] This observation came from Stephanie Charlton in a letter dated October 25, 2007.

Chapter 7

[1] Lisa Randall, *Knocking on Heaven's Door: How Physics and Scientific Thinking Illuminate the Universe and the Modern World* (New York: HarperCollins, 2011), p. 398.

Chapter 7 Endnotes, *continued*

[2] Lynn Sharratt and Michael Fullan, *Putting Faces on the Data: What Great Leaders Do* (Thousand Oaks, CA: Corwin, 2012), a joint publication with Learning Forward and The Ontario Principal's Council. "Putting faces on the data" is the term the authors use to emphasize that we are teaching and helping individual students and our commitment is to them first–to see the children who are behind the data.

[3] Kim Ball expressed her feelings in an e-mail on August 30, 2012.

[4] Alina Tugend, "Complaining Is Hard to Avoid, but Try to Do It with a Purpose," *The New York Times*, May 4, 2013, p. B7. In her article, Tugend cites the research-based viewpoints of Guy Winch, Joannna Wolfe, and Will Bowen.

[5] Lori Johnson shared this account of her experience in a letter on April 12, 2013.

[6] The quote is from Guy Winch, in Tugend, 2013, p. B7.

[7] Pasi Sahlberg, "What If Finland's Great Teachers Taught in U.S. Schools?" in "The Answer Sheet" blog by Valerie Strauss, *The Washington Post,* May 15, 2013.

[8] Laurie Espenel shared this comment during a phone conversation on September 19, 2012.

[9] Abigail Pinard provided this account in a personal letter dated July 19, 2013.

[10] Bill Preble and Larry Taylor, "School Climate Through Students' Eyes," *Educational Leadership,* December 2008/January 2009, p. 40. In their statement, the authors are reporting on the research of the Collaborative for Academic, Social, and Emotional Learning (CASEL). Also, Debra Viadero, "Social-Skills Programs Found to Yield Gains in Academic Subjects," *Education Week*, December 18, 2007, pp. 1, 15.

[11] Andy Hargreaves and Dennis Shirley, "The Persistence of Presentism," *Teachers College Record*, November 2009, pp. 2505–2534.

[12] Hargreaves and Shirley, 2009.

[13] Isaacson, p. 172, 173, 174.

[14] Michael Fullan and Andy Hargreaves, *What's Worth Fighting For in Your School?* (rev. ed.) New York: Teachers College Press, 1996).

[15] Michael Fullan, *Leading in a Culture of Change* (San Francisco: Jossey-Bass, 2001), pp. 40, 41.

[16] Adapted from Daniel Pink, *Drive: The Surprising Truth About What Motivates Us* (New York: Riverhead Books, 2009), pp. 204, 207–208.

[17] Laurie Espenal made this comment in a conversation on June 3, 2013.

[18] Laurie's additional comments came in an e-mail on June 12, 2013.

[19] Kathy Au, "Creating a Staircase Curriculum," *Reading Today*, August/September 2009, p. 15.

[20] Sharlline Markwardt, English language development teacher, made this comment during an interview on June 11, 2013.

[21] Regie Routman, *Literacy at the Crossroads: Crucial Talk About Reading, Writing, and Other Teaching Dilemmas* (Portsmouth, NH: Heinemann, 1996), pp. 147–165.

[22] Sharlline Markwardt shared this observation during a conversation on June 11, 2013.

[23] The bullet points are adapted from Regie Routman, "Mapping a Pathway to Schoolwide Highly Effective Teaching," *Phi Delta Kappan*, February 2012, p. 59.

[24] Nancy McLean, literacy coach, shared her thinking in an e-mail message on August 22, 2013.

Chapter 7 Endnotes, *continued*

[25] Bruce R. Joyce and Beverly Showers, *Student Achievement Through Staff Development,* 3rd ed. (Alexandria, VA: ASCD, 2002).

[26] Tracey Johnson made these comments and those in the next extract in an interview on January 28, 2013.

[27] The series is *Regie Routman in Residence: Transforming Our Teaching Through Reading/ Writing Connections* (Portsmouth, NH: Heinemann, 2008).

[28] Routman, 2008.

[29] Heather Khan, "Three Teachers' Perceptions of an Embedded Literacy-Based Professional Development Project (unpublished research, June 2012).

[30] Margaret Fair shared her enthusiasm in an e-mail on June 17, 2013.

[31] Jason Drysdale provided this account in an e-mail on July 17, 2013.

[32] Allyson Matczuk offered this description in an e-mail on August 2, 2013.

[33] Barb Ide offered this insight in response to the book manuscript, July 27, 2012.

[34] Motoko Rich, "Study Gauges Value of Technology in Schools," *The New York Times,* June 14, 2013, p. A17. Rich is quoting Ulrich Boser, a senior fellow at the nonprofit Center for American Progress and the coauthor of a report by the center.

[35] Amanda Ripley, *The Smartest Kids in the World and How They Got That Way* (New York: Simon & Schuster, 2013), p. 214, quoting Andreas Schleicher, who is the deputy director for education and skills for the Organisation for Economic Cooperation and Development, an international body of 30 member countries.

[36] Alice Munro, *Dear Life* (New York: Vintage, 2012).

References and Resources

Ackerman, R., & Mackenzie, S. V. (2006, May). Uncovering teacher leadership. *Educational Leadership, 63*(8), 66–70.

Afflerbach, P., Pearson, P. D., & S. G. Paris (2008, February). Clarifying differences between reading skills and reading strategies. *The Reading Teacher, 61*(5), pp. 364–373.

Alexander, K. L., Entwisle, D. R., & Olson, L. S. (2007, April). Lasting consequences of the summer learning gap. *American Sociological Review, 72*(2), 167–180.

Allington, R. L. (2002, June). What I've learned about effective reading instruction from a decade of studying exemplary elementary classroom teachers. *Phi Delta Kappan, 83*(10), 740–747.

Allington, R. L. (2008). *What really matters in Response to Intervention: Research-based designs*. Boston: Pearson.

Allington, R. L. (2011, March). What at-risk readers need. *Educational Leadership, 68*(6), 40–45. Available: http://www.ascd.org/publications/educational_leadership/mar11/vol68/num06/What_At-Risk_Readers_Need.aspx.

Allington, R. L. (2011, December). Reading intervention in the middle grades. *Voices from the Middle, 19*(2), 10–16.

Allington, R. L. (2012). *What really matters for struggling readers: Designing research-based programs* (3rd ed.). Boston: Pearson.

Allington, R. L., & Cunningham, P. M. (2006). *Schools that work: Where all children read and write* (3rd ed.). Boston: Pearson.

Allington, R. L., & McGill-Franzen, A. (2010). Why so much oral reading? In E. H. Hiebert & D. R. Reutzel (Eds.), *Revisiting silent reading: New directions for teachers and researchers* (pp. 45–56). Newark, DE: International Reading Association.

Allington, R. L., & McGill-Franzen, A. (Eds.). (2013). *Summer reading: Closing the rich/poor reading achievement gap*. New York: Teachers College Press.

Allison, N. (2009). *Middle school readers: Helping them read widely, helping them read well*. Portsmouth, NH: Heinemann.

Atwell, N. (2007). *The reading zone: How to help kids become skillful, passionate, habitual, critical readers*. New York: Scholastic.

Au, K. (2009, August/September). Creating a staircase curriculum. *Reading Today, 27*(1), 15.

Au, K. H., Raphael, T. E., & Mooney, K. C. (2008). What we have learned about teacher education to improve literacy achievement in urban schools. In *Improving literacy achievement in urban schools: Critical elements in teacher preparation* (pp. 159–184). Newark, DE: International Reading Association.

Bandura, A. (2006, June). Toward a psychology of human agency. *Perspectives on Psychological Science, 1*(2), 164–180.

Bauerlein, M., & Stotsky, S. (2012, September 18). "New study suggests remedies for Common Core's literature deficit" (Public Policy Research press release). Boston: Pioneer Institute. Based on the study at http://pioneerinstitute.org/education /new-study-suggests-remedies-for-common-core-literature-deficit/

Bazelon, B. (2013). *Sticks and stones: Defeating the culture of bullying and rediscovering the power of character and empathy.* New York: Random House.

Benkler, Y. (2011). *The penguin and the leviathan: How cooperation triumphs over self-interest.* New York: Crown Business.

Boo, K. (2012). *Behind the beautiful forevers: Life, death, and hope in a Mumbai undercity.* New York: Random House.

Boser, U., & Rosenthal, L. (2012). *Do schools challenge our students? What student surveys tell us about the state of education in the United States.* Center for American Progress. Report derived from student surveys that are part of the National Assessment of Educational Progress. Washington, DC: Center for American Progress. Available: http://www.americanprogress.org/issues/education/report/2012/07/10/11913 /do-schools-challenge-our-students/.

Brenner, D., & Hiebert, E. H. (2010, March). If I follow the teachers' editions, isn't that enough? Analyzing reading volume in six core reading programs. *Elementary School Journal, 110*(3), 347–363.

Bridges, L. (2010). *RTI: The best intervention is a good book* [White paper]. New York: Scholastic. Available: http://listbuilder.scholastic.com/content/stores/LibraryStore/pages /images/RTIwhitepaper_vFNL.pdf.

Brookhart, S. M., & Moss, C. M. (2013, May). Leading by learning. *Phi Delta Kappan, 94*(8), 13–17.

Brooks, D. (2013, February 15). When families fail. *The New York Times*, p. A23. Available: http://www.nytimes.com/2013/02/15/opinion/brooks-crayons-to-college.html.

Bryant, A. (2012, September 29). When humility and audacity go hand in hand. *The New York Times*, p. B2. Available: http://www.nytimes.com/2012/09/30/business/jacqueline -novogratz-of-acumen-fund-on-pairs-of-values.html.

Bryant, A. (2012, December 8). A good mentor never tramples on big dreams. *The New York Times*, p. B2. Available: http://www.nytimes.com/2012/12/09/business/tony-tjan-of -cue-ball-on-accepting-new-ideas.html.

Burke, J. (2010). *What's the big idea? Question-driven units to motivate reading, writing, and thinking.* Portsmouth, NH: Heinemann.

Calefati, J. (2012, December 9). N.J. educators unsure how to improve 4th-grade boys' reading scores on state test. *The [Newark] Star-Ledger*. Available: http://www.nj.com/news /index.ssf/2012/12/4th_grade_boys_in_nj_strugglin.html.

Calkins, L. (1986). *The art of teaching writing.* Portsmouth, NH: Heinemann.

Cambourne, B. (1988). *The whole story: Natural learning and the acquisition of literacy in the classroom.* Richmond Hill, Ontario, Canada: Scholastic.

Chen, M. (2010). *Education nation: Six leading edges of innovation in our schools.* San Francisco: Jossey-Bass.

City, E. A., Elmore, R. F., Fiarman, S. E., & Teitel, L. (2009). *Instructional rounds in education: A network approach to improving teaching and learning.* Cambridge, MA: Harvard Education Press.

Collier, L. (2013, March). Changes in writing instruction—the challenge and the promise. *Council Chronicle.* Urbana, IL: National Council of Teachers of English. Available: http://onlinedigitalpublishing.com/display_article.php?id=1332378

Commission on the Humanities and Social Sciences. (2013). *The heart of the matter: A report of the American Academy's Commission on the Humanities and Social Sciences.* Cambridge, MA: American Academy of Arts & Sciences. Available: http:/www.amacad.org

Daniels, H. (2002). *Literature circles: Voice and choice in book clubs and reading groups.* Portland, ME: Stenhouse.

Darling-Hammond, L. (2003, May). Keeping good teachers: Why it matters, what leaders can do. *Educational Leadership, 60*(8), 6–13.

Darling-Hammond, L. (2010, May 29). Restoring our schools. *The Nation.* Available: http://www.thenation.com/article/restoring-our-schools#.

Darling-Hammond, L., Barron, B., Pearson, P. D., Schoenfeld, A. H., Stage, E. K., Zimmerman, T. D., Cervett, G. N., & Tilson, J. L. (2008). *Powerful learning: What we know about teaching for understanding.* San Francisco: Jossey-Bass.

Darling-Hammond, L., & Richardson, N. (2009, February). Teacher learning: What matters? *Educational Leadership, 66*(5), 46–55.

Darling-Hammond, L., Wei, R. C., Andree, A., Richardson, N., & Orphanos, S. (2009). *Professional learning in the learning profession: A status report on teacher development in the United States and abroad.* Palo Alto, CA: School Redesign Network at Stanford University; and Oxford, OH: National Staff Development Council.

Dennis, B., Larson, K., & Nethery, M. (2009). *Nubs: The true story of a mutt, a Marine and a miracle.* New York: Little, Brown.

DeParle, J. (2012, December 23). For poor, leap to college often ends in a hard fall. *The New York Times.* Retrieved from http://www.nytimes.com/2012/12/23/education/poor-students-struggle-as-class-plays-a-greater-role-in-success.html?pagewanted=all.

Dewey, J. (1907). *The school and society.* Chicago: University of Chicago Press.

Dewitz, P., Jones, J., & Leahy, S. (2009, April/May/June). Comprehension strategy instruction in core reading programs. *Reading Research Quarterly, 44*(2), 102–126.

Dewitz, P., & Wolskee, J. (2012). *Making the most of your core reading program: Research-based essentials.* Portsmouth, NH: Heinemann.

Dickinson, D. K., & DiGisi, L. L. (1998, March). The many rewards of a literacy-rich classroom. *Educational Leadership, 55*(6), 23–26.

Duffy, G. G., Roehler, L. R., & Herrmann, B. A. (1988, April). Modeling mental processes helps poor readers become strategic readers. *The Reading Teacher, 41*(8), 762–767.

DuFour, R., & Eaker, R. (1998). *Professional learning communities at work: Best practices for enhancing student achievement.* Bloomington, IN: Solution Tree.

Duke, N. K. (2008, October). *Some key findings from research on reading comprehension and what they mean for classroom practice.* Presentation for the Texas Reading First Higher Education Collaborative, Austin, TX.

Duke, N. K., & Bennett-Armistead, V. S. (2003). *Reading and writing informational text in the primary grades.* New York: Scholastic.

Duke, N., Purcell-Gates, V., Hall, L. A., & Towers, C. (2006). Authentic literacy activities for developing comprehension and writing. *The Reading Teacher, 60*(4), 344–355.

Dweck, C. S. (2006). *Mindset: The new psychology of success.* New York: Random House.

Elley, W. (1991, September). Acquiring literacy in a second language: The effect of book-based programs. *Language Learning, 41*(3), 375–411.

Elmore, R. (2009). Institutions, improvement, and practice. In A. Hargreaves & M. Fullan (Eds.), *Change wars* (pp. 221–235). Bloomington, IN: Solution Tree.

Fielding, L. G., & Pearson, P. D. (1994, February). Synthesis of research/Reading comprehension: What works. *Educational Leadership, 51*(5), 62–68.

Fisher, D., & Frey, N. (2013). Engaging the adolescent learner: Text complexity and close reading. *IRA E-ssentials.* Newark, DE: International Reading Association.

Frankenberg, E., & Orfield, G. (Eds.). (2012). *The resegregation of suburban schools: A hidden crisis in American education.* Cambridge, MA: Harvard Education Press.

Fullan, M. (2000, April). The three stories of education reform. *Phi Delta Kappan, 81*(8), 581–584.

Fullan, M. (2001). *Leading in a culture of change.* San Francisco: Jossey-Bass.

Fullan, M. (2005). *Leadership and sustainability: System thinkers in action.* Thousand Oaks, CA: Corwin.

Fullan, M. (Ed.). (2010). *Motion leadership: The skinny on becoming change savvy.* Thousand Oaks, CA: Corwin.

Fullan, M., & Hargreaves, A. (1996). *What's worth fighting for in your school?* (Rev. ed.). New York: Teachers College.

Gallagher, K. (2009). *Readicide: How schools are killing reading and what you can do about it.* Portland, ME: Stenhouse.

Gallagher, K. (2011). *Write like this: Teaching real-world writing through modeling and mentor texts.* Portland, ME: Stenhouse.

Gallimore, R., & Ermeling, B. A. (2012). Why durable teaching changes are elusive and what might we do about it. *Journal of Reading Recovery, 12*(1), 41–53.

Gawande, A. (2007). *Better: A surgeon's notes on performance.* New York: Henry Holt.

Gilbert, J. K., Compton, D. L., Fuchs, D., Fuchs, L. S., Bouton, B., Barquero, L. A., and Cho, E. (2013, April/May/June). Efficacy of a first-grade Responsiveness-to-Intervention prevention model for struggling readers. *Reading Research Quarterly, 48*(2), 135–154.

Graham, S., & Hebert, M. (2010). *Writing to read: Evidence for how writing can improve. Carnegie Corporation Time to Act Report.* Washington, DC: Alliance for Excellent Education.

Graves, D. (1983). *Writing: Teachers and children at work.* Portsmouth, NH: Heinemann.

Guskie, T. R., & Yoon, K. S. (2009, March). What works in professional development? *Phi Delta Kappan, 90*(7), 495–500.

Guthrie, J. T., Wigfield, A., & You, W. (2012). Instructional contexts for engagement and achievement in reading. In S. L. Christenson, A. L. Reschly, & C. Wylie (Eds.), *Handbook of research on student engagement* (pp. 601–634). New York: Springer.

Hammond, W. D., & Nessel, D. D. (2011). *The comprehension experience: Engaging readers through effective inquiry and discussion.* Portsmouth, NH: Heinemann.

Hargreaves, A., & Shirley, D. (2009). *The fourth way: The inspiring future for educational change.* Thousand Oaks, CA: Corwin.

Hargreaves, A., & Shirley, D. (2009, November). The persistence of presentism. *Teachers College Record, 111*(11), 2505–2534.

Hattie, J. (2009). *Visible learning: A synthesis of over 800 meta-analyses relating to achievement.* New York: Routledge.

Herbert, B. (2005, February 14). The public thinker. *The New York Times,* p. A23.

Hiebert, E. H. (1999, December). Text matters in learning to read. *The Reading Teacher, 52*(6), 552–569. Also available as CIERA Report #1-009. Ann Arbor: CIERA/University of Michigan.

Hiebert, E. H. (2011, December/2012, January). The Common Core's staircase of text complexity: Getting the size of the first step right. *Reading Today, 29*(3), 26–27. Available: http://textproject.org/assets/news/Hiebert_Getting-the-Size-of-the-First-Step-Right.pdf.

Hiebert, E. H. (2013, March). Supporting students' movement up the staircase of text complexity. *The Reading Teacher, 66*(6), 459–468.

Hiebert, E. H., & Reutzel, D. R. (Eds.). (2010). *Revisiting silent reading: New directions for teachers and researchers.* Newark, DE: International Reading Association.

Hiebert, E. H., & Van Sluys, K. (2014). Standard 10 of the Common Core State Standards: Examining three assumptions about text complexity. In K. Goodman, R. C. Calfee, & Y. Goodman (Eds.), *Whose knowledge counts in government literacy policies? Why expertise matters* (pp. 144–160). New York: Routledge.

Higgins, A. (2012, November 14). Lessons for U.S. from a flood-prone land. *The New York Times,* p. A5.

Holdaway, D. (1979). *The foundations of literacy.* Portsmouth, NH: Heinemann.

Hord, S. M., & Sommers, W. A. (2008). *Leading professional learning communities: Voices from research and practice.* Thousand Oaks, CA: Corwin.

Horning, K. T., Lindgren, M. V., & Schliesman, M. (2013). *A few observations on publishing in 2012.* Madison, WI: University of WI–Madison, Cooperative Children's Book Center. Available: http://ccbc.education.wisc.edu/books/choiceintro13.asp.

Howard, M. (2009). *RTI from all sides: What every teacher needs to know.* Portsmouth, NH: Heinemann.

Innes, R. (2012, October 24). Commentary misleading on NAEP, dropouts (Letter to the Editor). *Education Week,* p. 26.

Isaacson, W. (2012). *Steve Jobs.* New York: Simon & Schuster.

Ivey, G., & Johnston, P. (2010, December). *Reading engagement, achievement, and moral development in adolescence.* Paper presented at the annual meeting of the National Reading Conference/Literacy Research Association, Fort Worth, TX.

Ivey, G., & Johnston, P. (2013, July/August/September). Engagement with young adult literature: Outcomes and processes. *Reading Research Quarterly, 48*(3), 355–375.

Jensen, E. (2013, May). How poverty affects classroom engagement. *Educational Leadership, 70*(8), 24–30.

Johnston, P. H. (2004). *Choice words: How our language affects children's learning.* Portland, ME: Stenhouse.

Johnston, P. H. (2012). *Opening minds: Using language to change lives.* Portland, ME: Stenhouse.

Johnston, P. H. (2012, July 23). Reducing instruction, increasing engagement [blog post]. Available: http://blog.stenhouse.com/archives/2012/07/23/blogstitute-week-5-reducing-instruction-increasing-engagement/

Johnston, P. H., & Ivey, G. (2013, July/August/September). Engagement with young adult literature. *Reading Research Quarterly, 48*(3), 255–275.

Joyce, B. R., & Showers, B. (2002). *Student achievement through staff development* (3rd ed.). Alexandria, VA: ASCD.

Khan, H. (2012, June). *Three teachers' perceptions of an embedded literacy-based professional development project.* (Unpublished research).

Kim, J. S. (2006). Effects of a voluntary summer reading intervention on reading achievement: Results from a randomized field trial. *Educational Evaluation and Policy Analysis, 28*(4), 335–355.

King, S. (2000). *On writing: A memoir of the craft.* New York: Scribner.

Kittle, P. (2013). *Book love: Developing depth, passion, and stamina in adolescent readers.* Portsmouth, NH: Heinemann.

Kozol, J. (2012). *Fire in the ashes: Twenty-five years among the poorest children in America.* New York: Crown.

Krashen, S. (2001). The Lexile framework: Unnecessary and potentially harmful. *CSLA* [California School Library Association] *Journal, 24*(2), 25–26.

Krashen, S., & McQuillan, J. (2007, October). The case for late intervention. *Educational Leadership, 65*(2), 68–73.

Kristof, N. (2011, September 14). Sewing her way out of poverty. *The New York Times.* Available: http://www.nytimes.com/2011/09/15/opinion/kristof-sewing-her-way-out-of-poverty.html

Lamy, C. (2013, May). How preschool fights poverty. *Educational Leadership, 70*(8), 32–36.

Learned, J. E., Stockdill, D., & Moje, E. B. (2011). Integrating reading strategies and knowledge building in adolescent literacy instruction. In S. Jay Samuels & Alan Farstrup (Eds.), *What research has to say about reading instruction* (4th ed., pp. 159–185). Newark, DE: International Reading Association.

Lesesne, T. (2010). *Reading ladders: Leading students from where they are to where we'd like them to be.* Portsmouth, NH: Heinemann.

Levin, B. (2012, October). The one-legged high jumper and the perils of prediction. *Phi Delta Kappan, 94*(2), 74–75.

Levin, H. M., Belfield, C., Muennig, P., & Rouse, C. (2007). *The costs and benefits of an excellent education for all of America's children.* New York: Teachers College Press.

Lipson, M. Y., & Wixson, K. K. (Eds.). (2010). *Successful approaches to RTI: Collaborative practices for improving K–12 literacy.* Newark, DE: International Reading Association.

Louis, K. S., Leithwood, K., Wahlstrom, K. L., & Anderson, S. E. (2010). *Learning from leadership: Investigating the links to improved student learning.* St. Paul, MN: Center for Applied Research and Educational Improvement, University of Minnesota; and Toronto, CA: Ontario Institute for Studies in Education, University of Toronto.

Loveless, T. (2012). *How well are American students learning? With sections on predicting the effect of the Common Core State Standards, achievement gaps on the two NAEP tests, and misinterpreting international test scores.* Washington, DC: Brookings Institution, Brown Center Report on American Education. Available: http://www.brookings.edu/~/media/newsletters/0216_brown_education_loveless.pdf

Maloch, B., & Bomer, R. (2013, July). Research and policy: Teaching about and with informational texts: What does research teach us? *Language Arts, 90*(6), 441–450.

Markle, B., & VanKoevering, S. (2013, May). Reviving Edward Bell. *Phi Delta Kappan, 94*(8), 8–12.

Maxwell, L. A. (2012, March 6). Growing gaps bring focus on poverty's role in schooling. *Education Week.* Retrieved from http://www.edweek.org/ew/articles/2012/03/07/23poverty_ep.h31.html?qs=Lesli+Maxwell

Maxwell, L. A. (2012, September 19). Calif. poised to spotlight ELLs stalled in schools. *Education Week.* Retrieved from http://www.edweek.org/ew/articles/2012/09/19/04ell_ep.h32.html?qs=long-term_ELLs

McGill-Franzen, A., & Allington, R. L. (2008, April). Got books? *Educational Leadership, 65*(7), 20–23.

McKenna, M. C., Conradi, K., Lawrence, C., Jang, B. G., & Meyer, J. P. (2012, July/August/September). Reading attitudes of middle school students: Results of a U.S. survey. *Reading Research Quarterly, 47*(3), 283–306.

McQuillan, J. (1998). *The literacy crisis: False claims, real solutions.* Portsmouth, NH: Heinemann.

Mesmer, H. A., Cunningham, J. W., & Hiebert, E. H. (2012, July/August/September). Toward a theoretical model of text complexity for the early grades: Learning from the past, anticipating the future. *Reading Research Quarterly, 47*(3), 235–258.

Miller, D. (2008). *The book whisperer: Awakening the inner reader in every child.* San Francisco: Jossey-Bass.

Moffett, C. (2000, April). Sustaining change: The answers are blowing in the wind. *Educational Leadership, 57*(7), 35–38.

Moje, E. B. (2011). Developing disciplinary discourses, literacies, and identities: What's knowledge got to do with it? In M. G. L. Bonilla & K. England (Eds.), *Discourses and identities in contexts of educational change* (pp. 49–74). New York: Peter Lang.

Moore, J. (2013, September). Research alert: The research on resilience. *Educational Leadership, 71*(1), 8. Available: http://www.ascd.org/publications/educational-leadership/sept13/vol71/num01/Double-Take.aspx

Munro, A. (2012). *Dear life.* New York: Vintage.

Murray, D. (1990). *Shoptalk: Learning to write with writers.* Portsmouth, NH: Heinemann.

Myers, W. D. (2012). *Just write: Here's how!* New York: HarperCollins.

Nagy, W., & Townsend, D. (2012, January/February/March). Words as tools: Learning academic vocabulary as language acquisition. *Reading Research Quarterly, 47*(1), 91–108.

National Center for Education Statistics. (2011). *Writing 2011: National Assessment of Educational Progress at Grades 8 and 12.* Washington, DC: U. S. Department of Education.

National Institute of Child Health and Human Development. (2000). *Report of the National Reading Panel: Teaching children to read: An evidence-based assessment of the scientific research literature on reading and its implications for reading instruction.* Available: http://www.nichd.nih.gov/publications/nrp/smallbook.htm.

National Reading Panel. (2000). *Report of the National Reading Panel. Teaching children to read: An evidence-based assessment of the scientific literature on reading and its implications for reading instruction.* Washington, DC: National Institute of Child Health and Human Development.

Neuman, S. B. (2013, May). The American dream: Slipping away? *Educational Leadership, 70*(8), 18–22.

Neuman, S. B., & Celano, D. C. (2001, January–March). Access to print in low-income and middle-income communities. *Reading Research Quarterly, 36*(1), 8–26.

Neuman, S. B., Celano, D. C., Greco, A. N., & Shue, P. (2001). *Access for all: Closing the book gap for children in early education.* Newark, DE: International Reading Association.

Newkirk, T. (2012). *The art of slow reading*. Portsmouth, NH: Heinemann.

Newkirk, T., & Kittle, P. (Eds.). (2013). *Children want to write: Donald Graves and the revolution in children's writing*. Portsmouth, NH: Heinemann.

New York Times. (2013, February 16). Getting preschool education right [Editorial], p. A16.

Nuthall, G. (2007). *The hidden lives of learners*. Wellington, NZ: New Zealand Council for Educational Research Press.

O'Brien, D., & Dillon, D. (1996, April/May). Engaging "at-risk" high school students: Perspectives from an innovative program. *Reading Today: Research Updates from the National Reading Research Center*, p. 18.

Pandolfo, N. (2011, October 19). New report: Dropout rate five times higher for poor students [blog post]. Retrieved from HechingerEd at http://hechingered.org/content/new-report-dropout-rates-five-times-higher-for-poor-students_4389/?utm_source=feedburner&utm_medium=feed&utm_campaign=Feed%3A+HechingerReport+%28Hechinger+Report%29

Pearson, P. D., & Gallagher, M. C. (1983). The instruction of reading comprehension. *Contemporary Educational Psychology*, 8(3), 317–344.

Peery, A. (2011). *The data team experience: A guide for effective meetings*. Englewood, CO: Lead and Learn Press.

Pink, D. H. (2005). *A whole new mind: Why right-brainers will rule the future*. New York: Riverhead Books.

Pink, D. H. (2009). *Drive: The surprising truth about what motivates us*. New York: Riverhead Books.

Preble, B., & Taylor, L. (2008, December/2009, January). School climate through students' eyes. *Educational Leadership*, 66(4), 35–40.

Purcell, K., Buchanan, J., & Friedrich, L. (2013, July 16). *The impact of digital tools on student writing and how writing is taught in schools*. Washington, DC: National Writing Project and Pew Research Center. Retrieved at http://pewinternet.org/Reports/2013/Teachers-technology-and-writing

Purcell-Gates, V., Duke, N. K., & Martineau, J. A. (2007, January/February/March). Learning to read and write genre-specific text: Roles of authentic experience and explicit teaching. *Reading Research Quarterly*, 42(1), 8–45.

Randall, L. (2011). *Knocking on heaven's door: How physics and scientific thinking illuminate the universe and the modern world*. New York: HarperCollins.

Ravitch, D. (2010). *The death and life of the great American school system: How testing and choice are undermining education*. New York: Basic Books.

Reardon, S. F. (2013, May). The widening income achievement gap. *Educational Leadership*, 70(8), 10–16.

Rebora, A. (2010, April 9). Responding to RTI. *Education Week, Teacher PD Sourcebook*. Available: http://www.edweek.org/tsb/articles/2010/04/12/02allington.h03.html.

Reeves, D. B. (2004 December/2005 January). If I said something wrong, I was afraid. *Educational Leadership*, 62(4), 72–74.

Reeves, D. B. (2009). *Leading change in your school: How to conquer myths, build commitment, and get results*. Alexandria, VA: ASCD.

Reiss, K. (2007). *Leadership coaching for educators: Bringing out the best in school administrators*. Thousand Oaks, CA: Corwin.

Renwick, M. (2013, January 22). Increasing engagement: A school revamps its reading intervention program [blog post]. Retrieved from *The Stenhouse Blog* at http://blog

.stenhouse.com/archives/2013/01/22/increasing-engagement-a-school-revamps-its -reading-invervention-program/

Renwick, M. (2013, February 10). How should social media etiquette be taught in schools? *EdTech*. Available: http://www.edtechmagazine.com/k12/article/2013/03/how-should -social-media-be-taught-schools

Reutzel, D. R., Jones, C. D., & Newman, T. H. (2010). Scaffolded silent reading: Improving the conditions of silent reading practice in classrooms. In E. H. Hiebert & D. R. Reutzel (Eds.), *Revisiting silent reading: New directions for teachers and researchers* (pp. 129–150). Newark, DE: International Reading Association.

Rich, M. (2013, February 14). Few states look to extend preschool to all 4-year-olds. *The New York Times: The State of the Union*, p. A15. Available: http://www.nytimes .com/2013/02/14/education/early-education-far-short-of-goal-in-obama-speech.html

Rich, M. (2013, June 14). Study gauges value of technology in schools. *The New York Times*, p. A17. Available: http://www.nytimes.com/2013/06/14/education/study-gauges-value -of-technology-in-schools.html?_r=0

Richardson, J. (2013, May). Highlighted and underlined: A notebook of short but worthy items. *Phi Delta Kappan*, *94*(8), 6–7.

Ripley, A. (2013). *The smartest kids in the world and how they got that way*. New York: Simon & Schuster.

Robinson, M. (2013, March 7). By the book. *The New York Times Sunday Book Review*, p. 9. Available: http://www.nytimes.com/2013/03/10/books/review/marilynne -robinson-by-the-book.html?_r=0

Ronka, D., Lachat, M. A., Slaughter, R., & Meltzer, J. (2008, December/2009, January). Answering the questions that count. *Educational Leadership*, *66*(4), 18–24.

Rothstein, D., & Santana, L. (2011). *Make just one change: Teach students to ask their own questions*. Cambridge, MA: Harvard Education Press.

Routman, R. (1988). *Transitions: From literature to literacy*. Portsmouth, NH: Heinemann.

Routman, R. (1996). *Literacy at the crossroads: Crucial talk about reading, writing, and other teaching dilemmas*. Portsmouth, NH: Heinemann.

Routman, R. (2000). *Kids' poems: Teaching first graders to love writing poetry*. New York: Scholastic.

Routman, R. (2000). Literature conversations. In *Conversations: Strategies for teaching, learning, and evaluating* (pp. 171–204). Portsmouth, NH: Heinemann.

Routman, R. (2003). *Reading essentials: The specifics you need to teach reading well*. Portsmouth, NH: Heinemann.

Routman, R. (2005). *Writing essentials: Raising expectations and results while simplifying teaching*. Portsmouth, NH: Heinemann.

Routman, R. (2008). *Teaching essentials: Expecting the most and getting the best from every learner, K–8*. Portsmouth, NH: Heinemann.

Routman, R. (2008, 2009, 2013). *Regie Routman in residence: Transforming our teaching* [video-based literacy series]. Portsmouth, NH: Heinemann.

Routman, R. (2012). *Literacy and learning lessons from a longtime teacher*. Newark, DE: International Reading Association.

Routman, R. (2012, February). Mapping a pathway to schoolwide highly effective teaching. *Phi Delta Kappan*, *93*(5), 56–61.

Routman, R. (2013, June/July). To raise achievement, let's celebrate teachers before we evaluate them. *Reading Today*, *30*(6), 10–12. Available: http://www.reading.org/general

/Publications/blog/BlogSinglePost/reading-today-online/2013/08/12/to-raise
-achievement-let-s-celebrate-teachers-before-we-evaluate-them#.Um7JW_mTjE0

Sahlberg, P. (2013, May 15). What if Finland's great teachers taught in U.S. schools? In Valerie Strauss, *The Answer Sheet* [blog]. *The Washington Post.* Available: http://www .washingtonpost.com/blogs/answer-sheet/wp/2013/05/15/what-if-finlands-great -teachers-taught-in-u-s-schools-not-what-you-think/

Scholastic. (2013). *Kids and family reading report* (4th ed.). Study by Scholastic in conjunction with Harrison Group. New York: Author.

Shannon, K. (2012, September 28). Researchers say nation's schools undergo more resegregation. *Education Week*, p. 5.

Sharratt, L., & Fullan, M. (2012). *Putting faces on the data: What great leaders do.* Thousand Oaks, CA: Corwin. A joint publication with Learning Forward and The Ontario Principal's Council.

Sotomayor, S. (2013). *My beloved world.* New York: Alfred A. Knopf.

Sparks, S. D. (2013, March 6). Principals lack training in shaping school climate. *Education Week*, 8. Available: http://www.edweek.org/ew/articles/2013/03/06/23principal.h32 .html

Speirs, T. (2011, June). Creating a self-sustaining school. Presentation at Literacy and Leadership Institute, Oshkosh, WI.

Stefanakis, E. H. (2004). Assessing young immigrant students: Are we finding their strengths? *Harvard Education Letter, 20*(3), 4–7.

Stengel, R. (2009). *Mandela's Way: Fifteen lessons on life, love, and courage.* New York: Random House.

Swan, E. A., Coddington, C. S., & Guthrie, J. T. (2010). Engaged silent reading. In E. H. Hiebert & D. R. Reutzel (Eds.), *Revisiting silent reading: New directions for teachers and researchers* (pp. 95–111). Newark, DE: International Reading Association.

Tatum, A. (2013). *Fearless voices: Engaging a new generation of African American adolescent male writers.* New York: Scholastic.

Taylor, B. M., Pearson, P. D., Clark, K. F., & Walpole, S. (1999, October). Effective schools, accomplished teachers. *The Reading Teacher, 53*(2), 156–159. Available: http://www .ciera.org/library/archive/1999-01/art-online-99-01.html

Taylor, B., Peterson, D., Pearson, P. D., & Rodrigues, M. (2002, November). Looking inside classrooms: Reflecting on the "how" as well as the "what" in effective reading instruction" *The Reading Teacher*, pp. 270–279.

Thompson, C. (2009, September 2009). Clive Thompson on the new literacy. *Wired, 17*(9). Available: http://www.wired.com/techbiz/people/magazine/17-09/st_thompson

Truebridge, S. (2010, November 29). "Resilience, research, and education reform." ASCD Whole Child blog, Accessed: www.wholechildeducation.org/blog /resilience-research-and-educational-reform

Ujiie, J., & Krashen, S. D. (1996). Comic book reading, reading enjoyment, and pleasure reading among middle class and Chapter I middle school students. *Reading Improvement, 33*(1), 51–54.

U.S. Department of Education, National Center for Education Statistics. (2012, December 6). *Vocabulary results from the 2009 and 2011 NAEP reading assessments.* Available: http:// nces.ed.gov/pubsearch/pubsinfo.asp?pubid=2013452

Valencia, S. W. (2011). Using assessment to improve teaching and learning. In S. J. Samuels & A. E. Farstrup (Eds.), *What research has to say about reading instruction* (4th ed., pp. 379–405). Newark, DE: International Reading Association.

Valencia, S. W., Pearson, P. D., & Wixson, K. K. (2011). Assessing and tracking progress in reading comprehension: The search for keystone elements in college and career readiness. Princeton, NJ: Center for K–12 Assessment & Performance Management at ETS. Available: http://www.k12center.org/publications/through_course.html

Valencia, S. W., & Wixson, K. K. (in press). CCSS in ELA: Suggestions and cautions for implementing the reading standards. *The Reading Teacher, 67*(3), pp. 181–185.

Van Gog, T., Ericsson, K. A., Rikers, R. M. J. P., & Paas, F. (2005). Instructional design for advanced learners: Establishing connections between the theoretical frameworks of cognitive load and deliberate practice. *Educational Technology, Research and Development, 53*(3), 73–81.

Van Keer, H., & Vanderlinde, R. (2013, May). A book for two: Explicitly taught reading comprehension strategies paired with peer tutoring can boost reading skills for elementary school students. *Phi Delta Kappan, 94*(8), 54–58.

Van Kraayenoord, C. E. (2010, July/August/September). Response to Intervention: New ways and wariness. *Reading Research Quarterly, 45*(3), 363–376.

Werner, E., & Smith, R. S. (1992). *Overcoming the odds: High-risk children from birth to adulthood.* Ithaca, NY: Cornell University Press.

Wiggins, G. (2009, May). Real-world writing: Making purpose and audience matter. *English Journal, 98*(5), 29–37.

Wiggins, G. (2012, September). Seven keys to effective feedback. *Educational Leadership, 70*(1), 10–16.

Wilhelm, J. D. (2012, September). CODA: Proactivity versus reactivity: Preparing students for success with the CCSS. *Voices from the Middle, 20*(1), 68–72.

Williamson, K. (2013, May 8). Teachers should receive more time to collaborate (Letter to the Editor). *Education Week*, p. 29. Available: http://www.edweek.org/ew/articles/2013/05/08/30letter-5.h32.html.

Wiseman, L., Allen, L., & Foster, E. (2013). *The multiplier effect: Tapping the genius inside our schools.* Thousand Oaks, CA: Corwin.

Index

Note: A *g* following a page number denotes a glossary term and a *q* denotes a Quick Win.

About the Author

Regie Routman is a longtime teacher, author, and speaker who is committed to improving the literacy and learning lives of children, especially those in high-challenge schools. Her current work involves weeklong school residencies where she demonstrates effective reading and writing practices in diverse classrooms, coaches teachers and principals, and facilitates ongoing professional conversations, all as a catalyst for sustainable, whole-school change. Regie's experiences as a classroom teacher, Reading Recovery teacher, language arts coach, and staff developer led her to see schoolwide collaboration and high-level, professional learning as a necessity for increasing and sustaining achievement. As a result, Regie created the residency model where she mentors an entire school to increase engagement, enjoyment, and literacy achievement for all learners. Because the number of residencies she is able to do is limited, she created the video-based and job-embedded literacy series *Regie Routman in Residence: Transforming Our Teaching.*

Read, Write, Lead: Breakthrough Strategies for Schoolwide Literacy Success is Regie's first book on school change and is based on the actions, practices, and priorities that lead to schoolwide literacy success. Drawing from her residency experiences, the text specifies how and why teachers and principals must collaborate as knowledgeable partners, that is, as joint experts in both leadership and literacy in a trusting school culture that becomes a Professional *Literacy* Community. Regie's earlier publications, especially her *Essentials* series—*Reading Essentials, Writing Essentials, and Teaching Essentials*—continue to support educators to teach reading and writing more effectively and joyfully. See www.regieroutman.org for more information on Regie's books and resources, blog, professional development offerings, Teacher Recognition Grant, and contact information. Regie lives in Seattle, WA, with her husband Frank.